# Essentials of Career-Focused Counseling

First Edition

Chad Luke

Tennessee Technological University

cognella® | ACADEMIC PUBLISHING

Bassim Hamadeh, CEO and Publisher
Kassie Graves, Director of Acquisitions and Sales
Jamie Giganti, Senior Managing Editor
Jess Estrella, Senior Graphic Designer
Kassie Graves, Director of Acquisitions
Claire Benson, Project Editor
Brian Fahey, Licensing Specialist
Christian Berk, Associate Production Editor
Don Kesner, Interior Designer



Printed in the United States of America.

ISBN: 978-1-5165-1329-1 (pbk) / 978-1-5165-1330-7 (br) / 978-1-5165-4630-5 (al)

cognella® | ACADEMIC PUBLISHING

# Essentials of Career-Focused Counseling

# Contents

# Preface

As most counselor educators know, whether explicitly or implicitly, career and mental health issues are intimately entwined. The task of a career theory and practice text then is to be very intentional about guiding readers in embracing this relationship and resist the urge to treat career and mental health issues as unrelated.

Essentials of Career-Focused Counseling transforms the approach to career and mental health, and as a result changes its applicability for the field: career-focused counseling, or counseling for career-related issues, is first and foremost about counseling; the presenting problem (or one of them) for clients relates to the world of work. It takes the position that "career counseling" *is* counseling ... related to career issues. The 2016 CACREP standards have increased from seven in 2009 to ten distinct standards related to career counseling. CACREP also accredits career counseling specialty masters programs, of which there are several across the US. Importantly, *all* of the CACREP core standards must be met, *in addition* to the specific career counseling standards. CACREP recognizes that as a field, we are counselors first, and then we specialize.

The purpose of this text is to build upon counselor identity and apply it to career issues that clients bring to counseling. It compares and contrasts current counseling theory and approaches with career theory toward more effective treatment of career and mental health issues. Little in the way of content is new in this book: career theory is career theory. What is new and cutting edge is the approach to career from the perspective of counseling, which is actually more inclusive than current approaches. It does not seek to integrate career and personal issues in counseling; instead, it presumes that these issues are already integrated. This approach is eminently practical—all conceptual, theoretical information is presented in a way that the reader/practitioner can use it with clients.

This text approaches these areas as complementary and builds connections toward application—areas that adult learners value. Consider, for example the approach to an assessment such as the Strong Interest Inventory. Career advisers use such a tool to help clients understand and explore their career options. From a counseling perspective, counselors should be able, through the use of well-honed attending skills, arrive at similar conclusions *without* the instrument. The instrument certainly has its uses, but must not be used in place of relationship and clinical skills.

The majority of texts approach theory and practice from a pedagogical framework: teaching content to children. The approach used in this text, in contrast, utilizes an andragogical approach, a model designed for adult learners. This approach presupposes that readers arrive at the text with their own unique experiences and knowledge, and this prior learning is then harnessed to build more effective learning strategies (see Luke, 2017 for discussion of this approach in counselor education). For example, many counseling students in graduate counseling programs—clearly adult learners—have already had a course in counseling theory. When career theory is taught or read about, it often is represented as separate from counseling theory, giving the appearance that students' prior learning is irrelevant, as this is a wholly new topic. In contrast, this text approaches career development and theory from the perspective that career is informed by counseling. Further, it views career/work/job as just one of many issues clients present.

## Features and Benefits

*Theory, Assessment. and Resource Integration*. Section Two, chapters 2-5, looks at counseling, assessment, and web-based information systems, and the interrelationships. It makes the case that assessment almost always must be combined with counseling or at least must be viewed in the context of relationship. This approach challenges readers to understand the connections between and among the three, rather than picking and choosing one without the concomitant foundations.

*Neuroscience.* Perhaps the most unique feature of this book is that it is the first of its kind (to my knowledge) to integrate neuroscience throughout, in a natural, non-forced way. For each section, a "Neuro-Perspective" is offered both to assist counselors in understanding their clients' issue, as well as supporting the natural connections between career and counseling.

*From Pedagogy to Andragogy.* One of the characteristics of adult learners, often ignored in popular texts, is that they must be convinced that the content presented is relevant, meaningful to their lives and for their practice. Every word and phrase of this text is scrutinized for applicability, rather than learning for the sake of learning. It assumes that readers can follow the references and suggested additional resources and readings to access additional materials, if they wish.

*Case Vignettes.* One of the most straightforward approaches to reader engagement is the use of case studies, including ***transcript excerpts***. As a former full-time clinician with many years of experience, I have a strong sense of how these issues both present and interact. In addition, the current approach lends itself well to case conceptualization in linking career theory with other mental health theory, while simultaneously exploring the reciprocal impact of career and mental health issues. Wherever feasible, the same vignettes are used throughout the book to illustrate with the same client, different approaches.

*Approach to Diversity.* Often in career texts, career and vocation are presented as normal ways of thinking about the world of work. Yet, for many, if not most in our world today, a job is just a job; issues of calling and deriving meaning from work are simply not on their radar. Appreciation for these differences, and for the privilege associated with career decision-making as choice, aids helpers in proceeding empathically and genuinely. This text utilizes both neuroscience in counseling and social justice models to assist readers in understanding various world of work perspectives.

*Integration of Career and Mental Health Assumed.* It seems reasonable in this approach to examine the interaction of specific types of mental health disorders with career and work; e.g., how do career-related issues lead to mental health issues, and how do mental health issues impact work performance, satisfaction and longevity?

*Contemporary Issues...* This feature is incorporated throughout each chapter and helps readers understand current trends in work and career against the backdrop of historical context.

Often, historical material is presented as a standalone chapter that readers resist engaging with. Here, these important developments are set with modern approaches to aid in understanding.

## Organization of this Book

This text accomplishes a lot in a little space. Chapter one offers introductory material to the study of career-focused counseling. Section one contains career theory, assessment and information resources. Students often struggle to make concrete connections between and among these three. Therefore, each chapter addresses all three and their relationship to one another. For example, chapter two discusses Trait and Factor theories, along with the commonly used assessments, followed by resources for clients when counselors operate from this theory. This pattern is repeated in chapter three, with developmental theories, in chapter four with social and cognitive theories, and chapter five with postmodern theories. Chapter six covers the application of counseling theory to career-focused counseling, in order to draw on students' prior learning.

A key role for counselors is advocacy and social justice. In section two we examine the issues associated with counseling marginalized and under-represented groups. In chapter seven we look at ethics associated with career-focused counseling. Chapter eight includes thorough coverage of multicultural issues. In chapter nine, we consider groups at risk. Lastly, chapter ten contains coverage of career-focused counseling and mental health issues.

In section three we examine career-focused counseling educational settings. This section falls near the end of the book because CFC in school settings subsumes all previous sections and considerations, so it is a capstone sections for counselors working in schools. Chapter eleven explores career-focused counseling in k-12 settings, with consideration of career-related issues across these developmental levels. Chapter twelve addresses career-focused counseling in college settings and includes considerations for issues in emerging adulthood. The section and text concludes with chapter thirteen, in which career-focused counseling is applied to the reader. Using this personal application, readers are then led through a summary and synthesis of career-focused counseling in daily clinical practice.

# CHAPTER ONE

# Job, Work, Career, and Vocation: Clarifying the Counselor's Role

### Chapter Goals

- Present a rationale for a career as a core counseling program component
- Discuss career counseling in light of counselor identity
- Explore and appreciate the relevant features of the history of this career field
- Introduce relevant career-related language
- Provide a framework for reflecting on one's own career experience and process

## Introduction

There is really no such thing as a "common" career-related problem that individuals would seek help for. It is important to recognize that not all career-related problems are created equally, and therefore, our approach must shift through our understanding of the client's concerns. The case conceptualization approach described here, alongside an orientation toward career as an inextricable component of mental health and school counseling, assist counselors in framing career issues strategically yet individually. At the same time, some of the more recurring categories of distinct career-related concerns include: career decision-making, career indecision, unemployment, underemployment, work adjustment, work-life balance, family conflict, and financial concerns.

### Opening Vignette: Joe and Jill

Joe is a thirty-something, male, married to Jill. The couple has two children under five years old: Hayden is their two-year-old daughter; Buddy is their four-year-old son. The two live in a two-bedroom apartment on the outskirts of a medium-sized metropolitan area. Joe has been the sole "bread winner" since the children came along. He works as an electrician's assistant and makes fifteen dollars per hour. He hopes to become a licensed electrician in a few years, which will increase his salary and his job prospects. Unfortunately, with the shifts in the global and local economies, Joe's job has reduced him to "on-call" status, and for the past six months, he has been averaging closer to thirty-two hours per week. This has put an incredible strain on the family's resources, and despite Jill's highly effective efforts to reduce expenditures, they have to rely on credit cards to make ends meet each month. In addition, as the children get older, sharing a bedroom becomes less desirable. Jill has explored work options to supplement their income; however, she has worked as a retail sales associate, and the jobs available to her pay ten dollars per hour—about two-thirds of the cost of daycare for two children, which would be required if the couple were both working. Joe has picked up side jobs in the evenings and on weekends to help. The result is that he is rarely at home with the family, Jill spends all her time at home with the children, so both are exhausted, disconnected from each other, and continue to work their way backwards financially each month. Joe reaches out to you for counseling for "stress."

Before we get into Joe and Jill's case, let's think through what their situation triggers in us. One of the unique features of career-focused counseling (CFC) is the fact that, unlike many mental health issues that counselors treat, career issues are fairly common among all people. A counselor may not have had personal experience with schizophrenia, bipolar disorder, or addiction, but it is highly likely they have personally or vicariously experienced career uncertainty, work-related stress, or periods of unemployment. This makes the career component of the presenting problem stand out and likely to trigger our own countertransference (addressing our own career-related concerns through our clients by giving advice, minimizing, etc.). Depending on our experiences with career development, counselors are susceptible to reverting to advice-giving, opining about the world of work, or even referring out to a career specialist. This is unfortunate, but also understandable. As the 1993 special issue of the Career Development Quarterly concluded, career counseling is personal counseling (Subich, 1993), and I would go one step further to assert that *career* is *personal* (Whiston & Oliver, 2005). It can strike at the core of who we are or think we are. There often exists a false dichotomy regarding whether career counseling is personal counseling. It does not get much more personal than career-related issues. This dichotomy may be true in one sense: when a client enters counseling for a diagnosis of post-traumatic stress disorder (PTSD) or major depressive disorder, it may not be that they also have a latent desire to find their perfect work, so to speak.

Before counselors step too far into learning the principles of CFC, they must examine their own assumptions, preconceptions, successes, and failures related to the world of work. As you read, I invite you to reflect on how successful you and those you know have been in finding a career; how effective you have been in communicating with significant others about career-related issues; how effective your models (parents, family, friends, mentors) have been in navigating career-related issues; and the strategies have you used to sort out fact from fiction in career development? In this way, we bracket our biases and decrease the likelihood that we will impose our beliefs about work on our clients; that we will unwittingly pass along the words of wisdom we gleaned through experience and relationships. I would invite you to add to this list your own words of wisdom that you have heard about career decisions and the world of work. Acknowledging these and testing them will aid in challenging your biases in session, as well as in your reading of this text.

- You can become anything you want
- A college degree will guarantee a good job
- If you want to know what to do for a career, take a career assessment
- Don't worry about it; things will all work out
- Select the right job starting out
- Just work hard

In order to appreciate the context in which these pieces of advice occur, it is important to understand their origins. To this end, we look briefly at the historical setting out of which CFC arose. During each epoch of career history, different "wisdom" emerged.

# History of Career and Guidance: Foundation of the Counseling Profession

Pope (2000) provides an impressive overview of the history of career development. He pulls from numerous sources (see Pope, 2000, for reference list) and then uses the development of career-related organizations to frame his Social Transitions Stage Model. His model covers six 10- to 20-year epochs in the development of career and vocational organizations. Table 1.1 summarizes his model. I have also included the period from 2000 to the present to address globalization and the global economy, a factor that has changed the vocational landscape in the U.S. and around the world for workers.

Pope (2013) summarized the objectives of the early days of the vocational guidance movement, a view he invites modern day readers to compare with contemporary career and vocational objectives:

> During the 1913 convention, papers were presented that provided insight on the most critical issues that vocational counselors were facing at the time. Many of these issues still resonate 100 years later.
>
> - Implementing some form of vocational guidance within the school system throughout the country and abolishing child labor.
> - Reforming education to make it more relevant to students by infusing vocational material throughout the curriculum.
> - Developing new psychological tests for vocational guidance to "choos(e) persons for positions rather than ... positions for persons" (Ayres, 1913, p. 37).

- Expanding the training of vocational counselors to include the use and interpretation of psychological tests and gaining the knowledge that would allow them to be able to work with diverse populations.
- Developing the skills of vocational counselors to conduct research in order to stay current in the field.
- Preparing vocational counselors to challenge each industry regarding wages, hours, working conditions, and unemployment and to advocate for workers (pp. 371–372).

Earlier on, career counseling and vocational guidance, as it was called prior to the 1950s, struggled regarding the role of professionals in career guidance (Super, 1955). Super illuminates the discrepant views between guidance professionals and counseling psychologists, "in the 1920s, of educators such as John Brewer (1932) with his stress on exploratory experiences in guidance, and of psychologists such as Clark Hull (1928), with his hopes for psychological tests as the basis of vocational counseling p. 3)". The difference is significant, and the enduring influence of this philosophical perspective can be seen today. Career counseling is largely dominated by a proliferation of career-based psychometric tests and assessments. Rogers' (1942) book strongly influenced the "push back" of guidance as psychometrics to that of relationship, such that "one counsels people rather than problems, of the fact that problems of adjustment in one aspect of living have effects on other aspects of life, and of the complexity of the processes of counseling concerning any type of individual adjustment, whether in the field of occupation, of group living, or of personal values" (Super, 1955, p. 4). This historical perspective sets the lens for viewing current trends, to which we turn next.

# EMERGING TRENDS IN CFC AT THIS POINT IN HISTORY

A notion we will return to throughout this text is the ever-changing nature of the world of work. This requires flexibility and adaptability on the part of the counselor and clients. Several categories of trends are relevant to the practice of CFC.

**Constant Connection (Wireless Devices)/Technology**. Regardless of how an individual feels personally about wireless technologies, we live in a connected world that shows no sign of slowing down. Social media—the use of technology to share thoughts and ideas with friends and the wider world—has ushered in a new form of communication. There is certainly a perspective that argues that social media and constant connection have resulted in personal *dis*connection. While this argument is outside the scope of the goals here, there are some palpable changes to the world of work as a result. One prominent effect is the reality that many workers today are always available, depending on the culture of their work environment. Many times, there is an expectation that, because there is the possibility of instant contact—via text and email—it can and should be required. Because of this, workers today have a trickier path to boundary setting between their personal self and their work self.

**Recession.** Until about 2007, a large proportion of the young workforce, as well as middle and high school students, had little experiential knowledge of national and global economic collapse. The certainty—the privilege of not having to think about it—of ready work and resources was replaced with fear and uncertainty. This generation of prospective and young (career-wise) workers have now lived through a national and worldwide economic trauma that changes both retirement prospects and attitudes toward work.

**White House Initiatives.** From No Child Left Behind (NCLB) to Reach Higher, the U.S. government continues to pump funds and legislation into initiatives to train and educate the American workforce. Now more than ever, America and Americans need to be able to compete in a global economy, where knowledge and skills become outdated at an increasingly rapid pace.

**Middle Class "Gap."** The working poor or what have been called wage-dependent earners (also often referred to as working paycheck to paycheck) is a growing group in the current economic climate. Debates regarding the one percent and the .01 percent highlight the distance between the "haves" and the "have-nots," but in a way, that feels increasingly insidious to a shrinking middle class. Skyrocketing college student loan debts push retirement planning and estate building further out from the reach of early career workers, while cost of living increases limit what minimum and low wages can purchase. At the same time, the public perception is that the wealthiest group of Americans continues to build wealth and influence public policy. Another trend involves dual-income families, which impose different stressors. The following case discussion combines the challenges.

# Reflecting on Joe and Jill's Case

In a later chapter, we will take a closer look at how to implement effective CFC strategies; for now, it is important to begin thinking through cases such as Joe and Jill's. In reflecting on the vignette at the beginning of the chapter, where would you want to begin? As I will ask in most vignettes, do you see this case as a career counseling issue or a mental health one, based on your own experiences with work and relationships? Many new counselors might be tempted to refer these clients to a career specialist in the community, one who focuses on job search preparation and exploration. The perspective this text takes is that counselors have a distinctive skill set and training history that prepares them to deal with a host of issues—and this is reflective in the 2014 American Counseling Association (ACA) Code of Ethics—so before referring, it is important to be certain that the issue is truly beyond our scope of practice and/or competence. In the majority of cases, counselors will be qualified and ethically accountable to provide CFC. This text is all about providing a map to success in this area—and even building a desire in counselors to do the work of CFC.

*New (and not-so-new) counselor mistakes in addressing career-related issues.* The first issue that will likely be a barrier to working effectively with clients like Joe and Jill is if the counselor internalizes the clients' pressure to figure out their finances and find a higher paying job. Getting clients more money or a job is not the role of the counselor! As soon as counselors take this on, they lose their objectivity and begin trouble-shooting and problem-solving. This is perhaps the number two reason counselors do not get energized by, nor feel successful, in counseling clients with career-related issues. The primary reason is that, often, counseling for career issues does not feel like real counseling. Throughout this text, you will experience ways that this does not need to be the case (and you may even want to pursue CFC in your practice, not just manage those issues when they walk through your door).

Once a counselor recognizes that they are not responsible for getting Joe and Jill more money and jobs, they can proceed with CFC by engaging in just that: counseling. The counselor can begin building the relationship by empathically listening as clients describe their situations and clarifying what the clients see is the problem (it is possible, even probable, that Joe and Jill will not agree on what the problem is). Likewise, the counselor will listen carefully and deeply to the goals these clients have in mind. In therapy, I will often ask, "at the end of our work together, when it has been successful, what will have changed? How will your behavior be different?" (If I only ask how differently they will feel, I may set myself up for vague goals that lack measurable progress markers. Experienced counselors know that clients often need to act differently before they feel or think differently). Once the outcomes goals and expectations are clear, the counselor can correct any client belief that the counselor will provide a better job by the end of their work together, or even that the counselor will tell them how to get a job. This is a key point that bears repeating. Counselors do not get clients jobs, nor do they tell clients how to get better jobs. And counselors do not apologize for these facts; in contrast, they embrace this role. The fact is, counselors are process experts who facilitate client development across multiple domains, thereby increasing the likelihood of success in multiple areas. I would go as far as to say that rarely do even clients come to counseling expecting their counselor to find them a job or more money. Instead, it is the counselor who often volunteers (implicitly, though at times explicitly, as well) to carry this load, often to negative effect.

Joe and Jill are concerned about money and employment. But they are also concerned about the stress they feel, their parenting, and the way they manage their relationship with one another. Therefore, the "answer" is not found just in finding a better job. The path forward is in asking betters questions, such as, "what are the things Joe and Jill can directly, immediately begin to change in the process?" Getting a job is analogous to "getting happiness;" we can really only act and think in ways that increase the likelihood that we will experience happiness. We cannot make it happen. Likewise, humans cannot make a job happen; instead, they can act and think in ways that will increase the likelihood of obtaining a job. Most importantly, in CFC, we assist clients in creating those circumstances that increase the likelihood of their success across life domains. This text guides readers in how to do this, and one way forward that might not be the first place you look, is in integrating neuroscience into counseling.

## The Role of Neuroscience Integration into CFC

Several decades of scholarship have demonstrated the connections between vocational identity and self-identity. Since the 1980s, John Holland has advanced the view that success work and careers are largely dependent upon a clear sense of self. It has been demonstrated that this clarity can positively impact multiple factors of well-being including career health. Despite the advances in this area of the career and vocational literature, limited attention has been paid to how this self develops in the brain—there is a plethora of research on identity and the brain; it just has not been connected to career identity and development. So, I do that here, beginning with one of the locations of identity: memory.

Autobiographical memory is a type of declarative memory that contains information about the self. It is the seat and function of one's identity. Without stepping on the toes of philosophers, in many ways the self—one's identity—resides in the memory. Memory, in turn, is stored in and controlled by specific brain regions. Importantly, autobiographical memory seems to be governed by two specific regions of the brain: the hippocampus and the ventromedial prefrontal cortex (vmPFC; Bonnici et al, 2012). This fact alone has implications for how one's self is experienced and expressed. As such, this pertains to the work of CFC. The hippocampus plays a key and almost exclusive role in the executive function of memory; it governs encoding and retrieval to a great extent. The vmPFC plays multiple roles in higher order cognitive functioning, namely in context-based and emotionally salient decision-making (Murayama et al., 2013). This means that the specific brain regions involved in goal-directed decision-making also manages memories related to the self: autobiographical memory. But what, then, is autobiographical memory, really?

Autobiographical memory is the repository of memories that involve the self and the self in context. But it is not just a warehouse; it works to consolidate memories passed along by the hippocampus, effectively shaping those memories (Bonnici et al., 2012). These memories involve relationships, experiences, and environments that give substance and texture to the neurobiological self (Frenton et al., 2013). The brain seems to weave these factors together into a whole that makes up the self. Later, this self is projected onto situations to assist in guiding decisions. But what material from relationships, experiences, and environments get to stay, and which are jettisoned? The answer remains murky. Nevertheless, it is important to note that this self (an admittedly Western construct) plays a key role in decision making. And decision making is a hallmark of career decision making. If Frank Parsons was perspicacious in his observations over 100 years ago—and he was—then how truly reasoned can career decisions be without knowledge of the self that goes beyond interests, abilities, personality, and values? Parsons' now-immortalized formula has been a cornerstone of career counseling for over a century. We will take a closer look in a later chapter, but in essence, self-knowledge + occupational knowledge + true reasoning = wise career choice.

One of the implications of this process is the perception (and reality) of self-directed choice (versus perceived or actual forced choice) related to career. Another contribution of neuroscience to this discussion involves the brain regions correlated with self-knowledge and goal orientation. For example, Murayama et al. (2013) demonstrated that self-directed task failure creates an almost positive feedback experience in the vmPFC (as opposed to a negative experience). In contrast, the reward-related structure, the striatum, was conspicuously uninvolved in failure during self-directed tasks. This is important, because the striatum is associated with unconscious reward, whereas the vmPFC is associated with conscious rewards involving higher-order thinking and behavior. The implications of Murayama's findings could indicate that, when individuals engage in a self-directed task in which they experience failure, this failure is seen (by the brain) as helpful information, rather than internalized as a negative reward.

It is at this juncture that neuroscience integration collides into CFC and is a dominant theme running through this text. Super recognized elements of this integration:

> The process of vocational development is essentially that of developing and implementing a self concept: it is a compromise process in which the self concept is a product of the interaction of inherited aptitudes, neural and endocrine make-up, opportunity to play various roles, and evaluations of the extent to which the results of role playing meet with the approval of superiors and fellows. (Super, 1951, p. 190).

You don't need to be a neuroscientist or even love brain science to appreciate the possible contributions it can make to CFC. Findings like these have important ramifications for CFC in that they support the need for a self-directed career choice, reframe failure as important feedback, and point to ways counselors can build resilience in their clients.

**Language in career counseling.** Language matters to the extent that it creates mental images of the words used to describe something. The catch is that the images created by those words are dependent on the meaning ascribed by the individual. That meaning is generated by experience, as well as the context of the word and the person. This is important, because as we look at language in CFC, the words used have different meanings to different people, so we do not want to get hung up on precise definitions. For example, career has been defined as "one's vocational behavior across the lifespan" (Ethridge, Burnhill, & Dong, 2009, citing Brown, 2002), yet counselors, students, and clients may struggle to see the practical value in definitions such as these. A couple of general descriptions and guidelines will be helpful as those terms are used throughout this text. So, in a sense, I operationally define these terms for our use throughout the book as we encounter them.

**Contemporary Issues in CFC: Work-Life Balance.** During the 2016 Republican Primary campaign, Florida Governor Jeb Bush made a damaging gaffe to the effect that one of his goals was to get Americans to work more (i.e. longer hours). For millions of Americans—and workers around the world—the workday/week/year feels increasingly longer, so to hear a politician demand more from them was too much. Every week, workers head off to work, enduring a long commute, arriving at a job that pays less than it did 10 years ago (when adjusted for inflation), requiring more work for the same or less pay, in order to keep hold of an increasingly undesirable job. However, despite their disdain, the scarcity of employment keeps them hanging on, while their work satisfaction plummets and, likely with it, their performance. Even when they do hang on, there is no guarantee that the company will hold on to them. This takes a toll on their physical, mental, and relational well-being. Regardless of the way a career-related issue presents in counseling, counselors must be prepared to empathize with the toll it takes on them. Despite the ubiquity of career experience, each individual's encounter with work-related issues is unique. Ironically, this ubiquity can make clients feel as if they are the only one going through these struggles and that they are somehow flawed because of it.

# Summary

Work is a vital part of culture and society but plays a key role in the identity development of the individual. Likewise, identity is often manifest through work. Counselors are critical to the advancement of society as they walk alongside individuals who are lost in the process of understanding themselves and their place in the world. As we will see throughout this text, CFC is a social justice, advocacy-oriented process, one that is interwoven into the fabric of counseling, guidance, and career counseling. Embracing this role more fully, counselors will be able to extend their impact in their local communities and beyond. This text serves as a guide in moving in that direction.

**Table 1.1. Pope's (2000) Social Transitions Stage Model (Adapted)**

| Stage | Time Period | Name | Description | Key Names / Dates |
|---|---|---|---|---|
| 1 | 1890–1919 | Job Placement Services | Confluence of social and industrial factors forced rethinking world of work: move from agrarian to industrial society; influx of workers from farms to factories (and cities); WWI veterans return and need work; increase in role of psychological testing; social reform movements; job placement was key | 1913: National Vocational Guidance Association (NVGA) established; Smith-Hughes Act of 1917 est. secondary school vocational training; Parson's *Choosing a Vocation* published posthumously in 1909 |
| 2 | 1920–1939 | Educational Guidance in the Schools | Increased need for literacy; continued advancement in psychometric testing, including vocational assessment; reformers Jesse B. Davis and Eli Weaver | 1921: *Principles and Practices of Vocational Guidance*;<br>1929: Stock Market crash leading to Great Depression of the 1930s;<br>1933: Civilian Conservation Corps (CCC) established;<br>1935: Works Progress Administration |

*(continued)*

Table 1.1. (***continued***)

| Stage | Time Period | Name | Description | Key Names / Dates |
|---|---|---|---|---|
| 3 | 1940–1959 | Colleges and Universities and the Training of Counselors | WWII results in Truman's Fair Deal (Veteran employment); Sputnik launch scares the U.S. in drafting National Defense Education Act (1957); NVGA becomes founding division of American Personnel Guidance Association—this more dramatically diminishes NVGA membership, as American Personnel and Guidance Association (APGA) became American Association for Counseling and Development and, later, the ACA | 1939–1945: WWII; 1957: Russia launches Sputnik; Army GI Bill |
| 4 | 1960–1979 | Meaningful Work and Organizational Career Development | Civil Rights Movement; Vietnam Conflict; press to find work that "matters"; explosion of social legislation focused on employment, including Head Start and Job Corps | 1963 (1968, 1976): Vocational Education Act; 1962: Manpower Development and Training Act to adjust for job loss from automation; 1966: Anne Roe receives inaugural Eminent Career Award from NVGA; 1967: Vocational Education Act initiates the development of the Bureau of Labor and Statistics |
| 5 | 1980–1989 | Independent Practice Career Counseling and Outplacement Services | Shift from industrial to information and technology; career counseling as private practice work; outplacement (i.e., downsizing, laying off, firing) takes center stage as companies try to adjust to transitions | c. 1982: National Certified Career Counselor Credential by NVGA; 1976 "ACES Position Paper on Counselor Preparation for Career Development"; 1984: Carl D. Perkins Vocational Education Act; 1984: NVGA becomes the National Career Development Association (NCDA) |

| Stage | Time Period | Name | Description | Key Names / Dates |
|---|---|---|---|---|
| 6 | 1990–1998 | A Focus on the School-to-Job Transition; Internalization of Career Counseling; Multicultural Career Counseling, and Increasing Sophistication in the use of Technology | Continued expansion of career counseling services; Americans With Disabilities Act of 1990 has significant impact on access and opportunities to work for all—covers physical and mental disabilities; increase in technology and "instant" communication and implications for world of work comes into great focus; Soviet Union dissolves during this period, increasing global economy, global workforce, and great international career counseling; increase in multicultural considerations in career counseling; women continue to be marginalized in workplace/workforce | 1998: Workforce Initiative Act;<br>1994: School-to-Work Opportunities Act;<br>1994: One-Stop Career Centers Act |
| 7* | 1999–Present (2017) | Globalization and an Aging Workforce | Shifts in worker demographics as Americans live and work longer; increasing numbers of retirees not fully replaced by successive generations; outsourcing of jobs reaching global (and epidemic?) proportions; increased pressures on school counselors to prepare and push students toward college | 2001: No Child Left Behind Act (NCLB);<br>2014: Workforce Innovation and Opportunity Act (WIOA);<br>Reach Higher Initiative:<br>https://www.whitehouse.gov/reach-higher |

What you can see from this table is that career development and counseling have been close companions for over 100 years. Time and time again, the U.S. government has called upon school and other counselors to support that national effort to educate and train the nation's workforce. This occurs in a variety of ways across numerous agencies, supported by copious legislation.

Table 1.2. 2016 CACREP Standards

| 4. CAREER DEVELOPMENT |
| --- |
| A. Theories and models of career development, counseling, and decision making |
| B. Approaches for conceptualizing the interrelationships among and between work, mental well-being, relationships, and other life roles and factors |
| C. Processes for identifying and using career, avocational, educational, occupational, and labor market information resources, technology, and information systems |
| D. Approaches for assessing the conditions of the work environment on clients' life experiences |
| E. Strategies for assessing abilities, interests, values, personality, and other factors that contribute to career development |
| F. Strategies for career development program planning, organization, implementation, administration, and evaluation |
| G. Strategies for advocating for diverse clients' career and educational development and employment opportunities in a global economy |
| a. Strategies for facilitating client skill development for career, educational, and life-work planning and management |
| 9. Methods of identifying and using assessment tools and techniques relevant to career planning and decision making |
| 10. Ethical and culturally relevant strategies for addressing career development |

Table 1.3. CFC Chapters by CACREP Standards.

| CAREER DEVELOPMENT F.1.4.a-j | *Essentials of CFC* Chapters |
| --- | --- |
| a. Theories and models of career development, counseling, and decision making | 2–6 |
| b. Approaches for conceptualizing the interrelationships among and between work, mental well-being, relationships, and other life roles and factors | 10 |
| c. Processes for identifying and using career, avocational, educational, occupational, and labor market information resources, technology, and information systems | 2–5 |
| d. Approaches for assessing the conditions of the work environment on clients' life experiences | 10 |
| e. Strategies for assessing abilities, interests, values, personality, and other factors that contribute to career development | 2–5 |
| f. Strategies for career development program planning, organization, implementation, administration, and evaluation | 11, 12 |
| g. Strategies for advocating for diverse clients' career and educational development and employment opportunities in a global economy | 8 |
| h. Strategies for facilitating client skill development for career, educational, and life-work planning and management | 13 |

| | |
|---|---|
| i. Methods of identifying and using assessment tools and techniques relevant to career planning and decision making | 2–5 |
| j. Ethical and culturally relevant strategies for addressing career development | 7–8 |

Abbreviations: CFC = career-focused counseling; CACREP = Council for Accreditation of Counseling & Related Educational Programs.

*It is important to note, at this point, that a little over half of masters counseling programs are accredited by the Council for Accreditation of Counseling & Related Educational Programs (CACREP), which is endorsed by the ACA. Because of their role in addressing national licensure portability, among other things, the standards are used as a compass for this text. There are many ways to address ethical, multiculturally-competent CFC; however, using the most stringent of program standards currently available will allow programs and readers to make the necessary adjustments as they proceed through the book.

# References

Bonnici, H. M., Chadwick, M. J., Lutti, A., Hassabis, D., Weiskopf, N., & Maguire, E. A. (2012). Detecting representations of recent and remote autobiographical memories in vmPFC and hippocampus. *The journal of neuroscience, 32*(47), 16982–16991.

Brewer, J. M., Cleary, E. J., Dunsmoor, C. C., Lake, J. S., Nichols, C. J., Smith, C. M., & Smith, H. P. C. (1942). *History of vocational guidance: Origins and early development.* New York: Harper and Bros.

Council for Accreditation of Counseling and Related Educational Programs (2015). 2016

CACREP Standards. Alexandria, VA. Retrieved from http://www.cacrep.org/for-programs/2016-cacrep-standards/.

Ethridge, G., Burnhill, D., & Dong, S. (2009). Career counseling across the life span. *The professional counselor's desk reference*, 443–453.

Erikson, E. H. (1968). *Identity: Youth and crisis.* New York, NY: W. W. Norton & Sons.

Freton, M., Lemogne, C., Bergouignan, L., Delaveau, P., Lehéricy, S., & Fossati, P. (2014). The eye of the self: precuneus volume and visual perspective during autobiographical memory retrieval. *Brain Structure and Function, 219*(3), 959–968.

Kelly, W. A. (1943). History of Vocational Guidance. *Thought, 18*(1), 146–147.

Luke, C. (2015). *Neuroscience for counselors and therapists: Integrating the sciences of mind and brain.* Thousand Oaks, CA: SAGE Publications.

Luke, C., Redekop, F., & Burgin, C. (2015). Psychological factors in community college student retention. *Community College Journal of Research and Practice, 39*(3), 222–234.

Luke, C., & Redekop, F. (2016). Supervision of co-occurring career and mental health concerns. *Career Planning and Adult Development Journal, 32*(1), 130–140.

Murayama, K., Matsumoto, M., Izuma, K., Sugiura, A., Ryan, R. M., Deci, E. L., &

Matsumoto, K. (2013). How self-determined choice facilitates performance: A key role of the ventromedial prefrontal cortex. *Cerebral Cortex, 25*(5), 1241-1251.

Pope, M. (2000). A brief history of career counseling in the United States. *Career Development Quarterly, 48*(3), 194–211.

Pope, M., Briddick, W. C., & Wilson, F. (2013). The historical importance of social justice in the founding of the national career development association. *The Career Development Quarterly, 61*(4), 368–373.

Remley, T. & Herlihy, B. (2009). Ethical, legal, and professional issues in counseling (3rd Ed.). New York, NY: Merrill.

Savickas, M. L., & Baker, D. B. (2005). The history of vocational psychology: Antecedents, origin, and early development. *Handbook of vocational psychology, 3*, 15–50.

Subich, L. M. (1993). How personal is career counseling?. *The Career Development Quarterly, 42*(2), 129–131.

Super, D. E. (1951). Vocational adjustment: implementing a self-concept. *Occupations.*

Super, D. E. (1955). Transition: from vocational guidance to counseling psychology. *Journal of Counseling Psychology, 2*(1), 3.

Whiston, S. C., & Oliver, L. W. (2005). Career counseling process and outcome. *Handbook of vocational psychology: Theory, research, and practice*, 155–194.

## Figure/Table Credits

Tab. 1.1: Mark Pope, "Social Transitions Stage Model (2000)," Adapted by Chad Luke.
Tab. 1.2: Copyright © 2016 by Council for Accreditation of Counseling & Related Educational Programs. Reprinted with permission.
Tab. 1.3: "CFC Chapters by CACREP Standards," Adapted by Chad Luke.

# SECTION ONE

# Theory, Assessment, Resources In Career-Focused Counseling

### School-Based Vignette: Xavier, 17

Xavier is a popular 17-year-old high school senior. He was referred to you for behavioral concerns, as he hasn't been paying attention in his classes. In an attempt to build rapport with Xavier, you ask him what he likes to do after school, to which he curtly replies, "I try to mind my own business." When you ask if he has an afterschool job, he shifts in his chair and tells you that his grandparents won't let him get one, so he "can focus on schoolwork." Xavier goes on to disclose that he makes straight As in his largely Advanced Placement coursework. He says that his grandparents, whom he lives with, had to give up their educations at early ages in order to provide for their families. While he says he understands his grandparents' concerns, Xavier says he feels stressed about paying for college, as his grandparents struggle to survive off of social security and their relatively meager retirement funds. You ask Xavier what he wants to study at university, and he tells you he's too stressed about finances to think about that. He says, "I need to be able to pay for college before I decide what to study."

CHAPTER TWO

# Career Development Theory, Assessment, & Counseling I: Trait and Factor

**Chapter Goals**

- Provide a brief overview of each of the most prevalent trait and factor theories
- Describe the career-focused counseling (CFC) implications of each theory discussed
- Utilize career theory to connect to clients' personal issues
- Articulate an integrated approach to theory, assessment, and resources

## Introduction

We will cover a lot of territory in the next few chapters, so I have enlisted the assistance of the two case vignettes for guidance. I would ask that you keep these two clients in mind as you review the theory descriptions that follow. Later, you will be provided with a brief session transcript that demonstrates the theory with each client. In this chapter, we begin by exploring the concept of theory in general, followed by a more detailed discussion of trait and factor theories. For each theory, you will encounter profiles of key theorists, along with essential points from the theory. We now turn our attention to theory.

# What is Theory?

Theory is a lens through which we view a phenomenon. If you have ever used a camera that had filters or used the tools on your smart phone for altering a picture, you may intuitively understand this: the filter affects the perception of the image being viewed without changing the actual image. Nothing has changed about that which is observed, only the lens or filter through which it is viewed. Career counseling theories, or filters, are grounded in repeated study and lead to a set of connected principles that describe, explain, predict, and seek to control a phenomenon (i.e., the scientific method). In CFC, we seek to find lenses that focus our view of the career-related issues of our clients in order to more adequately describe them, explain them to the client, predict what may happen, and provide the client with a sense of control over what comes next. Often our work in this area revolves around the decisions people make regarding their work or career.

As we begin to explore career theory over the next four chapters, you might take a moment to ask yourself what is required to make a decision about a job, work, career, or vocation. This could be a decision about applying for a job, getting an education and/or training for an occupation, transitioning from one job to the other, or many other things. For the last 100 hundred years, one theory (discussed below) has guided the discussion more than any other, and regardless of their appearance today, the majority of career theories contain components of, or at least owe portions of their existence to, it (Swanson & Fouad, 2015). I would go a bit further to say that any approach to CFC must contain the three vital components of Parson's seminal work, *Choosing a Vocation* (1909). It may be useful to reflect on your view of this as you read both Parson's profile, followed by a description of his theory.

***Choosing a Vocation.*** Parsons described three core components of the transition from not-work to work: self-knowledge, occupational knowledge, and bridging the gap between the two that he called "true reasoning." That's it. (This is obviously a reductive statement, and we will explore throughout this text how complex working with these three components can be.) Learn about oneself; learn about occupations; combine the two in a rational, meaningful way. All theory that has followed since

## Community-Based Vignette: Alexa, 21

**Alexa is a 21-year-old college student working in a local restaurant who comes to you for career counseling. She tells you that she switched from a major in special education to one in exercise science. After some inquiry, you learn that she initially chose special education, because a family member did that, and she then chose exercise science, because she ran cross-country all four years of high school. When asked what she wants to deal with in counseling, Alexa says, "Stress. Thinking about getting a job after graduation has been making me worry." She goes on to tell you that she switched out of special education after her first semester taking upper-division classes in her major. Alexa says that she wasn't sure if she wanted to teach, because she would "get too attached to the kids." She reports similar concerns with an exercise science job like gym teacher. She questions whether she wants to teach at all. Wiping away tears, Alexa discloses that she feels like she has been "trying to fill some kind of hole inside me" by finding a meaningful job in which she can help people, but to a greater extent than her restaurant server job.**

### Theorist Profile: Frank Parsons, Father of Career Counseling

**Engineer, art and history teacher, day laborer, lawyer, mayoral candidate of Boston, law professor, vocational activist ... these are just a few of the roles that occupied the career path of Frank Parsons prior to his founding of the vocational guidance movement at the turn of the 20th Century. Part of his work included opening the first clinic for vocational guidance (Zytowski 2001). He cemented his legacy through his establishment of the still-accepted foundations of career guidance: understanding the relationship between one's personal characteristics and the characteristics of the work environment. The true reasoning between these two aspects has formed the basis of trait and factor theory. Parsons worked primarily with young men and boys looking for work in an emerging industrial epoch. His key work, *Choosing a Vocation*, was published posthumously, the year following his death in 1909. Parsons heralded a new age of work-related decision-making by identifying vocation as a choice. This was a key transition in the thinking of many working class Americans who likely would continue on in the family trade or work. But in the changing landscape of American industry and agriculture—shifting away from an agrarian economy to an industrial one—people needed a way to navigate**

is predicated on this, regardless of the particular emphasis. This will frame the discussion of theory throughout this and subsequent chapters. I posit that all or most career theory subsequent to Parsons is related to one, two, or all three of these components, making them all look different on the surface, but containing the essence at their core. This section of the text explores the most current theories of relevance today in CFC and is divided into matching theories, developmental theories, learning (social and cognitive) theories, and postmodern, emergent theories. These are common, if artificial categories, necessary in some ways as a career theory heuristic. These individual theories and their respective categories will be viewed/reviewed in light of their correspondence (or not) to Parsons' three components.

There are many ways to categorize career theories in order to make them more digestible to students and practitioners. One common example is to group career theories into trait and factor theories, developmental theories, cognitive approaches, and all the rest. Another approach is to cover them chronologically, according to the time period in which they were developed. While a somewhat less common approach, this allows readers to better appreciate the social, economic, and political milieu in which these theories emerged. A third approach is the one used in this section and approaches career theory from the perspective of the client. In other words, how does the client frame the issue and the solution? Theory-based treatment should, of course, be client-centered, in the sense that the type of client and the client's presenting problem should really drive the approach used (Luke, 2015). While reasonable in concept, this can be quite challenging in application. For example, counselors, especially early in their careers, are more likely to select the counseling theory that best matches their orientation entering their training program. This does not reflect a conscious choice of a theoretical approach based on empirical evidence or even best practices. Instead, it is a theory chosen based on confirmation bias. This is common, even understandable, but may not always translate into positive client outcomes. Such is also the case in CFC.

Counselors may be inclined to select a theory based on the one that most closely reflects their worldview. In this section, I offer another approach to theory categorization that is intended to mitigate the effects of confirmation bias. In addition to grouping career theories according to their similarities and then by their chronological development, they are identified both by the category of career problem presented by the client, and by the counseling domain highlighted earlier and illuminated by Parsons over 100 years ago (1909). Table 2.1 contains a table that illustrates this grouping. There are many ways to challenge these groupings, but the approach is also meant to challenge students and practitioners in how they approach their clients: self-referentially or client-centered. A further distinction in this text and this section in particular is the way theory is connected to assessment and information gathering. As discussed below, the information gathered must connect logically to the assessments used and then to the lens or theory utilized. Furthermore, the theory used must connect logically to the type of client and type of client difficulty to be addressed.

**these decisions. It may seem foreign to many of us reading this to think of a time when career choice was negligible, if ever extant. In fact, the shift has been so thorough and enduring that career choice seems like a human right, rather than a luxury like it was in Parson's time.**

Table 2.1. Career Theory Summary

| Theory | Theorist | Parson's Component | Summary |
|---|---|---|---|
| Life-Span, Life-Space | Super (1951; 1955; 1980; 1990) | SK, TR | Developmental in nature—examines career factors at different stages in life and across career-related tasks |
| Trait and Factor | Holland (1996); Parsons (1909); E.K. Strong (1943) | SK | Seeks to understand the individual in terms of personality and match them with related careers |
| Theory of Work Adjustment | Dawis & Lofquist (1984) | SK, OK | Explores how individuals navigate transitions and obstacles in the workplace |
| Cognitive Information Processing | Peterson, Sampson, Reardon (1991); Peterson, Sampson, Reardon, & Lenz (2002) | TR | Approaches career decision-making as a problem to be solved and, therefore, amenable to cognitive decision-making models |
| Social Cognitive Career Theory | Brown & Lent (1996); Lent & Brown (2002) | SK, OK, TR | Combines constructs like self-efficacy, outcome expectations, and personal goals to explain and intervene with career-related barriers |
| Career Construction | Savickas (2005) | SK | Postmodern approach to career development wherein individuals construct their views of their career using life narratives that can support or inhibit success |

*(continued)*

Table 2.1. (*continued*)

| Theory | Theorist | Parson's Component | Summary |
|---|---|---|---|
| Happenstance Learning Theory | Krumboltz (1975, 2009) | SK, TR | Social learning model that promotes preparing the individual for unforeseen opportunities that can be encouraged through proactive behavior |
| Circumscription and Compromise | Gottfredson (1981, 2005) | SK, OK, TR | Social justice approach that examines the barriers that limit interests (circumscription) and challenges in accessing what is left (compromise) |

*SK—Self-Knowledge; OK—Occupational Knowledge; TR—True Reasoning*

# Trait and Factor Models

Parsons led the way in shaping a foundational approach to understanding the relationship between the individual and the world of work. His work lives on in the trait and factor models of career development, so named for the process of matching individual, relatively stable personal characteristics (traits) with markers in the work environment that indicate certain features of that work (factors). Trait-and-factor theories played a major role in the development of career and vocational counseling, beginning in the late 1800s with Frank Parsons, through the 1920s and 30s with the work of Strong on the Vocational Interest Blank (1929), and from the 1940s through today with John Holland's enduring work on personality and vocation. These theories are both simple and complex, and, at times, simplistic (Crites, 1981). They posit that the way to achieve success in the world of work is to use an understanding of the self (self-knowledge) in order to match personal characteristics with those in the work environment. While this sounds simple, it is rarely so, as anyone who has asked themselves who they are or what they want to do knows all too well. Additionally, as mentioned in an earlier chapter, the reality is that millions of Americans and hundreds of millions of humans around the world simply don't get the chance or privilege to self-reflect and choose; instead, they must simply act in order to survive.

***Multicultural Considerations from Trait and Factor Theory.*** A radical idea proposed by Strong in a 1936 article entitled "Interests of Men and Women," wherein Strong was among the first to articulate the inexplicable phenomenon that men and women had different vocational interests. By 1943, in his landmark book, Strong went further to exclaim that these differences are present despite the growing body of evidence that supported the notion that women were as intelligent and capable as men. The gender dynamics of the post-WWI industrial age must not be understated here: the nation and the world were reeling from a World War that saw millions of men shuttled off to battle, leaving women to run the machine of the nation and to support the war effort. Images of women working in munitions factories and otherwise performing "men's work" with aplomb left an indelible impression in the minds of many, creating dissonance along with it. Strong's writings were crucial and timely, and heralded a revolution in career guidance. Strong's voice resonates once again as the battle for equality has taken on the tone and tenor of "sameness". Strong's words from 1943 are prescient and relevant for our current cultural conversations,

> Before the advent of intelligence tests it was customary to view women as having intelligence inferior to that of men. Widespread use of these tests has demonstrated the fallacy of that view. But the fact that the two sexes obtain approximately equal scores in the tests does not mean that the character and quality of their intellectual processes is similar. They may have the same general capacity and at the same time use this capacity in different directions. (Strong, 1943, p. 216).

***Holland's Theory of Vocational Choice.*** In 1959, John Holland made his mark on the career and vocational development fields though the publication of *A Theory of Vocational Choice*. In it, he laid out another dimension relative to Parson's self-knowledge by describing the relationship between personality and career choice. Reflecting on his work, he proclaims, "I have become addicted to seeing careers from an individual's perspective—how can a person's difficulties be resolved within the present personal and environmental resources" (Holland, 1992, p. xi). As Walsh (2008) highlights, Holland was among the first to explore how individual differences related to environmental work differences. In essence, Holland proposed six dimensions of personality that matched with six dimensions of work environments. Holland outlined three postulates in this regard:

Holland proffered three key questions that defined his work and theory: What personal and environmental characteristics lead to satisfying career decisions, involvement, and achievement, and what characteristics lead to indecision, dissatisfying decisions, or lack of accomplishment? What personal and environmental characteristics lead to stability or change in the kind and level of work a person performs over a lifetime? What are the most effective methods for providing assistance to people with career problems (Holland, 1997, p. 1)?

Along with these key questions, Holland articulated four working assumptions: a) in our culture, most persons can be categorized as one of six personality types: Realistic, Investigative,

## Trait and Factor Essentials

**Self-Knowledge—In the post-war, post-agrarian world of a "reunited" America, there would have been little to no time to pause for reflection on one's interests, abilities, values, and preferences. These might have been present to a certain extent, but would have lived outside of awareness, pushed out by the need to survive and to take whatever was available. Self-knowledge, and personal reflection in particular, was a radical notion, one that would have seemed quite foreign to the boys and young men seeking help from Parson's clinic.**

**Occupational Knowledge - Occupational knowledge would have seemed similarly alien in Parson's time. There was limited mobility in terms of moving across the country to take a job. Instead, knowledge of work was word-of-mouth, rudimentary networking and depended on social status. The idea that a person could think of their personal characteristics and seek to intentionally match these with a job was a bit of a fantasy.**

**True Reasoning—Parsons mentioned this concept in his book but did not elaborate much on what this meant to him, at least not in his published writings. It seems a logical intuition, however, that Parsons believed in some active, intentional process whereby individuals looked into themselves and into the world of work and made pairings that increased the**

likelihood of a successful vocational match.

## Theorist Profile: E. K. Strong

If the Strong Interest Inventory (SSI) is based largely on John Holland's theory, where does the SSI get its name? In 1927, the Vocational Interest Blank became E. K. Strong's first occupational interest inventory and the very first of its kind. Strong explored and focused on the connection between interests and career decision making (Jo-Ida Hansen, 2008), a fairly radical concept in post–World War I America. Strong's work was an extension of Parsons in that Strong elaborated on the *interest* component of self-knowledge. This area of scholarly and applied inquiry served as a catalyst for the vocational guidance movement and generated copious amounts of research data and literature. It shifted the conversation from abilities alone to interests and abilities, based on what would prove to be, over subsequent decades, the utility of matching the two in career choice. The Strong Interest Inventory will be covered in greater detail in the chapter on assessment, but it may suffice to say the numerous versions of the instrument turned the field upside down and added to the U.S. Army's work in predicting soldier-duty matching (Hansen, 2008).

To return to the question posed above, the Strong Vocational Interest Blank, inaugurated in 1927, went

Artistic, Social, Enterprising, or Conventional; b) there are six model environments: Realistic, Investigative, Artistic, Social, Enterprising, or Conventional; c) people search for environments that will let them exercise their skills and abilities, express their attitudes and values, and take on agreeable problems and roles; and d) behavior is determined by an interaction between personality and environment (Holland, 1997, pp. 4–5). These assumptions define the work of the extended Parson's foundation by specifying the six personality and six work domains.

Holland's secondary assumptions articulated notable characteristics akin to true reasoning. These include consistency—"the degree of relatedness between personality types or environmental models" and affect preference; differentiation—"the degree to which a person or an environment is well defined;" identity—"possession of a clear and stable picture of one's goals, interests, and talents"; environment—"when an environment or an organization has clear and integrated goals, tasks, and rewards that are stable over long time intervals"; congruence—matching personality and environment, where rewards match desires; and calculus—the degree of relationship of factors measured by distance on the hexagon graphic (pp. 4–5).

As can be seen in the richness of the questions and the assumptions, Holland shifted the collective perspective of vocational development and provided a richness to the "matching" of self and the world of work. He took Parson's unfinished model (due to his untimely death) and elaborated on it to the state we find it in today: Holland's theory and the Strong Interest Inventory provide the "bread-and-butter" approach to career development we see today, from P–12 schools to career centers in the community. Holland proposed and demonstrated empirically that humans exhibit vocational personality characteristics that can be classified into six types, commonly referred to at the RIASEC Model. This theory is discussed in greater detail in the chapter on assessment. Holland also identified external factors, such as vocational opportunities and social pressures, as exerting potential negative impacts on the individual's ability to make effective vocational matches.

***Dawis and Lofquist—Theory of Work Adjustment (TWA).*** Whereas Holland theorized particularly about choosing a career and the initial procurement of work, Dawis and Lofquist extended Parsons' ideas to work satisfaction. Throughout the text, we will explore different models for understanding career-related presenting problems and covered in greater detail Busacca's taxonomy (2002): choosing an occupation, preparing to enter a chosen occupation, and coping with career. Dawis and Lofquist's Theory of Work Adjustment (TWA) is a trait and factor matching theory, and its import is demonstrated most clearly in the work adjustment domain, compared with theories that address career choice and career entry more explicitly.

"The major sets of variables used in the theory are abilities and needs to describe work personalities, ability requirements and reinforcer systems to describe work environments, and satisfactoriness, satisfaction, and tenure to describe outcomes of the interaction" (1976, p. 55). Rather than a static form of matching, Dawis and Lofquist (1976) describe the person and environment as mutually responsive to one another, "the continuous and dynamic process by which the individual seeks to achieve and maintain correspondence with his or her work environment" (p. 55). For Dawis and Lofquist, correspondence is the *mutual responsiveness* of an individual and his or her environment (1976).

# Trait-And-Factor Theories in Session

The brief descriptions of two prominent trait and factor theories above are intended to whet the reader's appetite for application. The work on understanding and applying this theory comes through case reflection. To that end, we now turn our focus toward our work with the two hypothetical clients, Xavier and Alexa. In applying a trait and factor approach to Xavier and Alexa, consider which of Parsons' three components a counselor would begin with in order to be most effective.

Parson's theory is a time-tested approach to the basic building blocks of career choice. The nuance comes in the approach the counselor takes in ascertaining client characteristics, on the one hand, and facilitating client's exploration of the world of work, on the other. As mentioned above, many times, clients enter the counseling room not having had the time, energy, or skill to reflect intentionally on their life and the major components of self-knowledge as described by Parsons:

through a few versions until 1974, when it underwent a radical transformation through the inclusion of a women's version, in addition to the addition of John Holland's six types of personality traits applied to the world of work. Hence, while the Strong Interest Inventory was initiated and innovated by E. K. Strong for many decades, the addition of Holland's personality typology brought about a tremendous shift in the measurement and application of interests in career choice.

### *Holland Essentials*:

### Background Principles

- The choice of a vocation is an expression of personality.
- Interest inventories are personality inventories.
- Vocational stereotypes have reliable and important psychological and sociological meanings.
- The members of a vocation have similar personalities and similar histories of personal development.
- Because people in a vocational group have similar personalities, they will respond to many situations and problems in similar ways, and they will create characteristic interpersonal environments.
- Vocational satisfaction, stability, and achievement depend on the congruence between one's personality and the

environment in which one works. (pp. 7–11).

### TWA Essentials

*Flexibility*—Tolerance of the discorrespondence between personality factors and work environmental factors. Correspondence increases with tenure, so it is assumed that individuals with greater flexibility will tolerate imperfect features until correspondence increases.

*Activeness*—Describes a personality feature wherein the individual actively seeks to impact the work environment with the intention of increasing correspondence.

*Reactiveness*—Describes a personality feature wherein the individual seeks to change his or her own self in order to increase correspondence.

*Celerity*—Describes a personality feature related to the speed at which an individual acts to increase correspondence.

### Xavier in Session

In Xavier's situation, it seems that exploring the self-knowledge component of the trait and factor approach is timely. However, the type of knowledge to explore extends beyond work-related attributes. Consider the following sample exchange:

CO: Xavier, I noticed that you have really good grades but that you have also been struggling to stay focused in some classes. What do you think is going on?

skills, abilities, preferences (1909). At the same time, client's career information is, many times, informed by assumption, word of mouth, and ill-informed intuition. Next, we view trait and factor through the lens of a community counseling session.

Alexa's case illustrates the challenge in practice as to how clients assemble these two bodies of information in order to make career choices. True reasoning can easily be interpreted as the filters humans use in gaining understanding and then applying these two informational components. Our own baggage can hinder how we move forward in reasoning through the meaning in these two areas, even if we were able to first gather accurate information in the domains of self and occupational knowledge. CFC recognizes the simplicity of the components of Parson's model, at least on the surface, but then demonstrate a vast appreciation for how individual and cultural differences impact the use of this information. Before we conclude this theory overview, it is important to consider the neuroscience implications for this theory.

## Summary

One of the barriers to effective CFC, particularly among newer counselors, is the belief that career theory requires us to jettison our counseling theories or basic skills. Nowhere is this truer than in the understanding and use of trait and factor theories. These theories have generated considerable development and use of assessment instruments. I argue throughout this book that CFC begins with the basics of counseling and adds specifics regarding career-related issues as a presenting problem—the counselor, in league with the client, is the most powerful and effective assessment instrument. The challenge is to maintain a perspective that builds on counseling, rather than moving out of the role of counselor to become a consultant or adviser. CFC is a developmental process that connects to multiple issues across the lifespan. These considerations are important to keep in mind as we discuss assessment in trait and factor approaches next.

# Assessment in Trait and Factor Models

Table 2.2. Theory → Assessment → Info/Resources

| Theory | Assessment | Resources |
|---|---|---|
| Trait and Factor<br><br>Person-Environment Fit<br><br>Work Adjustment | Interests—<br>-Strong Interest Inventory<br>-Minnesota Importance Questionnaire<br>-Kuder Occupational Skills Survey | www.careeronestop.org Interest Profile<br>http://vpr.psych.umn.edu/miq.html<br>http://www.kuder.com/who-we-help/educators-counselors-practitioners/<br>http://www.self-directed-search.com<br>http://www.valparint.com/sigi3.htm |
| | Personality—<br>-Myers-Briggs Type Indicator<br>-16PF<br>-NEO-PI-R | https://www.cpp.com/products/mbti/index.aspx<br>http://www.pearsonclinical.com/psychology/products/100000483/16pf-fifth-edition.html<br>http://www4.parinc.com/Products/Product.aspx?ProductID=NEO-PI-R<br>https://v6.typefocus.com |
| | Values—<br>-Values Card Sort<br>-Values Checklist | http://www.thegoodproject.org/toolkits-curricula/the-goodwork-toolkit/value-sort-activity/<br>https://www.onetonline.org/find/descriptor/browse/Work_Values/ |
| | Skills—<br>-Campbell Interests and Skills Survey<br>-General Aptitude Test Battery | http://www.pearsonclinical.com/talent/products/100000323/campbell-interest-and-skill-survey-ciss.html<br>http://www.careerchoiceguide.com/general-aptitude-test-battery.html<br>www.onetonline.org |

# Assessment Domains in CFC

Assessment has become an integral part of career counseling. However, in order to use assessment effectively, counselors must understand their construction and functions, instead of blithely accepting their value. Fred Borgen (2008, p. 1408) has identified 10 categories of career measures that can assist counselors in making effective use of assessment processes and have been summarized in Table 2.2. These categories serve to inform CFC in what assessments to select and why they should be used.

**Table 2.3. Borgen's Career Categories with the Addition of Sample Assessments**

| Borgen Category | Assessment |
|---|---|
| Comprehensive interest inventory with broad and specific measures | Strong Interest Inventory (SII) |
| | Self-Directed Search (SDS) |
| Comprehensive personality inventory identifying strengths in normal people | Myers-Briggs Type Indicator |
| | Neo-PI (Big 5) |
| | Firo-B |
| | 16PF |
| Comprehensive confidence inventory with broad and specific measures | Skills Confidence Inventory |
| Measure of work and life values | Values Cart Sort |
| | Work Values Inventory |
| Measure of career indecision | Career Thoughts Inventory |
| | Career Beliefs Inventory |
| | My Vocational Situation |
| Life satisfaction or well-being measure | The Salience Inventory |
| Job or college satisfaction measure | Minnesota Importance Questionnaire |
| Measure of career maturity | Career Maturity Inventory |
| Measure of career decision-making self-efficacy | Career Decision Self-Efficacy Scale |
| Career goal-setting inventory | Open-ended responses |

As you can see, there are many categories from which to choose, and the list can feel daunting. However, as you read, you will recognize that these categories can assist us in being judicious in the application of assessments. In this section, we take a closer look at specific instruments related to trait and factor theories. In fact, many authors divide career assessments based on the theory associated with them (see D. Sheperis in Capuzzi & Stauffer, 2012). Others describe them categorically, typically across four main factors: interests, skills, personality, and values (see Duggar, 2017). Both of these approaches have merit and have been used to great effect. Here, I also use Borgen's description in part because of its comprehensiveness, as well as it's conceptual simplicity.

But first, the Association for Assessment in Counseling and Education, a division of the American Counseling Association, provides guidance for counselors in the use of assessments with clients, particularly with considerations for diverse clients. Its Standards for Multicultural Assessment (2012) provides the following guidance (see its website for more detail:

http://aarc-counseling.org/assets/cms/uploads/files/AACE-AMCD.pdf ):

**ADVOCACY**

Culturally competent professional counselors recognize the importance of social justice advocacy; they integrate understanding of age, gender, ability, race, ethnic group, national origin, religion, sexual orientation, linguistic background, and other personal characteristics in order to provide appropriate assessment and diagnostic techniques.

**SELECTION OF ASSESSMENTS: CONTENT AND PURPOSE, NORMING, RELIABILITY AND VALIDITY**

Culturally competent professional counselors select assessments and diagnostic techniques that are appropriate and effective for diverse client populations.

**ADMINISTRATION AND SCORING OF ASSESSMENTS**

Culturally competent professional counselors recognize challenges inherent in assessment of persons and seek to provide administration and scoring of assessment to clients respecting age, gender, ability, race, ethnic group, national origin, religion, sexual orientation, linguistic background, and other personal characteristics.

**INTERPRETATION AND APPLICATION OF ASSESSMENT RESULTS**

Culturally competent professional counselors acknowledge the importance of social justice advocacy in interpretation and communication of assessment results with diverse populations.

**TRAINING IN THE USES OF ASSESSMENTS**

Culturally competent professional counselors seek training and supervised experience to ensure they provide appropriate assessment and diagnostic techniques for diverse client populations.

CL: I don't know, I guess I'm feeling some pressure from my school and family about figuring out the college thing.

CO: Okay, so rather than looking forward to graduation and the excitement of going to college, you are feeling stress?

CL: Yep. College is only an option if you can afford it ... oh yeah, and if you figure out what the heck you're supposed to pick for a career!

CO: There are two things going on in what you just said: even if you could pay for it, you don't know what you'd even major in.

CL: Exactly! It would be a huge waste of money to go without knowing! I can't do that to my family.

CO: Can I see if I understand your dilemma correctly?

CL: Yes.

CO: You see the value in attending college but are not sure what you'd major in, because you don't know what career to choose. Under those circumstances, it would be a waste to try to find funding for college. Is that close?

CL: That's definitely it and my family and counselor don't seem to get that.

CO: It can be tough to explain and to feel understood. What information about choosing a major/career is missing that might help you in this process?

CL: Well, everything! How am I supposed decide on the rest of my life? What if I make the wrong decision? This seems impossible, especially when I don't know what I want to do or who I want to be!

CO: This decision feels like more than selecting a starting point for college and instead feels like a life sentence. Is that right?

CL: That's because it is the rest of my life!

CO: Perhaps. It certainly feels like a daunting process for you. I wonder if we could back up a bit and talk a little about what you like, without making any decisions. Can you give me a couple of sessions to chat about yourself without feeling like I'm just another person pressuring you to make a lifelong decision?

CL: I'll try. That'd be really different from what I'm feeling now.

### Alexa in Session

For Alexa, she's already chosen a college major and is preparing to graduate. Yet, she seems unsure of how to blend her self-knowledge with occupational knowledge. Therefore, it seems she would benefit from a "true reasoning" approach, one that helps her refine her understanding of how these two knowledge domains come together.

CO: It certainly seems like the choices you're facing have an emotional weight to them, Alexa.

CL: I feel so much stress over making the right decision.

CO: How would you know if you'd made the right decision?

CL: I don't know. How does anyone know?

CO: It just sounds like this is an important issue for you

Next, we take a closer look at a few of the assessments listed above and how to use them with career-focused counseling (CFC) clients through the lens trait and factor theories.

## Assessing Interests—Strong Interest Inventory

As we discussed in a previous chapter, the Strong Interest Inventory (SII) that we know today is the culmination of the work of E. K. Strong, a Stanford University Business Professor, though his work with the instrument continued after his retirement. It has been revised many times and has evolved into its current form thanks to the research and work by John Holland (1959). The SII is comprised of 291 questions or items, using a 5-point Likert-type scale. For instance, respondents might read a question, such as "Making a speech" (*Technical Brief for the Newly Revised Strong Interest Inventory® Assessment* Copyright 2004 by CPP, Inc. All rights reserved.) and mark whether they Strongly Dislike, Like, Indifferent, Dislike, or Strongly Dislike. Responses are compared to normative samples of individuals working in a variety of fields and report at least moderate levels of satisfaction with their work. Please note, however, that the SII does not assess work performance! Over the course of the 291 items, the instrument is able to report on a set of responses using the following profile categories:

***General Occupational Themes***—these six categories (RIASEC) are based on Holland's (1959) theory and include the following:

- Realistic: This theme speaks to individuals who enjoy working with their hands over working with people. Examples include jobs working with tools, machines, or computers.
- Investigative: This theme involves using one's mind to solve problems or learn new information for learning's sake. Examples include college professor, scientist, or physicians.
- Artistic: In this theme, individuals prefer creative problem solving over structured work environments. Examples include the arts, performing, or other forms of personal expression.

- Social: This theme includes the helping professions, herein working with people takes priority over working with things. Examples include teachers, counselors, and clergy.
- Enterprising: Individuals in this theme prefer persuading and motivating. Examples include managers, salespeople, and other risk-taking fields.
- Conventional: These individuals prefer structured problem-solving, using rules and plans to complete work. Examples include accounting, data management, and other roles that support leadership positions.

The combination(s) of the top three scores in the six themes produce what is called a Holland code. These codes are paired with hundreds of possible careers.

***Basic Interest Scales (BIS)***—The SII is structured from broad themes to specific tasks and jobs. The BIS represent the next level of information from the SII. There are 30 BIS, in which the top five are highlighted in the score report. Examples include Counseling and Helping, Protective Services, and Visual Arts and Design.

***Occupational Scales (OS)***—Updated based on new research in 2012, the OS contains 244 occupations, or 122 pairs separated by gender. This 2012 revision was meant to encourage exploration of all occupations regardless of their historic gender over-representation.

***Personal Style Scales***—These scales are five characteristics rated on a continuum of clarity. They represent the manner in which an individual may approach the world of work, in terms of: work style, learning environment, leadership style, risk taking, team orientation.

***Profile Summary***—As the name implies, a score report includes a summary of all the major categories.

For additional information on the SII, you can visit the publisher's website at

www.cpp.com.

SII and CFC. The value of the SII rests in its ability to identify themes in one's interests, and then compare those interests

and it makes me wonder what kind of decision would ease your stress.

CL: Oh. Well, I'd have a job that matters, one that makes me feel fulfilled. And that I could make a living at so that my parents would not feel like they had wasted their money.

CO: I see. You have multiple sources of stressors impacting you. We know this about you: you want to help others; broadly defined, you like education; you want a job for which success is measured in broader impact; and you feel passionate about marginalized individuals.

CL: That's right, but how did you know that?!

CO: You told me. (smiles)

CL: Oh.

CO: Let's talk a little about the types of careers that do these things.

CL: There's probably a ton of those kinds of jobs.

CO: You are probably right, but not all of them will be right for you. How can we begin to look for areas of overlap with your training, your interests and the jobs that meet both. It won't happen in one session, but it might. How would that be?

CL: That would be amazing!

## BOX FEATURE: Neuro-Perspectives on Trait and Factor Approaches

The most straightforward application of neuroscience integration with counseling to trait and factor approaches involves the management of information. The purpose of these approaches is to combine two discrete bodies of information into a meaningful decision about next steps. An added dimension to a metaphoric approach to integrating neuroscience into CFC is self-knowledge. While the battle rages in various disciplines regarding the notion of hemispheric specialization in the brain, strong empirical literature supports the fact that the left hemisphere of the brain takes a leading role in language, literalness, logic, and linearity (Siegel, 2012), while the right hemisphere appears to specialize in creativity, holism, and particularly, emotion (Gainotti, 2012). It is also an anatomical reality that the corpus callosum is the dense nerve bundle that aids in the rapid communication and, therefore, integration across the two hemispheres. Additionally, most of the structures in the midbrain found in one hemisphere are symmetrically duplicated in the other hemisphere. These facts offer several helpful counseling perspectives for career issues.

The first is that the function of the left hemisphere is akin to the information-gathering role related to self-knowledge and occupational knowledge. It is helpful for clients to organize information about the world of work in a logical fashion based on literal data and not speculation. Once this information is obtained, it must be assembled in a holistic, meaningful way, similar to the documented specialization of the right hemisphere. For many clients, self-knowledge is limited or largely elusive; reflecting this back to them, however, can be quite challenging.

to those with similar interests and the work they are engaged in. It provides a level of credibility in the eyes of clients, that this instrument knows what they are thinking (even though it's reformulating their own thoughts). The main caveat in using the SII is that clients can cling to results as if they are *prescriptive* (telling them what that should do for a career) rather than *descriptive* (providing feedback about what their interests may mean).

It is also important to note that there are a number of variations of Web-based inventories that measure interests, as well as numerous other factors. These are listed later, at the end of the book, for reader reference. At this point, pause to consider the circumstances under which you would direct a client to complete the SII. Ethical use of assessments among counselors involves understanding what questions you would seek to address, how you might use the results to assist a client such as Xavier or Alexa, and if you decided to use the SII or another interest inventory, what sources or information you would want to direct your client to. We discuss this below, following a discussion of the Myers-Briggs Type Indicator (MBTI).

## Assessing Personality—Myers-Briggs Type Indicator

The MBTI is one of the most common and popular assessments used to measure personality. As you will recall from assessment and appraisal courses, personality is seen as a somewhat stable trait (versus a state, which is more temporary). The theory underlying the MBTI, Jungian typology, asserts that temperament is largely genetic and, therefore, present at birth. While susceptible to and masked by environmental and other factors, it remains the same throughout life. The MBTI measures four dimensions of temperament in pairs of dichotomous items. It is important for counselors to be aware of this in order to help normalize their experience of their temperament in light of the criticism they may have felt because of it/them. Certain types (all are susceptible) tend to be misunderstood by opposite types. Each of these is briefly identified immediately following the description of the dimension. As you read them, consider positive ways to reframe these traits. Remember, these are preferred ways of interacting with the world, not rigid categories; nor are they excuses for poor behavior.

- ***Extraversion–Introversion***: This dimension identifies how individuals derive energy from their environments. Extraverts may prefer talking through ideas to understand them, whereas introverts may prefer to think quietly about their ideas and then talk about them.
    - Introverts are often criticized for being un- or antisocial.
    - Extraverts are often criticized for being superficial and talkative.

  *This dimension is not "testing" social skills.
- ***Sensing–Intuition***: This dimension identifies how individuals approach the world. Sensing individuals may prefer tangible information, such as that gained through their five senses. In contrast, intuition types may prefer experiencing the world through a sixth sense, or intuition.
    - Sensing types are often criticized as being too concrete or rigid.
    - Intuitive types are often criticized as having their head in the clouds.

*This dimension is not "testing" rigidity.

- ***Thinking–Feeling***: This dimension identifies individual approaches to solving problems. Thinking types may prefer logic and rules in resolving conflict; whereas feeling types may prefer to consider relationships before rules.
    - Thinking types tend to be criticized as being cold and distant.
    - Feeling types are often criticized for being irrational and overly emotional.

*This dimension is not "testing" intelligence.

- ***Judging–Perceiving***: This dimension identifies how individuals approach time. Judging types may prefer to have a clear plan while perceiving types may prefer spontaneity.
    - Judging types are often criticized for being rigid and inflexible in planning.
    - Perceiving types are often criticized for being irresponsible

  *This dimension is not "testing" one's tendency to be judgmental.

CAVEAT: Except in rare cases with the use of inventories and checklists (rather than normed instruments), counselors and counselors-in-training should not feel qualified to administer these assessments and use the results merely from reading their descriptions in a textbook. In the majority of cases, career and other assessments have test manuals that provide an overview of the measure, the theoretical foundation, normative and sampling data, directions for administration, and instructions for scoring, interpreting, and sharing the results.

***MBTI and CFC.*** The MBTI measures *preferences*, not skills or abilities, yet that is how they are often framed, particularly in relational conflict. The value of the MBTI in CFC is that it informs clients about how they may prefer to experience the work world and how they might approach particular tasks. Again, this information is descriptive, not prescriptive. There would rarely, if ever, be a job that introverts could not do; they just may not experience a particular job as energizing or rewarding, or they might approach an occupation that is counter to their type in unique and novel ways.

# Assessing Career Needs/Values—Minnesota Importance Questionnaire

The Minnesota Importance Questionnaire (MIQ) is a self-report questionnaire that measures work needs and work values. It is based on Dawis and Lofquist's (1991) Theory of Work Adjustment (TWA). In TWA, job satisfaction results from the pairing of job conditions with one's own values and needs. In addition to outlining 20 work needs, the MIQ identifies six types of work values listed and described by R. Dawis (2008, p. 1575):

1. ***Achievement***—the importance of using one's abilities and having a sense of accomplishment
2. ***Altruism***—the importance of harmony with, and being of service to, others
3. ***Autonomy***—the importance of being independent and being in control
4. ***Comfort***—the importance of being comfortable and avoiding distress
5. ***Safety***—the importance of predictability, stability, and order
6. ***Status***—the importance of recognition, prestige, and being important

***MIQ and CFC.*** The Law of Parsimony, also referred to as Ockham's Razor, states that the simplest explanation is often preferable to more complex ones. In the TWA, client distress in the workplace and life in general may represent a poor fit between the client's values and needs and the demands of the work environment. It may not be a personality disorder or a recalcitrant employer; it may simply be a bad fit. This can clarify the role of the counselor and the goals of CFC. Once the client and counselor have a greater understanding of the qualities and characteristics of the client, the counselor will direct the client to information resources relative to trait and factor theories.

# Web-Based Information Systems Related to Trait and Factor Theories

Information systems and trait and factor–related theories are complementary in that the assessments that counselors use tend to cover the self-knowledge component, while the information resources cover occupational knowledge. CFC assists clients in obtaining and accessing these pockets of information and then connecting them in meaningful ways. It is important to note that many of the self-knowledge assessments discussed here are related to interests, personality, values, and client's perceived skills. We have covered very little on achievement and objectives abilities assessments. Those are typically accessible in limited formats, for limited client populations, and are restricted to certain professionals. One example of this is the Armed Services Vocational Assessment Battery (ASVAB), which is discussed in a later chapter.

For now, we stay close to those assessments counselors can readily implement, those related to client interests, values, and personality. The Strong Interest Inventory offers a wealth of information for those who take it, as well as directing users to additional information. But first, when you reflected on the decision to use the SII and subsequent information, what came to mind? In selecting any assessment instrument and related resources, begin with the publisher's own words to identify uses and implications. For example, the following excerpt is from the SII publisher, CPP, Inc's, website for using the instrument:

> The Strong Interest Inventory assessment is ideal for a wide range of applications, including the following:

https://www.cpp.com/products/strong/index.aspx

> Choosing a college major—helps students uncover their career interests and identify which areas of study are appropriate or required for a particular field
>
> Career exploration—opens up the world of work to first-time career seekers and those considering career transition by identifying their interests and demonstrating how they relate to various occupations and careers
>
> Career development—helps heighten individuals' self-awareness and provide deeper understanding of individual strengths and blind spots, including work style and risk-taking orientation
>
> Employee engagement—helps employees align their interests with areas of responsibility in their job that reflect those interests
>
> Reintegration—helps individuals navigate the reintroduction process after a period of disconnection (www.CPP.com)

Next, it is important to infer from such information how it matches (or doesn't) with your client's needs. The SII is really ideal for several types of clients, such as those who have no idea where to begin their search. It also is useful for clients who feel overwhelmed by options and need assistance in winnowing them. Another client well-served by the SII is the client who has very limited information about their interests and ways of being in the world. Lastly, it takes responses to what feel like random questions and converts them into meaningful next steps.

The above description should feel familiar. Think back to Parson's three-part model: self-knowledge, occupation knowledge, and true reasoning. In it you will see the logical, theory-based connections between the lens and the assessment, leading to information for follow up. As the SII has evolved, so have the information systems that accompany it. Companies like CPP, Inc. have packaged multiple informational products to accommodate the resources of the organization for which you work or the needs of the individual client,. That is to say, most commercial publishers of career-related assessments also offer many options for scoring and interpretation, but often at a cost. In addition, there exist a multitude of no-pay resources online and most significant are those offered by the U.S. government.

# U.S. Bureau of Labor and Statistics

As the name implies, the U.S. government's Bureau of Labor and Statistics (BLS), a division of the Department of Labor contains answers to virtually any data-based questions regarding work and occupational information. The resources discussed next are critical to the success of CFC and will be referenced in regards to most theories. Perhaps most importantly, in order

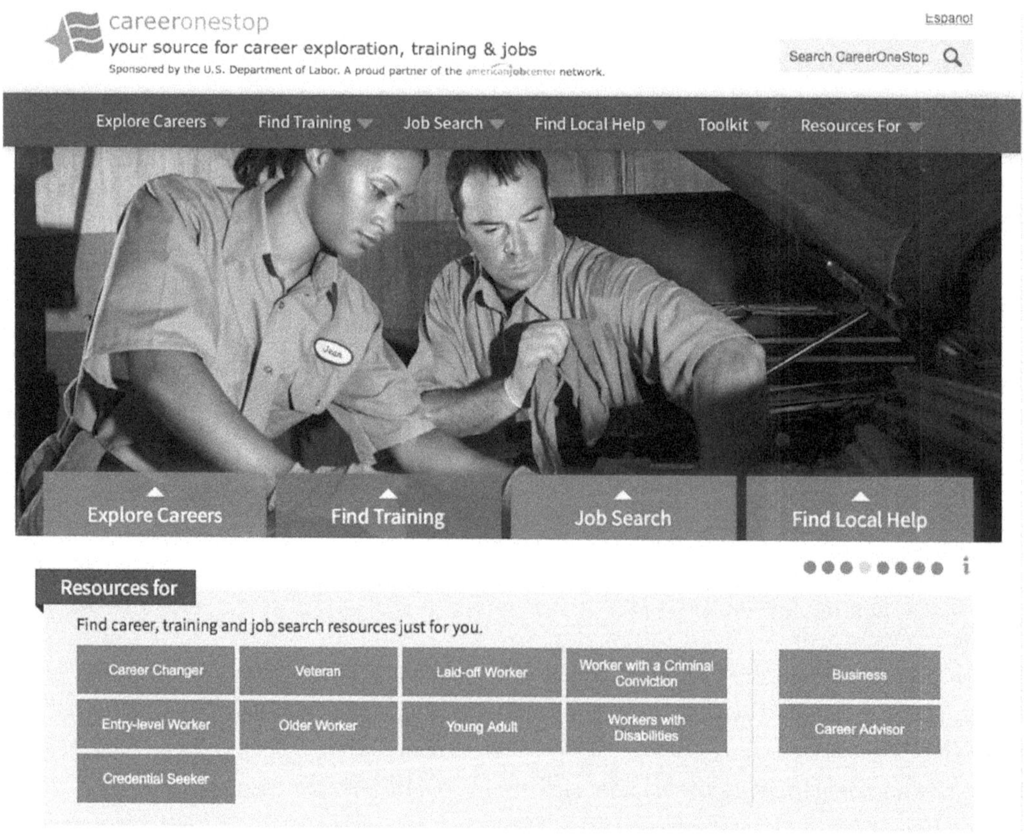


Figure 2.1. Screenshot of Careeronestop.org.

to be effective in CFC, counselors must know how to navigate this information and these sites (Duggar, 2017). Counselors do not have to memorize the material contained on the BLS website, but they need to be familiar with how and where to find it in order to assist clients in utilizing this information effectively and appropriately.

America's Career Infonet, now called Careeronestop, is perhaps the most user-friendly of the U.S.-backed Web resources.

It can be found at www.careeronestop.org, and the home page looks similar to this: It contains a considerable amount of information regarding career exploration, job training, job posting, and local resources. It is designed to be informative without being intimidating—a key to using informational resources effectively with individuals in a vulnerable position. It is strongly recommended that you invest an hour or so of your time to navigate the site, take the assessments and follow the information.

One of the most useful components of the website that pairs nicely with the results from the SII is the "Explore Careers" tab that identifies and explains the Occupational Profile and Codes. In a more paper-based time, several resources were printed regularly by the Department of Labor on occupational information, trends, and statistics. To access this information, you needed the book (often up to about five inches thick), the codes, and the legend to the codes. For decades, career texts have described and discussed this information, but with the Web-based nature of these resources, here is what counselors need to know for CFC, in tabular form. Table 2.3 lists and describes some other Web resources.

Table 2.4. Sources of Occupational Information

| Resource | Description |
|---|---|
| Occupational Outlook Handbook | • 2016-17 OOH released 12/17/2015<br>• Bureau of Labor and Statistics employment projections<br>• 329 occupational profiles<br>• 576 detailed occupations<br>• Available at:<br>www.bls.gov/ooh/about/occupational-information-included-in-the-ooh.htm.<br>• State-based links to Occupational Employment Statistics survey<br>• Labor Market Information (LMI) link to<br>www.projectionscentral.com for employment projections |
| Dictionary of Occupational Titles | List of occupational information that began in 1938 and was replaced in 1999 by O*NET, see below |

(continued)

Table 2.4. (***continued***)

| Resource | Description |
|---|---|
| O*NET | "The O*NET program is the nation's primary source of occupational information. Central to the project is the O*NET database, containing information on hundreds of standardized and occupation-specific descriptors. The database, which is available to the public at no cost, is continually updated by surveying a broad range of workers from each occupation. Information from this database forms the heart of O*NET OnLine, an interactive application for exploring and searching occupations. The database also provides the basis for our Career Exploration Tools, a set of valuable assessment instruments for workers and students looking to find or change careers." http://www.onetcenter.org/overview.html |
| Standard Occupational Classification | "System is used by Federal statistical agencies to classify workers into occupational categories for the purpose of collecting, calculating, or disseminating data. All workers are classified into one of 840 detailed occupations according to their occupational definition. To facilitate classification, detailed occupations are combined to form 461 broad occupations, 97 minor groups, and 23 major groups. Detailed occupations in the SOC with similar job duties, and in some cases skills, education, and/or training, are grouped together. General questions concerning the SOC may be sent by email or faxed to 202-691-6444." http://www.bls.gov/soc/ |
| Holland Codes | Codes implemented by the U.S. Department of Labor using John Holland's six occupation themes for categorizing work. They have been expanded and elaborated on, but they are based on the themes used in the SII. |

As you can see, there are quite a lot of Web-based resources to access. It is vital that the counselor obtain an accurate understanding of the client's familiarity with, and access to, Web-based information systems (NCDA, n. d.). For those with limited access and skill, steps will need to be taken to connect them with community resources via public transportation, the library system, and local career centers. These steps are crucial client advocacy. In the following table, you will find instructions for accessing two prominent Web-based, U.S. government-supported resources. Use this as a guide as you read the session transcript excerpts with Xavier and Alexa that follow.

Take a moment to navigate to www.careeronestop.org and www.onetonline.org and search careers. Type in mental health counselor and watch what happens. The following categories of information will be represented:

"What Do They Do?"

"Also Known As"

"Career Video"

"How Much Does It Pay?"

"Will There Be Jobs?"

"How Much Education Do You Need?"

"What Might You Do In A Day?"

In just a few clicks, a client can obtain a significant amount of information about a potential job or career. The page also identifies jobs based on Holland Codes! The next task, then, is to provide meaningful integration reflection for the client between this self- and occupational knowledge.

## Xavier in Session, Continued, Using the SII and Related Resources

Let's assume that Xavier has completed the SII and the MBTI between sessions and is meeting for a follow up to discuss the results. In this transcript, the emphasis is less on how to interpret the SII, and more on how to assist Xavier in using this self-knowledge.

CO: So Xavier, we have talked a bit about what is called your Holland Code, and that your code is SIA. This seems to indicate that you have similarities to people whose interests relate to helping (S), exploring ideas (I), and creativity (A). We've also discussed that the combination of letters is more than just the sum of each letter. I'm wondering, what was this like for you, and what is your reaction to the results?

CL: First of all, I've never spent this much time thinking about actual options. I mean, it's really always been about the "big ones" and whether I like those or not.

CO: Big ones?

CL: You know, doctor, lawyer, teacher, plumber, and stuff like that. Family asked me about those things, and since I don't see myself doing any of them, I say no, and the conversation sort of stops.

CO: And now?

CL: Now, I see that there are so many more options! The test is saying there's a lot of things I am good at!

CO: I can see you are a little more excited than before—that's good. I would like to remind you about a couple of things we mentioned earlier: the Strong Interest Inventory is not actually a test in the traditional sense—it's just asking you questions about you, and you cannot fail it. The second is that it's not measuring ability, but interest. You may or may not be good at the occupations listed.

CL: Oh yeah, I forgot. But it gives me a lot to think about.

CO: Just wait; there are a lot of things you can do next with this information.

CL: Uh oh. More? My brain is a little full.

CO: I'm glad you told me that. Let's take a minute to chat about the information in front of you and then schedule a time to meet again. How's that?

NEXT SESSION—Mid-way through

CL: You know, I said I want to help people, but I don't want to be a teacher or counselor or priest. What else is there?

CO: This is a great question! Let's go back to the Careeronestop site and look into this. Since your primary concern at this point is finding a viable career where jobs will be, take a look at the Career Profile in the Explore Careers tab. You see here that you can search by fastest growing occupations, which indicates that there will be jobs in this field. You can select the amount of education you plan to have and even the state you plan to work in.
CL: Oh, what's an occupational therapist assistant? It says you just need a 2-year degree.
CO: It does indeed. Take a look at the educational breakdown of occupational therapy assistants—it tells you the percentages across education levels. More than that, if we scroll to the bottom, you will see a list of related fields and occupations. It would be great if, by the next time we meet, you spent some time exploring, watching videos, making links and perhaps jotting down some notes. How does that sound?
CL: Good. I just wish I had this at the beginning of high school and not at the end.
CO: The truth may be closer to ... it might have been available; the problem is that it doesn't matter until it matters, like what's happening with you right now. Let's look at this from another perspective. If we navigate to www.onetonline.org and select explore user interests, we can actually look at careers related to your Holland Code SAI. This is an example of what comes up:

**Interests Search for:**

**Social, Artistic, Investigative** Save Table (XLS/CSV)

Selected occupations matching your chosen interest areas are displayed below. Occupations are sorted by Job Zone, to help you find occupations that match your current or expected level of education, training, and experience.

**Have a three-letter interest code?** You can focus your search by choosing up to three interest areas, to see the occupations which match your choices.

1st — Social (S) 2nd — Artistic (A) 3rd — Investigative (I) Go

**You have chosen: SAI**

28 occupations displayed.

| Interests (All) | Job Zone (All) | Code | Occupation |
|---|---|---|---|
| SAI | 4 | 29-1125.02 | Music Therapists Bright Outlook |
| SAI | 4 | 29-1125.00 | Recreational Therapists |
| SAI | 5 | 29-1125.01 | Art Therapists |
| SAI | 5 | 25-1121.00 | Art, Drama, and Music Teachers, Postsecondary |
| SAI | 5 | 25-1122.00 | Communications Teachers, Postsecondary |
| SAI | 5 | 25-1081.00 | Education Teachers, Postsecondary |
| SAI | 5 | 25-1123.00 | English Language and Literature Teachers, Postsecondary |
| SAI | 5 | 25-1124.00 | Foreign Language and Literature Teachers, Postsecondary |
| SAI | 5 | 21-1013.00 | Marriage and Family Therapists |
| SAI | 5 | 25-1126.00 | Philosophy and Religion Teachers, Postsecondary |
| SAI | 5 | 21-1011.00 | Substance Abuse and Behavioral Disorder Counselors |
| SIA | 5 | 25-1062.00 | Area, Ethnic, and Cultural Studies Teachers, Postsecondary |
| SIA | 5 | 19-3031.03 | Counseling Psychologists |
| SIA | 5 | 25-1053.00 | Environmental Science Teachers, Postsecondary |
| SIA | 5 | 29-9092.00 | Genetic Counselors |
| SIA | 5 | 25-1125.00 | History Teachers, Postsecondary |
| SIA | 5 | 25-1192.00 | Home Economics Teachers, Postsecondary |
| SIA | 5 | 25-1022.00 | Mathematical Science Teachers, Postsecondary |
| SIA | 5 | 21-1023.00 | Mental Health and Substance Abuse Social Workers |
| SIA | 5 | 21-1014.00 | Mental Health Counselors |
| SIA | 5 | 25-1066.00 | Psychology Teachers, Postsecondary |
| SIA | 5 | 25-1067.00 | Sociology Teachers, Postsecondary |
| SIA | 5 | 29-1127.00 | Speech-Language Pathologists |
| ISA | 5 | 19-3031.02 | Clinical Psychologists |
| ISA | 5 | 19-3039.01 | Neuropsychologists and Clinical Neuropsychologists |
| ISA | 5 | 29-1066.00 | Psychiatrists |
| IAS | 5 | 19-3094.00 | Political Scientists |
| IAS | 5 | 19-3041.00 | Sociologists |

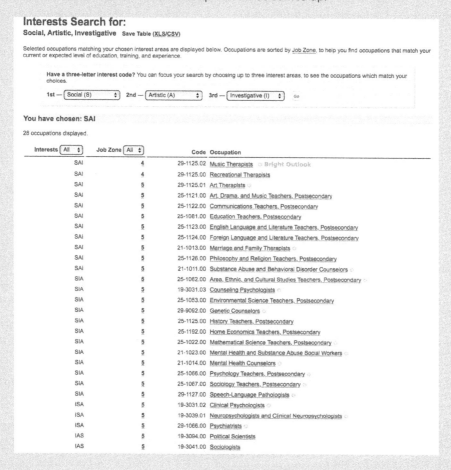

Figure 2.2. Search Results

You can see from this partial list that there are a number of positions that you said you weren't looking for, like teaching, counseling, and such. I wonder if we could speak a little more about how your profile—a result of your responses—highlights these careers as potentially satisfying ones for you, but not ones you like the sound of?
CL: I really like the thought of helping people, but you can't make any money in those fields. I can't be poor.
CO: Okay, thank you for your candor. Is there any other reason?
CL: (offers a sidelong glance) I get overwhelmed by the needs in the world. I mean, suffering people are so sad; I want to help, but am worried I'll end up being depressed.
CO: Those are real concerns. Would you say more about that fear?
CL: I've done some volunteering, and it was the same in the soup kitchen as it was at the seniors' center: I got stunned by the needs. I don't think I could do that for a living, much less go to school forever to do it!
CO: So, here's what we have so far: your response pattern to these almost 300 questions matches closely with those who are working in these fields. Do you think some of them might have felt the way you do?
CL: Oh, well I suppose. I never thought about that.
CO: I'm also wondering if perhaps their training helped protect them from getting so overwhelmed. Or if maybe there are ways to help without so much exposure to suffering up close.
CL: Really?
CO: Sure. When we select one of these occupations, we get a lot of information on that particular job, but also links to related one. Last but not least, we can switch around the letters in your Holland Code to see what other options may feel like a better fit.
CL: That's a huge relief. Everybody's always telling me I should be this or that, but I want to find my own path. This could help me do it! Thanks!

## Alexa in Session, Continued, Using the MBTI and Related Resources

In this scenario, Alexa has already committed to a college major and a career path in the short term. Hers is not a problem of access to educational or training opportunities, nor is it an issue of interests. Rather, she is seeking a different level of self-understanding that has limited her ability to apply true reasoning for the self- and occupational knowledge she has gained over her 4 years in college. The MBTI can often be useful in this regard and is used in this transcript to illustrate in practice. It is also used here to highlight the many ways that it can be misused with clients if counselors are not vigilant and well-trained to use it.

CO: We've talked a little bit about you feeling stuck regarding your next move or moves. How's that going?

CL: Probably about the same. I should already have a job, but I can't seem to get going.

CO: Okay. Let's see if we can untangle some of those feelings a little. You took the MBTI since our last meeting, and I wonder what you thought of it.

CL: I guess I enjoy taking personality tests and learning about myself.

CO: Good. You may recall that the MBTI is not a test, so much as it is an inventory of sorts. You can't fail it, and there are no right answers.

CL: Yeah, it said that, but it still feels like I have to get the right personality.

CO: What might that look like for you?

CL: That's just it; I think I'm supposed to get it right, but I don't know what "it" is, and I sure don't know what right looks like.

CO: You sound as lost as you do stuck.

CL: (tears up) Uh-huh.

CO: I suspect that talking through your results might offer some clarity. You may recall that the MBTI assesses preferences. It does not tell you who you should be or what you do. It describes how you may prefer to be in the world. Take a look at this chart from the publisher's website—you can go there on your on to get more information at https://www.cpp.com/products/mbti/index.aspx (pulls up chart on computer in order to discuss)

CL: That first box makes sense to me. I like people but I need plenty of time alone, reading or Web-surfing to be able to relax and think.

CO: So, this introversion preference makes sense to you.

CL: Sort of. I always thought I was socially awkward and shy in high school and college, because I did not like loud parties and did not have a ton of friends.

CO: So, you took this in-born preference for being in the world and turned it into tests that you were failing. That's a lot of pressure.

CL: I grew up in a home of extraverts, and they were exhausting. Don't get me wrong, I love my family, and we are very close, but they can wear me out.

CO: Makes sense. That would potentially create some internal conflict. Introversion does not mean that you don't like people or that you are weak socially. It just means you need a job with opportunities to recharge through working quietly or on your own. Let's take a look at this last dimension: Judging/Perceiving.

CL: I don't really see myself as a judgmental person but I came out very "J."

CO: Ah, this is making more sense now. First of all, a Judging temperament is not judgmental at all (well, anybody can be judgmental, regardless of type!). This dimension describes how we deal with tasks and deadlines. It may mean that you like to have a plan and work the plan, well in advance of deadlines.

CL: That's me exactly. In college, I've always mapped out assignments and responsibilities ahead of time.

CO: What happens when the plan hits a bump?

CL: (laughs) Chaos! I hate it when the plan does not work out!

CO: Kind of like what's happening with the next steps after college?
CL: (sighs) But I have no idea how to plan this. School papers and projects make sense to me. This stuff doesn't.
CO: So, one of the sources of conflict for you now is that you are having to operate against your type. You prefer a well-laid plan, but in career-planning, you feel lost in terms of planning, and you certainly can't execute a non-plan. You feel "chaotic" but that is actually quite normal for graduating seniors, and particularly for Js who don't have a plan.
CL: So, I'm not crazy?!
CO: Probably not. (smiles)
CL: So what do I do?
CO: We make a plan together, using what we've just learned about your temperament, along with the resources that tie type to work. Here, let's take a closer look at the information on the Myers & Briggs Foundation website at http://www.myersbriggs.org/my-mbti-personality-type/mbti-basics/
CL: Sounds like a plan!

# Summary

Trait and factor, person-environment-fit, true reasoning, and work adjustment all share matching in common. These approaches to matching can appear simplistic to the untrained eye, but counselors and clients both know very well how complex this matching process can be. The first step in matching involves gathering pertinent information to match. This involves assessments that fit the theory used—in this case trait and factor—and perhaps most importantly guide clients in an appropriate interpretation of these assessments—what they say and do not say. The other pieces of information come from occupational resources that inform clients accurately about the world of work. These two categories of knowledge set the stage for the all-important matching step. This is where a well-trained counselor can assist clients in gathering the right information at the right time so as not to overwhelm the client. Once the information pieces begin to fall into place, counselors use their prodigious relational skills to facilitate the client's matching process, or true reasoning. This is the point at which counselors "sit" with clients in their anxiety about this often-ambiguous process. Next, they return to the Web and other informational resources to design next steps for the client, so they can take action. It's a sophisticated process that looks simple from a distance, which is why clients struggle to navigate it.

# References

Badenoch, B. (2008). *Being a Brain-Wise Therapist: A Practical Guide to Interpersonal Neurobiology*. New York, NY: WW Norton & Company.

Brown, S. D. & Lent, R. W. (1996). A social cognitive framework for career choice counseling. *The Career Development Quarterly, 44*, 354–366.

Crites, J. O. (1981). *Career models: Models, methods and materials*. New York, NY: McGraw-Hill.

Cochran, L. (1997). *Career counseling: A narrative approach*. Thousand Oaks, CA: Sage.

Dawis, R. V., & Lofquist, L. H. (1976). Personality style and the process of work adjustment. *Journal of Counseling Psychology, 23*(1), 55–59. doi:10.1037/0022-0167.23.1.55

Lofquist, L. H., & Dawis, R. V. (1991). *Essentials of person-environment-correspondence counseling*. Minneapolis, MN: University of Minnesota Press.

Gainotti, G. (2012). Unconscious processing of emotions and the right hemisphere. *Neuropsychologia, 50*, 205–218. doi:10.1016/j.neuropsychologia.2011.12.005

Ginzberg, E., Ginsburg, J. W., Axelrod, S., & Herma, J. L. (1951). *Occupational choice*. New York, NY: Columbia University Press.

Gore, P. A., Leuwerke, W. C., & Kelly, A. R. (2013). Structure, sources, and uses of occupational information. In S. D. Brown & R. W., Lent (Eds.), *Career counseling and development: Putting theory and research to work*. (2nd ed., pp. 507–538). New York, NY: Wiley.

Gottfredson, L. S. (1981). Circumscription and compromise: A developmental theory of occupational aspirations. *Journal of Counseling Psychology, 28*(6), 545–579.

Gottfredson, L. S. (2005). Applying Gottfredson's theory of circumscription and compromise in career guidance and counseling. In S. D. Brown & R. W. Lent (Eds.), *Career development and counseling: Putting theory and research to work*. (pp. 71–100). Hoboken, NJ: Wiley.

Hansen, J. I. C. (2008). E. K. Strong, Jr. (1884–1963), In Frederick T. L. Leong, & W. Bruce Walsh (Eds.), *Encyclopedia of counseling* (Vol. 4). Thousand Oaks, CA: Sage.

Holland, J. L. (1966). *The psychology of vocational choice*. Waltham, MA: Blaisdell.

Holland, J. L. (1985). *Making vocational choices: A theory of careers* (2nd Ed.). Englewood Cliffs, CA: Prentice-Hall.

Holland, J. L. (1996). Exploring careers with a typology: What we have learned and some new directions. *American Psychologist, 51*, 397–406.

Krieshok, T. S., Black, M. D., & McKay, R. A. (2009). Career decision making: The limits of rationality and the abundance of non-conscious processes. *Journal of Vocational Behavior, 75*(3), 275–290.

Krumboltz, J. D., Mitchell, A. M., & Jones, G. B. (1976). A social learning theory of career selection. *The counseling psychologist, 6*(1), 71–81.

Krumboltz 2009). The happenstance learning theory. *Journal of Career Assessment, 17*(2), 135–154.

Krumboltz, J. D. (1998). Serendipity is not serendipitous. *Journal of Counseling Psychology, 45*(4), 390–392.

http://dx.doi.org/10.1037/0022-0167.45.4.390

Krumboltz, J. D. (1992). *Career Beliefs Inventory: Scoring Booklet*. Consulting Psychologists.

Krumboltz, J. D., & Levin, A. S. (2010). *Luck is no accident: Making the most of happenstance in your life and career*. Atascadero, CA: Impact Publishers.

Lent, R. W. (2002). Social cognitive career theory. In D. Brown & Associates (Eds.) *Career choice and development* (4th ed., pp. 255–312). San Francisco, CA: Jossey-Bass.

Luke, C. (2015). Neuroscience for counselors and therapists: Integrating the sciences of mind and brain. Thousand Oaks, CA: Sage.

Luke, C. & Redekop, F. (2014). Gottfredson's theory of career circumscription and compromise. In Eliason, G. T., Eliason, T., Samide, J. L., and Patrick, J. (Eds.). *Career counseling across the lifespan: Community, school, and higher education*. Information Age Publishing, Inc.: Charlotte, NC.

Miller, W. R., & Rollnick, S. (2013). *Motivational interviewing: Helping people change*. New York, NY: Guilford Press.

Norcross, J. C. (2010). The therapeutic relationship. In Duncan, Barry L., Miller, Scott D., Wampold, Bruce E., & Hubble, Mark A. (Eds), *The heart and soul of change: Delivering what works in therapy* (2nd ed.) (pp. 113–141). Washington, DC: American Psychological Association.

Parsons, F. (1909). Choosing a vocation. National Career Development Association.

Peavy, R. V. (1992). A constructivist model of training for career counselors. *Journal of Career Development, 18*(3), 215–228.

Peterson, G. W., Sampson Jr, J. P., & Reardon, R. C. (1991). *Career development and services: A cognitive approach*. Pacific Grove, CA: Brooks/Cole Publishing Co.

Peterson, G. W., Sampson Jr., J. P., Lenz, J. G., & Reardon, R. C. (2002). Becoming career problem solvers and decision makers: A cognitive information processing approach. In D. Brown & Associates (Eds.), *Career choice and development* (4th ed., pp. 312–369). San Francisco, CA: Jossey-Bass.

Prochaska, J. O., & DiClemente, C. C. (1984). *The transtheoretical approach: Crossing traditional boundaries of therapy*. Homewood, IL: Dow Jones-Irwin.

Rogers, C. (1961). *On being a person*. Boston, MA: Houghton Mifflin.

Savickas, M. L. (2005). The theory and practice of career construction. In S. D. Brown & R. W. Lent (Eds.), *Career development and counseling: Putting theory and research to work* (pp. 42–70). Hoboken, NJ: John Wiley.

Savickas, M. L. (2012). Life design: A paradigm for career intervention in the 21st century. *Journal of Counseling & Development, 90*(1), 13–19.

Savickas, M. L. (2014). Psychodynamic Career Counseling. *Career Counseling: Contemporary Topics in Vocational Psychology*, 79.

Sharf R. S. (2013). *Applying Career Development Theory to Counseling* (6th Ed). Belmont, CA: Brooks Cole.

Siegel, D. J. (2012). *Pocket Guide to Interpersonal Neurobiology: An Integrative Handbook of the Mind*. New York, NY: WW Norton & Company.

Strong, E. K. (1929). Diagnostic value of the vocational interest test. *Educational Record*.

Strong, E. K. (1943). *Vocational interests of men and women*. Stanford, CA: Stanford University Press.

Super, D. E. (1951). Vocational adjustment. *Occupations: The Vocational Guidance Journal, 30*(2), 88–92.

Super, D. E. (1953). A theory of vocational development. *American psychologist, 8*(5), 185.

Super, D. E. (1980). A life-span, life-space approach to career development. *Journal of vocational behavior, 16*(3), 282–298.

Super, D. E. (1988). Vocational adjustment: Implementing a Self-Concept. *The Career Development Quarterly, 36*(4), 351–357.

Swanson, J. L., & Fouad, N. A. (2014). *Career theory and practice: Learning through case studies*. Thousand Oaks, CA: Sage.

Wampold, B. E. (2010). The research evidence for the common factors models: A historically situated perspective. In Duncan, Barry L., Miller, Scott D., Wampold, Bruce E., & Hubble, Mark A. (Eds), *The heart and soul of change: Delivering what works in therapy* (2nd ed.) (pp. 49–81). Washington, DC: American Psychological Association.

Zytowski, D. G. (2001). Frank Parsons and the progressive movement. *The career development quarterly, 50*(1), 57.

## Figure/Image Credits

Fig. 2.1: Copyright © by the State of Minnesota.
Fig. 2.2: Copyright © 2017 by O*NET OnLine / U.S. Department of Labor, Employment and Training Administration, (CC BY 4.0) at https://www.onetonline.org/explore/interests/Social/Artistic/Investigative.

CHAPTER THREE

# Career Development Theory, Assessment, & Counseling II: Developmental Models

## Chapter Goals

- Provide a brief overview of each of the most prevalent development-related theories
- Describe the career-focused counseling (CFC) implications of developmental career theories
- Utilize developmental career theory to connect to clients' personal issues
- Articulate an integrated approach to theory, assessment, and resources

## Introduction

Development is one of those constructs that we live with everyday—so much so that we hardly recognize it. For example, the physical growth and development of a child feels different to those living in the home with them, than relatives who only see them every few months. A similar process happens with psychological and career development. The goal of developmental theorists is to, while living the development themselves, step back from the developmental process long enough to describe it. The same is true with developmental models of career. In this chapter, we examine two of the major developmental career theories, along with their implications for CFC. We begin with the best-known career theory: Donald Super's Life-Span, Life-Space theory.

### School-Based Vignette: Xavier, 17

Xavier is a popular 17-year-old high school senior. He was referred to you for mood concerns, as he hasn't been paying attention in his classes. In an attempt to build rapport with Xavier, you ask him what he likes to do after school, to which he curtly replies, "I mind my own business and do my school work." When you ask if he has an afterschool job, he shifts in his chair and tells you that his grandparents won't let him get one, so he "can focus on schoolwork." Xavier goes on to disclose that he makes straight As in his largely Advanced Placement coursework. He says that his grandparents, whom he lives with, had to give up their educations at early ages in order to provide for their families. While he says he understands his grandparents' concerns, Xavier says he feels stressed about paying for college, as his grandparents struggle to survive off of social security and their relatively meager retirement funds. You ask Xavier what he wants to study at university, and he tells you he's too stressed about finances to think about that. He says, "I need to be able to pay for college before I decide what to study."

## Developmental Models

The purpose of developmental career models in general is to describe the ways in which career changes over time, and with it, the tasks and needs related to career interventions. For example, vocational identity development at 11 years old looks considerably different at age 55. Developmental models provide ways for counselors to understand the developmental needs of clients across the lifespan, usually in terms of stages and tasks. As you read this chapter, reflect on how the way you think about work changed from your childhood, adolescence, and emerging adulthood to your current view.

### Community-Based Vignette: Alexa, 21

Alexa is a 21-year-old college student working at a local restaurant who comes to you for career counseling. She tells you that she switched from a major in special education to one in exercise science. After some inquiry, you learn that she initially chose special education because a family member did that, and she then chose exercise science because she ran cross-country all 4 years of high school. When asked what she wants to deal with in counseling, Alexa says, "Stress. Thinking about getting a job after graduation has been making me worry." She goes on to tell you that she switched out of special education after her first semester taking upper-division classes in her major. Alexa says that she wasn't sure if she wanted to teach, because she would "get too attached to the kids." She reports similar concerns with an exercise science job like being a gym teacher. She questions whether she wants to teach at all. Wiping away tears, Alexa discloses that she feels like she has been "trying to fill some kind of hole inside me" by finding a meaningful job in which she can help people but to a greater extent than her restaurant server job.

# Super's Life-Span, Life-Space Theory

One could spend a career learning the concepts and applications of Donald Super's Life-Span, Life-Space approach to career development, decision-making, and counseling. Here, I summarize the most salient features of his model, as it is more of a confluence of his many sub-theories. An essential feature of Super's model, particularly for our work in this text, is his view that vocation is the projection and then implementation of one's self-concept onto the world of work (1951; 1955; 1988). This emerges over time and in different contexts. Savickas (1997) offers a helpful framework for understanding this often unwieldy model, describing the components of Super's work in three stages, each of which reflects the name changes the theory has undergone:

> Developmental—This component "attends to how individuals construct and negotiate their work lives and specifies predictable tasks and coping behavior that individuals encounter as they develop their careers" (p. 248).

Self-Concept—This component describes the processes by which self-concept develops and how it is implemented in the world of work.

Contextual—This component represents the broadening of the model from primarily work roles to the myriad roles one plays across the life-span.

- Lifespan: Super was heavily influenced by his colleague Eli Ginzberg's developmental perspective of career development (Ginzberg, Ginsburg, Axelrod, & Herma, 1951; Super, 1951). An essential feature of the model is that career-related tasks are different at different ages (throughout the lifespan). He uses the example of career choice at 14 years old versus 21 years old. In Super's own words,
  "To the 14-year-old it means nothing more than preference, because at that age the need for realism is minimized by the fact that the preference does not need to be acted upon until the remote future. To the 21-year-old student of engineering, on the other hand, 'choice' means a preference which has already been acted upon in entering engineering school" (1951,p. 186).
- In discussing Super's lifespan stages, it is important to keep in mind that 1) the ages are somewhat arbitrary, 2) age does not equal development, 3) ages and developmental expectations can shift over generations, and 4) the stages are generalized. In this last instance, for example, it is really not reasonable to group 14-year-olds in with 24-year-olds in terms of development, even though in this and other models, they are both considered to be in the adolescent stage of development. These categories or stages are guidelines for consideration of developmental generalizations when working with different age groups. Super also described both mini- and maxi-cycles of development. In the maxi-cycle, the five stages occur over a lifetime: growth, exploration, establishment, maintenance, and decline. Within each of these stages are mini-cycles of the same process. In other words, the lifespan cycles (maxi) are also seen in any given stage as well (mini). Table 3.1 summarizes Super's life stages and tasks.
- Life-Space: this is Super's concept and articulation of the roles individuals play across their lifetimes. He described nine primary roles, along with other associated roles. The roles are important because of the ways they interact and, at times, exist in conflict with other roles (Super, 1980). These roles (child, student, "leisureitc", citizen, worker, spouse, homemaker, and parent) are played out in four social contexts, what super referred to as theatres (home, community, school, and workplace). Super's Life-Career Rainbow presents a graphic depiction of how these roles interact across different environments at different times. Super recognized that work occupies only one role—though a significant one—through which to enact one's self-concept
- Self-Concept: Super long maintained that work is the investment of oneself; therefore, in order to implement this self into the world of work, one must understand oneself. As mentioned above, the self is a mental representation (Hartung, 2013; Savickas, 1997; Super, 1980) of those characteristics of the individual, based in large part on a given role. Super's addition of self-concept theory involves the "formation, translation, and implementation

Table 3.1. Super's Developmental Life Stages (1990)

| Stage | Age | Tasks |
|---|---|---|
| Growth | Birth to 13 | Early formation of "mental representation of personal ***strengths, interests, values, abilities, talents, and personality traits***" (Hartung, 2013, p. 94) (emphasis mine). |
| Exploration | 14–24 | Adolescent and emerging adulthood stage toward "goal of ***crystalizing, specifying***, and ***implementing*** the vocational self-concept in an occupational role" (p. 94) (emphasis mine). |
| Establishment | 25–44 | Following implementation, adulthood involves "***stabilizing, consolidation***, and ***advancing*** the self-concept and a career pattern to develop a secure place in the world of work" (p. 95) (emphasis mine). |
| Maintenance | 45–64 | "Individuals ask themselves whether they want to continue in their established positions until retirement" (p. 95) or ***evaluating*** (emphasis mine). |
| Decline and Disengagement | 65+ | Major transition to retirement, wherein self-concept is implemented elsewhere besides work (Hartung, 2013). |

of a self-concept as well as how a self-concept affects vocational behavior" (Savickas, 1997, p. 248).

- Archway of Career Determinants: Super's way of conceptualizing and representing the interactions of life-span and life-space dynamics. In other words, age, stage, and role, interact with one another and with personal determinants to affect career maturity. Career maturity originated with Super and "is defined as the degree to which individuals are prepared to make good educational or vocational decisions" (Goodman, 2008). It is rooted in Parson's three key components and is assumed to occur over time.

Super's model is rich, complex, and ever-evolving. Mastery of the model takes time and experience, and much of its value rests in its explanatory power: it describes in rich detail how career development emerges over time. For beginning practitioners, however, it is recommended that you focus on the ways interventions come from the model.

# Gottfredson's Theory of Circumscription and Compromise

Linda Gottfredson proposed a theory of career development based on early experiences and one's perception of power and roles. These perceptions form the three core principles in her model: Self-Creation, Circumscription, and Compromise. Gottfredson (2002) expresses this succinctly in a question: "Why do children seem to re-create the social inequalities of their elders long before they themselves experience any barriers to pursuing their dreams?" (p. 85, as cited in Luke & Redekop, 2014). Table 3.2 highlights the ages and key features.

Circumscription: this is the process of refining interests and eliminating possibilities. The four factors (Table 3.2) that heavily influence this process are key to CFC from a social advocacy perspective. In circumscription, the individual "cuts out" careers that do not match his or her self-concept. This self-concept is derived and compared to the individual's perception of the world and of work across four stages:

Table 3.2. Stages of Circumscription

| Stage | Age | Description |
|---|---|---|
| Orientation to Size and Power | 3–5 | Increasing recognition of one's small size relative to adults; make simplistic categorizations of strong versus weak |
| Orientation to Sex Roles | 6–8 | Increasing recognition of sex and gender differences; self-selecting of same-sex playmates; dichotomizing work as "women's work" and "men's work" |
| Orientation to Social Valuation | 9–13 | Increasing recognition of the social status (real and perceived) that is associated with the work role; male-dominated careers tend to have greater status variability, whereas female-dominated careers have less; concept of tolerable-level boundary: minimum perceived status an individual can tolerate in a career (lower boundary) balanced with the highest perceived status that the individual has the potential to achieve (upper boundary) |
| Orientation to Internal, Unique Self | 14+ | Increasing recognition of the tension between idealistic goals and realistic ones; at younger end of the spectrum, closer to age 14, adolescents are expected to make this distinction without the requisite experience; begin to circumscribe career possibilities based on perception of self, and how that self would be in a career |

## Life-Span, Life-Span Essentials

Whole books have been written about the contributions of Donald Super to the field of career counseling, specifically, and counseling in general. Here's what counselors need to understand in order to use Super's work in CFC. The first issue is the time factor (1980). Career-related tasks require time in order to develop the skills to complete them. It is similar to infants crawling, then walking, and then running. Capacities must be built in order for the individual to complete increasingly complex tasks. In counseling, this means counselors sit with a fair amount of ambiguity, such as not giving answers to questions that clients must struggle with themselves as part of growth. Counselors must also foster their own development of patience, compassion, and empathy; as stated above, age is not tantamount to stage. A 26-year old client may exhibit the career maturity of the growth stage. This is not something to judge. Instead, counselors need to be sensitive to the developmental and environmental barriers to career maturity.

The second consideration for counselors is Super's connections between individual identity and vocational identity (1951; 1953; 1955). Knowing oneself and the relation of the self to the world of work is a vital component of career maturity. As we saw in chapter one, this sense of self is rooted in our neurobiology and indicates

- Compromise: Productive circumscription leads to making a career choice of the remaining options available that fit one's self-concept. This is the process of compromise. Compromise does not necessarily indicate a negative process, as in compromising one's values. It may simply represent resolution. At the same time, it can indicate that the individual must make a number of concessions regarding the career options left open to them after circumscription. Luke and Redekop (2014) use a corollary from politics: ideally, voters select a candidate that meets their circumscribed values and compromise by selecting their candidate. Realistically, it may be that voters may end up compromising by selecting the least-bad option. Career counseling clients often present in this second case, believing their options to be very limited and feeling dissatisfied with the ones that are available.
- Self-Creation: Gottfredson's work on intelligence is brought to bear in her formulation of self-concept and how the self is created as the result of the interaction between genetics and environment. In other words, "the self resides in these long-term consistencies in behavior, belief, and feeling, and self-insight lies in gaining a fuller, clearer-eyed view of them. The self-concept derives from our perceptions of this individual self and what we might want or fear it to be (2005, p. 76, as cited in Luke & Redekop, 2014).

Together, these factors, along with others, combine to create career choice. The choice may result in fulfillment as the self-concept at work or may be the least-bad option that feels very little like a match for one's self. This continuum of results has important implications for CFC.

Like many women's advocates before her, Gottfredson's model invites counselors to view career development through the lens of oppression. Circumscription and compromise assists counselors in exploring the systemic ways that individuals limit their career prospects, joining the ranks of social cognitive career theory (SCCT) and Super in advocating for marginalized individuals and populations. Readers are cautioned, however, about projecting their own experiences of oppression into their clients as they learn about theories such as this. Clients are unique and experience the world in ways that are their

that the self-knowledge required in Parsons' (1909) and Super's (1988) models goes beyond interests and values. A person's sense of self goes into our history or relationships, experiences, and environments, in connection with our genetic self. Understanding self at this level increases the chances for success in career decision-making, because vocational identity is a projection of one's identity onto the world of work (Super, 1988).

## Circumscription and Compromise Essentials

The first consideration for counselors from Gottfredson's model is the self-creation component. Gottfredson's model has a biological determinism component to it, so it informs the unseen predisposing factors that may support or limit the client's progress in counseling, before it even commences. At the same time, counselors and clients would rarely know these supports or limits at the beginning of counseling. Counselors must approach the relationship openly, recognizing that those things that hold clients back may include an inaccurate perception of both strengths and weaknesses: they may over- or underestimate their abilities.

Another important consideration is the process of circumscription across Gottfredson's four stages. The stages highlight the social justice components own. Next, we look at an example of developmental theory in practice with Xavier.

Xavier has magnified this decision to the point of distress, in part because he has limited experience that can inform the process. In addition, he is a first-generation college student, and has limited access to close relations who can advise him and assist him in chunking the tasks associated with college selection and career decision-making. His refusal to apply to college may also reflect his ambivalence about transitioning from child to adult roles. In Xavier's situation, Gottfredson's "optimizations" are particularly relevant, especially in the areas of learning and experience. Here is Alexa's experience in the context of developmental career theory.

The developmental perspective assumes a "typical" trajectory for individuals, though it also recognizes personal variability across stages. Alexa, despite her perceived stress level is not exactly in crisis, as much as she is in development. Individuating is a vital component of personal and vocational development; assisting clients like Alexa in determining her interests and bifurcating them from her social sphere is a vital step in CFC.

# Neuro-Perspectives on Developmental Approaches

A key feature of CFC is the incorporation of neuroscience literature integrated with career theory. Nowhere is this more appropriate or accessible than in the developmental models. Brain development is best understood from the inside out, and this can serve to inform career counseling. For example, in a feature article for *Counseling Today*, Luke and Redekop describe how this unfolds:

> One view of brain development is that brain regions developed as environmental needs required. The earliest of brain structures, the hindbrain, is focused on survival. It manages basic life functions such as regulating breathing and heart rate and includes an internal threat-detection system. Later, the limbic system developed to respond to a more social

inherent in CFC and offer implications for advocacy in career counseling across the lifespan. The crucial point here is that clients circumscribe careers based on perception; they create a list of possible careers based on the ways they see themselves and the world of work. One, the other, or both can be inaccurate, leading to premature and inappropriate circumscription of career options. Gottfredson (2005) proposes four ways counselors can assist clients in more appropriate, accurate circumscription:

- Optimize learning—counselors implement this intervention with clients by assisting in the reduction of task complexity (e.g., "what are the basic features of the task at hand?") and by accommodating cognitive "diversity" (i. e., using language and concepts appropriate to the client's level of social and cognitive development).
- Optimize experience—Clients often enter the counseling relationship having a shallow pool of resources available to them, including limited access to key experiences. This includes access to individuals with broad experiences, as well. Counseling supports clients as they gain new experiences that broaden their perspective of self and the world of work.
- Optimize self-insight—Here we can see another instance of self-knowledge that goes beyond the common conception of interests, values, and

environment that contained rewards. Therefore, the early parts of the forebrain developed a reward-detection system. Most recently, the cerebral cortex developed to adapt to increasingly complex social environs, adding to the system a context-detection system.

Therapy has been known to begin with interventions involving the most recently developed (in evolutionary terms) brain regions. In fact, cognitive behavior therapy and rational emotive behavior therapy are two of the main empirically supported treatments recognized by insurance companies and are often the most straightforward to measure for research purposes.

These approaches posit that abstract reasoning, critical thinking and problem-solving skills are essential early on in counseling so that problem thoughts, feelings and behaviors can be brought into alignment with individual and social expectations (i.e., top-down processing). However, it has been increasingly demonstrated that assisting clients in managing their breathing and heart rate and engaging in other mindfulness-based interventions aids them in thinking about their problems more clearly (i.e., bottom-up processing). (2016, p. 16)

skills. Counselors play a key role in facilitating clients' depth of understanding of self and, ultimately, how the self can exist in the world of work.

- Optimize self-investment—counselors can assist clients in directing finite personal resources by assessing the likelihood that certain behaviors will bear fruit. Not all effort will be equally rewarded, and not all paths lead to success. Counselors can facilitate self-investment by realistically determining pathways that have a higher likelihood of career and personal success.

### Xavier in Session

It will come as no surprise, at this point in the book, to read that the starting point with Xavier is rapport building. While self-evident, perhaps, this rapport is based on a developmental understanding of Xavier's struggle. From Super's perspective, Xavier is getting caught in the transition from a child student to an adult one, and this appears to be causing him stress. Part of the struggle is that Xavier, in all likelihood, has not made decisions that feel this life-altering before.

CO: Xavier, you are a senior, making really good grades in advanced courses, but things aren't going as smoothly for you as you or others would like. Is that a fair summary?

## Assessment in CFC Using Developmental Theories

Assessment in CFC is an exciting, informative, and illuminating process. It is also something of a two-edged sword, one that counselors must wield judiciously. For example, a classic caveat by psychologist and career counseling trailblazer, John Krumboltz, highlights the issue, "Career assessments are used to stimulate learning, not to match personal characteristics with occupational characteristics" (2009, p. 143). For Krumboltz, career assessments are conversation starters. This is important for counselors working to address career-related issues. With limited resources bearing down on counselors, administrators, and organizations, it can be natural to look toward computer-based guidance systems. The concern, echoed in the quote above, is that these tools should start conversations, not replace them. This chapter is less about cataloging the unending list of career-related assessments—later in Chapter I is a table of references for seeking additional information on career-related assessments, including publisher contact information, as this is where assessment manuals can also be procured. More on this later. Instead, this chapter focuses on helping counselors think through key questions regarding the use of assessments in CFC. Here are a few to consider as you read and think about your current or future clients: What do I want from a given assessment? How will it benefit my client? When is the best time to administer a given assessment? What do I want my client to do with the results? Why an assessment? In other words, what can I get from this assessment that I cannot obtain through talking with my client?

**Career Development Inventory.** The Career Development Inventory (CDI), is a 120-item instrument used to assess the career development needs of individuals and groups. The User Manual for the CDI (Thompson, Lindeman, Super, Jordaan, & Myers, 1981) describes the four most salient questions educators of adolescents might ask that can be addressed using the CDI (p. 1):

> 1) When should instruction in the special disciplines and in the various vocational and professional fields begin? 2) When should students be expected to choose between courses leading to different types of education and thus to different fields of work and occupations? 3) Is this student or group of students ready to make the choices called for by the school or college system and by the organization of the curriculum? 4) Does taking a certain course, studying a certain unit, engaging in a certain extracurricular activity, being enrolled in a work experience program, or being counseled by a professional counselor in any way affect the readiness of students to make these decisions? (Super, 1974, p. 9).

The CDI measures eight dimensions of career development: career planning, career exploration, decision-making, world-of-work information, knowledge of preferred occupational group,

CL: Yeah, that's pretty much it.

CO: How would you describe what's happening?

CL: I don't know ... I'm having trouble paying attention in my classes, and I've been biting the heads off some of my teachers.

CO: It sounds like you've been distracted and irritable.

CL: Definitely.

CO: Any guesses as to what is distracting and irritating you?

CL: It's just everything.

CO: Could you be a little more specific about how that feels to you?

CL: It just seems like everyone wants something from me, but I don't even know what I want?

CO: So "everything" feels like expectations and uncertainty?

CL: Yeah. How am I supposed to figure this stuff out, like the rest of my life stuff?

CO: You sound overwhelmed by the weight of these decisions. When is the last time you made a decision this big: "the rest of your life?"

CL: Never! I struggled to choose a prom date and the type of part-time job I would want (until I found out my grandparents wouldn't let me have one).

CO: It's no wonder then that making a decision about the rest of your life feels daunting. What if it was not as big as you think?

CL: That'd be great but it *is* big!

CO: What I mean is, what if you began looking at what

to do next instead of what to do forever?

CL: How's that?

CO: You've had great success academically in school, right? But you did not get there by taking all your high school classes at once. You took them in order. What if you could do that with this?

CL: What would that look like?

CO: I'm so glad you asked ...

## Alexa in Session

From a strict developmental perspective, Alexa is struggling with issues of identification and differentiation. Her identity to this point is derived from her proximity to close family members. This is normal and healthy and should be recognized as a part of development. Counseling seeks to support client autonomy through embracing these tasks without minimizing the client's struggles. Alexa has begun to express conflict within herself based on the roles she may be expected to play in her family culture and, perhaps, wider society. Gottfredson's theory predicts this dynamic in regard to social roles, as did Super in his description of roles. Let's look at how a culturally mindful, developmental approach might proceed.

CO: Alexa, if I understand correctly, you've had a certain career path planned, but it is one that did not fully emerge from you, as much as it did from some unchecked assumptions in your family. Is that correct?

career development-attitudes, career development-knowledge and skills, and career orientation-total.

A closer examination of the areas assessed can assist counselors in thinking and working with clients in more strategic ways. Table 3.3 contains a description of each dimension.

Table 3.3. CDI Dimensions and Descriptions

| Dimension | Description |
|---|---|
| Career Planning | Measures the degree of engagement in learning about careers (attitudinal more than cognitive) |
| Career Exploration | Measures client's sources of occupational knowledge and their perceptions of those sources (again, attitudinal more than cognitive) |
| Decision-Making | "Measures the ability to apply knowledge and insight to career planning and decision making" (p. 2). |
| World-of-Work Information | "Assesses general knowledge of occupations and understanding of how to attain and succeed in certain fields" (Rottinghaus, 2008, p. 1471). |
| Knowledge of Preferred Occupational Group | "First involves selecting one of 20 occupational groups (e.g., writing and law) to designate one's work interests. Next, the respondent's degree of knowledge regarding typical duties and personal characteristics of workers involved in that particular occupational group is examined" (Rottinghaus, 2008, p. 1471). |
| Career Development—Attitudes | Scale score that combines results from career-planning and career exploration subscales |
| Career Development—Knowledge and Skills | Scale score that combines results from decision-making and world-of-work information subscales |
| Career Orientation—Total | Combined score from the first four subscales and "is best viewed as a composite measure of four important aspects of career maturity" (Thompson, Lindeman, Super, Jordaan, & Myers, 1996). |

In using the CDI, the following recommendations highlight the value of the instrument with adolescent and emerging adulthood clients:

- "determine where the student is in his or her vocational development;"
- "identify how ready the student is to select among the available curricular and occupational choices;"
- "decide how the unprepared student can be helped" (p. 7).

Like other developmental assessments, and many other types described in this section of the text, these tools assist counselors in conceptualizing the client's struggles and identifying a path forward. In these developmental models, these assessments can identify stages of career development in which the client presents and, further, note the tasks completed and those yet to be completed relative to those stages.

**Career Maturity Inventory** (Crites, 1961; Crites & Savickas, 1996). www.vocopher.com "Career maturity is a prerequisite to the ability to make wise and realistic occupational choices" Busacca & Taber, 2002, p. 443). The Career Maturity Inventory was first developed by John Crites (1973; 1978) and was a modification of the original Vocational Development Inventory based on Super's theory (Crites and Savickas, 1996). In 1995, it was revised to its current form (Crites & Savickas, 1996). The Career Maturity Inventory (CMI) contains 50 items that are designed to measure students' and adults' approach to career development (Rottinghaus, 2008). It is modeled on Crites career maturity theory to assess how students approach career-related decisions across five competencies—self-appraisal, occupational information, goal selection, planning, and problem-solving. It also describes five attitudes: Decisiveness, Involvement in the Choice Process, Independence in Decision-Making, Orientation Toward Work, and Compromise (Crites, 1973). As you read these, you may recall that, in Motivational Interviewing (Miller & Rollnick, 2012), "resistance" in the client is actually the result of the counselor's attempts at applying an intervention geared toward a change for which the client is not ready. Likewise, in CFC, "resistance" in the form of not completing homework assignments (e.g., looking

CL: I guess so ... I hadn't really thought about it that way.

CO: How would you describe it?

CL: Well, I guess I never gave much thought to what I'd do, since it has felt clear for a while. Now that you mention it, I suppose it was an assumption based on my family, one that I just took for granted.

CO: But lately, you've been experiencing some internal conflict?

CL: Oh yeah! I want to be more than just a person who pursued a career without exploring all my options. Not that there is anything wrong with my family's jobs; I just don't know if that's for me.

CO: What is something you could see yourself doing instead?

CL: I don't know. I really like my job at the restaurant, though.

CO: I wonder if you could describe some things about it that you like.

CL: I love the customer interaction, but I also really enjoy being shift leader. I get to make sure everything is in order, problem-solve, and make people's days a little brighter. I also like checking the tills and making sure they balance.

CO: You seem pretty clear on those things. I might point out that your posture and vocal tone changed—a lot more energy!

CL: Yeah, I felt it. But admittedly, I don't love the food service part.

CO: Are there any career paths that you can picture that would allow you to continue to do this, but more of it, and perhaps in a more desirable setting?

CL: (nods)

CO: Let's talk about some and how you might describe this passion to your family in a way that feels right to you.

up information on career-related sites) or not showing up on time for appointments may actually be an indication that the client is not ready for the intervention. In another example from psychological theory, Prochaska and Norcross (2014) describe six steps in their stages of change model. Earlier stages respond to different interventions than later stages. Hammond, Michael, and Luke (2017) found support for this model in adapting the University of Rhode Island Change Assessment (URICA; McConnaughy, E.A., DiClemente, C.C. Prochaska, J.O., & Velicer, W.F., 1989) for career change. They found five career-related stages that may impact clients' readiness for career-related change. Table 3.4 highlights the stages, their description, and their potential application to career assessment and development.

Table 3.4. Stages of Change Comparison

| Stage of Change | Original Description | Translation to Career (Implicit Self-Statements) |
|---|---|---|
| Precontemplation | The client is both unaware of the problem and especially unaware of their role in it. | A career happens as the result of going to college, working hard, or luck; "there's nothing for me to do" |
| Contemplation | The client has moved into some awareness that there is a problem but is, at best, ambivalent about taking responsibility for the problem or the change that is needed. | "A career is something I'll get when I'm older, later on." |
| Preparation | The client has moved into greater ownership of both the problem and their role in it. They are beginning to explore options for change. | "Uh-oh, maybe this won't 'just happen' like I thought at first. Now what?" |
| Action | As the name implies, the client is actively taking steps for change that reflect personal responsibility for choices. | "If this is going to happen, I've got to take steps now. Here's what's next ... " |
| Maintenance | Making a change at a specific point in time is one thing; committing to making a change over time is a completely different one. | "Oh, I've got to keep this up. What things can I establish to help me keep up with my expectations?" |
| Relapse | Specific to substance and process addiction groups, this stage acknowledges that re-engaging in an old behavior is a part of the process of growth. | "I have fallen back into old patterns of self-defeating career thoughts and behaviors. I need to determine how to regroup" |

Prochaska and Norcross (2014) assert that clients in precontemplation and contemplation stages of change respond better to experiential and consciousness-raising interventions; whereas clients in preparation and action stages respond better to cognitive and behavioral interventions. This has clear implications for developmental career assessments, as described above. Let's look at how this might look in session with our clients, Xavier and Alexa.

# Developmental Theories in Session

In describing developmental theories in CFC, we return the same two vignettes to examine how counselors might utilize various theoretical approaches to the same clients, one in a high school setting (Xavier) and one in college (Alexa). This provides the opportunity to compare and contrast approaches with a thread of consistency throughout. Please keep in mind, however, that this approach is a learning device. Theory should be applied because it fits with the client and the presenting problem, not because it's most convenient or the one the counselor knows best.

### Xavier in Session with Developmental Theory

As we saw above in the transcript with Xavier, the counselor has already identified one hurdle to overcoming the stress and irritability that Xavier describes: he is a high-achieving student in new developmental territory. He and others around him may expect that he will transfer his academic success into success in career decision-making. For Xavier, it is far more complicated than that from a developmental perspective.

Cl: I know you gave me those websites to look at but honestly, they were too overwhelming. I stalled out and just didn't do it.

Co: That's okay. I appreciate you being open with me about this. Let's try this. Here is a site that might help us better understand what may be going on:

http://vocopher.com/ms/cmic/CMI_C_Master.pdf

Take a few minutes to complete this.

Cl: Here? In your office?

Co: Certainly. I want you to have the support you need as you take it. (I won't look over your shoulder.)

Cl: Did I pass? (smiles)

Co: You did (smiles)! Instead of scoring it, how about pointing to a couple of items that really stood out to you?

Cl: Okay, that's easy: This one, "I keep wondering how I can reconcile the kind of person I am with the kind of person I want to be in my occupation," and "There is no point in deciding on a job when the future is so uncertain."

Co: Oh, that's really helpful; thank you!

Cl: Are you kidding? This shows how bad it is!

Co: I can see how you might feel that way. Here's how I see it: in school, your role is clear, and your performance has been excellent, agreed?

Cl: Sure.

Co: Now you're in new territory, and it's getting to you. It is not that you don't know how to find information—you've done that your whole academic career. The two items you picked tell me you don't know who you are outside of a high school honors classroom and that uncertainty has you a little paralyzed. (pauses) What do you think?

Cl: I honestly never thought of it like that. I thought I was supposed to have it figured out but I don't have a clue!

Co: Yeah, you've been thinking of it as apathy, when I think paralysis is a better fit.

Cl: Yeah, and it's a little scary.

Co: I'll bet. Let's take a break from interest assessment and occupational information, and focus a little more on who you see yourself to be and how that might change over the next 4 to 6 years.

## Alexa in Session with Developmental Theory

Alexa's tension is highlighted in Gottfredson's stage four, orientation to one's unique self. Alexa seems more likely to stifle her sense of self in favor of meeting the expectation of others. We'll tread carefully here, so as not to vilify a family member or system, as these are often generational, not nefarious, behavioral assumptions.

Co: I thought we might talk a bit about the advantages to the situation you find yourself in, Alexa.

Cl: There aren't any! This is really stressful!

Co: You certainly seemed to feel stressed. Hypothetically speaking, though, if a person were to find an advantage to being in your situation, let's make some guesses ...

Cl: (thinking; appearing a little uncomfortable) Oh! You mean like, if my family pressures me, and I give in, then there's no tough decisions to make? Like that?

Co: Is that more what you're thinking, or what you think I'm thinking?

Cl: I guess I've heard that from some friends, "At least you have a direction/plan!" But it doesn't feel that way to me.

Co: But it does have its advantages?

Cl: Yeah. I mean, if it's a wrong decision then I'm not really to blame. Or, I don't have to put a lot of thought into it if I don't want to.

Co: But that's not quite working for you either, right?

Cl: Right!

Co: In career counseling work, we have this thing we call an elevator speech. It goes like this: suppose you find yourself in an elevator with a hiring manager for a job you'd be really interested in. She asks you about yourself, and you have only the time in the elevator—about 30 seconds—to appropriately describe yourself in a way that would make her interested to hire you. What would you say?

Cl: (blanches) No idea.

Co: No idea about what, exactly?

Cl: No idea who I am (tears up).

Co: So, that might be another advantage to your family situation: you don't have to feel what you're feeling this minute, because you'd likely not have to answers these questions.

Cl: Uh-huh.

Co: I can see this is tough for you, Alexa. You might call this growing pains: part of you wants to stretch and grow, but part of you wants to stay where it's safe and comfortable.

Cl: But it's not comfortable! I hate feeling like this.

Co: Okay. So what do you want to change first? (smiles)

Cl: (blanches again) I see what you mean. I'm scared to try something new.

Co: Perfectly natural. Now what do you want to do?

Cl: Well, how does a person figure out who they are, who they want to be, and what they want to do?

Co: Those are terrific questions! Let's talk that through ...

In this transcript, we can see the value in using a quick assessment (Form-C of the CMI) to highlight blocks for the client. He's not averse to working; he's averse to losing his identity that he's invested in. Giving him resources for occupational information is going to be met with the "resistance" describe above. Instead, we slow down to sit with his identity and the prospect of identity change.

Alexa's situation epitomizes in many ways Super's contention that career development is the process of implementing a self-concept into the world of work. It makes sense then that Alexa experiences conflict as she attempts to implement her family-concept, instead of her own, into the world of work. There may also be some evidence of gender-stereotyped thinking in her pursuit of this career field. This is not inherently a problem, but it may point to more unchecked assumptions about the role she is to play in an occupation. Next, we look at how we might transition to identifying and utilizing Web-based resources for our cases.

## Web-Based Information Systems Related to Developmental Theories

In this section, you will see demonstrated an example of how resources used with one theory, for one purpose, might also be used with another theory for another purpose. The first step in directing clients to relevant informational resources is to ask the right questions about where the client is in the information management process. For example, in thinking about a client's developmental needs, what stages are salient for consideration, and based on those stages, what tasks might be relevant? Once these are determined, the next question set involves what information is missing that would clarify the career picture for the client? I often ask something along the lines of, "what do you need to know now that would help you take your next steps?" Clients can breathe a small sigh of relief, because I'm not asking them the ultimate question of how will they get there; just what piece or pieces might be missing. This is best exemplified in our sample clients.

### *Xavier in Session with Developmental Informational Resources*

Xavier appears to be in the midst of an identity transition, leading to a kind of crisis. He's feeling and acting stuck in the process and has struggled to move forward with confidence and intentionality.

Co: Xavier, it sounds to me like you are at a bit of an impasse. You've been given these great cognitive resources that you've used wisely to be academically successful in high school. Is that fair to say?

Cl: Yeah, I'd say so. I like looking back and seeing how well I've done in school.

Co: Okay. So, what happens when you go to college, without a clear picture of what you want to do, and you don't achieve the same level of success?

Cl: Wow, you really cut right to the heart of it, don't you? (smiles, looks down) That would really suck.

Co: I'm familiar with the expression, but could you develop that a bit?

Cl: I don't know if I could take that—it feels like a big risk, and if I can't cut it there, then I'd have to leave on a negative note. Right now, I'm at the top of my game academically, but since high school has to end, I can just get some old job and not worry about my performance.

Co: So you like the success part; I wonder if there's some part of you that'd appreciate the challenge of college.

Cl: Well yeah, but it's way too risky!

Co: You need some guarantees.

Cl: You could say that.

Co: Is that what you'd say? (smiles)

Cl: (smiles back) Yeah, yeah, I'll own that. I'd like some guarantees.

Co: What would guarantees look like, for you, related to college?

Cl: Well, I don't really have any idea what to expect.

Co: Okay. Guarantee #1 would be to clarify expectations. What else? What's missing that would help you know what to expect?

Cl: I don't really know what the work is like; what the schedules are like; the people.

Co: Those are big things! Where would a student find answers to those things?

Cl: Where? The internet?

Co: Could be a good start. Can you be more specific?

Cl: Not really. I'm the first in my family to even think about college, so they aren't a lot of help about what to expect. My high school has some stuff, but I haven't really been into any of that.

Co: You've been a little down and disconnected?

Cl: Totally.

Co: I'll tell you what, let's look at this website together for a minute, http://knowhow2go.acenet.edu/index.html, and see if it comes close to filling in the gaps for you. Deal?

Cl: Sure.

Co: Here's something fun to start with:

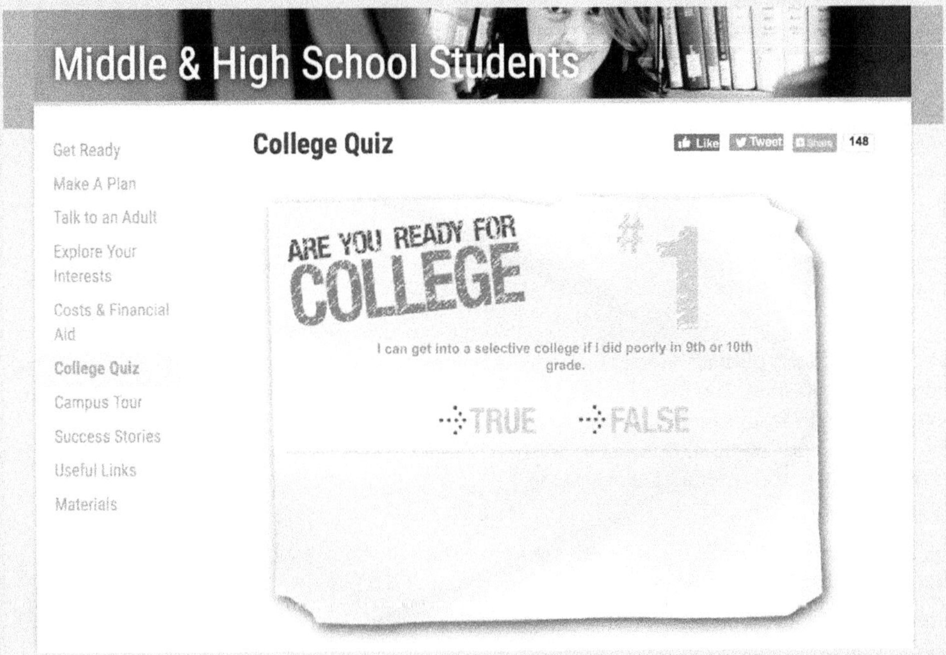


Figure 3.1. College Quiz

Quizzes and tools such as these help you chart where you are in the process, show you ideas, and help you take the next steps.

Cl: Yeah, this was pretty cool. But, it shows how much I don't know.

Co: But, there's a lot you do know. You also mentioned that your school counselor seems pretty cool. Why not talk to her?

Cl: I don't know what to say.

Co: Okay. How about these for starters:

## Your School Counselor

Your school counselor, or guidance counselor, is one of your best resources as you plan for college. Take the first step and make an appointment to discuss a plan for college. He or she has information about admission tests, college preparation and your education and career options.

**Here are some basic questions to help get you started:**

- Do you have any information to help me start exploring my interests and related careers?
- What are the required and recommended courses - for graduation and for college prep?
- How should I plan my schedule so I'll complete them?
- Do you have any after-school or evening sessions available for college planning?
- Do you have college handbooks or other guides I can browse or borrow?
- What activities can I do at home and over the summer to get ready for college?
- What kind of grades do different colleges require?
- Where do other kids from this school attend college?
- What are the requirements or standards for the honor society?

Figure 3.2. Your School Counselor

Co: There are tons of these kinds of resources online from reputable sources. I'll get you a list before we're finished. The point is that you don't have to reinvent the wheel, Xavier, and you certainly aren't responsible to know the things you can't know. You are responsible to seek and then act. You can do it. Before we finish, I'd like to take you through one other site that you might explore before we meet again, okay?

Cl: Yeah, okay.

Co: This website is hosted by the National Association of College Admissions Counselors (NACAC)

http://www.nacacnet.org/studentinfo/Pages/Default.aspx

It gives you the inside scoop on exploring and getting into college.

Co: One additional thing. These are resources that may generate even more questions, and that's okay. One step at a time.

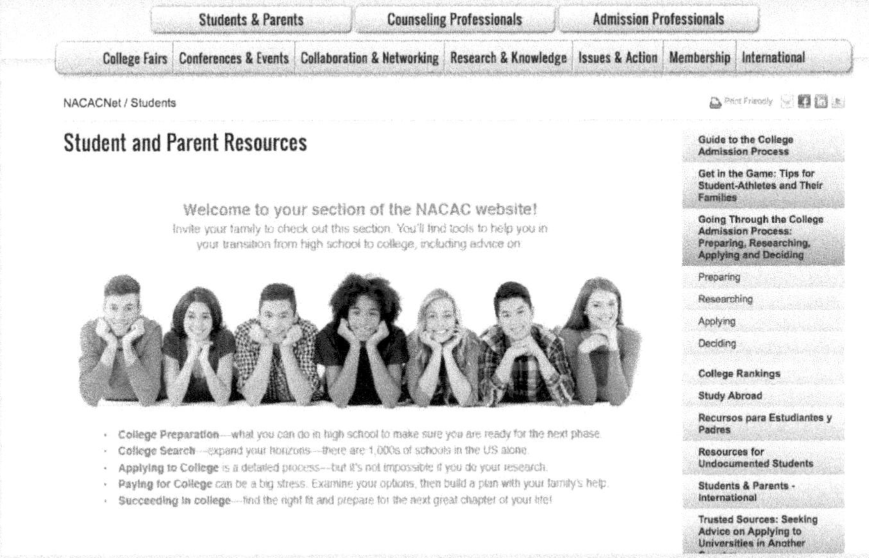


Figure 3.3. Student and Parent Resources

Counselors tend to be hesitant to give advice to clients, and well they should be—it's part of our ethics to bolster client autonomy, not undermine it, which is what advice-giving does. However, counselors often conflate resource sharing with advice-giving. In Xavier's case, the counselor is not advising him to go to college, where to go, or what to major in. They are responding to his conflict about college and his future by ensuring that he is equipped with the resources needed to make his own decisions and to support his decisions.

As we turn our attention to another example of applications of developmental theory-based informational resources, it is important to consider where to go to address clients who have asked great questions already. Alexa, for example, in the last transcript asked excellent questions, questions whose presence are quite challenging for clients and counselors alike. Vocational identity development sits at the intersection of who a person is and who they want to be as it pertains to the world of work. Counselors provide a powerful service to clients when they sit with clients in the ambiguity of their questions.

There is really nothing earth-shattering about the approach taken with Alexa, except that it started at the opposite end from which she was accustomed. To reiterate a thread that has run through this text, using Alexa as an example: there is nothing magical or particularly transformational about information, in and of itself. Rather, transformation comes through preparation of the individual to experience information in meaningful ways and then to use that information to take action. For Alexa, the counselor could have reflected these observations about her apparent work values (and very well may have). It is the process of walking with the client through their emotion and uncertainty that is the key. Stakeholders in her life don't have the benefit of emotional detachment like the counselor does. There is too much implicit pressure in their support in these types of cases for the client to be relaxed and move through the process.

### *Alexa in Session with Developmental Informational Resources*

Alexa has missed early opportunities for self-exploration and instead foreclosed on the process by accepting her role of carrying on her family's career traditions. Unfortunately, the lack of individuation and differentiation has ceased to work for her as she approaches the end of her undergraduate education.

Co: So, Alexa, in our last session you asked some outstanding questions. What additional thoughts do you have in regard to these since we last met?

Cl: I've felt pretty overwhelmed by the questions, but I do feel certain that I don't want to do something for a career, because others expect me to. I want to do something, because I feel it's right for me.

Co: I admire the courage it has taken to get you here. What a great start! Many times, we might start with individual values and move toward work values. In your case, your personal values are really tied to the expectations of others, so let's work backwards. I'll show you what I mean. Check out this site—it might look familiar to you, because it is the government career site, O*NET:

https://www.onetonline.org/find/descriptor/browse/Work_Values/

Under Advanced Search, we can explore by work values, like this:

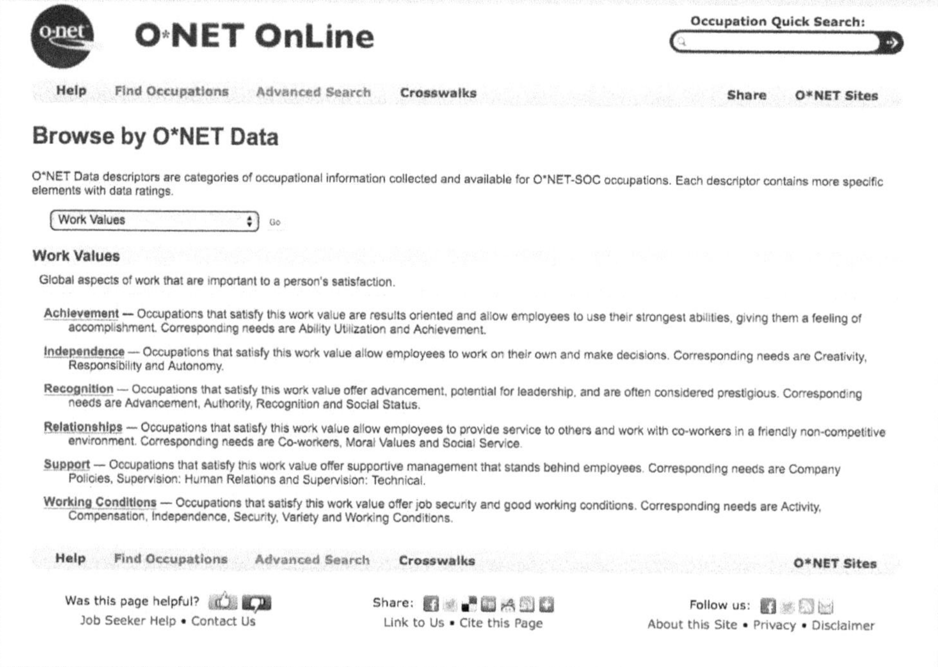


Figure 3.4. O-Net Online

Co: You can see the main work values. There are only six. Once you select one, it will then give you the option to select up to two additional ones for a more refined search. How about trying it now.

Cl: I think the Relationships work value stands out the most. One of the reasons I felt uneasy about education is that I was in the room on my own with the students. I could handle them okay, but I missed the connections to colleagues.

Co: Great! What else?

Cl: I notice right away that my family promotes education because of the Independence and Working Conditions values—they like working solo and having job security and a set schedule. Those sound okay, but they never really excited me. Support seems like the roles I've played in college. I never wanted to be out in front as much as I enjoyed the background preparation. Also, I really like a sense of accomplishment—getting things done and feeling good about it. I guess that fits with Achievement.

Co: Okay, good. Here's what comes up: There's a long list, from least to most job preparation. Anything stand out?

Cl: What is patient representation?

Co: I don't know; here's what it says ...

Cl: Oh my gosh! That sounds so much like me!

Co: Wow. Great. Tell me more ...

(later in session)

Co: You seem to have gotten a bump in your energy, Alexa. Can you tell me what's going on for you?

Cl: I'll be honest; I was skeptical that this approach would benefit me much. But trying to figure me out and matching that to a job has just not worked. I would have never considered working my way backward from job-related values to a greater understanding of myself. I mean, it gave me a new way to see myself—from the perspective of work. And, the site linked me to additional types of occupations that all seem interesting to me as well.

Co: I'm happy you're happy. Can you close the loop on your learning experience for me? What has this exercise shown you?

Cl: First of all, I guess it gave me permission to care about different things in the world than my family. It also put names to the things I've been feeling throughout college. It makes sense now the ways I approached classes and projects, friendships and student organizations. I was trying to fill a role that wasn't me.

Co: So, what's next?

Cl: I was going to ask you that!

Co: Now that you have these new realizations to work with, I would like to return to a couple of the assessments you took earlier to make sure we're not missing anything. I'm glad you are excited about this one job title, but I wonder how you might view the other options with this new mindset.

# Summary

Development, almost by definition, is a process. This process takes time and has different requirements at different points in time. These requirements each necessitate different skills. Developmental career theory caters to this understanding of human experience by articulating tasks and stages of career development that call on the counselor to use a variety of strategies. Assessment in these models is developmental in that it seeks to understand the needs of each individual, regardless of age, and facilitate the completion of tasks as appropriate (think learning to crawl, then walk, then run). Likewise, it is important when linking clients to resources that the depth and sophistication of the material matches their readiness to receive it. A final note regarding the value of developmental approaches to CFC is utility of the model across the lifespan, as it provides guidelines for clients at each stage.

# References


Busacca, L. A., & Taber, B. J. (2002). The Career maturity inventory-revised: A preliminary psychometric investigation. *Journal of Career Assessment*, *10*(4), 441–455.

Crites, J. O. (1961). A model for the measurement of vocational maturity. *Journal of counseling psychology*, *8*(3), 255.

Crites, J. O. (1973). Career Maturity. *NCME Measurement in Education*, *4*(2).

Crites, J. O. (1978). *Theory and research handbook for the Career Maturity Inventory* (2nd ed.).Monterey, CA: CTB/McGraw-Hill.

Crites, J. O. (1989). Career development in adolescence: Theory, measurement, and longitudinal findings. In D. Stern & D. Eichorn (Eds.), *Adolescence and work: Influences of social structure, labor markets, and culture* (pp. 141–156). Hillsdale, NJ: Lawrence Erlbaum.

Crites, J. O., & Savickas, M. L. (1996). Revision of the Career Maturity Inventory. *Journal of Career Assessment*, *4*, 131–138.

Ginzberg, E., Ginsburg, S. W., Axelrad, S., & Herma, J. L. (1951). *Occupational choice*. New York, NY: Columbia University Press.

Goodman, J. (2008). Career maturity, In F. T. L. Leung's (Ed.) *Encyclopedia of Counseling* (Vol. 4), pp. 1491–1492. Thousand Oaks, CA: SAGE.

Gottfredson, L. S. (1981). Circumscription and compromise: A developmental theory of occupational aspirations. *Journal of Counseling psychology*, *28*(6), 545.

Gottfredson, L. S. (2002). Gottfredson's theory of circumscription, compromise, and self-creation. *Career choice and development*, *4*, 85–148.

Gottfredson, L. S. (2005). Using Gottfredson's theory of circumscription and compromise in career guidance and counseling. *Career development and counseling: Putting theory and research to work*, 71–100.

Hammond, M. S., Michael, T., & Luke, C. (2017). Validating a measure of stages of change in career development. *International Journal for Educational and Vocational Guidance*, *17*(1), 39-59.

Harris-Bowlsbey, J., & Sampson, J. P., Jr. (2005). Use of technology in delivering career services worldwide. *The Career Development Quarterly*, *54*, 48-56.

Hartung, P. J. (2013). The life-span, life-space theory of careers, In S. D. Brown and R. W. Lent's (Eds.), *Career development and counseling: Putting theory and research to work* (2nd Ed.), pp. 83–114. Hoboken, NJ: Wiley.

Hirschi, A. (2009). Career adaptability development in adolescence: Multiple predictors and effect on sense of power and life satisfaction. *Journal of Vocational Behavior*, *74*(2), 145–155.

Krumboltz, J. D. (2009). The happenstance learning theory. *Journal of Career Assessment*, *17*(2), 135–154.

Luke, C., & Redekop, F. (2014a). Gottfredson's theory of circumscription and compromise. In G. Eliason, T. Eliason, J. Samide, & J. Patrick (Eds.) *Career development across the lifespan: Counseling for community, school, higher education, and beyond.* Charlotte, NC: Information Age.

Luke, C. & Redekop, F. (2016). Supervision of co-occurring career and mental health concerns: Application of an integrated approach. *Career Planning and Adult Development Journal, 32*(1) 130–140.

Luke, C. Redekop, F. (2016). Ethically integrating neuroscience into counseling: Nine key Considerations. *Counseling Today 58*(12) pp. 12–17.

McConnaughy, E. A., DiClemente, C. C. Prochaska, J. O., & Velicer, W. F. (1989). Stages of change in psychotherapy: A follow-up report. *Psychotherapy*, 26, 494–503.

Miller, W. R., & Rollnick, S. (2012). *Motivational interviewing: Helping people change*. New York, NY: Guilford Press.

Rottinghaus, P. J. (2008). Career development inventory, In F. T. L. Leung's (ed.) *Encyclopedia of Counseling* (Vol. 4), pp. 1471–1472. Thousand Oaks, CA: Sage.

Prochaska, J. O., & Norcross, J. C. (2013). *Systems of psychotherapy: A transtheoretical analysis*. Chicago, IL: Nelson Education.

Savickas, M. L. (1997). Career adaptability: An integrative construct for life-span, life-space theory. *The career development quarterly, 45*(3), 247–259.

Savickas, M. L. (2012). Life design: A paradigm for career intervention in the 21st century. *Journal of Counseling & Development, 90*(1), 13–19.

Super, D. E. (1951). Vocational adjustment. *Occupations: The Vocational Guidance Journal, 30*(2), 88–92.

Super, D. E. (1953). A theory of vocational development. *American psychologist, 8*(5), 185. Super, D. E. (1955). Transition: from vocational guidance to counseling psychology. *Journal of Counseling Psychology, 2*(1), 3.

Super, D. E. (1973). The career development inventory. *British Journal of Guidance and Counselling, 1*(2), 37–50.

Super, D. E. (1980). A life-span, life-space approach to career development. *Journal of vocational behavior, 16*(3), 282–298.

Super, D. E. (1983). Assessment in career guidance: Toward truly developmental counseling. *Personnel & Guidance Journal, 61*(9).

Super, D. E. (1988). Vocational adjustment: Implementing a Self-Concept. *The Career Development Quarterly, 36*(4), 351–357.

Super, D. E. (1980). A life-span, life-space approach to career development. *Journal of vocational behavior, 16*(3), 282–298.

Super, D. E., Crites, J. O., Hummel, R. C., Moser, H. P., Overstreet, P. L., & Warnath, C. F. (1957). Vocational development: A framework for research. New York, NY: Bureau of Publications, Teachers College, Columbia University.

Super, D. E., Thompson, A., Lindeman, R., Jordaan, J., & Myers, R. (1981). *The Career Development Inventory*. Palo Alto, CA: Consulting Psychologists Press.

Super, D. E., Osborne, W. L., Walsh, D. J., Brown, S. D., & Niles, S. G. (1992). Developmental career assessment and counseling: The C-DAC model. *Journal of Counseling and Development, 71*(1), 74–80.

Thompson, A. S., Lindeman, R. H., Super, D. E., Jordaan, J. P., & Myers, R. A. (1981). *Career development inventory* (Vol. 1). Palo Alto, CA: Consulting Psychologists Press.

University of Rhode Island Change Assessment (URICA). http://web.uri.edu/cprc/psychotherapy-urica/

## Figure/Image Credits

Fig. 3.1: Copyright © by American Council on Education.
Fig. 3.2: Copyright © by American Council on Education.
Fig. 3.3: Copyright © by National Association for College Admission Counseling.
Fig. 3.4: Copyright © 2017 by O*NET OnLine / U.S. Department of Labor, Employment and Training Administration, (CC BY 4.0) at https://www.onetonline.org/find/descriptor/browse/Work_Values.

### School-Based Vignette: Xavier, 17

Xavier is a popular 17-year-old high school senior. He was referred to you for mood concerns, as he hasn't been paying attention in his classes. In an attempt to build rapport with Xavier, you ask him what he likes to do after school, to which he curtly replies, "I mind my own business and do my school work." When you ask if he has an afterschool job, he shifts in his chair and tells you that his grandparents won't let him get one, so he "can focus on schoolwork." Xavier goes on to disclose that he makes straight As in his largely Advanced Placement coursework. He says that his grandparents, whom he lives with, had to give up their educations at early ages in order to provide for their families. While he says he understands his grandparents' concerns, Xavier says he feels stressed about paying for college, as his grandparents struggle to survive off of social security and their relatively meager retirement funds. You ask Xavier what he wants to study at university, and he tells you he's too stressed about finances to think about that. He says, "I need to be able to pay for college before I decide what to study."

CHAPTER FOUR

# Career Development Theory, Assessment, & Counseling III: Social- and Cognitive-Based Approaches

**Chapter Goals**

- Provide a brief overview of each of the most prevalent social and cognitive-related theories
- Describe the career-focused counseling (CFC) implications of social and cognitive-related theories
- Utilize social and cognitive-related career theory to connect to clients' personal issues
- Articulate an integrated approach to theory, assessment, and resources

## Introduction

In this chapter, we explore career theories that emphasize cognition and social influence. We cover social-cognitive models, as well as cognitive information-based approaches. You will notice right away that these build somewhat on the foundation laid by Parsons and trait and factor theorists. Try to resist viewing the models in this chapter as either/or—you do not have to choose between a belief in social influence or cognitive dominance. They should be viewed as complimentary. Theory development involves sharp dividing lines for the sake of clarity, but practitioners need not be so rigid in their thinking. We begin this process with an overview, followed by a description of what has become quite a dominant theory for CFC: Social Cognitive Career Theory (SCCT).

## Social And Cognitive Theory–Based Models

Many, if not most, career approaches can be linked back to counseling or psychological theory, as we saw in earlier chapters. This makes practical sense given that many were developed concurrently, if distinctly. Counseling theory-based career models have the most obvious and direct links back to psychological theory. Some theories are linked more explicitly than others. Some are based on theoretical models and some on applied models. Every model cannot be included; therefore, the most thoroughly researched are summarized here. The two primary theories covered in this chapter reflect social and cognitive psychologies. This category of career theories can be the most contentious, as many theories could be added, and different definitions used. Rather than getting too caught up in the categories, we shall focus in on the general "feel" for these theories and make the most of them in clinical practice. This chapter, rather than waiting until the end of the chapter to describe assessment and information resources, covers these elements immediately following the description of the two approaches. There is perhaps no better place to begin than with SCCT.

# Social Cognitive Career Theory

SCCT is based primarily on Albert Bandura's Social Cognitive Theory of behavior. Two defining components of Bandura's theory that have been adapted for SCCT are self-efficacy and triadic reciprocity. Triadic, or triarchic, reciprocity describes the bidirectional influence of any two of three groups of factors: behavior, environment, and personality and biological factors (picture the three points on a triangle). SCCT posits that the three components of career decision-making that are most relevant include self-efficacy, outcome expectations, and personal goals.

### Community-Based Vignette: Alexa, 21

Alexa is a 21-year-old college student working at a local restaurant who comes to you for career counseling. She tells you that she switched from a major in special education to one in exercise science. After some inquiry, you learn that she initially chose special education, because a family member did that, and she then chose exercise science, because she ran cross-country all four years of high school. When asked what she wants to deal with in counseling, Alexa says, "Stress. Thinking about getting a job after graduation has been making me worry." She goes on to tell you that she switched out of special education after her first semester taking upper-division classes in her major. Alexa says that she wasn't sure if she wanted to teach, because she would "get too attached to the kids." She reports similar concerns with an exercise science job like gym teacher. She questions whether she wants to teach at all. Wiping away tears, Alexa discloses that she feels like she has been "trying to fill some kind of void inside" by finding a meaningful job in which she can help people, but to a greater extent than her restaurant server job.

SCCT is a model that describes learning processes in a social context and how these interact to affect behaviors. As such, it offers practical approaches to corrective, facilitative learning experiences for clients. The first is self-efficacy. CFC uses the power of this construct by facilitating with clients opportunities to build mastery, to observe mastery in others, to find encouragement from appropriate resources, and to regulate their physiological response to the process.

*Personal Mastery*: In the first case, counselors draw out experiences wherein clients have achieved some parallel success. Clients often filter out positive experiences or minimize them in the face of new decisions or anxiety. It is important here, in working with younger clients, to take into consideration that their limited life experience may have afforded them fewer opportunities to build mastery in decision-making regarding their vocational future. These clients often assume a greater level of intensity than is warranted, which may be developmentally appropriate. In these cases, clients can be directed to look for analogs to their decision-making process, by gleaning principles from previous experiences, while keeping the decision-making process in healthful perspective.

*Vicarious Experience*: Second, it is important to identify career role models outside of their immediate circle of relationships, as the influence of these individuals can safely be assumed to be present. Instead, counselors assist clients in identifying key individuals from the community from which they can learn and draw inspiration.

*Verbal Persuasion:* Next, counselors can assist clients in analyzing the career-related messages they have received from significant others. One technique from SCCT for approaching this is utilizing an occupational card sort, wherein careers are listed and sorted according to certain criteria. Excluded careers can be explored and the reasons behind those exclusions discussed in therapy in order to determine the potential faulty beliefs underlying those exclusions.

*Physiological Arousal*: Lastly, it is important for counselors to assist clients in managing their thoughts and feelings about the process. In particular, clients can benefit from learning to manage their breathing and heart rate, as these can indicate anxiety or fear, negatively impacting self-efficacy. Guided imagery and progressive muscle relaxation are two such techniques.

## SCCT Essentials

*Self-Efficacy*: Self-efficacy is the belief that a person can accomplish a given task. It is domain-specific and is distinct from self-esteem and emotion-based confidence. Self-efficacy has been tied to myriad outcomes in behavioral research. Higher task self-efficacy predicts level of effort and length of effort (Luke, Redekop, & Burgin, 2015). Bandura described four processes involved in increasing self-efficacy, and these have implications for CFC (discussed further below): personal mastery (success in a task builds self-efficacy in completing similar tasks in the future); vicarious experience (seeing or knowing someone who is similar in some meaningful way succeeding in a task increases self-efficacy); verbal persuasion (when an individual of some meaningful stature or relation provides encouragement, self-efficacy increases); and physiological arousal (anxious arousal is often tied to lower self-efficacy, so moderating this arousal can increase self-efficacy).

*Outcome expectations*: Outcome expectations are beliefs about the result related to one's efforts. It is difficult to convince an individual to take some action in a meaningful way when they believe the effort will be fruitless. A significant body of literature supports this, as well. Outcome expectations are learned based on experiences in one's environment. Realistic outcome expectations are vital to learning effective ways of achieving goals.

Taken together, these influences offer not only explanations of beliefs and behaviors, but a way forward in terms of intervention. Counselors can leverage these to intervene in numerous ways with clients, from relaxation exercises (to address physiological arousal) to reflection exercises focusing on past success (personal mastery). This expands the intervention repertoir of counselors and instills hope for change in clients in regards to to career-related issues.

As you can see in the transcript excerpt with Xavier, SCCT theory emphasizes the role of social learning. In other words, Xavier's environment is key to the development of his beliefs. Therefore, assessing these environments and the beliefs that emerge offer a path forward to intervention. In the next section, we examine some of the assessments counselors can use to better understand these factors.

# Assessment in SCCT—Self-Efficacy

***Career Decision Self-Efficacy Scale.*** The Career Decision Self-Efficacy Scale (CDSES; Taylor & Betz, 1983) and the Short Form (CDSES-SF; Betz, Klein, & Taylor, 1996) are 50- and 25-item, respectively, assessment instruments designed to measure individuals' perception of their ability to complete tasks related to career decision-making (Betz & Luzzo, 1996). It is based on Bandura's Social Cognitive Theory (1977) wherein self-efficacy is a core component of cognitions related to other factors in the model. In assessing self-efficacy, Bandura asserts that self-efficacy is domain-specific and must be measured specifically (1986), as opposed to a more global measure of self-efficacy. It is task-specific, so assessing requires identification of discrete tasks. Therefore, the CDSES-SF measures self-efficacy in the career decision-making domain, which is comprised of five subscales, or sub-tasks (Taylor & Betz, 1983). Research has demonstrated the practical utility of CDSES in many types of studies and suggests using it as a general measure of career decision-making self-efficacy, rather than overly attending to the subscales. However, in CFC, it is suggested that the subscales offer a breakdown of the target areas in career decision self-efficacy and can be instructive to clients. The

*Personal goals*: Agency is Bandura's name for self-directedness, or the sense that one is responsible for outcomes. Personal goals are beliefs about the purpose behind behaviors and are tied to effortful action. Individuals benefit from having refinement in personal goals that are desirable and attainable.

## Xavier in Session with SCCT

From a social cognitive perspective, Xavier's thoughts concerning his future have been largely informed by his environment. He appears to have learned from his grandparents that life and work are hard, and it's important to *work* for certainty. These behaviors and attitudes were modeled for Xavier as he grew up, so despite their encouragement to pursue a college education, his grandparents' words may become drowned out by their modeling. In counseling Xavier from an SCCT perspective, he will benefit from recognizing this learning process.

Co: It seems that you feel strongly about working hard, and working for a "sure thing" (like a paycheck) rather than a college education, which might feel like a gamble. Is that close?

Cl: Yeah. I mean, why would I give up the chance to work and make money just to go to college and lose money?

Co: You seem passionate about this. I wonder where you learned this perspective?

Cl: What do you mean?

manual to the CDSES, for example, takes individuals through the challenges and opportunities associated with scores in each subscale (see table below).

**Unskilled and Unaware in Counseling for Career (CFC)—A Caveat to Self-Efficacy.** Kruger and Dunning (1999) demonstrated over studies spanning almost two decades that individuals' ability to reflect on a behavior and to accurately assess their performance was vital for growth and future success. Unfortunately, they identified a critical error in the metacognitive judgments of low-performing task completers: the worse an individual did, the more they artificially inflated their assessment of that performance. The researchers further found that this was a pairing that seemed to be outside the awareness of the individual—they were not aware that they did poorly and mis-assessed their performance. This led to the description of the unskilled and unaware phenomenon: lower performance positively correlated with inaccurate assessment. In addition, these and subsequent researchers went on to describe the opposite effect, as well: the better the performance, the less likely subjects were to see it as such. This phenomenon, which came to be known as undue modesty, highlighted these two opposing findings. This series of studies has important implications for CFC vis-à-vis the CDSES subscale, accurate self-appraisal. Counselors often struggle to challenge clients in their own self-assessment by looking for evidence of efforts and successes, or failures, for that matter. Clients, and humans in general, often struggle in their self-appraisal. Metacognitive judgments appear to be the flipside of self-efficacy.

Table 4.1. CDSES Information from the website and manual

http://www.mindgarden.com/79-career-decision-self-efficacy-scale#horizontalTab3

*Adapted from the CDSES Manual*

Although the concept of self-efficacy expectations provided the primary theoretical basis for scale development, Crites' (1978)

Co: Well, from my perspective, people don't just happen upon their beliefs and attitudes; they learn them from someone or something.

Cl: I had not thought of it like that. I just have always thought this way.

Co: Makes sense. If you were to have learned it, where might that have come from?

Cl: (goes on to describe how he came to live with his grandparents and their financial struggles, fixed, concrete attitudes, and lack of experience related to college-going behaviors.)

But why does any of that matter? I don't want to go to college.

Co: Okay. Remind me why you are here, if you don't mind.

Cl: (pauses, thinking) My teachers and counselor at school are worried about me.

Co: Could you say a little more about that?

Cl: Well, I've been pretty unfocused and irritable—that's what they tell me.

Co: So why do they care? (challenging his perspective, beliefs)

Cl: I don't know ... I get really good grades and scored pretty high on my SATs, and I guess I have felt pretty tired and frustrated lately.

Co: Okay, so they are concerned, because there may be reason to be concerned (smiles). Thanks for sharing that with me. I want to suggest one idea to you about your beliefs about work and college, okay?

Cl: Okay.

model of career maturity provided the original scale authors (Taylor & Betz, 1983) with a framework for deciding how to define and operationalize the skills required in career decision-making. More specifically, Crites (1978) in his model of career maturity hypothesized that "good" career decisions will be facilitated by competence with respect to five career choice processes and by mature versus immature attitudes regarding the career choice process. Because self-efficacy theory is defined in relationship to competence in specific behavioral domains, Crites' five career choice competencies were used to define the domain of interest, that of competent career decision-making. These five competencies and, subsequently, the subscales of the CDMSE, were: 1) accurate self-appraisal; 2) gathering occupational information; 3) goal selection; 4) making plans for the future; and 5) problem solving. Thus, the conceptualization and measurement of career decision self-efficacy involved the integration of two major theories, one originally stemming from clinical/social psychology and the other having its origins in counseling/vocational psychology.

— Nancy E. Betz and Karen M. Taylor, Career Decision Self-Efficacy Scale Manual

"Uses of the CDSE

Indicates an individual's pattern of higher and/or lower confidence areas as they relate to career decision making competencies

Identifies students at high risk for academic or decisional difficulties and, hence, those students needing career or academic intervention. Suggests which areas of decision are most in need of intervention. Evaluation of the effectiveness of educational and career interventions (such as DISCOVER, or administration of interest or values inventories).

**Scales**

Self-Appraisal: The ability to accurately appraise one's own abilities, interests, and values as they related to educational and career decisions.

Occupational Information: The ability to locate sources of information about college majors and occupations, including the ability to identify and talk with people employed in the occupations of interest.

Goal Selection: The ability to match one's own characteristics to the demands and rewards of careers so as to identify one or more majors or careers to pursue.

Planning: Knowing how to implement an educational or career choice, including enrolling in educational programs, job search, resume writing and job interviewing.

Problem Solving: Being able to figure out alternative plans or coping strategies when plans do not go as intended."

Co: The way I see it (that is, from SCCT) if you learned one set of beliefs regarding anything, work and college in this case, then you could also learn different beliefs that might help with the frustration, fatigue, and irritability. If that's even partly true, would you be interested in exploring it?

Cl: Yeah, if it helps and gets them to stop worrying about me.

**Outcome Expectations.** Outcome expectations can be assessed using interviews and other qualitative methods of assessment. Outcome expectations involve individuals' predictions regarding what will happen as a result of their efforts. Bandura (1977; 1987) asserted that self-efficacy expectations function similarly to outcome expectancies in that the belief in one's ability in a task predicts effort and time spent (1997). In the same way, beliefs in the outcomes—both the quality likelihood—predict the same (Fouad & Guillen, 2006). In essence, individuals' outcome expectations can be expressed as "If I do ____, ____ will happen." For example, in CFC with a displaced retail services worker, "if I spend five hours per week in researching occupations and companies, learning to write a compelling resume and cover letter, and visiting potential employers, I will be able to become employed again in four months." In assessing outcome expectations, it is important to determine the reality base of those expectations. As in the case above, a frustrated client may be assessed by asking, "what steps have you taken and what were you expecting from taking those steps?" If the client responds that they looked up jobs on Monster.com for 10 minutes late one night, thinking they would get a job the next day, their frustration makes sense. Further assessment involves how they arrived at their expectations, both for the amount of time and effort required and for the results. Often, it will be the result of faulty information and assumptions, and in many cases, it may be related to their low self-efficacy in this area, resulting in avoidant patterns of behavior. This dynamic is not remedied by information only, but through a relational process of self-efficacy and expectancy evaluation.

**Personal Goals.** Goals are the end product of individual effort, and they can be short-, long-, or mid-term. Goals in SCCT are the drivers of behavior to the extent that the individual believes that their goals are positive and self-directed. Helping a client to pursue a goal set by another person is rarely effective long-term. Likewise, goals are best set in terms of positive pursuits, rather than avoidance of negative events. For example, our client above may want to avoid unemployment, but this is not sufficient to sustain their efforts; instead, they will need to identify a future self that is framed in the affirmative sense. One excellent way of assessing client goals in CFC is to apply the goals rubric used in Reality Therapy (Glasser, 1998; Wubbolding, 1991). The SAMIC3 is a mnemonic for assessing goals in general and can be used in assessing career-related goals. While largely intuitive, they are vital to effective goal-setting:

Simple—helps ensure that the goal is comprehensible and easy to conceptualize
Attainable—helps ensure that motivation and self-efficacy remain high by increasing chances of success
Measurable—helps ensure that the client will be able to discern when the goal is met
Immediate—helps strengthen cause and effect linking
Controllable—helps ensure that the goal is within the sphere of the client's influence
Consistent—helps ensure that the goal remains the same and does not shift based on emotion
Commitment—helps ensure that the client is invested in the goal

These characteristics provide a clear rubric for evaluating the nature of the client's goal and their potential for success. Recall that personal mastery is the strongest way to build self-efficacy and setting goals that meet the above criteria is one effective way of accomplishing this. It is also important to keep clients mindful that they can have multiple goals along the way towards much larger goals. A key in building self-efficacy is setting goals that can be met, thus building mastery.

**Barriers and Supports.** One of the key factors of SCCT that distinguishes it from other cognitive and decision-making theories is its recognition and treatment of contextual factors—the "social" part of SCCT. One way that these contextual factors manifest is through environmental barriers and supports. Lent (2013) describes a model of assessing these factors using four steps:

> (a) anticipate possible barriers to implementing their choices, (b) analyze the likelihood of encountering these barriers, (c) prepare barrier-coping strategies (i.e., methods for preventing or managing likely barriers), and (d) build supports for their goals within their family, peer, and other social networks. (p. 139)

This approach is really less about the counselor assessing the client and more about teaching the client to assess their own goals (a cognitive component). Lent recommends a modified decisional balance sheet, so here a modification of their (Lent, 2013) worksheet:

Goal A: ______________________________

1. Possible barrier: ______________
2. Likelihood of encountering barrier (1–10): ____
3. Coping Strategies for barrier: ____________
4. Supports related to barrier: ____________

SCCT offers a rich description of the development of career beliefs and behaviors. The assessments include a combination of quantitative and qualitative approaches beyond those relational assessments career-focused counselors use in session. Here is an example of how this might look in session.

## Xavier in Session with SCCT-Based Assessments

Co: Xavier, I thought we might chat for a minute about the assessment you just took (CDSES-SF). What stood out to you as you took it?

Cl: I don't know; it asks about a lot of things I had not thought about.

Co. Oh? Like what?

Cl: You know how you said I learned to think a certain way? Well, it asked about my confidence in all kinds of things, but there were some I did not even know how to answer.

Co: Oh, really?

Cl: There was one question that asked about lifestyle decisions ["Define the type of lifestyle you would like to live"], and I had no idea.

Co: Okay. And, you think that ties into something you have learned?

Cl: I learned that step one is to survive. But I don't know what to do beyond that. My teachers talk to me about all the things I could be or do, but I don't see it. That's why I feel frustrated sometimes.

Co: You feel like they see potential in you that you can't see, and since you've learned to "survive," their support feels like expectations.

Cl: That's exactly how it feels!

Co: Well, it's interesting, because the category that you identified with this question is called self-appraisal. It just looks at how well you know yourself and your abilities. What that means is that you know you can "survive," but others around you believe you can thrive. You just may not have learned how to see that yet.

Cl: Okay. Makes sense.

Co: Interested in learning how to thrive?

Cl: Yes.

Note that, in this transcript excerpt, CFC assessment is not a superficial or trivial approach to client care. Counseling clients with career issues is a truly counseling-based enterprise. Once assessed in the context of the counseling relationship, clients can be directed to SCCT-related information.

# Information Resources for SCCT

One of the most practical aspects of social and cognitive approaches to CFC is their level of concreteness and ability to assess and take action. In this section, rather than covering one key Web-based resource, you will find a listing of each component of the assessment processes in SCCT and a description of how to obtain and use specific information.

## From the CDSES-SF Subscales.

1. **Accurate self-appraisal**—Accurate self-appraisal requires accurate sources of information about oneself. Here, SCCT relies on more traditional approaches of self-knowledge, including interests, values, personality, and abilities. Abilities is a tricky component to assess and to gather information on. As discussed an earlier chapter, resources like www.onetonline.org can assist clients in identifying skills and abilities required for particular fields and occupations. However, many, if not most, online resources that are freely available to clients and counselors are self-report—they measure and report on the client's perception of their abilities. Counselors can assist clients in gathering information about their abilities by promoting information-seeking of those who know the client well, but are also willing to provide candid feedback about abilities.
2. **Gathering occupational information**—Again, this category is not a domain unique to SCCT, but its use in the context of the other steps listed here, is.

3 **Goal selection**—If you're a client unused to selecting personal and occupational goals, this can be daunting. Therefore, one of the best sources of information on goal-setting may be the professionals in the role to which a client might aspire. Case studies and personal accounts of vocational decision-making also allow clients to internalize components of goal-setting that may fit them. For example, books like Po Bronson's *What Should I Do With My Life?*, Paul and Sarah Edwards' *Finding Your Perfect Work*, and Richard Bolles' *What Color is your Parachute?* all provide relational, relatable information on the career development processes of individuals and groups. Strictly speaking, in the counseling and psychology realms, "prescribing" books for clients is called bibliotherapy. On a practical side, working through the resource with the client can reduce the anxiety and sense of being overwhelmed by looking through a 500-page book. Having the resources on hand with the appropriate pages or chapters marked can help clients use these resources more efficiently and effectively.

4 **Making plans for the future**—In this domain, as with all domains, the National Career Development Association provides a wealth of resources for counselors and clients looking for information related to these subscales. The website, http://www.ncda.org/aws/NCDA/pt/sp/resources, is below:

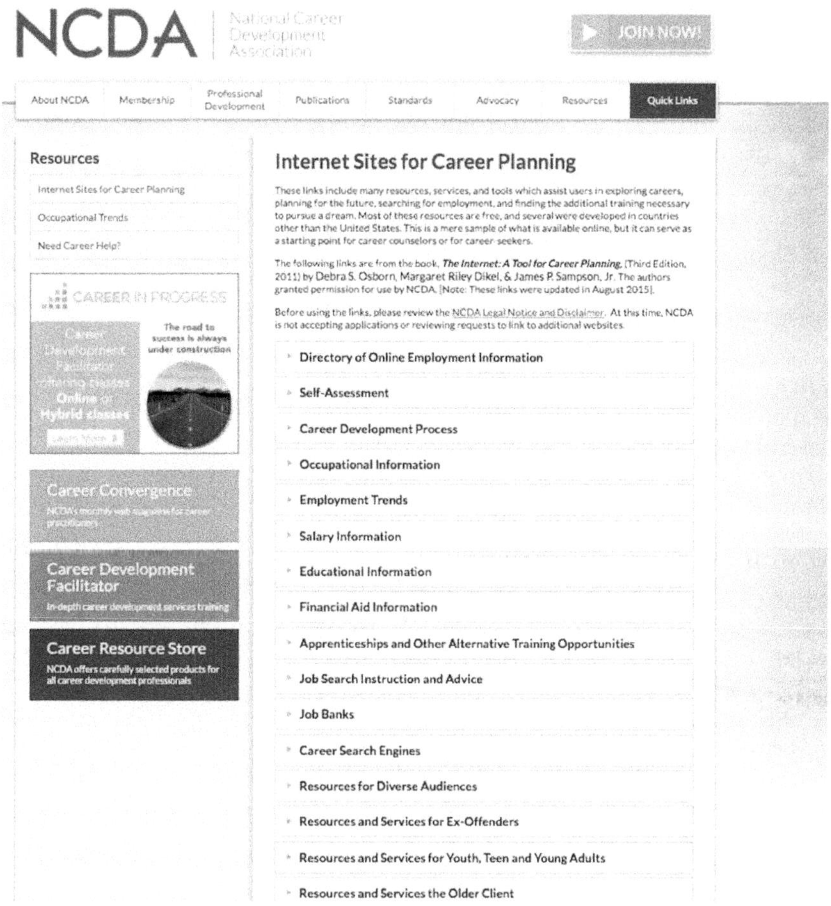


NCDA screenshot

5 **Problem solving**—The process of problem solving can be obtained and facilitated using any number of Web-based resources. The point of teaching/learning a process is less about the content of any step or the "rightness" of the move. It is far more about how clients manage information relative to a problem. The first problem to overcome is where to find information on problem solving! One immediate example of the skills being modeled for clients in this area is a Google Search for "problem solving." In the top 10 results is a link to Wikipedia (students and clients are using this regardless of the consternation of academics). On that page is an outline that highlights strategies and models. It is beyond the scope of this chapter, or SCCT for that matter, to outline these here (one model is already discussed in the context of Cognitive Information Processing (CIP)). It suffices to know where to find these resources, model the search for clients, and then facilitate their application relative to their particular career-related problem.

**Outcome Expectations; Goals; Barriers/Supports.** As discussed earlier, there are a multitude of Web- and print-based options for assisting clients in reality testing their career-related expectations and goals. We have seen that basic Web searches, career-specific Web searches, and indexing popular career-related books and other print materials can be utilized to assist clients in reality-testing their next steps. It is important to highlight here that, as counselors, we want to try to remain detached from specific choices and their consequences of our clients. Instead, we want to facilitate the client's exploration of such resources and evaluate their relative merits. We do this to foster client autonomy (in contrast to dependence) such that they leave with tools and strategies for further exploration.

SCCT-based, CFC is a hopeful, strength-based approach. As with the transcript excerpt above, it can be used to generate energy in the client and help them find the motivation to persist in their career development. Xavier's experience is fairly common in experiencing insight into the lessons learned that may have held him back. When exposed, they lose power over his behavior, and he experiences more freedom to seek new beliefs and actions.

## Xavier and SCCT-Based Information Sources

Co: So, Xavier, we've looked at several resources related to self-appraisal, the item you identified that you'd be interested in working on. What made the most impact?

Cl: Well, I guess you talked to my school counselor, and she was able to set me up with some aptitude or achievement tests, or something. They showed that I'm a pretty good writer and problem-solver.

Co: "Pretty good?"

Cl: Okay, I'm good at writing and problem-solving, among other things.

Co: And these results surprised you?

Cl: Yeah. I was very surprised. Especially since I can't problem-solve my own future!

Co: Cannot? Or have not yet?

Cl: Okay, okay. I get it (smiles).

Co: So, you have some abilities and potential, but you've been pretty unaware of those up to this point. I wonder if that has played into your survival mode of "I just want to work."

Cl: I can see that more now. A part of me has been really scared of failing. I mean, I can do the high school thing pretty well, and it comes easy to me, but what if I can't cut it in college? That's embarrassing and lot of wasted time and money.

Co: So, now that you have a little more self-awareness, and dare I say, confidence,

# Summary

SCCT has generated a prodigious amount of research literature (Flores, Navarro, & Ali, 2017). This is for a good reason. The model is highly testable, meaning that the components allowed for assessment and measurement. SCCT also has demonstrable effectiveness with clients. It gives the counselor a number of tools to use in intervening with clients. In the next section, we explore a similarly applicable model.

# Cognitive Information Processing Model (CIP)

Cognition has long held a prominent place in counseling theory in general. It makes sense, then, that career theory would also access its utility in working with clients. In this section, we take a closer look at a significant career theory based on cognition, and more specifically, information processing. Sampson, Peterson, Reardon, and Lenz (2002) described a model of career decision-making using cognitive and decisional sciences. They approach career decision-making as a problem to be solved, and therefore, career-related issues respond well to decisional models. Their approach has generated considerable research and has demonstrated its efficacy in moving clients through the process of career decision-making. They caution that this approach, while cognitive in nature, does not disparage the role of emotion in the experience of individuals (Sampson et al., 2002). They outline several key components of effective decision-making. It begins with several assumptions and is based on the pyramid of information processing and decision-making. It comprises knowledge domain, decisional domain, and executive domain.

*Knowledge Domain*: This domain includes understanding oneself and the world of work. Self-knowledge involves understanding oneself in light of the way individual memories are stored, processed, and recalled (Sampson et al., 2004, as cited in Sharf, 2013). Much like the approach in cognitive therapy, self-knowledge in CIP is an individual's interpretation of their experiences—their self-talk—as much as any objective

tell me what you thought of those few readings I gave you.

Cl: They really helped! I read cases that sounded a lot like me—people who were scared to go to college but were able to use the skills from high school to be successful in college.

Co: Okay, so those people you read about both seemed like you and were also able to make it in college.

Cl: Yeah, absolutely.

Co: Great. So what's next?

Cl: I have a meeting with my school counselor to make a plan to talk to some college admissions folks.

Co: Wow! That's a big step! What is that like for you?

Cl: I'm still scared ...

## CIP Essentials

Counselors will recognize in CIP characteristics that are similar conceptually and in application to CBT. In the first case, CIP promotes a very intentional relationship that includes treatment planning, goal-setting for the working relationship, and an educational component. Psychoeducation is a key component in that clients need to understand the model (as do counselors) in order to understand the expectations and roles at each level and across each domain. Clients walk away from CIP with a structured outline for how to proceed in making effective career decisions (or employment choices in CIP).

One of the major contributions of CIP to career development is in extending the trait and factor approach to include a cognitive decision-making model of "true reasoning." The CASVE decision-making approach's inherent value rests in its ability to assist clients in structuring their thinking about decisions, goals, problems, and the like. Clients often enter into CFC bewildered and overwhelmed with the process, unsure of where to even begin. Counseling using the CIP approach and the CASVE model in particular provide a framework for helping clients think through their goals and even their emotions related to the process. Lastly, the meta-cognitive domain opens the door to greater personality analysis of the barriers found within an individual. Increased understanding of self-talk, self-awareness,

knowledge of the self. Sampson et al., (2000) add to the more common knowledge of interests, values and skills, employment preferences, and family situations. The second component of the knowledge domain involves occupational knowledge. This is composed of the accumulated information about occupations and the world of work. Like most career theories, CIP emphasizes that this knowledge domain is dependent upon what one does with the information—how one processes the information. In this way, it is similar to cognitive-behavioral approach to counseling in that it looks at the beliefs about knowledge and decisions and how these influence behaviors.

*Decision-Making Domain*: Sampson et al. (2000) describe a decision-making model using the CASVE cycle, Communication→Analysis→Synthesis→Valuing→Execution, which essentially addresses what people need to do to solve problems. Communication means recognizing the gap between where one is and where one wants to be. This gap can be the result of internal or external cues or factors. Examples of these cues include anxiety about job choice (internal) and being asked by a friend or family member what one will do after graduation (external). Analysis is described as a mental model the individual creates in order to begin to understand relationships between what they know about themselves and about the world of work. Self-talk plays a role in how individuals make these linkages. Synthesis involves expanding one's options and then narrowing them back down. Valuing is really about clients assessing the value of their options and decisions about those options, both on themselves and those around them. And lastly, Execution involves making a plan and putting it into action, returning again to communication in order to reflect on the degree to which the decision completes this CASVE cycle.

*Executive Processing Domain*: This domain involves metacognitive processes, or thinking about how ones thinking influences thinking and subsequent behaviors. It is composed of three components: self-talk, self-awareness, and monitoring and control (Peterson et al., 1991). Sampson et al. (2000) describe self-talk as "the silent conversations clients have with themselves about their past, present, and future capability to complete a specific task" (p. 13). Like its Cognitive Behavior Therapy (CBT) counterpart, self-talk in CIP can have both beneficial and deleterious effects. Positive self-talk in career decision-making can increase one's level and duration of effort despite setbacks; in contrast, negative self-talk can short circuit a client with great potential by undercutting their efforts and perceptions. Self-awareness is "an awareness of the interaction among thoughts, feelings, and behaviors, especially the debilitating impact of negative self-talk on employment choice" (Sampson et al., 2000, p. 13). Monitoring is the process of maintaining awareness of where one stands in terms of gathering information, making decisions, and asking for help. Control is similar to the concept of agency and includes purposeful action related to career decision-making.

CIP offers numerous tools for harnessing the power of cognition in managing decision-making. One of its values rests in the description of decision-making's various components. Rather than allowing client's to own beliefs such as "I can't make decisions," CIP looks at the steps in decision-making to identify the element that is disruptive to the overall process. This challenges, first and foremost, client's self-limiting, all-or-nothing thinking, and it provides direction for breaking down decisions into smaller, more manageable tasks. Look for this in the transcript excerpt with Xavier.

You may have noticed the way the counseling leveraged the counseling relationship to facilitate Xavier's challenges of his own thinking. Regardless of the theory, it is the client's experience in the counseling relationship that evokes changes in thinking. One of the significant features of career focused counseling, as opposed to career guidance or advisement, is the process leading clients into *experience* knowledge or information. Our information-saturated environment can lead clients to believe that the answer is "out there" somewhere; whereas, counselors lead clients to answers "in there." It is the process of engaging information that transforms, not the information itself. We see this play out in Alexa's case.

Alexa may be outsourcing her sense of agency due to a lack of specific skills in decision-making and career decision-making in particular. The key strength of CIP and the CASVE model is that it provides a framework for clients to learn to make decisions. After reading and reflecting on the neuro-informed perspectives, we consider assessment strategies with these models.

**and monitoring and control gives clients tools for greater success in many areas of their lives in general, not just in career-related issues. In this way, CIP has a strong advocacy and autonomy component as clients enter counseling for career issues as a result of other systematic life problems for which career decision-making is a symptom; therefore, CIP provides a metaphor for addressing problems in other life domains.**

## Xavier in Session

Cognitive-based career counseling models offer a wide array of intervention and techniques for counselors. The challenge is to forestall problem-solving implements until rapport is built and the situation is understood well. At the same time, their structured perspectives can bolster counselors' confidence through the use of assessments and treatment plans. Xavier can certainly benefit from having his thinking about careers structured. For example, the CIP perspective offers an assessment that can assist in locating the source of his struggle. It turns out that of the three problem areas—decision-making confusion, commitment anxiety, and external conflict—Xavier is able to identify commitment anxiety as the most problematic for him.

CO: Xavier, according to the results of the Career Thoughts Inventory, it seems that you might feel a great amount of pressure to make the most-right decision about your future.

CL: That sounds right ... it *is* a lot of pressure to figure all of this out!

CO: So, it sounds like you are telling yourself that you get one shot at this and if you get it wrong, then what?

CL: I don't know, I'll be a loser bum with no money and no career!

CO: This feels like a really high stakes decision then.

CL: The biggest! How in the heck am I supposed to do this? Better to just get a job and not waste the money.

CO: I wonder if we could take a closer look at what you are saying to yourself about this process?

CL: Okay. What do you mean?

CO: Well, if I understand correctly, you have reduced your whole future down to this one decision, and I'm thinking I'd be pretty stressed out, as well.

CL: It's not this one decision, but it is pretty important.

CO: Okay, well those two statements seem different to me; they even feel different.

CL: Yeah, I guess.

CO: Can you think of a time that you had to make a decision or accomplish something that you were uncertain about in the beginning?

CL: Well, yeah, a ton of stuff.

CO: Like what?

CL: (discusses a number of developmentally appropriate achievements)

CO: So you've had a number of successes. What are the chances that this could be similar to those?

CL: The difference is those were relatively small, and this is HUGE!

CO: Okay. First, I'm not so sure the examples you gave were so small; second, what if this one decision you've been looking at is really a number of smaller decisions?

CL: What do you mean?

CO: You're not really making one decision for forever; you're actually making a choice to explore several schools, and at each school, there are several majors to explore, and each of those majors leads to a variety of careers, each of which you can change at almost any time.

CL: I never looked at it that way. So, I could make a decision about my top three majors at first.

CO: That's the idea. Let's play that out a bit further ...

### Alexa in Session

From a CIP or SCCT perspective, Alexa's dilemma is one of problem-solving related to accurate goal setting or outcome expectations. She is struggling with her own self-efficacy in terms of implementing her passions and values onto the world of work. Her goals seem distant, almost disconnected from herself. SCCT speaks to Bandura's concept of agency through the empowerment of clients to take ownership of the areas of career decision-making that are within their control.

CO: Alexa, I can't help but think, as I listen to you describe your situation, that it feels like something someone else should have done for you, rather than something you can take control of. What are your thoughts about this?

CL: I know I feel a lot of pressure to make the right decision ...

CO: What is the right decision?

CL: I know my parents and family would like to see me continue the family tradition of becoming an educator, though they would never say they pressure me.

CO: But, you're not sure it's what you want.

CL: I want to find something meaningful.

CO: Here's the conflict, as I see it: the language you're using, "find" implies passivity, and I wonder if it is contributing to those tears there.

CL: What do you mean? I'll do what I need to do.

CO: What is it that you need to do?

CL: (silence)

CO: How about this: what can you do?

CL: What do you mean?

CO: (silence)

CL: What? Do you think I should tell my parents I don't want to be an educator?

CO: (silence)

CL: What?!

CO: It sounds like you have a problem to solve. Let's assume I don't have any answers. What would be your next step in solving a problem?

CL: (tears)

CO: While I don't have an answer to your career problem, I do have some experience walking with people through the process of making decisions. How would that be?

# Neuro-Perspectives on Social and Cognitive Approaches

One of the first things that readers will notice about SCCT and CIP is their respective emphases on cognition. From a neuroscience perspective, this would be referred to as top-down processing, in contrast with bottom-up processing referred to in the previous section. In this view, conscious, cognitive processes occupy a superordinate position in making decisions. Top-down processes include using the executive function of the cerebral and prefrontal cortices to subordinate emotion and bodily processes (like respiration and heart rate). For example, exploration of self-talk, rationality, and dysfunctional thinking analyses provide mechanisms for regulating emotion. This will be familiar to students of counseling theory, particularly CBT, Rational Emotive Behavior Therapy (REBT), and Reality Therapy. These processes are particularly effective in executing predictable, "invariant" steps or tasks (Badenoch, 2008). Therefore, in order to harness the full power of top-down processing, models such as SCCT and CIP analyze and articulate sequential processes in career decision-making. The risk in this model is accounting for unpredictable experiences that can derail the process. In anticipation of these events, these models identify safeguards in thinking and behaving that can inoculate the individual from such experiences.

## Assessment Using Intake Interviewing in Social and Cognitive Approaches

Clients seek counseling for a variety of reasons, typically because of some pain or discomfort in their life, self-directed or mandated. They may have a clear sense of what is wrong and what they want to change; other times, they know something is "off" but are unsure what exactly needs to change. This can also be the case with counselors, as well. At times, supervisees have said to me, "It's just a career issue, so I'm not sure how I can help" or "My client seems depressed but they really just need a different job. Is that legit for counseling?" The issue of counselors and clients being uncertain about how to deal with career-related issues has already been discussed, but it can help to address it in terms of career assessment and intake, as well.

> This [intake} information allows a counselor to develop a framework in which to understand the clinical issue presented (diagnosis) and to collaboratively plan the counseling experience with the client (treatment plan). Developing rapport with the client is a primary concern during an intake interview and attention to cultural considerations is essential. (Mears, 2009, p.127)

Effective career assessment begins with effective intake assessment in general. As the quote above highlights, the approach to gathering information by a counselor sets the tone of the rest of the work they will do with their client. In structuring intake interviews, many agencies and organizations will have specific intake protocols, but here, I identify a couple of intake models that can be modified for career intake, in addition to setting the stage for effective CFC.

Ivey, Ivey, & Zalaquett (2013) outline a five-step narrative model for interviewing clients, one which lends itself well to career intake. From this perspective, all theoretical approaches to helping are storied (Ivey et al., 2013). In Table 4.1, I have included the model of Ivey et al, as well as a version modified for CFC intakes. It is important to keep in mind that these types of models are stand-alone and are helpful in counseling in general but also add to the process of career-related intake interviewing.

Table 4.2. Ivey's Stages of Counseling with Career-Focused Application

| Ivey Stage | CFC application |
|---|---|
| Empathic Relationship—In an age on constant information flow, knowledge is rarely the solution to a person's presenting concern. Rather, a caring relationship provides the framework for a client to do the work they likely already know they need to do—integrating information or knowledge in a way that changes behavior. The relationship is the vehicle to get them to this destination. | There is a surprising amount of shame and embarrassment around career-related issues. Perhaps because almost everyone works, it seems like it should be simple to work or because of clients' view that "I just need a job." Regardless, it is of tangible importance that a career counseling client feel accepted and understood by their counselor. Otherwise, it may take numerous sessions to get to the real barriers to career success, if you get them there at all. Everyone has an opinion about the world of work, so the last person that needs to express an opinion is the counselor; instead, they need to provide a space for the client. |
| Story and Strengths—Every client has a story and it is the counselor's job to help them tell it. The questions we ask shape the flow of the narrative, so we should be cautious in how we gather the client's story. For example, consider the last time you wanted to tell a story of something meaningful and were interrupted by the listener's questions. These questions can be listener-centered or teller-centered. Counselors are teller-centered and, in the process, learn to hear and highlight client strengths. | Typically, clients in CFC arrive to counseling with what are referred to as problem-saturated stories—stories of pain and set-backs, disappointment and discouragement, when it comes to the world of work. These perceptions are often based on "real" world-of-work-related events, but the story built around these experiences shape future behaviors—and these behaviors are typically ineffective. Often, these stories are reactive, meaning they are knee-jerks to some negative stimulus rather than proactive ones. They ignore client strengths and assets. In some ways, this simplifies the CFC process in that it empowers the counselor to sleuth out strengths—this model assumes the strengths are there just waiting to be identified. In the career domain, clients who enter counseling having constructed a story based on their deficits and are likely to be unaccustomed to focusing on the positives. |
| Goals—Once the safe context has been established, and the story has been elicited and strengths identified, both the client and the counselor have a better sense of what goals will be both effective and desirable. These goals have an important temporal sense, in that they are focused both on individual sessions, as well as the whole of the counseling relationship. It has been said that counselors must counsel in each session as if it is the only one we get, yet be invitational enough that the client wants to return. | Career goals are tricky in CFC, because clients (and, at times, counselors) may have limited experience with effective goal-setting. For goals to be successful in the career domain, they must be:<br>• Attainable—Can the client reach this career-related goal realistically and in a reasonable amount of time? Can they obtain the resources needed to make this happen?<br>• Desirable—Is this something that the client wants, or is it someone else's plan for them?<br>• Measurable—How will they know when/if they reach their goal, or is it ambiguous?<br>• Specific or concrete—What are the actual steps that need to be taken to move toward this career goal? |

| Ivey Stage | CFC application |
|---|---|
| Re-story—In the postmodern tradition, people have the ability to construct, reconstruct, and co-construct their life story. This does not mean they can immediately change their present circumstances and certainly not that they can change another person's behaviors. It does mean that through their language, they can change the story of their lives, from one of helplessness, for example, to one of empowerment. Counselors assist clients in changing their language and, therefore, their story to enable them to take a desired action or make a change. | In terms of career, as with many areas of life, history is often the best predictor of the future. History is also what we lean on when approaching new or novel tasks. Unfortunately, many CFC clients struggle to generalize problem-solving skills from one area of their life to the career domain—there just is so much anticipation of the unknown. Counselors are privileged to explore alternate versions of their realty—past, present, and future. For example, in CFC, I often ask clients to construct a "today resume." It is an assessment of where they are and have been in terms of education and work. The resume often accompanies apologies, excuses, and a variety of self-denigrating comments from the client. Next, we construct an ideal resume focused on about five years out, depending on the needs of the client. I then work with them to proceed backwards from that resume to today, identifying the steps needed to get them to that ideal resume. In doing so, they begin to re-story their career process. |
| Action—As I have asserted elsewhere (Luke, 2015), behavior matters. Behavior is the clearest indicator of change, but it is also the most effective way to cement learning. Action, or the lack thereof, is extremely informative feedback for a counselor in working with a client. | Arguably, the most challenging part of the CFC or any counseling endeavor, for that matter, is converting relationship, story, goals and re-story into action. It is through action that counseling success is identified and measured. However, if the re-story phase has been effective, clients will begin to own the action to be taken, in much the same way Motivational Interviewing assists clients in internalizing change leading to external behavior. |

Abbreviations: CFC = career-focused counseling.

As you may have noted in the table above, assessment is an ongoing, relational process that serves the client, not the needs of the counselor.

# Assessing Career Decision-Making Barriers—*Career Thoughts Inventory (CTI)*

A key assessment used in CFC through the CIP approach is the CTI. "Career thoughts include the feelings, thoughts, attitudes, beliefs, and expectations that relate to one's effectiveness in career problem solving and decision making" (Galles & Lenz, 2013, p. 240). The CTI, developed by James P. Sampson, Jr., PhD; Gary W. Peterson, PhD; Janet G. Lenz, PhD; Robert C. Reardon, PhD; and Denise E. Saunders, PhD, at the University of Florida over the past 30 years. It is a 48-item self-report instrument based in the theory of CIP. Scores in the CTI identify problem areas in three conceptual categories. The first is Decision-Making Confusion, wherein, "Items in this scale indicate feelings of depression and anxiety, or confusing thoughts that interfere with the acquisition of self knowledge and occupational knowledge and in identifying and considering plausible career options" (Saunders, Peterson, Sampson, & Reardon, 2000) (Lenz, Peterson, Reardon, & Saunders, 2010, p. 6). The second problem area is Commitment Anxiety, which "measures the extent to which individuals experience fear and trepidation in implementing a first choice of a course of action" (Sampson et al., 1996). The anxieties associated with committing to a career option may be specifically related to the career choice in the present (i.e., state anxiety), or they could be exacerbated by more fundamental personality proclivity (i.e., trait anxiety; Saunders et al., 2000) (Lenz, Peterson, Reardon, & Saunders, 2010, p. 6). The final area is External Conflict, which "assesses the extent to which individuals can balance the views of significant others with their own values in the career decision-making process" (Lenz, Peterson, Reardon, & Saunders, 2010, p. 6). Table 4.2 displays information from the CTI publisher's website to guide further exploration of this assessment.

**Table 4.3. CTI Publisher Information**

From the website:
http://www4.parinc.com/Products/Product.aspx?ProductID=CTI#
*The CTI is "a self-administered and objectively scored assessment, the CTI is designed to identify individuals who would benefit from counseling assistance and pinpoint the nature of their career problems ... Helps individuals to identify, challenge, and alter negative career thoughts that interfere with effective career decision making. The CTI yields a Total score (a single global indicator of negative thinking in career problem solving and decision making), as well as scores on three construct scales: Decision-Making Confusion, Commitment Anxiety, and External Conflict. A learning resource, the CTI Workbook includes information and exercises designed to help your clients identify the number and nature of their negative career thoughts, challenge and alter these thoughts, and take concrete action to make career decisions."*

The CTI is a useful tool for teaching clients about the reasons decisions are challenging. It provides insights to clients and a roadmap to counselors in overcoming barriers in the process of making career-related decisions. The following transcript excerpt demonstrates the use of the CTI with Alexa.

Self-talk reveals itself in a variety of ways in counseling. One way it materializes is in interactions like the one with Alexa above. CIP-oriented counselors listen for nuance and subtle language cues in clients, in order to determine the types of thinking exhibited. Asking directly rarely yields direct answers. This highlights the nature and value of strong listening skills, regardless of the theory used. Once again, these skills set up the role of information resources, to which we turn next.

# Information Resources for CIP

CIP offers a cognitively-oriented approach to understanding career-related decisions. It is also illuminating about other ways clients process information and make decisions outside of career. Likewise, it offers a plan for addressing the various kinds of information-processing issues in the CTI user's manual. In fact, one of the reasons CIP and the CTI were selected for this chapter, among the many options available, is the developmental, applied nature of the user's manual. The manual is the first stop in the process of teaching clients about the decision-making process relative to career (CIP is a highly cognitive, didactic approach to career development). One area of value beyond the three subscales of the CTI is its connection to the overall CIP theory. Because of this, the results can then be tied back into the various elements of the theory. You will recall the didactic nature of cognitive approaches, and CIP is no different, so the *Professional Manual* takes counselors though the career process. Two significant examples are particularly relevant for our purposes here.

In the first instance, the manual contains an appendix wherein the CTI questions are broken down according to the pyramid of information processing domains (Peterson et al., 1991). Figure 4.1 contains a representation of the pyramid showing the relevant domains.

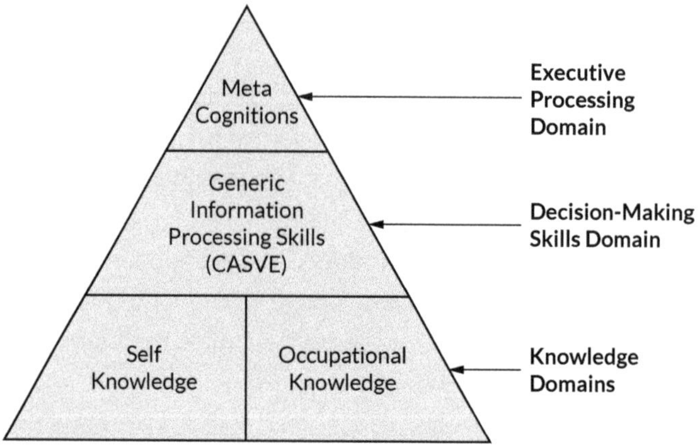


Figure 4.1. Information Processing Domains in CIP

## Alexa in Session with the CTI

Alexa has all but laid her concerns out for the counselor: her conflict is based on her parents' expectations for her career and those of herself. This epitomizes the External Conflict scale on the CTI. Walking her through this using the assessment may enable her to view the situation with a measure of objectivity.

Co: So Alexa, now that you've taken the CTI, I'm wondering if it brought up anything for you that you may want to talk about?

Cl: (chuckles) It made it pretty obvious that I'm really struggling in my relationship with my parents.

Co: Really? How so?

Cl: Well, it is like we've been talking about: I have my own career goals, and they have theirs for me, and the two don't line up!

Co: We have certainly talked around this issue. What did you see in the CTI?

Cl: It just made my struggles kind of jump off the page at me. I've been letting this conflict paralyze me.

Co: That seems like a pretty important insight for you.

Cl: It make sense why I've felt so upset. I just don't know what to do next.

Co: The action step is a pretty challenging one. What do you want to do?

Cl: I don't know what I should do!

Co: What do you *want* to do?

Cl: I told you, I don't know!

Co: Well, let's start with the fact that you may be answering a different question than I've asked.

Cl: What do you mean?

http://www.career.fsu.edu/content/download/283149/1982427/PPT_CoreConceptsofCIP_2003.pdf

The questions on the CTI are broken down into the three domains, better enabling the counselor to guide the client in understanding their place in the process. The self-knowledge and occupational-knowledge domains are quite literally taken from Parsons' model (1909), and the information resources for this model have been discussed throughout. The other questions fall into the categories in the CASVE cycle (see Figure 4.2).

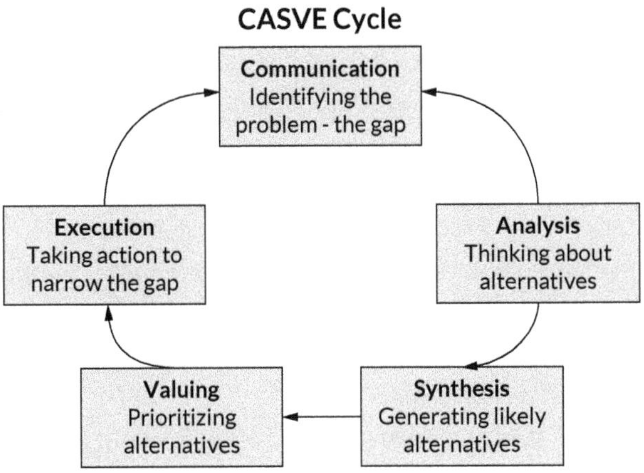


Figure 4.2. CASVE Cycle in CIP

These questions assist clients in identifying where exactly in the decision-making process the challenge exists. This empowers them to hone in on the trouble spot, rather than exacerbating any issues by globalizing the problem (e.g., "I'm terrible at making decisions"). In examining the CASVE cycle and thinking about information resources, the type of resource for each step becomes more apparent: ***Communication*** is the first step in realizing that there is an issue that needs to be addressed, that they are missing some fundamental pieces to the puzzle. The informational resources needed at the stage involve a basic understanding and overview of the process. This is where rapport building at the initiation of CFC is vital. During ***Analysis***, individuals are beginning to explore their self and occupational

CO: I asked you what you want to do and you responded that you did not know what you should do. Do you see any difference in those two?

Cl: I guess. Okay, no, not really.

Co: Thank you for your candor. It seems that you have conflated what you should do (someone else's expectations for you) with your own desires. (pauses)

Cl: (tears up) I really can't tell the difference.

Co: And so, that's the direction our work together will go next. Let's talk about the two and how they are producing tearful frustration for you.

Cl: Okay.

## Alexa in Session with CIP-Related Information Resources

Co: I appreciate your willingness to explore this with me; even I can see how disquieting it might be.

Cl: (sniffs and nods)

Co: Because of the emotional content of this topic, I thought we could start with a cognitive component of the approach (used here not to avoid painful emotions as if something is wrong with them, but to allow the client to feel composed in the moment—a way to provide privacy in the presence of another).

Cl: Okay, that's good.

Co: In this approach, metacognitions refer to the things we say to ourselves about decisions, how we think about ourselves while making a decision, and how we think about those things at any given time in the process (Sampson et al., 1996). That's kind of a mouthful, so let's look first at your self-talk about what is happening right now. What kinds of statements are flowing through your mind?

Cl: Uh, I don't know. "I can't do this." "There's no way to please my parents and myself at the same time."

Co: Those are some strong thoughts. What are the feelings that accompany them?

Cl: I feel helpless and hopeless about this!

Co: I imagine so. I wonder if we could work together to challenge some of these?

Cl: How do you mean?

Co: Well, let's look at a few facts to get us started: 1) You have to make a decision about your next steps (right?); 2) Your family will have an opinion about any decision (right?); 3) And you have to live with your decision one way or the other (right?).

Cl: That's all true, but I just don't know what decision is the right one!

Co: That's right. It sounds like the next decision you make feels like the ultimate decision that cannot be changed. It also sounds like agreement with your family is a really high priority.

Cl: That's how it feels.

Co: Good; now we're back to the core conflict: what you want versus what you should do. It appears that you are telling yourself (self-talk) that you must make the most-right decision that will please everyone. I wonder if there's something a little more accurate you might replace this statement with?

knowledge. Sampson et al. (1996) note that they often use information in the occupational domain to clarify self-knowledge. This is where it is important to be able to assist clients in finding accurate sources of occupational information that can serve as a catalyst for realistic self-understanding. ***Synthesis*** consists of elaboration and crystallization, this stage comprises the processes of expanding and narrowing options, a skill all its own (Lent, 2013). Sampson et al. (1996) identify the skill of convergent thinking in taking the information from Web-based guidance systems and distilling alternatives down to a plausible, manageable amount. In ***Valuing***, clients engage in cost-benefit analysis. They must incorporate additional occupation information beyond basic descriptions of work. This information may include growth potential, educational preparation and other information found on the websites discussed in previous chapters, like www.onetonline.org. Modified cost-benefit analysis, as described in the transcript below, may help move clients forward in this often-tricky step. ***Execution*** is the action step with which many clients struggle. It requires movement beyond exploration and cognition. Sampson et al. discuss components such as preparation program enrollment, reality testing plans, and employment seeking.

As you can see, this approach, along with the CTI, is information-rich. It can be easy for counselors to become overwhelmed by the levels and layers in this and other theoretical approaches. Counselors can, however, stick to the area of focus that is most relevant to their clients at a given time. A CFC session might address this in the following way.

Through the process of CIP-based intervention and information resources, Alexa comes to a greater appreciation for the power and control she has at her disposal. She can now choose whether to cling to her self-limiting thoughts or release them in favor of more strategic thinking. She is now ready, as a result of the counseling relationship, to engage in a structured approach to decision-making.

## Summary

Social and cognitive approaches to CFC are direct, didactic, and exist somewhat outside the traditional matching approaches.

They augment matching and developmental approaches by focusing in on the "true reasoning" component. They identify the environmental and decisional barriers that clients often face in working with copious amounts of information, along with missing data. They offer highly complementary, directive approaches to the CFC process.

## References

Badenoch, B. (2008). *Being a Brain-Wise Therapist: A Practical Guide to Interpersonal Neurobiology*. New York, NY: WW Norton & Company.

Bandura, A. (1977). Self-efficacy: Toward a unifying theory of behavioral change. *Psychological Review, 84*(2), 191–215.

Bandura, A. (1986). *Social foundations of thought and action: A social-cognitive theory*. Englewood Cliffs, NJ: Prentice-Hall.

Bandura, A. (1997). *Self-efficacy: The exercise of control*. New York, NY: W. H. Freeman & Co.

Betz, N. E., Klein, K., & Taylor, K. M. (1996). Evaluation of a short form of the career decision making self-efficacy scale. *Journal of Career Assessment*, 4(1), 47–57.

Betz, N. E. (2007). Career self-efficacy: Exemplary recent research and emerging directions. *Journal of Career Assessment*, *15*(4), 403–422.

Betz, N., & Hackett, G. (2006). Career self-efficacy: Back to the future. *Journal of Career Assessment*, 14, 3–11.

Betz, N., Hammond, M., & Multon, K. (2005). Reliability and validity of five-level response Continua for the Career Decision Self-Efficacy Scale. *Journal of Career Assessment*, 13, 131–149.

Brown, S. D., & Lent, R. W. (2017). Social Cognitive Career Theory in a Diverse World: Closing Thoughts. *Journal of Career Assessment*, *25*(1), 173–180.

Crites, J. O. (1978a). *The Career Maturity Inventory* (2nd ed.). Monterey, CA: CTB/McGraw-Hill.

Flores, L. Y., Navarro, R. L., & Ali, S. R. (2017). The state of SCCT research in relation to social class: Future directions. *Journal of Career Assessment*, *25*(1), 6–23.

Fouad, N. A., & Guillen, A. (2006). Outcome expectations: Looking to the past and potential future. *Journal of Career Assessment*, 14, 130–142.

Galles, J. A., & Lenz, J. G. (2013). Relationships among career thoughts, vocational identity, and calling: Implications for practice. *The Career Development Quarterly*, *61*(3), 240–248.

Glasser, W. (1998). *Choice Theory: A New Psychology of Personal Freedom*. New York, NY: HarperPerennial.

Hackett, G., & Betz, N. E. (1981). A self-efficacy approach to the career development of women. *Journal of Vocational Behavior*, 18, 326–339.

Cl: I guess I could say that I don't want to disappoint my family, but I have to act on the best information available to me? How's that?

Co: It depends ... what's it like to say that?

Cl: It feels pretty good.

Co: Does it feel good enough to try replacing the previous statements with the current one?

Cl: I guess I could.

Co: Okay, because this seems to get to the heart of the valuing step we discussed earlier. Up to this point, your self-talk has backed you into a no-win cost-benefit analysis: all cost, no benefit. I suspect that substituted statements like the ones we've been working on may help.

Cl: It's gotta be better than what I've been putting myself through!

Co: I agree. Here is the workbook that provides additional examples of the unhelpful self-talk we often engage in, along with suggestions for replacing them. Let's try this for a week or two and then meet again to see how things are going. How's that?

Cl: Sounds good.

Ivey, A. E., Ivey, M., & Zalaquett, C. P. (2013). *Intentional interviewing and counseling: Facilitating client development in a multicultural society*. Belmont, CA: Brooks/Cole.

Lent, R. W., Brown, S. D., & Hackett, G. (1994). Toward a unifying social cognitive theory of career and academic interest, choice, and performance. *Journal of Vocational Behavior*, 45, 79–122.

Lent, R. W., Brown, S. D., & Hackett, G. (2000). Contextual supports and barriers to career choice: A social cognitive analysis. *Journal of Counseling Psychology*, 31, 356–362.

Lent, R. W. (2013). Social Cognitive Career Theory. In S. D. Brown and R. W. Lent (Eds.) *Career development and counseling: Putting theory and research to work*, pp.115-147. Hoboken, NJ: Wiley.

Lenz, J. G., Peterson, G. W., Reardon, R. C., & Saunders, D. E. (2010). Connecting career and mental health counseling: Integrating theory and practice. *VISTAS 2010*.

Luke, C., Redekop, F., & Burgin, C. (2015). Psychological factors in community college student retention. *Community College Journal of Research and Practice*, *39*(3), 222–234.

Mears, G. (2008). Conducting an intake interview. In I. Marini & M. A. Stebnecki's (Eds.) *The Professional Counselor's Desk Reference* (p. 127) New York, NY: Springer.

Parsons, F. (1909). *Choosing a vocation*. National Career Development Association.

Peterson, G. W., Sampson, J. P., Jr., & Reardon, R. C. 1991). *Career development and services: A cognitive approach*. Pacific Grove, CA: Brooks/Cole.

Sampson, J. P., Jr., Reardon, R. C., Peterson, G. W., & Lenz, J. G. (2004). *Career counseling & service: A cognitive information processing approach*. Belmont, CA: Brooks/Cole.

Peterson, G. W., Sampson, J. P., Jr., Lenz, J. G., & Reardon, R. C. (2002). Becoming career problem solvers and decision makers: A cognitive-information processing approach. In D. Brown & Associates (Eds.), *Career choice and development* (4th ed., pp. 312-369). San Francisco, CA: Jossey-Bass.

Sampson, J. P., Lenz, J. G., Reardon, R. C., & Peterson, G. W. (2000). A cognitive information processing approach to employment problem solving and decision making. *The Career Development Quarterly*, *48*(1), 3–18.

Taylor, K. M., & Betz, N. E. (1983). Application of self-efficacy theory to the understanding and treatment of career indecision. *Journal of Vocational Behavior*, *22*(1), 63–81.

Taylor, K. M., & Popma, J. (1990). An examination of the relationships among career decision-making self-efficacy, career salience, locus of control, and vocational indecision. *Journal of Vocational Behavior*, *37*(1), 17–31.

Weiner, B. (1985). An attributional theory of achievement motivation and emotion. *Psychological Review*, *92*(4), 548–573.

Wubbolding, R. E. (1991). *Understanding Reality Therapy: A Metaphorical Approach*. New York, NY: HarperCollins.

## Figure/Table Credits

Tab. 4.1: Copyright © 2012 by Nancy E. Betz and Karen M. Taylor.
NCDA Screenshot: Copyright © by National Career Development Association.
Tab. 4.3: James P. Sampson, Jr., et al., "CTI Publisher Information," Career Thoughts Inventory. Copyright © by Par, Inc.
Fig. 4.1: Gary W. Peterson, James P. Sampson, Jr., and Robert C. Reardon, "Information Processing Domains in CIP," Adapted by Chad Luke.
Fig. 4.2: Gary W. Peterson, James P. Sampson, Jr., and Robert C. Reardon, "CASVE Cycle in CIP," Adapted by Chad Luke.

# CHAPTER FIVE

# Career Development Theory, Assessment, & Counseling IV: Postmodern and Emergent Approaches

### Chapter Goals

- Provide a brief overview of each of the most prevalent emergent theories
- Describe the career-focused counseling (CFC) implications of post-modern and emergent theories
- Utilize emergent theory to connect to clients' personal issues
- Articulate an integrated approach to theory, assessment, and resources

## Introduction

Career theory, like other theories of human development, have continued to evolve as new research and practices have expanded. While postmodern thought is not new, its application to counseling and career development has continued to generate scholarly interests. In particular, as the nature of work has changed dramatically in the face of technological advances and globalization, career models that emphasize adjustment to change have received increased attention. This chapter addresses two such approaches to understanding career development in the modern world, career construction and happenstance learning theory.

### School-Based Vignette: Xavier, 17

Xavier is a popular 17-year-old high school senior. He was referred to you for behavioral concerns, as he hasn't been paying attention in his classes. In an attempt to build rapport with Xavier, you ask him what he likes to do after school, to which he curtly replies, "I mind my own business and look out for my own." When you ask if he has an afterschool job, he shifts in his chair and tells you that his grandparents won't let him get one, so he "can focus on schoolwork." Xavier goes on to disclose that he makes straight As in his largely Advanced Placement coursework. He says that his grandparents, whom he lives with, had to give up their educations at early ages in order to provide for their families. While he says he understands his grandparents' concerns, Xavier says he feels stressed about paying for college, as his grandparents struggle to survive off of social security and their relatively meager retirement funds. You ask Xavier what he wants to study at university, and he tells you he's too stressed about finances to think about that. He says, "I need to be able to pay for college before I decide what to study."[1]

[1] Credit: Nathan

# Constructivist and Emergent Models

Super (1980) described vocational identity as the projection of one's identity onto the world of work; postmodern and constructivist models describe reality as the projection of one's self onto the world. Reality is created as the individual experiencing the events interprets them. As such, reality can shift and be recreated in ways that increase one's ability to function effectively. The same applies to career development.

## Savickas's Career Construction Theory

Savickas (2012), building on the developmental foundation laid by Super, notes that, because we live in a rapidly changing world of work, it is necessary now, more than ever, to cultivate skills of adaptability. Previously, the work world was fairly predictable, with 30-year career workers, where the bulk of the career was in one company. Nowadays, this has shifted dramatically, particularly in the wake of the global recession in 2007–2008. Savickas calls for "constructing a self and designing a career as many career counselors now concentrate on identity rather than personality, adaptability rather than maturity, intentionality rather than decidedness, and stories rather than scores" (2012, p.14) . Savickas includes the self and identity into his model, and because of his postmodern orientation, includes construction, deconstruction, reconstruction, co-construction, and action into his approach to intervention. These are the result of the model's roots in Super's developmental perspective, where self is projected onto the world of work.

***Self:*** Core essence of a person that is created using the language of the person. Rather than self-actualization—the acting on a pre-existing self on the world of work—self-construction is the creating of the self one wants. This creation takes place through the words one uses to describe themself.

***Identity*** is the self in context; it is the essence of an individual in their social role and is much more variable than self. The

### Community-Based Vignette: Alexa, 21

Alexa is a 21-year-old college student who comes to you for career counseling. She tells you that she switched from a major in special education to one in exercise science. After some inquiry, you learn that she initially chose special education, because a family member did that, and she then chose exercise science, because she ran cross-country all four years of high school. When asked what she wants to deal with in counseling, Alexa says, "Stress. Thinking about getting a job after graduation has been making me worry." She goes on to tell you that she switched out of special education after her first semester taking upper-division classes in her major. Alexa says that she wasn't sure if she wanted to teach, because she would "get too attached to the kids." She reports similar concerns with an exercise science job, like being a gym teacher. She questions whether she wants to teach at all. Wiping away tears, Alexa discloses that she feels like she has been "trying to fill some kind of hole inside me" by finding a meaningful job in which she can help people but to a greater extent than her restaurant server job.

### Life Design Essentials

It may be tempting to feel daunted by the apparent esoteric nature of Savickas's approach. However, it makes sense in light of what interplay between self and identity forms the basis for one's narrative.

***Life Design*** is Savickas's model for creating a career identity that reflects accurate knowledge of self. It draws from narrative career counseling (Cochran, 1997), constructivist career counseling (Peavy, 1992), and multiple others in order "to prompt meaningful activities that further self-making, identity shaping, and career constructing (Savickas, 2010)" (2012, p. 15). Life design involves the following postmodern facets: *construction*—creation of micronarratives about one's self; *deconstruction*—process of micronarrative analysis that seeks to "undo a story's uncritical domination over the client's thinking, not destroy the story" (p. 15); and *reconstruction*—"gathers micronarratives about important incidents, recurrent episodes, significant figures, self-defining moments, and life-changing experiences" (p. 16). This process involves the reconsolidation of life themes into a coherence that clients can make sense of and upon which they take action. *Co-construction*, through the relationship between counselor and client, seeks to create a narrative that includes changes to one's identity that the client would like to implement. This aids in impelling them to action. *Action*, then, is a type of working ahead of oneself "through action, not verbal expressions of decidedness, clients engage the world" (Krieshok, Black, & McKay, 2009, p. 17).

counselors already do at some level with their clients; he has just made this process more explicit. Therefore, the model works well in CFC as well as counseling for other specific issues. Clients live out their stories—small and large—often without ever realizing it. Counseling draws out these stories from clients through listening, reflecting, and probing. Once "out there," clients have the freedom and ability to examine each component, revealing previously implicit assumptions, biases, and other contaminants to the story (Savickas, 2012). They can then appreciate and exercise their options for rebuilding their story, having stripped out or at least confronted those things that poison their larger narrative. Counselors then step in again to assist in building in additional healthful components of the story to replace the ones that were removed. All of this sets the client up for implementing this revised story of self and identity into the world of work.

## Krumboltz, Social Learning, and Happenstance

John Krumboltz has parlayed his 40-plus years of theory development into its current iteration, called Happenstance Learning Theory (HLT; 2009). He spent many years refining models of career development based on Social Learning Theory (1975, 1979, 1988, 1994). His focus has been on the way individuals learn and how this learning influences behavior. In HLT, he makes a somewhat radical departure from traditional approaches, like trait and factor, and provides a rare exception to Parsons' (1909) tripartite model. For Krumboltz, HLT is a humility-based learning model that posits that the field gives too much credence to intentionality in career decision-making. Instead, he advocates for intentionality in learning from each

### HLT Essentials

Clients facing career-related issues are adept at transferring their anxiety about work onto their counselors, most often unwittingly. Perhaps it is because the need for work is imbedded in our collective unconscious as a means of proving our worth. Regardless, when counselors take ownership of and responsibility for finding clients jobs, they almost invariably will resist engaging in CFC. However, step on the job path, recognizing that more times than not, careers develop serendipitously (1998; 2010), despite our intentions, not necessarily because of them. However, Krumboltz is not advocating for a hands-off, luck-be-your-guide approach. He describes four key assumptions from his model that indicate an active role for clients in learning and behaving (2009, p. 135).

1. *The goal of career counseling is to help clients learn to take actions to achieve more satisfying career and personal lives—not to make a single career decision:* For Krumboltz, career counseling is about assisting clients in life transitions, not in choosing a career. "Naming a future occupation is amazingly simple and can easily be faked. When asked about a future occupational goal, children can easily please their parents by naming some high prestige occupation" (2009, p. 142). He further notes what career counselors have long known to be true, that CFC can seem as simple as choosing an occupation, when this understanding of our work is simplistic and reductive.

2. *Assessments are used to stimulate learning, not to match personal characteristics with occupational characteristics:* Krumboltz maintains that career-related assessments are meant to spark conversations and stimulate further learning, not attempt to make a match between a person and work. An example of this perspective is the Career Beliefs Inventory (Krumboltz, 1992), in which attitudes and beliefs about career development are assessed, not interests, skills, or values.

3. *Clients learn to engage in exploratory actions as a way of generating beneficial unplanned events:* "Unplanned event" is not the same as saying out of control events. On the contrary, Krumboltz (2009) has long maintained that the value in happenstance is the way in which clients can both prepare themselves for when these serendipitous events come along, as well as taking action that increases the likelihood that these unforeseen events might occur. He describes the following potential considerations: 1) Before the unplanned event, you take actions that position you to experience it; 2) During the event, you remain alert and sensitive to recognize potential opportunities;

HLT offers a useful reframe of the role of counselors in this process. The first is to hand ownership back to the client by redefining the purpose of counseling. The counselor is not present in the relationship to help the client find a job or make a career choice. Instead, the role of the counselor is to increase client learning and motivate the client to take some action or actions. This is a completely different process from the former, and it leads to different outcomes. Success is not job-based; it is process-based. If this sounds conspicuously like "regular" counseling, it is because it is! Counselors are process experts who facilitate client learning and action, at least according to Social Learning Theory (Krumboltz, 1975, 1979, 1988, 1994).

## Xavier in Session

For Xavier, career choice, in the form of attending college and selecting the right major, is a finite, foreknowledge-dependent process. He seems to have convinced himself that he needs to have the answers prior to having the right questions. In doing so, he has bailed out of the process by avoiding college and career decision making altogether. A large part of this stems from his difficulty recognizing how his past experiences in high school can inform his next steps and create opportunities for continued learning (not making a single, right decision).

CL: I just need to work for a while instead of going to college.

3) After the event, you initiate actions that enable you to benefit from it. (2009, p. 144); 4) *The success of counseling is assessed by what the client accomplishes in the real world outside the counseling session:* CFC can be an intimidating process for counselors to embrace, particularly when they evaluate "success" as a binary system: either the client gets the job they want right away or they don't (Luke & Redekop, 2016). In Happenstance Learning Theory (HLT), the focus is on preparing the client to take action—any action. It is this action that supports their motivation and increases their readiness for and the likelihood of serendipitous, happenstance events. Success in counseling is tantamount to action. Therefore, counselors focus on moving clients to take action at every stage of development.

In addition to these assumptions, Krumboltz recognizes and describes the influences of the following in learning: genetics, learning experiences—including both instrumental and associative learning experiences, environmental conditions and events, parents and caretakers, peer groups, structured education settings, and an imperfect world. Learning does not place in a vacuum and requires appreciation of the influence of these factors in learning and taking action. After discussing "essentials" we look at these theories in practice with Xavier and Alexa.

As this transcript excerpt demonstrates, career construction is not simply a matter of explaining the model to a client and asking them to see things differently. A bright client like Xavier will be able to verbally spar with a counselor in order to maintain his view. Instead, a counselor might look for opportunities to connect Xavier's experience or way of thinking to the ways the counseling model works. Rather than asking him to give up the pressure to make the one right decision, his counselor will help him see the multiple solutions to other, real-world problems, and then make connections to career decision making.

As this transcript excerpt demonstrates, the career problem is rarely the *actual* problem. Decoding the client's narrative helps to determine the career decision-making barriers that underlie other issues, and vice versa. Rather than finding a career, the session turns toward communication in relationships.

CO: Getting a job seems so much simpler and straightforward at this point.

CL: Exactly, and no one seems to understand that.

CO: Okay. Tell me.

CL: I've been in these AP classes for 3 years, and I can do well, but they are boring. It's hard to see them leading to anything substantial.

CO: Whereas working a job is tangible, with clear outcomes (a paycheck).

CL: Yeah, I'm sick of seeing my grandparents struggle and feeling broke all the time too.

CO: They sense that as well, but their solution is a college education while yours is to get any 9 to 5 job. Is that right?

CL: I just don't know how to make them understand.

CO: What would it take for them to understand your perspective?

CL: They can't.

CO: Let's assume that's accurate. What about their perspective can you agree with?

CL: Oh, I know a college degree is the way to go. The statistics on salary and employment rates are clear.

CO: Okay, but ... ?

CL: But I don't know what to pick. What happens if I pick the wrong one?

CO: I don't know; what?

CL: I don't know either, and that's the problem!

CO: Oh, I think I'm catching up now. I wonder if the situation you find yourself in now is related to being a high-performing high school student, which translates into being a high-performing career selector.

CL: Well, yeah. I don't want to screw it up and disappoint my grandparents. They have done so much for me.

CO: I see. Knowing that employers value employees who can analyze problems, let's take some time to look at the differences between finding *a* solution to a problem versus gathering information to prepare for multiple possible solutions.

### Alexa in Session

Alexa has created for herself a world of work based on *shoulds*. She appears caught between a family narrative about what makes a career meaningful and her own pull toward something else that feels meaningful. She is struggling to experience actively (rather than passively) creating her own career path; as she moves away from the family narrative of educator-based career meaning, she feels increasingly uncertain about what this might look like. Let's examine how a clinical conversation around this might explore and begin to modify this narrative.

CO: So Alexa, it sounds like your family is hopeful that you will continue to pursue a career in education.

CL: That's a nice way of putting it!

CO: What would be the not-nice way of putting it? How would you state it?

CL: They think I should stay in the education field for job security and because they had very meaningful careers there.

Clients often struggle in these areas, so a counselor can be led down a primrose path of career problem solving and miss the more fundamental relational issues that can impede progress. Taking time to help the client narrative unfold aids in career-focused counseling.

## Assessment in Postmodern and Emergent Theories

Assessment in the form of questions help career-focused counselors address what the counselor wants the client to get from the assessment process. Options include the following:

1. Client insight—what can a client gain in self-understanding from an assessment that has yet to be gleaned from the counseling relationship?
2. Idea generation—have we exhausted brainstorming approaches to developing client options that an assessment will take to the next step?
3. "Objective" Information—are clients mistrustful of their own thinking about career-related issues, and do they need some form of formal, quantitative feedback to spur them to action? (Counselors understand that assessments are reports of information given by the clients.)

Another consideration as we continue down the primrose path of career-related assessments involves the connections between the assessments themselves and the theoretical constructs that underpin them. It is important to the CFC endeavor for counselors to use an assessment largely within the confines of the theory upon which it is grounded, in order to ensure greater ethical use of the assessment. For example, if a counselor decides to use the Career Thoughts Inventory (CTI) to identify the primary barriers for a client in committing to a career path, it is important that that counselor also recognizes the role that cognition plays in decision-making and problem-solving with Cognitive Information Processing (CIP), the theory foundation from the CTI. In particular, Herr (2009) asserts the value in using career assessments to bridge theory and practice; some instruments and developers do this more clearly than others.

One additional disclaimer before we proceed: while counselors utilize questions sparingly, so as not to overwhelm the client or convince them that counseling is question-answer time, they use questions strategically. In many cases, the assessment question *is* the intervention. J. Sommers-Flanagan and R. Sommers-Flanagan (2012) enumerate multiple clinical interview questions useful as interventions, as well. This is similar in CFC, wherein assessments in general, and individual questions in particular, can be used as catalysts for change or reflection. For example, I might ask a client, "Where and when did you learn to doubt your abilities so thoroughly?" While I am asking for information, I am also communicating to the client 1) counseling will address beliefs and thought processes, and 2) these beliefs were learned over a period of time in certain contexts. Further, if these are beliefs and they have been learned, they are also able to be over-learned, in that those messages can be overwritten in the course of counseling. The point is that assessments need not always be simply a means to an end; they can, at times, be an end in themselves.

Students of counseling begin to recognize that thus far I have not included a biopsychosocial assessment. These assessments explore clients' (bio) physical health, including any issues in utero or during birth; (psycho) cognitive and emotional functioning; and (social) family, social, and work relationships. There's a good reason for this omission. There are two important considerations with regard to intake that correlate with two distinct directions. These directions will be dictated both by the counselor's place of employment and the client's needs. In the first instance, sometimes it is prudent to gather all the information possible through intake and background forms followed by a thorough intake interview that covers the above categories. This is often effective in making a preliminary diagnosis and identifying complicating or mitigating circumstances relative to the client's presenting problem. This is also a common approach in community or campus mental health centers and is appropriate when clients present with a mental health issue outside of career in which career issues emerge later.

The second approach is to begin with a very open-ended question like "What brings you in today?" It addresses some concerns I have with the biopsychosocial model described above: first, intake interviews like those above tend to be

CO: But you are not sure that is for you?

CL: I'm just not feeling it in those courses. I want something more.

CO: Let's try something: if you are living out the plot to a book, and this process to this point is one chapter, what would you title it?

CL: Huh? Oh, you mean like in a novel?

CO: Yes, or an autobiography.

CL: I don't know ... Family Pressure?

CO: Okay. Good. Now let yourself be as creative as you want to be in turning this into a compelling chapter title.

CL: Hmmm ... "Lost in Education"

CO: Mmm, I see. Good. Now let's take it to the next step. If this next chapter of your life—selecting a major and career that matter to you, and finishing your degree and getting a good job—what would that title be?

CL: "Peace of Mind?"

CO: That sounded like a question.

CL: Well, I guess that's what I'd want to have, but it's a side effect of a good career choice.

CO: Okay. Let's make that a little more concrete.

CL: "Making My Mark but Taking a Stand"

CO: That sounds clear. Can you tell me more?

CL: I guess this is making me see that I've been feeling all this frustration at my family and it's made me want to run, which I have. I think the next thing I want to do is tell them what I'm feeling about this, whether they listen or not.

CO: So this is about more than picking the "right" major or career; it sounds like it's about asserting yourself in a series of conversations with your family.

CL: Yeah, it's not really about a job at all!

CO: How about if we plan to practice those conversations in here by role playing? Here's how that would look ...

## BOX FEATURE: Neuro-Perspectives on Postmodern,

counselor-focused, even though the information is about the client. It says to the client, "Before we get to your needs, let's talk about mine." Second, the deluge of client information can overwhelm counselors, especially new ones, and result in either misdiagnosis or the counselor having to ask for the same information again, because it was forgotten—not good for rapport building. In contrast, a gather-info-as-we-go approach to Career Focused Counseling (CFC) in particular helps the client and counselor keep pace with one another. It also keeps the information fresh and relevant to the moment, a type of just-in-time manufacturing approach to gathering information. As an adjunct to this approach, I incorporate a brainstorming of life domains inventory:

Figure 5.1.a highlights just a handful of the domains of life that may affect or be affected by career-related issues. Each of these contains a narrative that most likely connects to the other domains. In CFC, I might ask clients to first identify their feelings related to the diagram. Almost without exception, they express feelings of being overwhelmed by the magnitude of the issues. Therefore, the first step is to identify the domain most strongly related to their career-related issue. Figure 5.1.b highlights the next step in the process: covering the other domains in order to provide perspective on addressing the most salient issue. This also provides a sense of relief as it reminds clients that they may not need to attempt to address every domain at once.

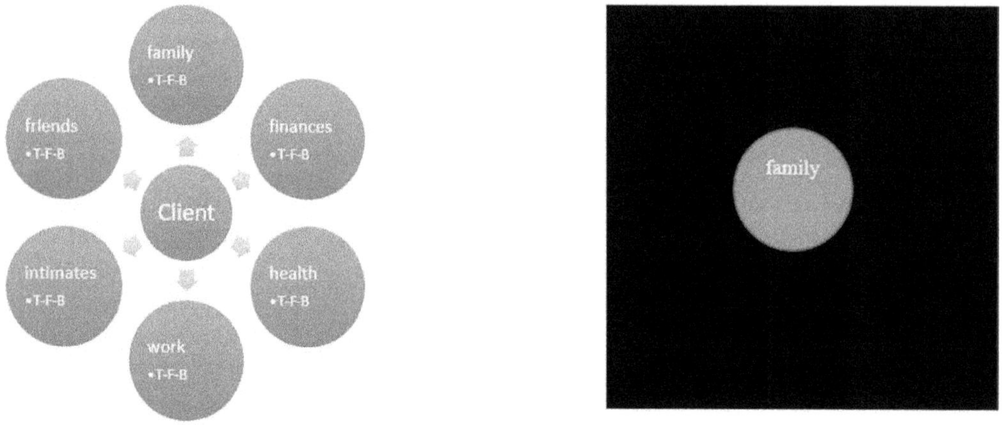


Figure 5.1.a and 5.1.b Brainstorming Activity

# Vocational Card Sorts in CFC

Card sorts are qualitative assessment instruments (Sheperis, 2012). While they are not inherently postmodern, card sorts, and qualitative assessment in general, are more open-ended by design allowing for more client projection and interpretation. For example, values card sorts are quite literally cards with values listed on them, one on each card, that clients then sort into piles by priority. There are also blank cards that allow clients to add their own values or values in their own language. Card sorts are more interactive initially in that they ask clients to be active in the assessment process (quantitative measures can feel passive in that clients are primarily answering someone else's questions). In contrast, card sorts require clients to ask their own questions. Further, they are more kinesthetically engaging for clients who may be distractible or who otherwise need varied engagement. For the sake of concrete understanding of card sorts, figures 5.2.a and 5.2.b represent a prominent card sort system developed by Richard Knowdell and found at:

http://www.careernetwork.org/WorkSheets/Values%20Work%20Sheet%20Jan%20'11.pdf

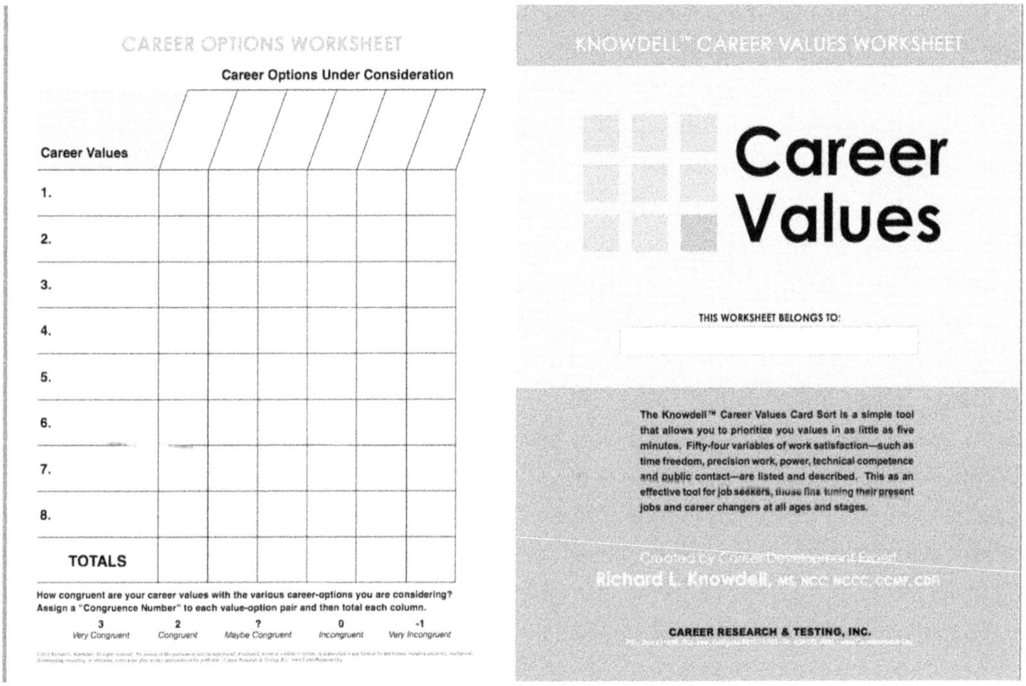


Figure 5.2. a and 5.2.b. Sample Card Sort Activity from Richard Knowdell

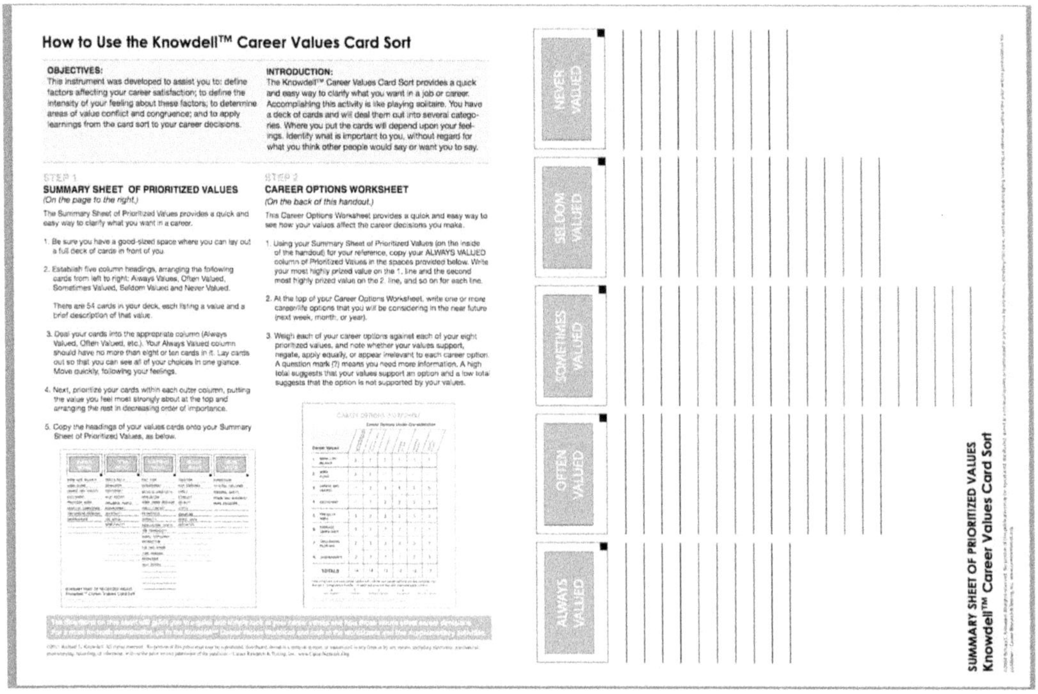

## How to Use the Knowdell™ Career Values Card Sort

**OBJECTIVES:**
This instrument was developed to assist you to: define factors affecting your career satisfaction; to define the intensity of your feeling about these factors; to determine areas of value conflict and congruence; and to apply learnings from the card sort to your career decisions.

**INTRODUCTION:**
The Knowdell™ Career Values Card Sort provides a quick and easy way to clarify what you want in a job or career. Accomplishing this activity is like playing solitaire. You have a deck of cards and will deal them out into several categories. Where you put the cards will depend upon your feelings. Identify what is important to you, without regard for what you think other people would say or want you to say.

STEP 1

**SUMMARY SHEET OF PRIORITIZED VALUES**
*(On the page to the right.)*

The Summary Sheet of Prioritized Values provides a quick and easy way to clarify what you want in a career.

1. Be sure you have a good-sized space where you can lay out a full deck of cards in front of you.
2. Establish five column headings, arranging the following cards from left to right: Always Values, Often Valued, Sometimes Valued, Seldom Valued and Never Valued.

   There are 54 cards in your deck, each listing a value and a brief description of that value.
3. Deal your cards into the appropriate column (Always Valued, Often Valued, etc.). Your Always Valued column should have no more than eight or ten cards in it. Lay cards out so that you can see all of your choices in one glance. Move quickly, following your feelings.
4. Next, prioritize your cards within each outer column, putting the value you feel most strongly about at the top and arranging the rest in decreasing order of importance.
5. Copy the headings of your values cards onto your Summary Sheet of Prioritized Values, as below.

STEP 2

**CAREER OPTIONS WORKSHEET**
*(On the back of this handout.)*

This Career Options Worksheet provides a quick and easy way to see how your values affect the career decisions you make.

1. Using your Summary Sheet of Prioritized Values (on the inside of the handout) for your reference, copy your ALWAYS VALUED column of Prioritized Values in the spaces provided below. Write your most highly prized value on the 1. line and the second most highly prized value on the 2. line, and so on for each line.
2. At the top of your Career Options Worksheet, write one or more career/life options that you will be considering in the near future (next week, month, or year).
3. Weigh each of your career options against each of your eight prioritized values, and note whether your values support, negate, apply equally, or appear irrelevant to each career option. A question mark (?) means you need more information. A high total suggests that your values support an option and a low total suggests that the option is not supported by your values.



***Career Futures Inventory—Revised.*** The Career Futures Inventory (Rottinghaus, 2005) and the Career Futures Inventory-Revised (CFI-R; Rottinghaus et al., 2012) was developed to assess career adaptability in the light of Savickas' (2012) approach. "The 28-item CFI-R assesses aspects of career adaptability, including positive career planning attitudes, general outcome expectations, and components of Parsons' tripartite model and Bandura's personal agency" (Rottinghaus, et al., 2012, p. 123). The revised instrument identifies five subscales: career agency, occupational awareness, support, work–life balance, and negative career outlook. The CFI-R assesses how adaptable clients are in the face of changing occupational climates and explores their optimism about adjusting to these eminent changes.

***Career Beliefs Inventory (CBI).*** The CBI is a 96-item instrument used to "Measure participants' assumptions, generalizations, and beliefs about themselves and the world of work" CBI manual). It emerged from the work of John Krumboltz and his Learning Theory of Career Counseling (LTCC; 1988). His theory of career development has metamorphosed over the four decades of research but remains anchored in the CBI as it relates to the ways beliefs influence behavior. The CBI continues to be an instrument of value in identifying how CFC clients might self-sabotage their efforts via their career beliefs. Identifying these beliefs and their impact on career risk-taking can empower clients to challenge these beliefs and to take different action.

Step five in HLT (2009) involves
Overcome Blocks to Action
Goal: Help clients to overcome dysfunctional beliefs that block constructive action.
Counselors may ask questions similar to the following:

- What do you believe is stopping you from doing what you really want to do?
- What do you believe is a first step you could take now to move closer to what you want?
- What do you believe is stopping you from taking that first step?
- How would your life become more satisfying if you were to take appropriate action?
- What action will you take before we meet next?
- By what date and time will you e-mail me a report of your action? (2009, 148)

Any of these sample questions might enable Xavier to think differently about his future and the role that additional education may play in it.

One important consideration in using career assessments is that the questions individually and the assessment process can be an intervention in and of itself. This is just as true for the CBI, for example (Krumboltz & Vosvick, 1996). As most students of an introductory or developmental psychology course will recognize, attending to an issue alone exerts influence on that issue. The so-called Hawthorne Effect reflects the power of observation in making changes. In the same way, asking assessment questions focuses the observation of the individual on a particular aspect of a problem. Let's take a look at how the questions from the Krumboltz's CBI, for example, might fit with his HLT.

# Narrative Career Assessment

## Career Construction Interview

In 1989, Mark Savickas developed the career style/story interview, which has been modified and renamed the Career Construction Interview (Savickas, 2011, 2013). As described earlier, Savickas describes the process of a career self in five stages: construction, deconstruction, reconstruction, co-construction, and action. Now, Savickas is as much a philosopher as he is a theorist, so readers are cautioned not to get too bogged down in the language. Within each stage, the Career Construction Interview asks a series of questions, again for the purpose of individual learning.

## Xavier in Session with Postmodern Career Assessments

Co: So Xavier, here's a sample of your CBI score profile. I thought we might take a quick look at it and discuss what stands out to you.
Cl: That is okay with me. (together, they look at the article)
(from Krumboltz & Vosvick, 1996, p. 349)
Co: Look for a moment at the dimension "Effort I am willing to initiate". What stands out for you?
Cl: I see that on the items "Persisting while uncertain" and "Taking risks" I have really low scores.
Co: I see that as well.
Cl: It makes sense considering how stuck I've felt recently.
Co: You've certainly described some struggles in pursuing a path to a future that you can't see clearly from where you currently sit ... (continued below)
Co: I've heard you say that you'd like to move forward, and I have also heard you say that certainty and risks are concerns for you. If you were to begin addressing this area of your career and life development, what might be the first step?
Cl: I guess I haven't thought of it as a step—more of jumping off a cliff.
Co: Thanks for that analogy, as if it paints an even clearer picture for me of your struggles. Say more about the cliff.
Cl: It has felt like I have to leap into the unknown, and it feels perilous. I don't want to do it!
Co: But when I asked about a step, you seemed a little relieved, if skeptical.
Cl: Yeah, if it was a step and not a "leap of faith," that'd be much better.
Co: What do you imagine that step might look like? Pick anything.
Cl: Find a couple of possible careers of interest?
Co: Great! Let's start there. Now what do you imagine is the biggest barrier to finding these?
Cl: Well, I think we just addressed it: exploring possibilities feels way better than committing to an uncertain career.
Co: Okay, so a type of Xavier-formula is emerging, one that takes leaps and turns them into steps.
Cl: Yeah, that sounds like me and like a me I'd rather be.
Co: Good. Let's look at this a little closer next time.

***Construction***—This stage of the process asks about the following five areas: 1) Who were their role models, as they represent possible selves? 2) What are their "manifest" interests, rather than "inventoried" interests? In other words, how have they seen their interests play out in their life, instead of how they scored on an interest inventory? 3) In thinking about a favorite book or movie, how would they describe the script and its importance to them? 4) What is their favorite saying, as "a motto usually advises clients about the adaptability resources and adapting actions required to move to the next episodes in the occupational plot?" (2013, p. 169) 5) How would they describe their character arc, carefully shifting them from the inevitable past core conflict onto a future perspective that will guide action?

***Deconstruction***—This stage involves eliciting self-defeating aspects of their narrative and is often related to cultural biases (e.g., race, SES, gender). The purpose of breaking down these stories into their component parts is to allow access to and make vulnerable the "self-limiting ideas, confining roles, and cultural barriers" (p. 169). In this, we might ask how the client how they can re-remember this limiting memories and orient themselves toward a future, contrary action than that which they learned and have been living out.

***Reconstruction***—This stage involves assembly and re-assembly of a grand narrative, which enables the client to see beyond their past and current circumstances out toward the future they plan to create. In this step, Savickas cautions counselors to avoid getting too caught up in the data of the client's story, not confusing facts for substance. In this approach, substance refers to the connective tissue of the story, the "glue" that holds the narrative together. Counselors who over-focus on data and details can miss important themes that run through the facts.

***Co-construction***—this step invites the client to participate in refining the new picture of their story and asks if there are any edits needed as they prepare for action. The impetus for these revisions rests with the client, not the counselor, and as such, creates more predictable success (Savickas, 2013).

***Action***—Just as interests enacted are more reliable than interests inventoried, self-in-action is the logical next step of a created self. The counselor's role in this is assist in

## Constructivist Approaches

**The brain makes meaning by drawing on past experiences (stored in memory systems), environmental conditions, and relationships. Meaning, in this way, is very much constructed in such a way that each individual's perception of experiences, environments, and relationships are highly phenomenological. This means that any individual can create a reality all their own, whether in the world of work or the world in general. It will be immediately obvious that these models are not suggesting that one can create their own reality about gravity, making it appear or disappear. However—and this is key—they can construct their own reality about what gravity means for their ability to function in the world. In counseling and in teaching counseling, I often use the example of the training of circus elephant to remain where their trainers want them. Early in their lives, baby elephants have a shackle placed around their ankle attached to a stake in the ground. At this tender age and size, they experience the limit and cease pulling against it. As they grow, as the narrative goes, the shackle can remain without being tethered to anything (not that it would do any good anyway, given the size and power of the animal). The adult elephant has crafted a narrative—a view of reality—that restricts its behavior. The brain arranges itself in ways that internalize these views in order to increase efficiency (no need**

to waste time and energy pulling against something immovable, especially when that energy could be directed toward finding food). Likewise, clients enter CFC possessing learning experiences that have shaped their views of reality. Counseling offers a context and process that permits challenging these realities through brain change, called neuroplasticity.

developing an "agenda" for action that moves from storytelling to story-living.

Watch for these as you read Alexa's interaction.

## Alexa in Session with Narrative Assessment

Co: So Alexa, we've done a little role-playing for how to communicate with your folks and that's working ok, I think.
Cl: Yeah, I guess so.
Co: And you've taken some career assessments, right?
Cl: Yeah.
Co: I wonder if we could approach this a little differently ... the narrative approach that I introduced you to a couple of sessions ago says that it's better to look at the expression of interests, not the inventorying of interests. Could I ask you a few questions about that?
Cl: Sure.
Co: We've discussed in some length how influential your family has been in shaping your career direction, at least up to this point. Who else has been influential in your life, career or otherwise? Like role models?
Cl: (describes several key figures in her life that had not previously been explored)
Co: Wow, your energy seemed to shoot up when you discussed those folks!
Cl: Well, I've only ever thought about who I needed to please, not who I might want to emulate!
Co: This is a good start—let's follow that energy ... What are some things you do in your regular life that, if I saw you doing those things, I might think, "Hey, I wonder if that's an interest are for Alexa?"
Cl: You mean like hobbies?
Co: Actually, I mean anything that you do that is self-directed and may reflect an interest (something you do rather than something you check on an inventory).
Cl: Oh, I see what you mean. Well ... (Alexa goes on to describe a variety of activities that are part of her daily life).

Co: Again, there's a visible increase in your energy level. You have described parts of your life that we have not discussed before.
Cl: I never thought of them as career-related.
Co: And they may not be directly career-related, but recall that we're working together to co-construct a life, not just a career. It may be that these will be avocational parts of your life.
Cl: Okay. I don't know what avocational means but I'll take your word for it (smiles).
Co: Good point. I was using "shop talk." Avocation simply means things you take part in that exist outside of your employment but that represent your contribution to your piece of the world.
Cl: Got it.
Co: Okay. When you think of your favorite movie or book, what is it about the script or plot that really captures your attention?
Cl: Oh that's easy (describes in great detail her favorite television series and the lead character's role and storyline).
Co: That came right to mind! Continue.
Cl: Well, the character is a problem-solver, innovative, and creative. She's the opposite of those in shows I hate, where they do the same thing over and over (pauses).
Co: (silence)
Cl: The shows I hate feel like education—training to do what seems like the same thing every day, all day!
Co: And in contrast you want to ...
Cl: Create! Solve puzzles!
Co: I can see that. Well, now that you have experienced that a little, let's look at how you might turn this into a vocational path.
Cl: Great!
(Interview continues through additional two *construction* questions)

## Web-Based Information Systems Related to Postmodern and Emergent Theories

In the HLT, Krumboltz suggests four key propositions, described earlier in this chapter, one of which has vast implications for career assessment. As noted throughout this section, postmodern assessment is best used to create learning opportunities, not to deliver information and answers (2009). In a similar way, career construction approaches assessment from the perspective of the client, not the assessment instrument. In fact, Savickas describes the Career Story Interview. This influence of career construction, now called life design, is highlighted in the special issue of the Career Developmental Quarterly (2016). The editor, Paul Hartung, highlights four features of the approaches, each with implications for career assessment (p. 2):

> (a) activity to shape interests, capacities, and aspirations; (b) career adaptability to cope with changes in self and situation; (c) narratability to articulate a clear identity and coherent personal life/career story; and (d) intentionality to give meaning to activities and experiences related to life career.

In approaching sources of occupational information, this section deviates somewhat from the previous chapters. Here, I describe the use of a Card Sort assessment with a client in order to demonstrate the multiple variables involved and how each might lead to the same or a very different source of information. Earlier in the chapter, we described Knowdell's system. Here, we take a closer look as a modified version of this approach.

In working with Xavier or Alexa, we might build on the career construction interview by asking them to list behaviors that highlight their interest, values, and personal style. Readers will note that in this approach, I am combining assessment categories rather than isolating just interest, for example. In practice, these areas overlap considerably, and it is just not always useful to make artificial divides when encouraging exploration with clients. Here in Table 5.2 is a sample list, representing an amalgam of the two:

**Table 5.2. Eliciting and Translating Client Characteristics**

| Activity | Translation |
|---|---|
| • Going to movies with friends | • Social, artistic |
| • Solving word puzzles | • Linguistic problem-solving |
| • Solving number puzzles | • Logical problem-solving |
| • Quiet conversations with one or two close friends | • Closeness in personal connections |
| • Cooking | • Artistic expression |
| • Modifying recipes when cooking | • Playful, experimental artistic expression |
| • Collectibles | • Patterns, ritual, themes |
| • High-intensity exercise | • Indication of task completion approach? |
| • Fantasy sports | • Systematic "play" |
| • Reading novels | • Learning through abstraction |
| • Reading scientific blogs | • Learning them concrete empiricism |
| • Playing online role-playing games | • Virtual self-expression |
| • Others | • ? |

One practical information-based intervention can be to then rank and order the activities and use the top ones in a search, like "careers for people who like role-playing games." This is best done in the office with the client, as the results can be unpredictable, as you might imagine. These searches assist in generating ideas and connecting themes, without the onus being placed on the counselor or client to generate these from scratch.

## Alexa in Session with Information Systems

Co: Alexa, we've spoken quite a bit regarding how you feel in conflict with your family about your career path. You've done really good work describing what you want, in terms of an occupational path. What remains for you to work on in your communication with your family about your goals?
Cl: Well, I guess I spoke with my mom this last week, as I do every day, and she asked me again about career stuff. I froze up.
Co: That sounds difficult. What would like to have done instead?
Cl: I want to talk with her about our work together and to be able to explain what I want to do next and why I want to do it.
Co: Okay.
Cl: (pauses)
Co: But you don't know what to say?
Cl: Yeah. I forget what to say and all the things I've learned go out the window!
Co: I can see that is frustrating for you. How about this: we design a way for you to teach your mom what you've learned by showing her?
Cl: Uh, how would that work?
Co: I'm thinking that, first of all, you could use a card sort with her. (See figure below.) You could list out with me, and then repeat with her, those things you do in your daily life. Then, you can translate those into what you know about yourself. Next, take these insights to the Web. You can use the www.onetonline.org site to search for career possibilities that correspond with your values, interests, and abilities. In essence, you'd let the card sort and website speak for you. How'd that be? It's similar to what we discussed last time.
Co: I can definitely do that!
Cl: Good. Let's practice. On the site, select Advanced Search and then select Browse By ... and select Work Context. This will take us a little different route than before, since you told me that innovation and problem-solving are important to you. Then select Structural Job Characteristics.

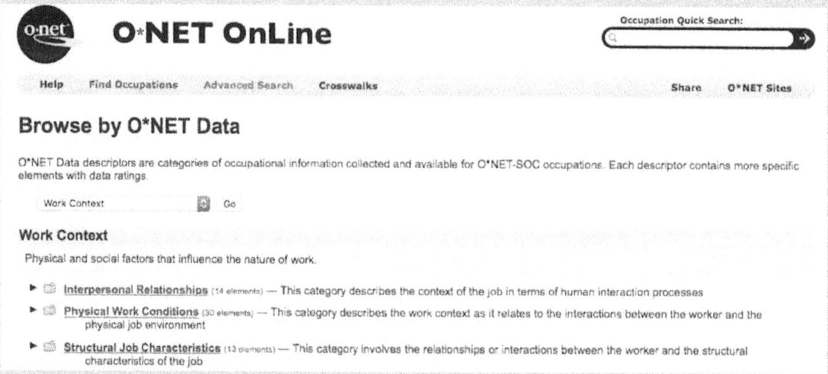

O*NET OnLine

Occupation Quick Search:

Help Find Occupations Advanced Search Crosswalks Share O*NET Sites

**Browse by O*NET Data**

O*NET Data descriptors are categories of occupational information collected and available for O*NET-SOC occupations. Each descriptor contains more specific elements with data ratings.

Work Context Go

**Work Context**

Physical and social factors that influence the nature of work.

- Interpersonal Relationships (14 elements) — This category describes the context of the job in terms of human interaction processes
- Physical Work Conditions (30 elements) — This category describes the work context as it relates to the interactions between the worker and the physical job environment
- Structural Job Characteristics (13 elements) — This category involves the relationships or interactions between the worker and the structural characteristics of the job

Co: Let's take a look at these categories and see what stands out to you.

Cl: Oh, this looks interesting.

Co: You can see how this becomes its own work context values card sort. Each selection will take you to occupations that fit the context to a certain extent.

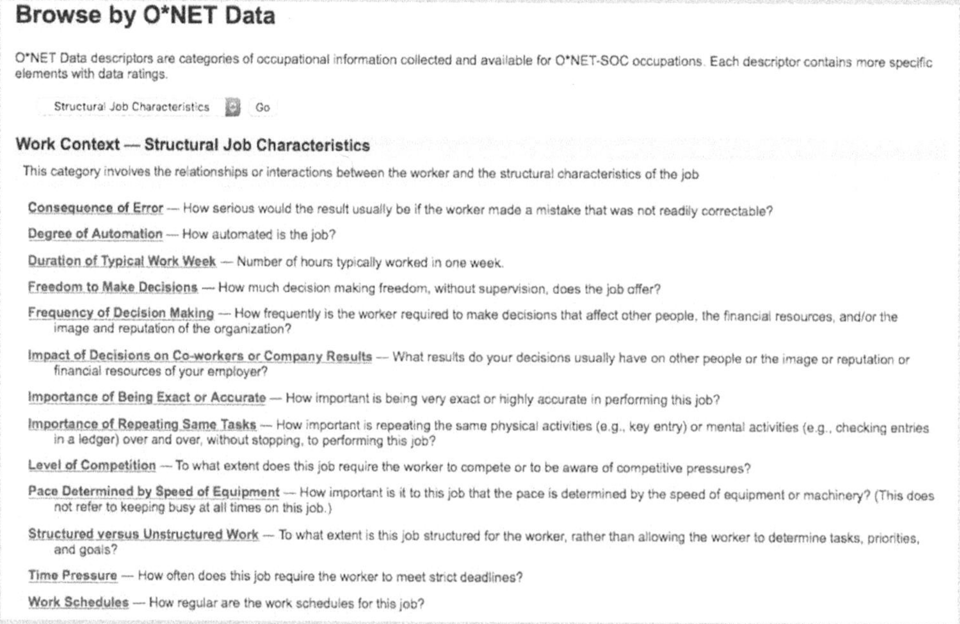

**Browse by O*NET Data**

O*NET Data descriptors are categories of occupational information collected and available for O*NET-SOC occupations. Each descriptor contains more specific elements with data ratings.

Structural Job Characteristics Go

**Work Context — Structural Job Characteristics**

This category involves the relationships or interactions between the worker and the structural characteristics of the job

Consequence of Error — How serious would the result usually be if the worker made a mistake that was not readily correctable?

Degree of Automation — How automated is the job?

Duration of Typical Work Week — Number of hours typically worked in one week.

Freedom to Make Decisions — How much decision making freedom, without supervision, does the job offer?

Frequency of Decision Making — How frequently is the worker required to make decisions that affect other people, the financial resources, and/or the image and reputation of the organization?

Impact of Decisions on Co-workers or Company Results — What results do your decisions usually have on other people or the image or reputation or financial resources of your employer?

Importance of Being Exact or Accurate — How important is being very exact or highly accurate in performing this job?

Importance of Repeating Same Tasks — How important is repeating the same physical activities (e.g., key entry) or mental activities (e.g., checking entries in a ledger) over and over, without stopping, to performing this job?

Level of Competition — To what extent does this job require the worker to compete or to be aware of competitive pressures?

Pace Determined by Speed of Equipment — How important is it to this job that the pace is determined by the speed of equipment or machinery? (This does not refer to keeping busy at all times on this job.)

Structured versus Unstructured Work — To what extent is this job structured for the worker, rather than allowing the worker to determine tasks, priorities, and goals?

Time Pressure — How often does this job require the worker to meet strict deadlines?

Work Schedules — How regular are the work schedules for this job?

Cl: What if I don't know which occupation I want to go into from the list?

Co: Good question! I'd emphasize that this activity is more about finding a way to communicate with your mom about who you see yourself to be in the world of work. Like with most career planning, it's more about the process of selection and the communication about the selection than it is about the actual end product. That comes later. Could you see yourself taking your mom through this process?

Cl: I think I can. It helps to not have to get to the right job at the end.

Alexa's case is so reflective of the dilemma many of us face when asked a "why" question from those we hold in high regard. When the response is not immediate or does not seem to be readily accepted, we can experience self doubt. CFC from a postmodern perspective is particularly focused on the process. This process is about exploring how and what we have learned about ourselves and how that translates into the world of work. In it, the information resources are similar to other approaches, but they are nuanced in their application.

# Summary

Postmodern and emergent approaches to CFC harness the power of curiosity, optimism, risk-taking, flexibility, and persistence (Mitchell, Levin, & Krumboltz, 1999). These approaches view indecision as opportunities. They seek better career-related questions rather than answers. Clients are free to explore how learning experiences from their environment have informed the ways in which they view themselves in the present, and how the current view of the self impacts their decisions for the future. Clients are seen as the drivers of their narrative, both in how they interpret the past and how they construct their career futures.

# References


Cochran, L. (1997). *Career counseling: A narrative approach*. Thousand Oaks, CA: Sage.

Hartung, P. J. (2016). Introduction to the Special Issue: Advancing Career Intervention for Life Design. *The Career Development Quarterly*, *64*(1), 2–3.

Herr, E. L. (2009). Career assessment: Perspectives on trends and issues. In E. A. Whitfield, R. W. Feller, & C. Wood (Eds.) *A counselor's guide to career assessment instruments* (5th ed.), pp. 13–26. Broken Arrow, OK: National Career Development Association.

Krieshok, T. S., Black, M. D., & McKay, R. A. (2009). Career decision making: The limits of rationality and the abundance of non-conscious processes. *Journal of Vocational Behavior*, *75*(3), 275–290.

Krumboltz, J. D., Mitchell, A. M., & Jones, G. B. (1976). A social learning theory of career selection. *The counseling psychologist*.

Krumboltz, T. D. (1988). *Career beliefs inventory.* Palo Alto, CA: Consulting Psychologists Press.

Krumboltz, J. D. (2009). The happenstance learning theory. *Journal of Career Assessment*, *17*(2), 135–154

Krumboltz, J. D., & Vosvick, M. A. (1996). Career assessment and the career beliefs inventory. *Journal of Career Assessment*, *4*(4), 345–361.

Krumboltz, J. D., & Levin, A. S. (2010). *Luck is no accident: Making the most of happenstance in your life and career (2nd Ed.)*. Atascadero, CA: Impact Publishers.

Krumboltz, J. D., Fuqua, D. R., Newman, J. L., & Walsh, W. B. (1994). The Career Beliefs Inventory—Comment/reply. *Journal of Counseling and Development: JCD*, *72*(4), 424.

Krumboltz, J. D. (2015). Practical career counseling applications of the happenstance learning theory. In P. J. Hartung, M. L. Savickas, & B. W. Walsh, (Eds), *APA handbook of career intervention, Volume 2: Applications.*, (pp. 283-292). Washington, DC: American Psychological Association.

Luke, C., & Redekop, F. (2016). Supervision of co-occurring career and mental health concerns: Application of an integrated approach. *Career Planning and Adult Development Journal*, *32*(1), 130.

Mitchell, K. E., Levin, S., & Krumboltz, J. D. (1999). Planned happenstance: Constructing unexpected career opportunities. *Journal of Counseling & Development*, *77*(2), 115–124.

Parsons, F. (1909). *Choosing a vocation*. New York, NY: Houghton Mifflin. Reprinted by the National Career Development Association.

Peavy, R. V. (1992). A constructivist model of training for career counselors. Journal of Career Development, 18(3), 215–228.

Rottinghaus, P. J., Day, S. X., & Borgen, F. H. (2005). The Career Futures Inventory: A measure of career-related adaptability and optimism. *Journal of Career Assessment*, *13*(1), 3–24.

Rottinghaus, P. J., Buelow, K. L., Matyja, A., & Schneider, M. R. (2012). The career futures inventory-revised measuring dimensions of career adaptability. *Journal of Career Assessment*, *20*(2), 123–139.

Savickas, M. L. (1997). Career adaptability: An integrative construct for life-span, life-space theory. *The career development quarterly*, *45*(3), 247–259.

Savickas, M. L., & Porfeli, E. J. (2012). Career Adapt-Abilities Scale: Construction, reliability, and measurement equivalence across 13 countries. *Journal of Vocational Behavior*, *80*(3), 661–673.

Savickas, M. L. (2012). Life design: A paradigm for career intervention in the 21st century. *Journal of Counseling & Development*, *90*(1), 13–19.

Savickas, M. L. (2013). Ten ideas that changed career development. *Ten ideas that changed career development*, pp. 1–3.

Savickas, M. L. (2013). Career construction theory and practice. *Career development and counseling: Putting theory and research to work*, pp. 147–183.

Savickas, M. L. (2011). The self in vocational psychology: Object, subject, and project. In P. J. Hartung, & L. M. Subich, (Eds), *Developing self in work and career: Concepts, cases, and contexts*, (pp. 17-33). Washington, DC: American Psychological Association.

Sheperis, D. S., Perpiczka, M., & Limoges, C. (2012). Individual and group assessment and appraisal. In D. Capuzzi, & M. D. Stauffer (Eds.), *Career counseling: Foundations, perspectives, and applications*. New York, NY: Routledge.

Sommers-Flanagan, J., & Sommers-Flanagan, R. (2015). *Counseling and psychotherapy theories in context and practice: Skills, strategies, and techniques*. Hoboken, NJ: John Wiley & Sons.

Super, D. E. (1980). A life-span, life-space approach to career development. *Journal of vocational behavior*, *16*(3), 282–298.

## Figure/Table Credits

Fig. 5.2a: Richard L. Knowdell, from Knowdell Career Values Worksheet. Copyright © 2011 by Richard L. Knowdell/Career Network, Inc. Reprinted with permission.
Fig. 5.2b: Richard L. Knowdell, from Knowdell Career Values Worksheet. Copyright © 2011 by Richard L. Knowdell/Career Network, Inc. Reprinted with permission.
O*Net Online: Copyright © 2017 by O*NET OnLine / U.S. Department of Labor, Employment and Training Administration, (CC BY 4.0) at www.onetonline.org.
O*Net Online: Copyright © 2017 by O*NET OnLine / U.S. Department of Labor, Employment and Training Administration, (CC BY 4.0) at www.onetonline.org.

CHAPTER SIX

# Counseling Theory Applied to Career Development

**Chapter Goals**

- Identify the primary career-specific issues clients face, or for which they seek counseling
- Explore these issues from the four primary categories of counseling theory
- Utilize these counseling theories to inform our understanding of career theory
- Identify gaps in application of counseling theory for career-focused counseling (CFC)

## Introduction

The fields of career counseling and vocational psychology have contributed invaluable knowledge and practice resources to CFC. It is an important transition step to discuss career-related issues from the vantage point of counseling theory in general. Rounds and Tinsley (1996) view career intervention as a form of psychotherapy: " ... career interventions can be practiced and evaluated within the context of more general behavior theories that provide models of behavior change, and can benefit from what has been learned in the methodologically advanced psychotherapy outcome literatures" (p. 138). After all, CFC, like all of counseling, ultimately seeks to facilitate client change in affective, cognitive, behavioral, and social domains of human experience. Rounds and Tinsley clearly assert this point, highlighting the developmental nature of the field of counseling,

> Most of those individuals who seek vocational counseling do not have a generalized deficit in their information-processing system. Rather, their problems can be traced to cognitions pertaining to some specific content domain that is a product of their social learning history (Mischel, 1973) ... Although the problem content involves vocational or work-related areas, the problem processes are cognitive and behavioral (p. 141).

These authors are arguing for a deeper level of theoretical and empirical approaches to career theory and interventions, highlighting the role of classification in communication and prediction, which increase in complexity. This chapter stops short of prediction, focusing instead on understanding and intervention. Furthermore, there are hundreds of career-related interventions that can easily overwhelm students of career counseling when returning to foundational approaches (often already learned in a theories course that precedes a career course) can advance the understanding and application of career theory.

When you think of career-related issues, what comes to mind? This question is especially highlighted in the mere presence of a chapter such as this: applying mental health counseling theory to career issues. It is an important topic given the challenges counselors face in incorporating career theory into their practice. As noted in chapter one, this has not, historically, been the most enticing focus area for counselors. And yet, clients come to counseling with a host of issues, many of which are entangled with career issues. So, what are these career issues, and how does counseling speak to them? To begin to address this, it is helpful to explore the eight-factor meta-model of conceptualizing client issues (Luke, 2015), this time applied specifically to career-related issues (Table 6.1. A tremendous amount of career-counseling literature is dedicated to career decision-making, but this is only a fraction of the issues that clients face related to career. At the same time, career decision-making has major implications for individual's functioning in career and other domains of life. First, let's take a broad look at career, followed by a narrowing in on the issues connected to career decision-making:

**Table 6.1. 8-Factor Meta-Model of Career Problem Domains**

| Domain | Career Problem Examples | Observations |
|---|---|---|
| Relationships | • Relational conflict at work<br>• Conflict at "home" over work<br>• Intrapersonal conflict | Many career issues materialize *after* a job choice has been made, resulting in and from issues in interpersonal relationships; these issues are reciprocal with home and work:<br>one affects the other |
| Sociocultural milieu | • Social and cultural expectations about what work should be | Virtually every culture has their own expectations about productivity and contributions to the larger community, whether implicit or explicit, whether high or low; most bring these expectations into career-decision-making |

| Domain | Career Problem Examples | Observations |
|---|---|---|
| Thoughts/Cognitions | • Self-defeating | Cognitive distortions underlie many, perhaps most, career-related issues, either as precursors to or results of career-related issues |
| Emotions/Affect | • Negative emotional experience of work | Emotions are real, though they don't always reflect reality; this does not preclude them from influencing and even exacerbating career-related issues |
| Behavior/Volition | • Poor or lack of motivation<br>• Problematic behaviors at work | Most people make a change when the pain of stasis exceeds the pain of change; career-related issues in the behavior domain can be explicit (e.g., acting out, substance use, etc.) or implicit as in passivity on the job or in seeking change |
| Environment | • Work environment and impact of work on other environments (like home) | It is important to understand the individual's work environment (real and perceived) as well as their desired environment; in addition, examine how the home or other environments are impacting career-related issues |
| Experiences | • Various negative experiences finding, maintaining, transitioning through work | One of perhaps the most common and influential involves both early experiences related to the perception of work, as well as individual experiences in the workplace and out that shape perceptions and expectations |
| Bio/Genetic/Neuro | • Physical, cognitive, emotional abilities that may be limited | A key component of diversity competencies involves able-ness and its impact on work options; in addition, the brain changes in response to repetitive behaviors, so work transitions can be impacted by change across job types |

As this table shows, career issues pervade each and every domain of this model, and every domain exerts at least some influence or impact on career-related issues. But this is just a starting point. In order to make career interventions meaningful from the perspective of counseling theory, it is necessary to "zoom in" on the categories of career issues. For this chapter, we will begin with what are perhaps the most obvious connections: using counseling theory to address intrapersonal career-related issues. In order to accomplish this, we need a conceptual map of sorts to illustrate how the various categories of counseling theories map onto the intrapersonal career issues. Later, we will return to this for a similar application to the interpersonal career issues domains.

# A Taxonomy of Career-Related Issues

In order to apply counseling theory to career-related issues, it is vital that we first identify meaningful categories of career-related issues—where does one begin? There are myriad ways to do this, each with its respective strengths and weaknesses (see Brown & Krane, 2000; Busacca, 2002; Campbell & Cellini, 1981; Gati et al., 2007; Gati & Levin, 2014; Moulton et al., 2007, for just a few examples). For efficiency and effectiveness here, I begin with a tabular overview of career-related issues sampled from the literature (see Table 6.2). At first this table adds extra complexity to our understanding of career-related issues, which is important, because it is incredibly complex, and counselors do their clients a disservice when career-issues are minimized. However, in order to get us started with understanding these complexities, we'll begin with Busacca's (2002) conceptualization of career related issues, as presented in Table 6.2.

**Table 6.2. Career Problem Conceptualization**

| Multon et al., 2007 (adapted here) | Gati et al., 2011 | Busacca, 2002 | Gati and Levin, 2014 |
|---|---|---|---|
| Psychologically healthy but not clear about career paths and expressed discomfort about career decisions. Recommend good career assessment and high-quality career information over a few sessions. | Pessimistic views<br>• About the process<br>• About the world of work<br>• About individual's control | Lack of information | Lack of readiness<br>• Lack of motivation<br>• General indecisiveness<br>• Dysfunctional beliefs |
| Psychologically healthy and clear about career choices and uses all available resources to affirm own decisions; may simply need reassurance and affirmation | Anxiety<br>• About the process<br>• Uncertainty in choosing<br>• About making a choice<br>• About outcome of choices | Lack of skill | Lack of information<br>• About the career decision-making (CDM) process itself<br>• About the self<br>• About occupations or majors<br>• About ways of obtaining information and help |
| High levels of psychological distress but moderate decidedness about career paths.<br>Recommend interventions that reduce distress and assess and reinforce career direction | Self-concept and identity<br>• Trait anxiety<br>• Low self-worth<br>• Uncrystalized identity<br>• Conflictual attachment and separation | Lack of experience | Difficulty using career information<br>• Unreliable information<br>• Internal conflicts<br>• External conflicts |

| Multon et al., 2007 (adapted here) | Gati et al., 2011 | Busacca, 2002 | Gati and Levin, 2014 |
|---|---|---|---|
| Highly distressed but were undecided and uncomfortable with where they were in their careers as well; constellation of problems that requires a counselor to have a host of skills to work on helping reduce high levels of psychological distress and helping achieve satisfying life goals. | | Self-actualization | |
| | | Lack of self-understanding and awareness | |
| | | External and internal conflict | |

The taxonomy of career issues presented by Busacca (2002) builds on the work of Savickas (1996; 1998) and others (Brown & Krane, 2000; Gati, Krause, & Osipow, 1996; Parsons, 1909) going all the way back to Parsons' tripartite model, and divides career-related issues into two domains, for the sake of conceptual simplicity, *inter*personal and *intra*personal. Interpersonal domain issues involve external environments and a great deal of social contact with others (2002). The intrapersonal domains involve "growth seeking and discomfort reducing" (p. 133). These two domains contain discrete roles and objectives, as presented in the following two tables.

**Table 6.3.a Typical Counselor Question and Objective—Interpersonal (adapted from Busacca, 2002)**

| Level | Career Service Area | Counselor Question | Counselor Objective | Key Problem | Savickas' Implicit Problem | Client Question |
|---|---|---|---|---|---|---|
| A | A. Career Guidance | Does client wish to begin new job/or change old position? | Explore match between self-concept and jobs | Lack of Information | Making career choice | "What shall I choose?" |
| | B. Career Placement | How is client attaining new position? | Prepare, refine, and help secure a position | Lack of Skill | Starting a career | "How do I get a position?" |
| C | C. Career Education | Does client express immature attitudes and lack competencies? | Foster autonomy, foresight, and self-management attitudes | Lack of Experience | Developing Career | "Why Career?" |

Table 6.3.b Typical Counselor Question and Objective—Intrapersonal (adapted from Busacca, 2002)

| Level | Career Service Area | Counselor Question | Counselor Objective | Key Problem | Savickas' Implicit Problem | Client Question |
|---|---|---|---|---|---|---|
| B | A. Career Counseling | Does client have vague self-concept and lack meaning-making? | Develop self-concept, insight, self-reflection, and healthy cognitions | Self-Actualization | Self-Conception | "Who am I within a career?" |
| | B. Career Development | How is client coping with normal life/ career tasks? | Enhance awareness and develop skills to negotiate career tasks | Lack of self-understanding | Managing and Coping | "What should I expect?" |
| C | C. Career Adjustment | How is client adapting to thwarting conditions? | Increase personal flexibility, adaptive skills, and resilience | External and internal conflict | Adaptation | "What is getting in the way of my career?" |

It is easy to see that the simplicity fades quickly, but this demonstrates the complexity of dealing with career. In spite of the categorization of career issues into interpersonal and intrapersonal, within these two domains, there are many areas for conflict as well as points of intervention. Determining the nature of the career issue, in terms of problem domain, can aid in more efficient and effective case conceptualization. (More on this below). It is very important to remember that 1) career issues are far more complex than virtually any heuristic can demonstrate, and 2) Busacca's model is one of many. It was chosen for its relative straight-forwardness and its ability to be integrated into the case conceptualization model presented here. Busacca's (2002) three descriptive categories of career-related problems that can assist in guiding counselors is conceptualizing client issues that include both inter- and intra-personal domains:

A. Level A: Choosing an occupation—

a. Interpersonal: The guidance component of this domain comprises career-related information and its use. Individuals who have a stable vocational identity need awareness of and access to reliable career information that they are ready to implement. This is embodied in the question from above, ***"What shall I choose"*** (p. 133).
b. Intrapersonal: The career counseling component of this domain comprises a willingness on the part of the individual to explore issues related to self-concept and identity on the path to knowing how to identify career of interests. This is embodied in the question, ***"Who am I within a career?"*** (p. 133).

B. Level B: Preparing to enter a chosen occupation—

a. Interpersonal: The career placement component of this domain comprises assisting individuals in identifying and developing the skills related to beginning a profession. Individuals who have clear sense of their career choice and commitment to that choice are often ready for implementation of career placement. This is embodied in the question from above, ***"How do I get a position?"*** (p. 134).
a. Intrapersonal: The career development component of this domain comprises assisting individuals in self-understanding, awareness, and assertiveness related to getting prepared to explore the world of work. This is embodied in the question from above, ***"What should I expect?"*** (p. 134).

C. Level C: Coping with a career—

a. Interpersonal: The career education component of this domain comprises assisting individuals in working through developmental issues of motivation and of implementing self-concept in the world of work. This is embodied in the question from above as, ***"Why choose a career?"*** (p. 135).
a. Intrapersonal: The career adjustment component of this domain comprises assisting the individual in navigating internal and external conflicts related to career behaviors and choices. These individuals need assistance in developing adaptive capacities. This is embodied in the question from above, ***"What is getting in the way of my career?"*** (p. 135).

It should become apparent in the description of the domains described above that, at least in Busacca's conceptualization, CFC can emphasize *informational approaches to address interpersonal domains* and/or *developmental approaches to address intrapersonal barriers*. All conceptual schemes are necessarily reductive in that they are seeking to describe complex phenomena in digestible ways. Busacca's scheme is particularly useful in that it clarifies the counselor's role in CFC by bifurcating content delivery progression:

interpersonal → informational

from process delivery progression:

intrapersonal → developmental

In the former's case, counselors may find themselves in less familiar territory in emphasizing resources and information, which can lead to the perception of a less-than counseling approache. At the same time, counselors, who likely gravitate toward the wellness, developmental paradigm of human functioning (as described in Chapter 1) will see the whole as a continuum of developmental care, as opposed to a dichotomous one. In order to make the above information more concrete, I have included a case conceptualization component.

# Career-Focused Case Conceptualization

One additional component is needed in order to effectively apply counseling theory to CFC. Case conceptualization has been described as resembling an inverted triangle, or a funnel, in that the counselor begins with voluminous information and slowly winnows it into a narrower set of directions. It might more reasonably be conceived of as an hourglass, because from a cognitive complexity perspective, clients only get more complex the more we learn about them, and as counselors narrow their focus, they are much more likely to miss vital pieces of the client's behaviors or experiences.

For example, in the case of diagnostic- (Reiss, Levitan, & Szysko, 1982) or vocational-overshadowing (Magee & Whiston, 2010; Rogers & Whiston, 2014), a client may report concerns about a variety of issues, including career-related concerns and mental health concerns, like anxiety. In the inverted pyramid perspective, the counselor might identify anxiety—social anxiety—as the "AHA!" of counseling and narrow their focus to social anxiety, which overshadows career-related issues. In contrast, a pyramid model, in combination with CFC, sees the client issues as increasing in complexity. This in itself is not a problem, because simplicity is not the goal in this approach to case conceptualization. Instead, it serves as a poignant reminder to the counselor that we only ever see part of the client and, therefore, eschew reductive conceptions of them. This both adds to and relieves pressure from the counselor.

This chapter represents a return to a model of career intervention that is based in counseling theory. Career theory in many ways predates certain psychological theories, was articulated concurrently with psychological theory, and follows in the footsteps of psychological theory in other ways. On one end of this spectrum, for example, philosophers have mused about the role of work in the lives of individuals and society for millennia. On the other end is the career theory derived from psychological theories, as in the case of social cognitive career theory (Lent, Brown, & Hackett, 1994), cognitive information processing theory (Sampson, Peterson, Lenz, & Reardon, 1992), and Roe's personality development theory (Roe, 1956; Roe & Lunneborg, 1990), to cite just a few examples. In the middle of the continuum, wherein career and psychological theory appeared to develop concurrently, we find Parson's vocational model, culminating in the posthumous publication of his book *Choosing a Vocation* in 1909 while Freud's psychoanalytic model was gaining notoriety. Similarly, Donald Super was writing about the life-span, life-space model of vocational development (1957; 1996) around the time Erik Erikson was describing a psychosocial model of human development (1963; 1980). All of these examples illustrate that career theory and psychological/counseling theory have revolved around one another, even as they simultaneously orbited the human experience. This brings us back to the rationale for exploring counseling theory as a means of understanding career-related issues and how a case conceptualization model of career issues assists in effective, efficient paths to intervention.

Typically, counseling interventions, and their precursor, counseling theory, will be used most commonly with what have traditionally been viewed as intrapersonal domains. Even problems of workplace conflict and poor work performance can be traced most often back to intrapersonal issues. A couple of questions arise here, in light of Busacca's (2002) description of career-related issues: first, what utility do counseling theories offer for interpersonal career issues like, as Savickas (1996; 1998) notes, career choice, starting a career, and developing a career, when not attributable to intrapersonal issues? The second question that arises, therefore, is whether counseling theories are most appropriate for the intrapersonal career-related issues of self-conception and adaptation (Savickas, 1996) and managing and coping (Busacca, 2002)? And if the answer to this question is yes, is it then appropriate to begin addressing these issues from a career-theory perspective ... unless the two—career and counseling theories—are already linked implicitly, if not explicitly?

As we explore this, it is important to keep a couple of points in mind: the first is that, when modifying this perspective using counseling theory, the "key problem," "counselor objective," "counselor question," and "counselor objective" all change. These questions are theory-based and lead to a specific case conceptualization. For example, a psychoanalytic approach will define the problem differently, ask different questions and have different objectives, etc. More specifically, even the "key problem" shifts as it becomes the client's description of the problem, but recall that from a case conceptualization perspective, the theory drives the *actual* problem. This is not as un-humanistic as it might sound at first. People approach life with a particular worldview, whether explicitly stated or implicitly influencing their thinking and behavior. Part of the value of case conceptualization is in the way it draws out counseling assumptions and makes them explicit.

Let's begin with an outline for using the case conceptualization method. When we get to the theoretical orientation section of the model, I'll describe how each of the theory categories would address the presenting problem discussed. The first table, Table 6.4, offers a condensed overview of the steps involved. The table that follows, Table 6.5, expands upon this. In step one, the client's view is solicited. This aids in client buy-in but is also a reflection of their specific worldview. It must be combined with the information gleaned from step two, wherein the counselor gathers information they know may be relevant, in contrast to how the client might view it. Together—the client's view, against the backdrop of this clinical information—creates a clinical picture for the counselor, assisting them in gauging their client's awareness of the big picture. Step four takes this impression and measures it against more established diagnostic criteria. In essence, they are translating client symptoms and descriptions into diagnostic criteria. These form the basis of a diagnosis. The fifth step is deceptively recursive in that, while it is positioned here in an idealistic sense, the reality is that the counselor's theory guides the questions they ask early on and shapes their clinical impression and, ultimately, the diagnosis. At step five, the theoretical orientation shapes the treatment approach, which directs the subsequent steps of goals, objectives, strategies, interventions, and techniques. These last steps use terms that are interchangeable to a certain extent, based on the setting in which they are used. Table 6.4 contains a brief outline of the case conceptualization format.

Table 6.4. Case Conceptualization Outline—Brief

| | |
|---|---|
| 1 | Presenting Problem—What does the client think is wrong? |
| 2 | Psychosocial Assessment—What is the client's multi-domain background? |
| 3 | Clinical Impression—What do you think about what you've seen, heard, and read? |
| 4 | Diagnostic Formulation—What is your diagnostic impression? |
| 5 | Theoretical Approach—What approach best fits with preceding formulation? |
| 6 | Treatment plan—What goals (in client's words), objectives, and strategies should be pursued? |
| 7 | Specific Interventions—How will you move client through the treatment plan? |

Table 6.5. Case Conceptualization Outline—Expanded

| |
|---|
| **Presenting Problem**—In client's own words. (**1-2 sentences**)<br>*"What brings you into (career-focused) counseling?"*<br>*"How may I help you?"*<br>*"If (career-focused) counseling is effective, what will be different?* |
| **Psychosocial Assessment**<br>(Brief summary: ***3-5 sentences***)<br>*"How long have you had this (career-related) issue? When did it start? What else was happening at that time?"*<br>*"Tell me about family, friends, work, school, physical health, etc."* |
| **Clinical Impression**—Brief summary statement blending subjective client report with more objective counselor observations (***1-2 sentences***)<br>*Ex. "Client reports feeling 'depressed' and appears disheveled with flat affect, which tells me that ... "*<br>*Ex. "Client states there is no alcohol problem but is court-referred for 3rd DUI"* |
| **Diagnostic Formulation**<br>**DSM-5 Diagnosis**—Translation of client concern (a) with background information (b) and clinical impression (c) moves from symptoms to criteria to diagnosis |
| **Theoretical Approach**<br>Briefly summarize how a specific theoretical approach would describe/explain Dx (***+/- 3 sentences***)<br>*Ex. "ACT has been demonstrated to be highly effective with certain types of depression, i.e ct appears to experientially avoid emotions, resulting in withdrawal and exacerbation of symptoms"* |
| **Psychoanalytic Approaches** |
| **Humanistic Approaches** |
| **Cognitive and Behavioral Approaches** |
| **Postmodern Approaches** |
| **Neuroscience Integration** |

**Career Development Theory**

**Treatment Plan**

Goal: *"Ct states that s/he wants to 'feel better' and to be able to engage in the world more actively"*

Objective: *"Ct will quantify 'feeling better' by measuring moods on a daily basis"*

Strategy: *"Ct will identify negative self-talk, along with defusion techniques for dealing with depressing emotions"*

**Specific Interventions**—Discuss how you will move client through the treatment plan (***3 interventions***)

*"Ct will complete a CBT/ACT thought log for one month"*

*"Ct will identify two core beliefs underlying feelings of depression"*

*"Ct will use defusion worksheet to become mindful of unwanted feelings instead of trying to avoid them"*

It is also notable that this case conceptualization format includes five categories of theory orientation. In this chapter, I use the same three case examples, two for community and one for school, to examine how each of the three categories of career-related concerns might be addressed across the four main categories of theoretical approaches, along with an application of neuroscience integration. Before looking at the vignettes, I provide a summary of each of the theoretical perspectives and how they might view career-related issues.

# Psychodynamic Approaches and Career

It is challenging to condense 120 years of psychoanalytic/psychodynamic thought down to a couple of pages in a career counseling textbook; and yet, that's my aim here. Many readers will have already taken a course in counseling theories, but many may not have. Even if you have, a reminder of the key components of this category of approaches is well in order, as these models are applied in fairly unique ways. There is little empirical and conceptual literature upon which to lean as this discussion proceeds. Nevo and Wiseman (2002) offer a theoretical perspective on applying brief dynamic theory to career counseling, but the examples of this type of work are limited. Other work in this area focuses on psychodynamic explanations of work (e.g., work as sublimation of sexual energy; see Walsh & Osipow's edited text, 1990). While interesting to contemplate, for our purposes here, I will examine a few foundational tenets of psychoanalytic theory and its application to CFC, as well as drawing in extrapolative forms of analytic thinking. For example, Adlerian psychology, or Individual Psychology (1925/1963) has a lot to offer CFC, as does Erikson's Psychosocial model (1982). Adler's work, while an extension of Freud's work, is its own theory, which is part of the reason I don't refer to it in my writings as neo-Freudian. Likewise, Erikson's model is in part a reaction to psychosexual explanations of development in Freud's conceptions, yet Erikson's work is wholly his own (to the extent that any work can be independent of all that has been seen, heard, read and experienced as a theorist approaches a subject). We are all, at some level, neo-Freudians, whether our work is seen as a continuation or a reaction to him.

There are myriad concepts of import in analytic theory, and every reader could add his or her own favorite to the list. However, there are a few that not only bear special relevance to

CFC, but also have gained traction in the research literature, further validating their existence and impact. Three psychoanalytic constructs or domains of particular relevance here are early relational patterns, implicit dynamics in the relationship between the counselor and the client, and the role of memory function in interpreting the past in the process of present decision-making.

**Early Relational Patterns.** One of the key characteristics of psychoanalytic thought and practice is the pattern of early relational interactions, especially with the primary caregiver. Far removed from the sexual foundation of early Freudian thought, contemporary counseling interpretations view Freud's biased emphasis on sexual energy as more generic psychic energy (Redekop, 2014). For example, emotions create energy. This energy has to have someplace to go. Appropriately discharged, this energy can be incredibly productive, as in the case of an electrical circuit in the wiring of a modern home, the result of which is the powering of electrical appliances. On the other hand, when stifled or inappropriately discharged, the results can range from less-than functional (blown electrical fuse) to catastrophic (lightening strike). As articulated by object relations theory, early relationships with primary caregivers (objects) assist individuals in managing the emotions that come with navigating developmental tasks and the energy that accompanies them (Redekop, 2014). When these early objects resonate acceptance and support of the needs expressed by the child, the children are able to internalize the object's acceptance and support, thereby experiencing themselves as acceptable and secure. When the object's treatment of the child's experience of the emotions associated with a developmental task is rejecting and unsupportive, the child likewise internalizes this as he or she is unacceptable or insecure. Or, more precisely, their emotions are unacceptable and must remain hidden, or they risk rejection. One way to frame these developmental tasks is Mann's (1973) short-term dynamic psychotherapy, as discussed in Nevo and Wiseman (2002). These tasks are framed as essential (and universal) conflicts that are central to the human experience: 1) Independence versus dependence; 2) Activity versus passivity; 3) Adequate self-esteem versus diminished or low self-esteem; 4) Unresolved or delayed grief. The applications of these tasks to CFC become almost self-evident.

**Implicit Dynamics in the Relationship between Counselor and Client.** The couch in psychoanalysis has long been the object of criticism and jests, yet Freud was on to something that only would be validated by neuroscience many decades later. Humans in general and counselors specifically exert virtually continual influence over their clients, often in ways that are outside of awareness. Likewise, clients exert a similar influence over counselors. This reciprocal influence takes a significant amount of energy to manage, and must be addressed in some way throughout the course of counseling. Freud seemed to have a prescient sense of this in utilizing *the couch*, which here is used as a metaphor for the counseling relationship. The couch offers liberation from the constant implicit messages that are ongoing in the counseling session when counselor and client are seated facing one another (Redekop, Luke, & Malone, 2017). Let us assume for example that the counselor is working with a client who is looking to find a more meaningful career outside of the business world in which he or she is currently employed. The client shares that he would like to become a painter and make a living expressing himself through his art. The counselor, whether explicitly aware of this or not, has a negative visceral reaction to this goal and communicates this without knowing it. The client, already primed to be sensitive to skepticism of this goal, becomes almost immediately aware of the counselor's feelings. Both, then, need to work to keep their feelings in check as they seek to work together in a productive manner. This example is not meant to be an argument for using the couch in CFC; it is merely a basic example of the energy flowing between the counselor and client, a phenomenon long recognized and appreciated by psychoanalytic theory.

**Role and Function of Memory**. When you ask a person, client, counselor, or other person what experience is, what would they say? How would you describe experience? I submit that experience is memory—the way our brains/minds encode thoughts, feelings, and events—and store/retrieve them. Experience—something you get right after you need it—is the way our brains shape meaning into memory and then recall it for later use. Interesting ... but what does this have to contribute to CFC? Here's one answer in the form of a reflection activity:

> Try to recall your first memory of the world of work. It may have been a conversation, a jobsite, a uniform, or sometime from television or the Internet. What are the thoughts, emotions, and otherwise visceral reactions you have toward that work moment?

Whatever your recollection, we know from recent neuroscience findings—which offer support for psychoanalytic theory—that memories are almost always suspect (Wright & Panskepp, 2012). Events, and perceptions of events, are most often encoded in context, along with emotions and relational data. Therefore, objective memories do not really exist. What this means for work memories is that these phenomena are recalled in their own context of emotional experiences and relationships and other contextual factors, further shaping the meaning ascribed to that memory. Let's return to the reflection activity. Assume that you perceived at a young age that work was gendered—some jobs were "women's work," some were "men's work"—which is not a stretch by any means (Gottfredson & Lapan, 1997). Perhaps you are now a female adolescent with an aptitude for math and chemistry, yet your memories are of male physicians and mathematicians. Furthermore, your primary caregivers fulfilled stereotypical work roles according to gender. How might these "memories" when recalled in the context of career decision-making confusion impact your process? You might be more likely to pursue a gender-congruent (stereotyped) career path in order to minimize gender role conflict in your family and to match the internalized expectations based on your memories of work and related work roles.

# Cognitive-Behavioral Approaches and Career

As behaviorists have heralded for many decades, *behavior matters*. But what does this mean for career? One expression of this meaning is contained in the saying, "I can't hear what you're saying because your behavior is speaking too loudly," or variously, "actions speak louder than words." In counseling, this is especially important, because counselors listen to what clients cannot or will not say, particularly with their words. Speaking is a behavior, but so is not speaking, along with all of the other actions that occur in a session that inform counselors about what might be going on with their client. Behavior matters just as much outside the consulting room, as well. Clients will often try to use their words in session to describe events in their life that occur, naturally, outside of the session. In describing these events or phenomena, they create an image of what is happening for the counselor, but often this image obfuscates what may actually be occurring. For example, clients will often describe their experiences in vague terms, such as "I tried to complete my therapy homework this week" or "I worked really hard on my homework this week." However, when pressed to be concrete, trying and working hard may be utterly subjective and ultimately empty. At other times, a focus on client behaviors in relationships can assist greatly in making the client concern concrete. Borrowing from the cognitive-behaviorists, counselors might perform a "camera-check" (Maultsby, 1990). During a session, a client might describe a recent conflict with a loved one in which they very much felt in the right and, thus, a victim of their partner's behavior. "What did you do?" the counselor might ask. The client, responding reflexively, might say, "Nothing!" The counselor then might ask the client the following, "I hear you say you did nothing but were attacked. If there was a camera in the room, recording you 'doing nothing' and you played it back for me in here, what would I see?" As the client starts to respond, retreating into their world of words, the counselor interrupts politely, "Please show me instead of telling me." Over the next several minutes, the clients demonstrate facial expressions and other body language that, when combined with their "innocent, nothing" statements, paint a very different picture. As the counselor mirrors their movements, it becomes (somewhat painfully) apparent that "doing nothing" actually contributed in tangible ways to their partner's perception and negative feelings. But what benefit might this pattern of communication serve? The behaviorally-oriented counselor is extremely interested in the answer to this type of question in that the antecedents (precursors) to the behavior reinforce the behavior. Likewise, the consequences of this behavioral pattern also increase the likelihood that this pattern of behavior will continue. "It's the only way I can get him/her to listen to me!" is a common refrain. The behavior that the client purportedly wants to change serves a far too valuable purpose for them to simply relinquish. At this point, therapy can begin in earnest.

Consider this dynamic in CFC. This might be applied to any and all of the three categories of career issues in the taxonomy described above, but one example might suffice. A client enters counseling at the behest of the company's human resources office (Employee Assistance Program) to address a pattern of belligerence with colleagues and supervisors. The client is baffled by this accusation. Upon further exploration, the client acknowledges a tendency to grimace with given directions and mumbles under his breath when colleagues make a request or take issue with his suggestions in staff meetings. The counselor would likely want to explore the antecedents of these responses. For example, the client, after two weeks of self-monitoring, reports that he feels sick to his stomach, feels the "blood rush behind my eyes," and he clinches his fists. These antecedents are reinforcing his defensive, and at times aggressive, behaviors due to his sensing of a threat. The consequents? Supervisors and colleagues tend to back away physically but also relationally. While the client claims he does not want to be isolated, there is some relief knowing that his coworkers are less likely to talk to him and, thereby, possibly criticize him. These behaviors are working for him to keep him feeling safe from criticism, or at least, they were working until he was mandated into counseling.

**Experiential Avoidance.** Freezing is a behavior, and thus is open to analysis by a behaviorally-oriented counselor. Freezing is one type of avoidance and is common among clients with chronic indecisiveness (Gati et al., 2010). The problem with any and most forms of avoidance, particularly in the presence of some anxiety-provoking stimulus, is the avoidance reinforce the stimulus by giving credence to the fear. This is the rationale behind the *flooding* technique some behaviorists use (Wolpe, 1973). Avoidance of a negative stimulus strengthens it, so confronting it helps to extinguish it. Experiential avoidance is a powerful concept in cognitive-behaviorally oriented counseling, particularly in the view of Acceptance and Commitment Therapy, a mindfulness-based spin on Cognitive Behavioral Therapy (CBT; Hayes, 2004). The problem with avoidance, beyond convincing clients that their anxieties and fears are well founded, is that they lead to inaction and developmental regression. Clients actually move backward, living in an ever-shrinking bubble of certainty and perceived competence (their comfort zone shrinks as they validate their fears). While flooding has been shown to be efficacious in certain circumstances (Wolpe, 1973), there are obvious limits. The mindfulness-based CBT (MBCBT) approach (e.g., Dialectical Behavior Therapy, Acceptance and Commitment Therapy, and MBCBT), offers a more palatable option. Rather than attempting to change the avoidance behavior directly and immediately, these approaches invite the client to increase their awareness of when they are actively (or passively) avoiding an anxiety-provoking stimulus (e.g., breaking up with a partner, choosing a career, making a job change, etc.) by highlighting that it is happening, without focusing on changing it. These approaches assert that the compounding factors in experiential avoidance include both failed attempts to change in the past, as well as the loads of judgment and self-flagellation clients heap on themselves for not changing. This is often reinforcing in that clients may believe to themselves, "I may not be making changes but at least I feel bad about it and take it out on myself." What purpose does experiential avoidance serve in, for example, career decision-making? First and foremost, it delays making a decision that could be the wrong one. In addition, the counselor would want to inquire where and how the client learned to think and act in these ways.

**Thinking Errors/Self-Defeating Thinking.** The brain is easily tricked, unfortunately, and will believe what we tell it. If we tell it lies and inaccuracies, it's tendency is to believe them. This is particularly true if past events have been viewed from a certain perspective that seems to support these lies. One of the places counselors see this is in the career development process. As we'll see in greater detail later, Nancy Betz (1983) reported over three decades ago on the deleterious effects of telling one's brain lies. In the Science, Technology, Engineering and Math (STEM) fields, women have always been at a social disadvantage, though not necessarily a cognitive one. At that time (and to some extent still today) STEM fields have been viewed as the province of white men. Through socialization, women and people of color came to believe that perhaps they weren't allowed in the STEM fields, because they were not capable of being successful there. Betz tested this by assessing men and women's capabilities in STEM content and then assessed their beliefs in their capabilities. Women, somewhat naturally, rated themselves significantly lower than did men in their own capabilities in STEM. However, when their *actual* capabilities were measured, women performed equal to and in many cases outperformed the men in the study. What is the outcome of women's inaccurate beliefs about their abilities/capabilities? Experiential avoidance. Women have been and are far less likely to pursue careers in STEM fields, in part due to their socially derived thinking errors. Thinking errors affect far more than just women and just STEM fields, but this example highlights the power of the beliefs in influencing subsequent beliefs and behaviors.

# Existential-Humanistic Approaches and Career

**Core Conditions.** Try to imagine the last time you spoke with someone either in a position of authority or with whom you are in a close relationship. Was that person able to convince you that they were at least invested in trying to understand your perspective or at best able to see the world through your eyes. They may have said they understood you, but were they able to communicate it to you in a way that you believed it? If any of these were the case, what was that like for you? What feelings did that evoke from you? What were your behaviors like in response? It most likely felt positive or good, to state it simplistically and generically. You might have felt understood, and that feeling may have led to you share more of yourself with that person—perhaps something you had not shared with another person previously. Now, consider that all or any of these factors did not happen, and you perceived that the other person was not making a true attempt to understand you by seeing the experience from your first-person view. What feelings are likely to be evoked? How about subsequent behaviors? Even before you read further, it is likely that the contrast is stark. Why would a person volunteer to give additional information, much less share deeper, more meaningful parts of themselves? This empathic exercise is analogous to what we could also consider genuineness and acceptance, the other two core conditions in Person-Centered Therapy (PCT). Without these core conditions, I would argue that clients with career-related issues are far less likely to disclose their most person barriers to navigating career concerns. However, when these conditions are present, clients are more likely to move from "I can't find a job" to a more accurate reflection of their experience of, "I'm not capable of obtaining the type of job I think will be fulfilling." These are two entirely different career concerns and can result in the red herring phenomenon, wherein a great deal of time and energy are spent pursuing a path that is largely inconsequential relative to the actual path.

A caveat about the core conditions: It is important to note at this point what I call the confrontational nature of intense listening. Listening at the level that Rogers described (1961), while often described as non-directive counseling, is not passive. It is actually quite intrusive in that it takes the counselor right into the most personal space of their clients. This is not a benign intervention; it is invasive and must be used with caution.

**Motivational Interviewing.** We might ask at this point, how do people change? And more specifically here, how do clients in CFC change? The answer, while irritatingly obvious is also deceptively simple: they make a decision to change. So, the question might then shift to what makes people decide to change? Motivation Interviewing's (MI's; Miller & Rollnick, 2012) answer to this is that people decide to change when the pain of staying the same exceeds the pain of not changing. The crux of MI is accepting that ambivalence is a natural state of change to be embraced, not judged or fixed. This is where MI's foundation in PCT becomes very apparent: unconditional positive regard is really based in a tolerance for ambiguity—the ability to suspend judgments and endure the absence of explicit direction in a session. Clients (and all humans) are frequently "of two minds" regarding change. When a counselor's own need to perform in a session or to resolve his or her own anxiety about finding a solution to the client's problem, they miss a valuable opportunity to facilitate the client's own exploration of both the reasons to change and the barriers to that change.

Clients experiencing a career-related concern are often in the dilemma because of their ambivalence regarding some action that may need to be taken or change that needs to be made. Take, for example, when a client working in a day-labor position for minimum wage, is introduced to the notion of obtaining a professional certification in their field that would require 10 months of college. They face a difficult choice: stay on the same, safe path or take a risk and possibly fail. One of the reasons stasis is so attractive is its familiarity. It is a known quantity (even if that quantity is poor or less than desirable). Change means uncertainty, loss of the familiar. It can be easy to assume that of course, any client would like to improve the quality of their life, but those are not safe assumptions, and MI gives counselors permission—a mandate even—to consider any discrepancies that reveal client ambivalence.

*Meaning Making*: As we have seen and will continue to see throughout this text, vocational identity and "finding" meaning in a career are often signs of privilege that many, if not the majority of individuals in the workforce, do not have access to. Finding perfect work, our "bliss," our vocation, and the other various names it has been called, is simply not an option for the working poor, but also for those who experience material success in their work but not existential success. For many, meaning is made outside of work through volunteering, family, hobbies, and the like. For others, work is seen as the primary path to meaning. For these individuals—and they are legion—finding meaning in their work has proven fruitless, and may leave them feeling despondent and unsatisfied in their work (the difference between satisfaction and satisfactoriness according to Dawis and Lofquist (1984)). This can lead to under-performance and a degree of "job-hopping"—changing jobs often in search of meaning. This is a critical issue for CFC.

First of all, from the humanistic-existential perspective, meaning is *made*, not *found*. Counselors are often led down a slippery slope when they try to help clients find meaning through work, as opposed to facilitating the creation of meaning, through work or other places. From an existential perspective, work is simply one path to creating meaning. This view gets occluded in popular culture that uses the language related to finding and matching, rather than building, making, and creating. The founder of existential therapy, Victor Frankl, illuminated this principal during his time in Auschwitz, the German internment (death) camp during World War II (1959). Some, even Frankl himself might, at times, even use the term finding meaning in misery, but the meaning to be literally found in the senseless slaughter of millions is a fool's errand. Taken to an extreme, this line of reasoning can lead to justification for inducing tragedy so that meaning might be found. Instead, Frankl's actions in Auschwitz were more akin to the creation of meaning—there was no meaning in the suffering for him to find, so he created the meaning. Finding meaning implies a passiveness: if there is none to be found, that's too bad. In contrast, if meaning is be made or created, this implies an active, even proactive, stance. This might explain why clients, and people in general, may search for meaning in work rather than creating meaning in work: it's far simpler and provides a rationale for their lack of success. This is not a character flaw so much as it is an outgrowth of a cultural worldview: "find a job that gives you meaning," versus Frankl's admonition to create meaning through whatever means possible, in whatever circumstance you might find yourself.

# Postmodern Approaches and Career

**Reality Therapy—We are responsible; we have options; we must choose.** No one would likely accuse William Glasser of being passive or subtle in conceptualizing mental health from a reality therapy perspective. He even gets downright close to blaming the client for their symptoms. However, his approach has tremendous applicability to CFC owing to its directive, postmodern orientation. For example, in the previous section, I described passive versus active orientations toward career development among clients. Reality Therapy (RT) invokes language choice and mental health as a fallacy in order to highlight for clients that they are, in the tradition of the existentialists: free to choose, responsible to choose, and therefore, must choose. Glasser's (1998) assumption is that clients are always choosing. The question is whether they are choosing responsibility or, through a mental health diagnosis and other means, choosing to abdicate responsibility. RT utilizes many Socratic-type questions, including four main ones developed by Robert Wubbolding in the WDEP model (2013). The questions, in their most simplistic form are: "What do you *want*?" "What are you *doing* (to get what you want)?" "How is that working?" (*evaluation*) "What is next (based on responses above)?" (*planning*). The simplicity of these questions is deceptive, because they rest on complex foundations related to the client's quality world. I've added my own question to this set, "How do your responses indicate what it is you may really want (compared to what you answered in question 1)?"

For example, in CFC, a client might have the following responses to these questions in regard to career choice:

1 What do you want? "I want to be happy in my career"

2 What are you doing? "I have been struggling to get started on my resume, and on looking into careers that might make me happy"

3 How is that working? "I suppose it's not working"

4 What's next? "I guess I need to start looking more"

5 Based on these responses, what might you really want? "I want to keep myself from being disappointed about not finding an awesome career, so I've avoided even looking or preparing"

Even in this highly reductive exchange, it is apparent that this client's behaviors are serving the purpose of staying un-responsible for his own dissatisfaction. Glasser and Wubbolding would quickly cue into this client's passive, externalizing language and would challenge it through subsequent questions.

**Narrative.** Constructing career narratives has actually found its way across the counseling–career counseling divide to become its own system of career counseling. This specific approach (Savickas in particular, 2012) is discussed in more detail in Chapter 3, so for now, we can explore the use of narrative therapy in CFC. The foundation of narrative approaches is a postmodern view of the world that includes the creation of reality. More specifically, this involves the creation of one's own perception of reality, which leads to thoughts, feelings, and behaviors consistent with this view of reality, thereby creating this reality. This is not the same as the creation of some objective, external reality. For example, an individual, say a politician, who believes that there is no systemic racism in the hiring of underrepresented groups does not create this as a reality for everyone. It does mean, however, that his reality of this is reflected in a passive state on affirmative action or other policies intended to level the playing field for these marginalized groups. Likewise, a client who has been marginalized in previous employment situations may have internalized this bias and will, therefore, be more likely to see it in other work environments, regardless of any external, objective reality. This has become their reality, their career narrative.

One way to use this theory with clients with career-related issues is to work with them to write out this narrative explicitly, identifying perceived barriers (this perception makes them real for the client). Because reality in this model is constructed, the client can begin to construct solutions to these barriers and begin to rewrite the career narrative they want to live. This may not change the world, but it will change *their* world. This shift in perspective will impact their behaviors, as described earlier in the text about training circus elephants. Perceived restraints becomes their reality and directs subsequent behaviors: inaction and passivity.

**Solution-Focused Therapy (SFT).** SFT, grounded in postmodern philosophy, and as the name applies, assumes that solutions are just lying around waiting to be picked up and used (Luke & Redekop, 2016). This is not to minimize the client's experience or pain; it is merely a reorientation to their worldview. An example of this is learning to drive a car. The hands steer where the eyes look. Early on, fears of running off the road can lead to looking at the side of the road. The result? The car follows the eyes, and before long, the new driver is heading toward the problem. The solution to this problem is to refocus of the desired path instead of the dreaded one. This refocusing is a hallmark of SFT. It assumes that clients are capable of finding and using solutions and that these solutions are often in front of them, if they would only avert their gaze from the cliff to be avoided long enough to see them. Brief by definition and name (Solution-Focused Brief Therapy it is often called) clients find relief not by exploring problems but by exploring solutions. This is incredibly important in CFC. Clients are often in counseling for career-related issues because of barriers and, more to the point, a fixation on those barriers.

# Neuroscience, Counseling, and Career—Three Models

We are not yet at the point in the counseling profession wherein neuroscience would be called a *force* in counseling (as with multicultural counseling or postmodernism). Nevertheless, the field is rapidly expanding to include brain-based applications to counseling. In order to keep this valuable resource in perspective, even as the field seems to be on a trajectory leading to the intersection of neuroscience and counseling, it is important to begin to understand how neuroscience is and may be conceptualized. The first thing for counselors to recognize is there are facts about the brain and then there applications of these facts. The facts, even though some are debated, are often far more tangible than the applications often are. In the understanding-gap, stand models of brain-based applications—not yet theories, per se, but models and approaches. For the purposes of CFC and this chapter, it is less important that the "right" one is selected, and more that counselors are aware that, when discussing the integration of neuroscience and counseling, not everyone is talking about the same thing.

**Neuroscience as a Theory.** The neuroscience of human behavior, motivation and relationships has developed into a framework for understanding the relationship between the brain and human emotions and interactions. One of the clearest examples of this is Interpersonal Neurobiology (IPBN; Siegel, 2006; 2015). Siegel's model, well on its way to a theory of brain-based human interaction, attempts to takes the facts of the brain—functions and processes—and present them as a unified approach to understanding mental health-related and other issues. For example, Siegel articulates to specific qualities as examples of a unified brain-based theory of behavior: lateral integration and horizontal integration. Briefly, vertical integration involves creating healthy connections between and among the three regions of the brain viewed vertically: the hindbrain (brainstem), the midbrain (including limbic system), and the forebrain (cerebral cortex). He posits that when these three structures operate independently, in disintegrated ways, one part may override the other parts, leading to dysfunction. For example, in CFC, clients often will respond to the career development process with fear and trepidation, acting out of their mid-brain's fear responses, leading the hindbrain to react by stimulating fight or flight behaviors, rather than using the regulatory capacity of the forebrain to balance anxiety with logic, in order to exercise regulated basic life functions and thereby successfully navigate decision-making. Similarly, in horizontal integration, the left hemisphere—which has a primary role in language, logic, linearity (Siegel, 2012; 2015)—works in harmony with the right hemisphere—which has primary responsibility for emotion, creativity, and holistic thinking. For instance, in CFC, clients can often miss the big picture of career development (right hemispheric function) by getting distracted by the details and rules involved in the process (left hemispheric function). In other words, they cannot see the forest for the trees. However, when the left and right hemispheres are integrated, the sides work in complimentary ways, balancing logistics with creativity.

**Translational Approaches.** A second approach to harnessing the power of neuroscience for mental health treatment is exemplified in Feldstein-Ewing's Translational Model (Feldstein-Ewing & Chung, 2013; Ewing, Witkiewitz, & Filbey, 2015). In this approach, there is no attempt at a unified theory of brain and mind; rather, it seeks to identify and communicate what is happening in the brain during counseling interventions and where these neural events are taking place in the brain. Quite literally, this approach seeks to translate the therapeutic events during clinical interventions to their phenomena in the brain. It is an explanatory approach to treatment. For example, in CFC, a counselor utilizing MI (as in the primary case in Feldstein-Ewing's research) would attempt to locate the neural processes activated during, for instance, a client's use of change language.

**Metaphoric Models**. Siegel is a psychiatrist. Feldstein-Ewing is a neuroscientist. I am a counselor and counselor educator. As such, I'm a synthesizer and application specialist. Therefore, a metaphor model may make the most sense in terms of clinical application of neuroscience to counseling. The metaphoric model, first articulated in Luke (2015), offers a third category of approaches that utilizes basic (and not-so-basic) neuroscience research to assist clients in understanding their thoughts, behaviors, and emotions in terms of brain phenomena. For example, in CFC, the metaphoric model might highlight the philosophical reality that humans see with their brains, not with their eyes. Through the use of simple demonstrations in session (non-invasive, non-contact) clients can experience this reality as a metaphor for how their beliefs about the world of work shape their perceptions and, ultimately, their own reality and subsequent behaviors and emotions. The metaphoric model offers a complimentary, synergistic approach to integrating neuroscience with counseling. We now turn our attention to concluding this chapter with an applied case conceptualization that integrates each theory in the case of Andre. Naturally, the treatment plan and specific interventions sections remain blank, as these will be determined by the theory selected.

### Issues in CFC:
### Problem Area 2 in Community Counseling
### Andre and Preparing to Enter an Occupation (adapting)

Andre is a 27-year-old recent graduate of an MBA program. He is self-referred for concerns related to anxiety and indecision about career. He was fairly successful in his undergraduate education: selecting business administration as a major early in his academic career. He worked for a bank for two years before deciding to return to school. He thought an MBA was a "sure thing" in terms of finding a meaningful, successful career. However, after receiving several interviews followed by job offers, his confidence is shaken, and he is uncertain about what he should do about his anxiety and uncertainty. He remarks, "I now have all this education, but I'm not sure I'll like the career."

Table 6.6. CFC Based Case Conceptualization #2—Andre and Problem Cluster #2: Preparing to Enter an Occupation

| | |
|---|---|
| **Presenting Problem**—In client's own words. (***1–2 sentences***)<br>*"What brings you into treatment?"*<br>*"How may I help you?"* | *Andre: "I don't know who I am in terms of my career and don't know how to build a meaningful career. I'm afraid I've chosen the wrong path, and now, I'm not sure what to do. What should I do?!"* |
| **Psychosocial Assessment** (Brief summary: ***3–5 sentences***)<br>What information would PA/PD approaches attend to?<br>*"How long have you had this issue?"*<br>*"Tell me about family, friends, work, school, etc."* | Andre has always struggled with making decisions. |
| **Clinical Impression**—Brief summary statement blending client statement about the problem and your observations. (***1–2 sentences***)<br>*Ex. "Client reports feeling 'depressed' and appears disheveled with flat affect, which tells me that ... "* | Lack of self-understanding |
| **Diagnostic Formulation**<br>***DSM-5 Diagnosis*** | Deferred |
| **Theoretical Approach**<br>Briefly summarize how a specific theoretical approach would describe/explain Dx (***+/- 3 sentences***)<br>*Ex. "ACT has been demonstrated to be highly effective with certain types of depression, i.e,. Ct appears to experientially avoid emotions, resulting in withdrawal and exacerbation of symptoms."*<br>**Psychoanalytic Approaches** | ***See Following*** |
| ***Psychodynamic*** | How would you characterize your early relationships with your primary caregivers? What stands out to you about those relationships? Strengths? Weaknesses? In what ways do you see those relationships playing out in your current or recent relationships? How might those relationships, or the ways in which you perceive and/or approach those relationships, impact the career-related issues you are currently facing? |
| ***Adlerian*** | What are your earliest memories regarding work? What stands out to you about the attitudes related to work among those around you early on? In terms of flagging the minefield, what are some work-related stumbling block you have or might one day encounter related to these early memories or work? |

| | |
|---|---|
| *Erikson* | How would you describe your early development and your adolescent development? If I asked you about your identity, what would you say? What is the construct "Andre" composed of? If I had folks in the room that once knew and currently know you extremely well, and they were willing to be highly candid about their impressions, what words would they use to describe you? |
| Humanistic Approaches | |
| *Rogerian* | How have you experienced conditions of worth in your life in general, and in your career-decision-making process? What are the indicators from your primary relationships that you've made a decision or taken an action that they approve of? Disapprove of? What would it look like for me to fully understand your experience of your situation? |
| *Motivational Interviewing* | Would you describe for me the reasons you see to continue on in the career path you've been on? Would you now describe for me the reasons you see to discontinue in the career path you've been on? What might you pursue instead? What would it mean for you to change careers at this point, and to whom would it matter? What are the costs associated with being successful in a career? With maturing in general? |
| *Existential* | What might you be avoiding in being stuck in this process? What would taking responsibility for your career development look like? What would avoiding responsibility for it look like? Where is the sense of meaning for you personally in the work you've been preparing to do? What would creating meaning in this particular field look like? |
| *Gestalt* | Can you develop the discrepancy between the parts of you that want to be successful and the parts of you that do not want to be successful? Can you do the same for the part of you that wants to continue on in your chosen path? How about for the part of you that does not want to continue in this path? |
| Cognitive and Behavioral Approaches | |
| *Behavioral* | How is it benefitting you to be stuck in the position you are currently in? What does success in this area equate to? Or, what have you paired success or moving forward with in your mind? Can you describe other examples where you've made decisions, taken some action, and experienced negative consequences? |
| *Cognitive/Cognitive-Behavioral* | What are you telling yourself about your career development? When you are feeling your worst about the career-related situation in which you find yourself? What are the statements you say to yourself repeatedly? Are these statements grounded in fact or fantasy? How might your thinking patterns be limiting your chances for success in navigating this career decision-making process? |

(*continued*)

Table 6.6. (***continued***)

| | |
|---|---|
| *ACT* | What language are you using to describe this career issues, and how might it be affecting your decisions? What thoughts, feelings, or behaviors are you clinging to as if they are reality, rather than mere reflections of reality? |
| Postmodern Approaches | |
| *Solution-Focused* | If you awoke in the morning and this career issue was resolved, what would be different? Specifically, what in your behaviors would change? How might you act such that upon observation, others might say, "Hey, Andre's career issue has been resolved?" On a scale of 1–10, how would you rate the difficulty of this career situation? What number would it be if we make progress? And if we are successful, what would that new number look like, in terms of your thoughts, feelings, and behaviors? |
| *Narrative* | What is the story you are living out in this career situation? If this chapter of your life—this career-related issue—what title would you give to it? What would you prefer the title of this chapter to be? How might we rewrite the story of your career development? |
| *Reality Therapy* | How does your behavior in this current career situation tell us about what you really want, in contrast perhaps to what you said you wanted when we first began? |
| **Treatment plan**<br>*Goal: "Ct states that s/he wants to 'feel better' and to be able to engage in the world more actively"*<br>*Objective: "Ct will quantify 'feeling better' by measuring moods on a daily basis"*<br>*Strategy: "Ct will identify negative self-talk, along with defusion techniques for dealing with depressing emotions"* | |
| **Specific Interventions**—Discuss how you will move client through the treatment plan (***3 interventions***).<br>*"Ct will complete a CBT/ACT thought log for 1 month"*<br>*"Ct will identify two core beliefs underlying feelings of depression"*<br>*"Ct will use defusion worksheet to become mindful of unwanted feelings instead of trying to avoid them"* | |

Abbreviations: ACT = Acceptance and Commitment Therapy; CBT = cognitive behavioral therapy; CFC = career-focused counseling; DSM-5 = Diagnostic and Statistical Manual of Mental Disorders, 5th Edition; PA/PD = psychoanalytic/psychodynamic approaches.

# Summary

Case conceptualization, treatment planning, and applying counseling theory in meaningful ways is difficult, and it takes quite a bit of skill to master and even perform well. On the surface, it may appear that CFC plays by a different set of rules in these regards. However, treating career issues as counseling issues, wherein career-related issues are the presenting problems, allows counselors to utilize the skills they have been building throughout the course of their training. In doing so, they can become more proficient at identifying the relationships between career issues and other areas of functioning, even when career is not listed as the main area of concern by the client. In addition, applying their knowledge and skill in the area of counseling theory can assist counselors in providing a richer counseling experience for clients with career-related issues.

# References


Adler, A. (1963). *The practice and theory of individual psychology*. (P. Radin, Trans.). Patterson, NJ: Littlefield, Adams, & Co. (Original work published in 1925).

Betz, N. E., & Hackett, G. (1983). The relationship of mathematics self-efficacy expectations to the selection of science-based college majors. *Journal of Vocational behavior, 23*(3), 329–345.

Campbell, R. E., & Cellini, J. V. (1981). A diagnostic taxonomy of adult career problems. *Journal of Vocational Behavior, 19*(2), 175–190.

Dawis, R. V., & Lofquist, L. H. (1984). *A psychological theory of work adjustment: An individual-differences model and its applications*. Minneapolis, MN: University of Minnesota Press.

Erikson, E. H. (1963). *Childhood and society*. (2nd ed.). New York, NY: Norton.

Erikson, E. H. (1968). *Identity: Youth and crisis*. New York, NY: Norton.

Erikson, E. H. (1980). *Identity and the life cycle*. New York, NY: Norton.

Erikson, E. H. (1982). *The life cycle completed*. New York, NY: Norton.

Ewing, S. W. F., Witkiewitz, K., & Filbey, F. M. (2015). How to Practically Apply lessons learned from Translational Neuroscience to intervention development: ideas for the road Ahead. In *Neuroimaging and Psychosocial Addiction Treatment* (pp. 25–264). New York, NY: Palgrave Macmillan UK.

Feldstein Ewing, S. W., & Chung, T. (2013). Neuroimaging mechanisms of change in psychotherapy for addictive behaviors: emerging translational approaches that bridge biology and behavior. *Psychology of Addictive Behaviors, 27*(2), 329.

Frankl, V. E. (1959). Man's search for meaning in life. Cutchogue, NY: Buccaneer Books, Inc.

Gati, I., Gadassi, R., Saka, N., Hadadi, Y., Ansenberg, N., Friedmann, R., & Asulin-Peretz, L. (2011). Emotional and personality-related aspects of career decision-making difficulties: Facets of career indecisiveness. *Journal of Career Assessment, 19*(1), 3-20.

Glasser, W. (1998). *Choice theory*. New York, NY: HarperCollins.

Gottfredson, L. S., & Lapan, R. T. (1997). Assessing gender-based circumscription of occupational aspirations. *Journal of Career Assessment, 5*(4), 419–441.

Gunz, H. P., & Peiperl, M. (2007). *Handbook of career studies*. Thousand Oaks, CA: Sage.

Hayes, S. C. (2004). Acceptance and commitment therapy, relational frame theory, and the third wave of behavioral and cognitive therapies. *Behavior Therapy, 35*(4), 639–665.

Luke, C. (2015). *Neuroscience for counselors and therapists: Integrating the sciences of mind and brain.* Thousand Oaks, CA: Sage.

Luke, C., & Redekop, F. (2016). Supervision of co-occurring career and mental health concerns. *Career Planning and Adult Development Journal, 32*(1), 130–140.

Magee, I. M., & Whiston, S. C. (2010). Casting no shadow: Assessing vocational overshadowing. *Journal of Career Assessment, 18*(3), 239–249.

Mann, J. (1973). *Time-limited psychotherapy*. Oxford, England: Harvard Press.

Miller, W. R., & Rollnick, S. (2012). *Motivational interviewing: Helping people change*. New York, NY: Guilford press.

Nevo, O., & Wiseman, H. (2002). Incorporating short term dynamic psychotherapy principles into career counseling: A theoretical and practical approach. *Journal of Career Development, 28*(4), 227–245.

Reiss, S., Levitan, G. W., & Szyszko, J. (1982). Emotional disturbance and mental retardation: diagnostic overshadowing. *American journal of mental deficiency*. 86(6), 567–574.

Rogers, C. R. (1961). *On becoming a person: A therapist's view of psychotherapy*. Boston, MA: Houghton Mifflin.

Rogers, D. R., & Whiston, S. C. (2014). Qualitative analysis of clinical notes do counselors ignore work and academic concerns? *Journal of Career Assessment, 22*(2), 207–220.

Savickas, M. L. (2012). Life design: A paradigm for career intervention in the 21st century. *Journal of Counseling & Development, 90*(1), 13–19.

Siegel, D. J. (2006). An interpersonal neurobiology approach to psychotherapy. *Psychiatric Annals, 36*(4), pp. 248-256.

Siegel, D. J. (2015). *The developing mind: How relationships and the brain interact to shape who we are*. New York, NY: Guilford.

Wright, J. S. & Panksepp, J (2012) An evolutionary framework to understand foraging, wanting, and desire: The neuropsychology of the SEEKING system. *Neuropsychoanalysis: An Interdisciplinary Journal for Psychoanalysis and the Neurosciences, 14*(1), 5–39, DOI: 10.1080/15294145.2012.10773683.

Wolpe, J. (1973). *The practice of behavior therapy.* Oxford, England: Pergamon.Wubbolding, R. E. (2013). *Reality therapy for the 21st century*. Bridgeport, NJ: Routledge.

# SECTION TWO

# PROFESSIONAL ISSUES AND APPLICATIONS IN CAREER-FOCUSED COUNSELING

# CHAPTER SEVEN

# Ethical Considerations for Career-Focused Counseling

## Chapter Goals

- Provide an overview of counselor professional ethics
- Apply counselor professional ethics to career-focused counseling (CFC)
- Use an ethical decision-making model for CFC
- Describe the role of ethics in the professional identity of counselors engaged in CFC

As you read the opening case, what thoughts come to mind? As a counseling student or practicing counselor, your immediate reaction is likely that you can't share any information with the grandparents without Xavier's consent, or can you? He is 17 years old and still in high school, legally a minor, yet depending on the state in which you practice, he is old enough to sign and consent to his own treatment. Hopefully, as a result of going through this text, a few additional areas of reflection will come to mind as well. For example, If you decide that you can't share this information with the grandparents, you will need a clear rationale for this. Once decided on, how you communicate this to the grandparents will affect their receptivity to it. You must then decide whether or not you will share this process with Xavier. Another example involves the determination that you can share the information with the grandparents. The same concerns about rationale and communication occur here as well. Finally, the implications of the request may change if the request for information is being made by a teacher or your high school principal. Each decision has potential legal ramifications and must be considered carefully.

### Opening Vignette

Xavier's grandparents have been increasingly concerned with his distracted, sullen demeanor at home. They contact you at the high school to inquire about your work together. They state that they want to be able to assist him more effectively and ask you what he talks about in session. Below is a reminder of the overview of Xavier's case.

Xavier is a popular 17-year-old high school senior. He was referred to you for behavioral concerns, as he hasn't been paying attention in his classes. In an attempt to build rapport with Xavier, you ask him what he likes to do after school, to which he curtly replies, "I mind my own business and look out for my own." When you ask if he has an afterschool job, he shifts in his chair and tells you that his grandparents won't let him get one so he "can focus on schoolwork." Xavier goes on to disclose that he makes straight As in his largely Advanced Placement coursework. He says that his grandparents, whom he lives with, had to give up their educations at early ages in order to provide for their families. While he says he understands his grandparents' concerns, Xavier says he feels stressed about paying for college, as his grandparents struggle to survive off of social security and their relatively meager retirement funds. You ask Xavier what he wants to study at university, and he tells you he's too stressed about finances to think about that. He says, "I need to be able to pay for college before I decide what to study."

As you can see, it does not take long for a "simple" CFC session in a high school setting, or with an adolescent in general, to become complicated. Issues like these are the daily experience of counselors today. There are often many others involved and invested in the client, even if the client is the only one in your office. To further complicate things, K–12 settings bring in an additional level of rules and complications for counselors. Legal definitions of minors also shift in terms of *consent* and *assent*, as they relate to counseling services. Counselors in training often struggle to know what to do and why they should do it, yet counselors are being held to increasingly strict standards about how they make decisions about their clients. This chapter is written to assist counselors in training engaged in CFC better understand what to do, why they should/shouldn't do it, when and how to do it, and under what circumstances. And this process begins—and ends—with counselor identity. However, it is neither an exhaustive guide to counseling and career counseling ethics, nor can it substitute for reading the ACA Code of Ethics for oneself.

# Ethics and Counselor Identity

Ethical decision making in CFC is grounded in counselor identity. Remley and Herlihy (2010) outlined four key characteristics of counselor identity. These characteristics define who we are as individual professionals and collectively as a profession, if, that is, we allow them to. Counselors and counseling espouse a *wellness orientation* to helping relationships. This has become increasingly challenging as the Diagnostic and Statistical Manual of Mental Disorders (DSM-5) continues to build in prominence and influence and is increasingly recognized by third-party payers. Counselors are challenged to think in terms of pathology—of what *is not* working—rather than wellness—what *is* working. This is a necessity of our modern counseling age, as least to a certain extent, but the ethos of counseling calls us to return to finding what is working in the lives of our clients. No one in our clients' lives knows better than they do what is going wrong; where they need help is in shifting perspective, and that shift begins with counselor orientation toward wellness. The *developmental focus* builds on the wellness principle in viewing the human experience as proceeding along predictable stages or steps in their lives. At each stage, completion of a task is required, and success builds capacity for approaching the next stage. Some of these stages are task focused and some are age based and further outside one's direct control (e.g., puberty). Client dysfunction is framed in counseling as difficulties related to stage-task completion and the role of the counselor is to provide support and resources for the individual as they revisit earlier stages and tasks, and seek to build the skills and capacities for getting back—and staying on—track. The assumption here is that nature has built in a process of challenge-growth (Erikson, 1968) that enables organisms to survive and thrive. Counselors resist the pull of the medical model to view clients primarily in terms of deficits and damage and diagnosis.

*Prevention and Early Intervention*, the third counselor identity principle is particularly challenging, as counselors rarely encounter clients before there is a problem. The problem is salient, which is what motivates clients to seek assistance and also assures that third-party payers will reimburse for services. Counselors are empowered, however, to treat the presenting issue, while looking for developmental, systemic roots that aid in preventing the same or similar issues from retaking over the individual or family. When it does begin to resurface, counselors have built in protective mechanisms that clients can use as their own sort of early intervention.

Lastly, and this is a big one, is client *autonomy*. Clients come to counseling at some of their most vulnerable moments and, as such, are incredibly susceptible to becoming dependent on their counselors. Counselors know this and actively look for indicators of this dependence in their clients. They take action to bolster the client's own resources. Essentially, counselors are in the business of working themselves out of a job with their clients. Dignity accompanies autonomy, and counselors do everything they can to point back to the client's work as a way to promote their dignity.

# Ethics and Counselor Identity in CFC

There is perhaps no better resource to use for this discussion than the 2014 American Counseling Association's (ACA) Code of Ethics. The revised preamble to the ACA ethics code firmly establishes the professional identity from which each standard is derived. Counselors who understand the role and purpose of the profession can more readily apprehend our professional identity—who we are as counselors—and, therefore, proceed to make ethical decisions about professional practice and clinical care. Table 7.1 includes the ACA Code of Ethics Preamble that will guide this discussion.

Table 7.1. 2014 ACA Code of Ethics Preamble

ACA Code of Ethics Preamble

The American Counseling Association (ACA) is an educational, scientific, and professional organization whose members work in a variety of settings and serve in multiple capacities. ***Counseling is a professional relationship that empowers diverse individuals, families, and groups to accomplish mental health, wellness, education, and career goals*** [1] (emphasis added). Professional values are an important way of living out an ethical commitment. The following are core professional values of the counseling profession:

1 enhancing human development throughout the life span;

2 honoring diversity and embracing a multicultural approach in support of the worth, dignity, potential, and uniqueness of people within their social and cultural contexts;

3 promoting social justice;

4 safeguarding the integrity of the counselor–client relationship; and

5 practicing in a competent and ethical manner.

These professional values provide a conceptual basis for the ethical principles enumerated below. These principles are the foundation for ethical behavior and decision making. The fundamental principles of professional ethical behavior are

- *autonomy*, or fostering the right to control the direction of one's life;
- *nonmaleficence*, or avoiding actions that cause harm;
- *beneficence*, or working for the good of the individual and society by promoting mental health and well-being;
- *justice*, or treating individuals equitably and fostering fairness and equality;
- *fidelity*, or honoring commitments and keeping promises, including fulfilling one's responsibilities of trust in professional relationships; and
- *veracity*, or dealing truthfully with individuals with whom counselors come into professional contact.



1. This *is* the definition of counseling from the largest counseling organization in the world, and it includes career counseling.

The ACA defines counselling as, ***"a professional relationship that empowers diverse individuals, families, and groups to accomplish mental health, wellness, education, and career goals"*** (emphasis added). It is no coincidence that the definition includes career goals as a core component of the work of counselors. Therefore, it is incumbent upon counselors in training and professional counselors that counseling include assessment of clients' career-related concerns and that CFC remain an option for working with clients. This definition sets the stage for the six ethical principles that have become established best practices for counselors:

The ethical principles outlined in Table 7.2 have clear implications for CFC. The table lays out the principle ethics of counselors, the ACA description, and the implications for CFC.

Table 7.2. Ethical Principles Applied to CFC

| Ethical Principle | ACA Description | Implications for CFC |
| --- | --- | --- |
| *autonomy* | fostering the right to control the direction of one's life | Clients in CFC are provided the tools as well as the means to find and use additional tools in making career-related decisions. |
| *nonmaleficence* | avoiding actions that cause harm | Rarely do counselors intend to do harm; instead harm most commonly results from counselor ignorance or negligence, so CFCs take great care in learning and self-reflection. |
| *beneficence* | working for the good of the individual and society by promoting mental health and well-being | CFCs take the extra step, go the extra mile in providing quality care for clients; this includes career-related assessment of clients even if that is not the presenting problem as expressed by the client. |
| *justice* | treating individuals equitably and fostering fairness and equality | CFCs don't eliminate career options for clients as a result of making biased assumptions about client abilities/capacities. |
| *fidelity* | honoring commitments and keeping promises, including fulfilling one's responsibilities of trust in professional relationships | CFCs follow through on promised resources and information and that pause before making promises to clients that they can't keep. |
| *veracity* | dealing truthfully with individuals with whom counselors come into professional contact | While clients don't limit client career-related options for them, neither do they over-estimate the potential of a client in a career-related area when contrary to objective information. |

Abbreviations: CFC = career-focused counselor.

In addition to the principle ethics that guide the counseling profession, four characteristics define the worldview, in general, of counselors. These characteristics assist in guiding counselors in thinking through the variety of career-related issues. Table 7.3 contains a comparison of the these characteristics across the three types of career issues identified in this text.

Table 7.3. Summary of Counselor Identity Applied to Career Issues

| | Career Decision-Making | Work Entry | Work Adjustment |
|---|---|---|---|
| Developmental | One of the biggest decisions a person can make, but also one for which previous experience is not always helpful; life experience may be limited depending on age | Each transition into a new job or work role brings anticipation for most people, so it is important to normalize this experience; it is part of the process | It is important to determine which work issues are internal and which are external; what changes can the individual make in the themselves in order to facilitate increased effectiveness in the work environment? |
| Wellness | Because this is developmental the stress associated with it can be normalized to some extent and the decision can be framed as healthful | Work transition brings with it the opportunity for growth, so it can be embraced as a type of strength training | Counselors assist clients in managing their health in multiple life domains so that struggles at work can be moderated by healthful practices in other domains |
| Prevention | Inoculating students and clients against faulty assumptions about career decision-making and inaccurate information is key to wellness | Assumptions about work entry are potentially harmful so keeping expectations moderated is vital to healthful work entry | Flagging the minefield (Adler) is a counseling technique that, when applied to CFC, assists clients in identifying where they are likely to encounter challenges in the workplace and begin to strategize about dealing with them in advance |
| Autonomy | Students and clients often look to other to make the decision for them (for a variety of reasons discussed throughout), but it is vital that they be given appropriate levels of support to make these decisions themselves, according to their developmental level | There are many elements of control that have to be sacrificed or suspended during these transitions, so counselors help clients sit with the ambiguity until autonomy can be restored | Counselors assess whether clients are able to increase their ability to self-assess and then to plan intentional coping behaviors in the work environment |

Abbreviations: CFC=career-focused counseling.

These tables underscore the point that was stated earlier—that career development issues are closely related to both counselor identity and to ethical practice. Over 100 years of counseling practice and identity development affirm the integral role that career plays in the life of individuals and is foundational to counseling. In the next section, we look more closely at the tools of the CFC trade.

## Section E. Evaluation, Assessment, and Interpretation

Introduction

Counselors use assessment as one component of the counseling process, taking into account the clients' personal and cultural context. Counselors promote the well-being of individual clients or groups of clients by developing and using appropriate educational, mental health, psychological, and career assessments.

## E.1. General

E.1.a. Assessment

The primary purpose of educational, mental health, psychological, and career assessment is to gather information regarding the client for a variety of purposes, including, but not limited to, client decision making, treatment planning, and forensic proceedings. Assessment may include both qualitative and quantitative methodologies.

Source: American Counseling Association, from the 2014 ACA Code of Ethics, p. 11. 

The ACA Code of Ethics outlines ethical guidelines for counselors using evaluation procedures, assessment instruments, and the interpretation and application of these results. The Code is summarized below. It is important to note that ACA Code is a broad set of guidelines; therefore, the National Career Development Association (NCDA) has taken the ACA Code and created its own, which is a practical and focused elaboration on the practice of counseling applied to career issues.

There are many times when a document like a code of ethics is included in a text of this nature in an appendix. The same is true here; however, the NCDA's Career Counseling Competencies figures prominently in the identity and practice of counseling for career issues. Therefore, the NCDA Competencies, which include both ethics and multicultural considerations, is addressed throughout this chapter. It is not something to read "later" but a living document that guides practice.

# Ethical Considerations from the NCDA Code

"When career professionals are faced with ethical dilemmas that are difficult to resolve, they are expected to engage in a carefully considered ethical decision-making process" (p. 2). So, where does all this information leave us with Xavier and his grandparents? It leaves us wanting an ethical decision-making model like that called for by the NCDA code. There are precious few models from which to draw that are specifically focused on career counseling. Many exist as more general models applied to career counseling (see Niles & Harris-Bowlsbey, 2013 for an example of this approach). In a monograph using a case study approach to career-related ethical decision-making, Makela (2009) synthesizes the extant decision-making models and applies the result to career-related ethical principles. In the synthesis, she identifies nine common components:

1 *Identify and define the problem.* As basic as this sounds, in clinical consultation with counselors in CFC dilemmas, refinement of the problem at hand leads more expeditiously to resolution simply by reducing the

number of conceptual red herrings. Thinking deeply about the actual problem leads to asking additional questions and gathering more information to ensure the problem is clearly comprehended.

2 *Consider foundational ethical issues involved.* This seems basic at first, too, but it means looking past behavioral questions, such as "What should I do?" to conceptual, client-centered questions like, "What is my ultimate responsibility to my client?" This means a return to those core counselor identity issues, such as client autonomy, nonmaleficience, beneficence, justice, veracity, and fidelity. It extends further to the role of the counselor discussed earlier, including a developmental perspective, a wellness orientation, and prevention/early intervention, as well as client autonomy, as previously identified.

3 *Tune into feelings.* Encountering an ethical decision-making issue in CFC can be—and usually is—anxiety-provoking, especially early in your career, but throughout as well. While natural, these feelings—fear, anxiety, overwhelmed—can constrain ethical decision-making. They enable in that they can be a signal to the counselor that something may be amiss and direct them to attend more closely to these feelings and what they may be communicating about what is happening with the client. They inhibit when the negative feelings about taking a stand ethically lead to the variety of avoidance, whether that be avoiding consultation or avoiding confrontational interactions with clients and stakeholders.

4 *Consult the Code of Ethics.* Here is where ethical decision-making in CFC can get frustrating. The code is a set of guidelines for practice, but is not a system wherein a counselor can enter an ethical question and receive a black and white answer. Some issues are clearer than others, but ultimately, many issues are personal and individual. This is why knowledge of the Code is very important so that a counselor does not take a myopic view of the Code and miss the broader context in which the Code is presented. One way in which this broader context is exhibited is the ways in which the NCDA Code is situated within the broader framework of the ACA Code.

*Xavier*: What is the problem in the scenario with Xavier and his grandparents? What information is missing that would assist you in clearly identifying the problem?

*Xavier:* what are the foundational ethical issues involved here? How might the counselor's behaviors effect these as they relate to Xavier?

*Xavier*: How did you feel when you read about Xavier's *grandparents' request*? If you were actually in that situation, how would you feel? When you feel those types of feelings—fear, anxiety, and uncertainty, for example—what behavior typically follows in your experience of yourself?

5 *Seek appropriate consultation.* When it comes to non-emergency ethical dilemmas, a career-focused counselor's best friend is the following statement: "I'm not quite sure; I'll need some time to consult with my colleague (or supervisor)." In the majority of cases, the issue can wait for consultation. This is highlighted in the situation with Xavier. The counselor does not need to give the grandparents an immediate answer. This does not mean that the counselor will not feel pressure to answer or anxiety about putting them off. Counselors get into trouble when they practice in isolation and fail to consult about ethical issues.

6 *Identify desired outcomes.* The value in asking yourself what you want from this situation is the recognition that, depending on the situation, often someone involved in the situation will be dissatisfied with the outcome. If your desired outcome is that all parties are happy with your decision, you are set up to make questionable ethical decisions. Part of the reason these issues are so challenging to navigate is their existence in a gray area, which means the "right" answer is often a matter of interpretation.

7 *Consider possible actions and their consequences.* This step involves if-then thinking. As you begin to list possible ways to proceed, picture in your mind, or better yet, write them out, how your actions may play out. This helps to consider multiple perspectives, but can also help reduce surprise from the client in response to those actions.

8 *Select and implement an action.* Ethical decision-making in CFC requires action. Even inaction is a type of action for which counselors are responsible. Decide a course of action with appropriate consultation and exploration and reflection, and take the steps necessary to implement that decision, recognizing that, afterward, it will be you who must take responsibility for the action to take (or not take).

9 *Document the process and reflect on the outcome.* One of the ways that counselors can be held responsible for negative outcomes in ethical decision-making in CFC is by not following an ethical decision-making

*Xavier:* what specific components of the code are relevant for Xavier's situation? Is this issue related more to client confidentiality? What are the additional code components that can clarify the issue and your next steps?

*Xavier:* Is the situation emergent: are you making a decision that relates to Xavier's immediate safety or the safety of a vulnerable population? What are your supervision and consultation resources?

*Xavier:* What is your goal in this situation with Xavier and his grandparents? Is it to make a decision that makes everyone happy (this would be a normal experience earlier in your training)? How closely are your desired outcomes in line with ethical principles?

*Xavier:* As you anticipate what steps to take regarding Xavier and his grandparents' request, what are the possible results? How does thinking through these potential outcomes affect your thought process and intention to act?

*Xavier:* At the moment that Xavier's grandparents make their request, you must recognize that you must act. It would not be ethically or professionally appropriate to act as if the request had never been made. What actions could you take, and what are their potential effects? How will you proceed in implementing your plan of action?

*Xavier:* Would beginning to document your intended plan of action help you clarify and refine your

> model. The only way to demonstrate that this was done is to document the process. The temptation is to try to put it out of your mind and not think about it, but documenting the process, while challenging, is essential. Furthermore, it is vital to reflect on the decision, process, action, and outcome, and in case where, upon reflection, you would not take the same action the same way with the client, own this. It may even include going back to the client and discussing this; seek consultation!

**action? What might you do differently next time something like this comes up?**

Makela (2009) adds one additional piece that can assist counselors throughout the process. Consider these areas and the questions she poses as you think through the action you do or do not take:

> Justice—Would I treat others the same way in a similar situation?
>
> Publicity—How comfortable would I be if my actions were to become known by others?
>
> Universality—Would I recommend my course of action to others who were faced with a similar situation or ethical dilemma? (p. 13)

As indicated in step four, I do not offer advice as to the "right" way to resolve the issue with Xavier and his grandparents. This is intentional to assist you in wrestling with these issues—to develop of *tolerance for ambiguity* in counseling. Counselors who are able to sit with clients without having answers are better able to promote client autonomy by not yielding to pressure—both from the client and internally—to give answers.

# Building Career Theory on Foundation of Ethical Counseling Practice

As we saw in chapter two, counseling theory, as a whole, has quite a lot to contribute to our thinking about and practice of CFC. One key to utilizing counseling theory is in the way one conceptualizes career-related issues when they present in session, not to mention how important it is that counselors look for these issues. As we approach discrete career counseling theories and applications, it will be helpful to watch for ways these theories grew out of counseling theory. This plays an important role in learning these theories, as is seeing them as complimentary, not competing.

As we proceed through the ethical considerations of CFC, keep in mind that, in this modern age, client access to career information is unprecedented. It is a cultural reminder that it is not the data that transforms. Counseling holds the view that it is the interpersonal relationship that transforms (Rogers, 1961). As we reviewed previously, humans in general, and clients in particular, enter counseling possessing a full measure of ambivalence regarding taking action toward change (Miller & Rollnick, 2012). Clients rarely grow through or take action in the presence of ambivalence simply through information gaining. This is true now more than ever in the digital/quantum age. Before undertaking any approaches or interventions, counselors must display basic helper characteristics and skills. It is vitally important from an ethical perspective that CFC emphasizes relationship-building over directing clients to data alone.

The characteristics of relevance here are those found in Rogers' Person-Centered Therapy, (PCT; 1961) integral findings in the study of common factors, (Wampold, 2010) and the Transtheoretical Model of psychotherapy (TTM; Prochaksa & DiClemente, 1984). Simply stated, about 40% of client change is related to extra-therapeutic factors—those client characteristics and experiences that occur outside of the therapeutic relationship, such as motivation, hope for change, supportive relationships, etc. In contrast, 30% of change occurs as a result of the therapeutic relationship—the conditions that occur in session as a result of a counselor's intentionality in communicating empathy, genuineness, unconditional positive regard, and so on. So, why not let clients sort things out on their own, since these extra-therapeutic factors account for so much change? Because through the relationship, counselors can evoke and influence the extra-therapeutic factors for the client's benefit through, again, motivation, hope, and relationship support. Fifteen percent of change is related to client expectancy regarding change. Here is where it is vital to keep in mind that through the therapeutic relationship, clients can develop increased expectancy for change—a precursor to change. Fifteen percent of change occurs because of the specific therapeutic interventions—15%! Once again, these are impacted by the relationship: clients are unlikely to respond to interventions devoid of a safe, supportive context. So, how do we build a therapeutic relationship as a catalyst for developing these other factors? Skillful, deep listening. Sharf (2013) provides a thorough summary in his book on career theory; here, I lay out the seven most foundational skills gleaned from the literature on counselor effectiveness.

**Attending Behaviors.** Attending behaviors communicate to the client that the counselor is tuned in and interested in their experience. They include body language and question asking. Body language involves nonverbals, such as posture, gestures, and the myriad ways humans communicate without words. Paraverbals are the "mmmhs" and "uh-huhs" that indicate verbal tracking without interrupting the client's flow of thought. Asking questions comprises learning about the client through the expression of respectful curiosity about their experience (imagine leaning in slightly toward the client in an attempt to learn from them about their experience). It is about treating the individual and not a diagnosis or stereotype.

**Reflecting/Responding.** Once the client senses that the counselor is invested in their story, they share additional information. Counselors can ensure both that they understand the client and that the client feels understood via the skills of clarifying, paraphrasing, and summarizing. Restating/clarifying means using clients' own words verbatim, at times, but largely for the sake of checking out what has been heard for accuracy. It is a form of verbal tracking that communicates that the counselor is "with" the client. Paraphrasing involves the reflection of a larger body of client information in such a way that helps the counselor and the client begin to understand larger sections of the puzzle that is the client's situation. Summarizing is restating plus paraphrasing over a session's worth of material, or block of client material that needs to be framed. It serves to help the counselor keep up with the volume of client material, as well as to indicate to client a shift in focus or some call to action.

**Redirecting.** Redirection is the process of shaping the clinical conversation toward client growth. It involves the skills of reflecting and pointing out discrepancies. Reflecting is the process of using a verbal mirror held up to client's communication as a way of helping them hear themselves, perhaps differently than ever before. Three general types or levels include reflection of content, affect, and meaning. Reflection of thinking (content) are often the accuracy checks of client information: facts, dates, names, and connections between ideas. Reflection of feeling (affect) is often reflecting the emotion a client appears to be experiencing or might reasonably expect to feel. It benefits the client by providing a concrete label for their emotional experience and is often followed by a check out (an implied question mark at the end (e.g., you feel angry ... ?). Reflection of meaning (content + affect in context) is one of the most sophisticated reflections. This is the combination of content and affect into a coherent whole that aids the client in reaching a new level of self-understanding. Pointing out incongruence or discrepancies is a way to challenge client ambivalence about change and taking action. Ambivalence often emerges via discrepant statements or incongruity between words and behaviors. Strategically highlighting or reflecting these inconsistencies in a gracious manner affords clients the opportunity to look at them (if they choose) and determine if they want to move toward reconciliation—an indicator of movement through ambivalence.

As the field of career counseling, and CFC especially, moves forward from the old (and disparaged) paradigm of "test them and tell them," listening skills are vital. Early career approaches were often criticized for viewing career counseling as given an assessment or three and sharing the results, or as Crites puts it, "three interviews and a cloud of dust" (1981). Listening skills, in contrast, are not only vital, but they are active. Even more than that, they are challenging and can even be confrontational, yet they pave the way for infusing theory into the work of counseling.

# Neuro-Informed, CFC

The role of (ethical) decision-making in the brain is relegated to the prefrontal cortex and associated structures, depending on the specific nature of a given decision. However, decision-making is not a purely reason-based system neurologically, as cogitation is balanced with emotional reasoning, which is situated in emotional memory. In other words, fear circuits are also involved in making decisions in case evasive (fight or flight) maneuvers are required that would preempt higher order decisions. The inverse is also true; emotional reasoning in the limbic system must be balanced with the cognitive reasoning in the prefrontal cortex in order to make decisions that may represent a conflict between safety and "rightness." For example, in ethical decision-making, many times the initial rush of emotion a counselor feels can affect their ability to make well-reasoned decisions. Therefore, having an established process, such as the one described in this chapter, can aid in regulating these fight or flight responses in the midst of an ethical issue.

This whole process mirrors the challenges clients face when encountering career-related crises (e.g., job loss, career decision-making, work conflict, job interviews). When we as counselors have a working knowledge of the brain-body connection, along with cognitive and emotional reasoning in the brain, we pass this along to our clients, both through modeling regulation, as well as through psychoeducation. Clients come to a deeper understanding of the processes that influence their choices, thereby gaining more control over those processes. In practice, clients will present with what appears to be illogical reasoning or poor decision-making. This may not be due to a lack of skills, per se, but may be due more to a lack of self-regulation—a common theme in understanding the struggles of humans through the lens of neurobiology. Therefore, interventions designed to restore regulation and homeostasis allow clients to move through the processes of addressing career crises with more aplomb. Counselors can, in turn, be reminded that their own efforts at self-regulation in the context of ethical decision-making to clarify the path ahead.

# Summary

It has been said that experience is something you get right after you need it. This is especially true for ethical decision-making in CFC. Experience brings new insights, but the only way to gain this crucial experience is to have experiences. Ethical decision-making processes provide a framework for structuring thinking about ethical issues and guide behavior. Through the process, counselors refine their beliefs and learn firsthand the strengths, limitations, and likely outcomes of their behaviors. Prior to this experience, it is critical to think, practice, read, consult, and get regular supervision in order to cultivate these ethical decision-making skills.

# References


American Psychiatric Association. (2013). *DSM 5*.

Betz, N. E., & Corning, A. F. (1993). The inseparability of "career" and "personal" counseling. *The Career Development Quarterly*, *42*(2), 137–142.

Bronfenbrenner, U. (1977). Toward an experimental ecology of human development. *American psychologist*, *32*(7), 513.

Bronfenbrenner, U., and Morris, P. A. (2007). The Bioecological Model of Human Development. *Handbook of Child Psychology*, pp. 793-828.

Crites, J. O. (1981). *Career counseling: Models, methods, and materials.* New York, NY: McGraw-Hill.
Erikson, E. H. (1968). *Youth and crisis.* New York, NY: WW Norton & Company.

Gelso, C. J., Prince, J., Cornfeld, J. L., Payne, A. B., Royalty, G., & Wiley, M. O. L. (1985). Quality of counselors' intake evaluations for clients with problems that are primarily vocational versus personal. *Journal of Counseling Psychology, 32*(3), 339.

Hayden, W., Seth, C., & Osborn, D. (2016). Introduction to This Issue. *Career Planning and Adult Development Journal, 32*(1), 6.

Ladany, N., & O'Shaughnessy, T. (2015). Training and supervision in career counseling. In Hartung, Paul J. (Ed); M. L. Savickas, W. B. Walsh, (Eds) *APA handbook of career intervention, Volume 1: Foundations.*, (pp. 375–387). Washington, DC: American Psychological Association.

Lara, T. M., Kline, W. B., & Paulson, D. (2011). Attitudes regarding career counseling: Perceptions and experiences of counselors-in-training. *The Career Development Quarterly, 59*(5), 428–440.

Luke, C. (2015). *Neuroscience for counselors and therapists: Integrating the sciences of mind and brain.* Thousand Oaks, CA: Sage.

Luke, C., Redekop, F., & Burgin, C. (2015). Psychological factors in community college student retention. *Community College Journal of Research and Practice, 39*(3), 222–234.

Luke, C., & Redekop, F. (2016). Supervision of co-occurring career and mental health concerns: Application of an integrated approach. *Career Planning and Adult Development Journal, 32*(1), 130.

Magee, I. M., & Whiston, S. C. (2010). Casting no shadow: Assessing vocational overshadowing. *Journal of Career Assessment, 18*(3), 239–249.

Miller, W. R., & Rollnick, S. (2012). *Motivational interviewing: Helping people change.* New York, NY: Guilford Press.

Pedersen, P. B., Lonner, W. J., Draguns, J. G., Trimble, J. E., & Scharron-del Rio, M. R. (2015). *Counseling across cultures.* Thousand Oaks, CA: Sage

Prieto, L. R., & Betsworth, D. G. (1999). Supervision of career counseling: Current knowledge and new directions. *The Clinical Supervisor, 18*(1), 173–189.

Prochaska, J. O., & DiClemente, C. C. (1984). Self change processes, self efficacy and decisional balance across five stages of smoking cessation. *Progress in clinical and biological research, 156,* 131.

Reiss, S., Levitan, G. W., & Szyszko, J. (1982). Emotional disturbance and mental retardation: diagnostic overshadowing. *American journal of mental deficiency 86*(6):567-74.

Remley, T. P. Jr., & Herlihy, B. P. (2010). *Ethical, Legal, and Professional Issues in Counseling* (3rd ed.).

Rogers, C. R. (1961). *On becoming a person: A therapist's view of psychology.* Boston, MA:

Houghton-Mifflin.

Rogers, D. R., & Whiston, S. C. (2014). Qualitative Analysis of Clinical Notes Do Counselors Ignore Work and Academic Concerns? *Journal of Career Assessment, 22*(2), 207–220.

Sharf, R. S. (2013). *Applying Career Development Theory to Counseling* (6th ed.). Belmont, CA: Brooks/Cole.

Spengler, P. M., Blustein, D. L., & Strohmer, D. C. (1990). Diagnostic and treatment overshadowing of vocational problems by personal problems. *Journal of Counseling Psychology, 37*(4), 372.

Subich, L. M. (1993). How personal is career counseling? *The Career Development Quarterly, 42*(2), 129–131.

Swanson, J. L. (2002). Understanding the Complexity of Clients' Lives Infusing a Truly Integrative Career-Personal Perspective into Graduate Training. *The Counseling Psychologist, 30*(6), 815–832.

Wampold, B. E. (2010). The research evidence for the common factors models: A historically situated perspective. In B. L. Duncan, S. D. Miller, B. E. Wampold, & M. A. Hubble (Eds.). *The heart and soul of change: Delivering what works in therapy* (2nd ed), pp. 49–81. Washington, DC: American Psychological Association.

Uthayakumar, R., Schimmack, U., Hartung, P. J., & Rogers, J. R. (2010). Career decidedness as a predictor of subjective well-being. *Journal of Vocational Behavior, 77*(2), 196–204.

# Appendix A

10/02/2009 Career Counseling Competencies ***National Career Development Association***
Career Counseling Competencies ***(Revised Version, 1997)***

NOTE: IN 2009, NCDA updated these Career Counseling Competencies to infuse multicultural competencies. See the Multi-Cultural Career Counseling Minimum Competencies for the most up-to-date information.

### Introduction to Career Counseling Competency Statements

These competency statements are for those professionals interested and trained in the field of career counseling. For the purpose of these statements, career counseling is defined as the process of assisting individuals in the development of a life-career with focus on the definition of the worker role and how that role interacts with other life roles.

NCDA's Career Counseling Competencies are intended to represent minimum competencies for those professionals at or above the Master's degree level of education. These competencies are reviewed on an ongoing basis by the NCDA Professional Standards Committee, the NCDA Board, and other relevant associations.

Professional competency statements provide guidance for the minimum competencies necessary to perform effectively a particular occupation or job within a particular field. Professional career counselors (Master's degree or higher) or persons in career development positions must demonstrate the knowledge and skills for a specialty in career counseling that the generalist counselor might not possess. Skills and knowledge are represented by designated competency areas, which have been developed by professional career counselors and counselor educators. The Career Counseling Competency Statements can serve as a guide for career counseling training programs or as a checklist for persons wanting to acquire or to enhance their skills in career counseling.

### Minimum Competencies

In order to work as a professional engaged in Career Counseling, the individual must demonstrate minimum competencies in eleven designated areas. These eleven areas are: Career Development Theory, Individual and Group Counseling Skills, Individual/Group Assessment, Information/Resources, Program Management and Implementation, Consultation, Diverse Populations, Supervision, Ethical/Legal Issues, Research/Evaluation, and Technology. These areas are briefly defined as follows:

**Career Development Theory:** Theory base and knowledge considered essential for professionals engaging in career counseling and development.

- **Individual and Group Counseling Skills:** Individual and group counseling competencies considered essential for effective career counseling.
- **Individual/Group Assessment:** Individual/group assessment skills considered essential for professionals engaging in career counseling.
- **Information/Resources:** Information/resource base and knowledge essential for professionals engaging in career counseling.
- **Program Promotion, Management and Implementation:** Skills necessary to develop, plan, implement, and manage comprehensive career development programs in a variety of settings.
- **Coaching, Consultation, and Performance Improvement:** Knowledge and skills considered essential in enabling individuals and organizations to impact effectively upon the career counseling and development process.
- **Diverse Populations:** Knowledge and skills considered essential in providing career counseling and development processes to diverse populations.
- **Supervision:** Knowledge and skills considered essential in critically evaluating counselor performance, maintaining and improving professional skills, and seeking assistance for others when needed in career counseling.
- **Ethical/Legal Issues:** Information base and knowledge essential for the ethical and legal practice of career counseling.
- **Research/Evaluation:** Knowledge and skills considered essential in understanding and conducting research and evaluation in career counseling and development.
- **Technology:** Knowledge and skills considered essential in using technology to assist individuals with career planning.

### Professional Preparation

The competency statements were developed to serve as guidelines for persons interested in career development occupations. They are intended for persons training at the Master's level or higher with a specialty in career counseling. However, this intention does not prevent other types of career development professionals from using the competencies as guidelines for their own training. The competency statements provide counselor educators, supervisors, and other interested groups with guidelines for the minimum training required for counselors interested in the career counseling specialty. The statements might also serve as guidelines for professional counselors who seek in-service training to qualify as career counselors.

### Ethical Responsibilities

Career development professionals must only perform activities for which they "possess or have access to the necessary skills and resources for giving the kind of help that is needed" (see NCDA and ACA Ethical Standards). If a professional does not have the appropriate training or resources for the type of career concern presented, an appropriate referral must be made. No person should attempt to use skills (within these competency statements) for which he/she has not been trained. For additional ethical guidelines, refer to the NCDA Ethical Standards for Career Counselors.

**Career Counseling Competencies and Performance Indicators**
**Career Development Theory**
Theory base and knowledge considered essential for professionals engaging in career counseling and development. Demonstration of knowledge of:

Counseling theories and associated techniques.

1 Theories and models of career development.

2 Individual differences related to gender, sexual orientation, race, ethnicity, and physical and mental capacities.

3 Theoretical models for career development and associated counseling and information-delivery techniques and resources.

4 Human growth and development throughout the life span.

5 Role relationships which facilitate life-work planning.

6 Information, techniques, and models related to career planning and placement

**Individual and Group Counseling Skills**
Individual and group counseling competencies considered essential to effective career counseling. Demonstration of ability to:

Establish and maintain productive personal relationships with individuals.

1 Establish and maintain a productive group climate.

2 Collaborate with clients in identifying personal goals.

3 Identify and select techniques appropriate to client or group goals and client needs, psychological states, and developmental tasks.

4 Identify and understand clients' personal characteristics related to career.

5 Identify and understand social contextual conditions affecting clients' careers.

6 Identify and understand familial, sub-cultural and cultural structures and functions as they are related to clients' careers.

7 Identify and understand clients' career decision-making processes.

8 Identify and understand clients' attitudes toward work and workers.

9 Identify and understand clients' biases toward work and workers based on gender, race, and cultural stereotypes.

10 Challenge and encourage clients to take action to prepare for and initiate role transitions by:

- locating sources of relevant information and experience,
- obtaining and interpreting information and experiences, and acquiring skills needed to make role transitions.

11 Assist the client to acquire a set of employability and job search skills.

12 Support and challenge clients to examine life-work roles, including the balance of work, leisure, family, and community in their careers.

**Individual/Group Assessment**

Individual/group assessment skills considered essential for professionals engaging in career counseling. Demonstration of ability to:

Assess personal characteristics such as aptitude, achievement, interests, values, and personality traits.

- Assess leisure interests, learning style, life roles, self-concept, career maturity, vocational identity, career indecision, work environment preference (e.g., work satisfaction), and other related life style/development issues.
- Assess conditions of the work environment (such as tasks, expectations, norms, and qualities of the physical and social settings).
- Evaluate and select valid and reliable instruments appropriate to the client's gender, sexual orientation, race, ethnicity, and physical and mental capacities.
- Use computer-delivered assessment measures effectively and appropriately.
- Select assessment techniques appropriate for group administration and those appropriate for individual administration.
- Administer, score, and report findings from career assessment instruments appropriately.
- Interpret data from assessment instruments and present the results to clients and to others.
- Assist the client and others designated by the client to interpret data from assessment instruments.
- Write an accurate report of assessment results.

**Information/Resources**

Information/resource base and knowledge essential for professionals engaging in career counseling. Demonstration of knowledge of:

Education, training, and employment trends; labor market information and resources that provide information about job tasks, functions, salaries, requirements and future outlooks related to broad occupational fields and individual occupations.

- Resources and skills that clients utilize in life-work planning and management.
- Community/professional resources available to assist clients in career planning, including job search.
- Changing roles of women and men and the implications that this has for education, family, and leisure.
- Methods of good use of computer-based career information delivery systems (CIDS) and computer-assisted career guidance systems (CACGS) to assist with career planning.

**Program Promotion, Management, and Implementation**

Knowledge and skills necessary to develop, plan, implement, and manage comprehensive career development programs in a variety of settings. Demonstration of knowledge of:

Designs that can be used in the organization of career development programs.

- Needs assessment and evaluation techniques and practices.
- Organizational theories, including diagnosis, behavior, planning, organizational communication, and management useful in implementing and administering career development programs.
- Methods of forecasting, budgeting, planning, costing, policy analysis, resource allocation, and quality control.
- Leadership theories and approaches for evaluation and feedback, organizational change, decision-making, and conflict resolution.
- Professional standards and criteria for career development programs.
- Societal trends and state and federal legislation that influence the development and implementation of career development programs.

*Demonstration of ability to:*

Implement individual and group programs in career development for specified populations.

- Train others about the appropriate use of computer-based systems for career information and planning.
- Plan, organize, and manage a comprehensive career resource center.
- Implement career development programs in collaboration with others.

- Identify and evaluate staff competencies.
- Mount a marketing and public relations campaign in behalf of career development activities and services.

**Coaching, Consultation, and Performance Improvement**

Knowledge and skills considered essential in relating to individuals and organizations that impact the career counseling and development process. Demonstration of ability to:

Use consultation theories, strategies, and models.

- Establish and maintain a productive consultative relationship with people who can influence a client's career.
- Help the general public and legislators to understand the importance of career counseling, career development, and life-work planning.
- Impact public policy as it relates to career development and workforce planning.
- Analyze future organizational needs and current level of employee skills and develop performance improvement training.
- Mentor and coach employees.

**Diverse Populations**

Knowledge and skills considered essential in relating to diverse populations that impact career counseling and development processes. Demonstration of ability to:

Identify development models and multicultural counseling competencies.

- Identify developmental needs unique to various diverse populations, including those of different gender, sexual orientation, ethnic group, race, and physical or mental capacity.
- Define career development programs to accommodate needs unique to various diverse populations.
- Find appropriate methods or resources to communicate with limited-English-proficient individuals.
- Identify alternative approaches to meet career planning needs for individuals of various diverse populations.
- Identify community resources and establish linkages to assist clients with specific needs.
- Assist other staff members, professionals, and community members in understanding the unique needs/characteristics of diverse populations with regard to career exploration, employment expectations, and economic/social issues.
- Advocate for the career development and employment of diverse populations.
- Design and deliver career development programs and materials to hard-to-reach populations.

**Supervision**

Knowledge and skills considered essential in critically evaluating counselor or career development facilitator performance, maintaining and improving professional skills. Demonstration of:

Ability to recognize own limitations as a career counselor and to seek supervision or refer clients when appropriate.

- Ability to utilize supervision on a regular basis to maintain and improve counselor skills.
- Ability to consult with supervisors and colleagues regarding client and counseling issues and issues related to one's own professional development as a career counselor.
- Knowledge of supervision models and theories.
- Ability to provide effective supervision to career counselors and career development facilitators at different levels of experience.
- Ability to provide effective supervision to career development facilitators at different levels of experience by:
    - knowledge of their roles, competencies, and ethical standards
    - determining their competence in each of the areas included in their certification
    - further training them in competencies, including interpretation of assessment instruments
    - monitoring and mentoring their activities in support of the professional career counselor; and scheduling regular consultations for the purpose of reviewing their activities

**Ethical/Legal Issues**

Information base and knowledge essential for the ethical and legal practice of career counseling. Demonstration of knowledge of:

Adherence to ethical codes and standards relevant to the profession of career counseling (e.g. NBCC, NCDA, and ACA).

- Current ethical and legal issues which affect the practice of career counseling with all populations.
- Current ethical/legal issues with regard to the use of computer-assisted career guidance systems.
- Ethical standards relating to consultation issues.
- State and federal statutes relating to client confidentiality.

**Research/Evaluation**

Knowledge and skills considered essential in understanding and conducting research and evaluation in career counseling and development. Demonstration of ability to:

- Write a research proposal.
- Use types of research and research designs appropriate to career counseling and development research.
- Convey research findings related to the effectiveness of career counseling programs.
- Design, conduct, and use the results of evaluation programs.
- Design evaluation programs which take into account the need of various diverse populations, including persons of both genders, differing sexual orientations, different ethnic and racial backgrounds, and differing physical and mental capacities.
- Apply appropriate statistical procedures to career development research.

**Technology**

Knowledge and skills considered essential in using technology to assist individuals with career planning. Demonstration of knowledge of:

- Various computer-based guidance and information systems as well as services available on the Internet.
- Standards by which such systems and services are evaluated (e.g. NCDA and ACSCI).
- Ways in which to use computer-based systems and Internet services to assist individuals with career planning that are consistent with ethical standards.
- Characteristics of clients which make them profit more or less from use of technology-driven systems.
- Methods to evaluate and select a system to meet local needs.

*NCDA Headquarters*
*305 N. Beech Circle*
*Broken Arrow, OK 74012*
*918/663-7060 Toll-free 866-FOR-NCDA*
*Fax: 918/663-7058*

*www.ncda.org*

*Retrieved from*

*http://www.ncda.org/aws/NCDA/pt/sd/news_article/37798/_self/layout_ccmsearch/true October 21, 2016.*

# CHAPTER EIGHT

# Career-Focused Counseling in a Diverse World

## Chapter Goals

- To present an overview of the issues involved in career-focused counseling (CFC) with diverse clients
- To illustrate the personal, individual nature of culture as it exists in the context of group cultural characteristics
- To apply a reasoned, empathic approach to assisting diverse individuals with career-related issues
- To identify ways counselors in a variety of work settings can advocate for social justice in the world of work related to the systematic oppression of many individuals and groups

## Introduction

> B.1.a. Multicultural/Diversity Considerations
> Career professionals maintain awareness and sensitivity regarding cultural meanings of confidentiality and privacy. Career professionals respect differing views toward disclosure of information. Career professionals hold ongoing discussions with clients as to how, when, and with whom information is to be shared. (NCDA Code of Ethics, 2015, p. 6)

In spite of the polarizing mindsets that pervade our contemporary society, our world is getting increasingly diverse. This increased diversity has important implications for CFC. In this

### Opening Vignette

For this vignette, I offer the one used in the preceding chapters, but with a twist. First of all, which cultural characteristics could change, and how might they affect how you would approach this client? Which characteristics "matter" in terms of CFC? The changes are highlighted in italics.

Krystal is a 21-year-old *African American,* college student who comes to you for career counseling *with her same-sex intimate partner*. She tells you that she switched from a major in special education to one in exercise science. After some inquiry, you learn that she initially chose special education, because a family member did that, and she then chose exercise science, because she ran cross-country all 4 years of high school. When asked what she wants to deal with in counseling, Krystal says, "Stress. Thinking about getting a job after graduation has been making me worry. *I've been praying and believe God will tell me what I should do, but so far He has been silent.*" She goes on to tell you that she switched out of special education after her first semester taking upper-division classes in her major. *She fears that because being a lesbian (her term) conflicts with her conservative faith, God is punishing her by remaining silent*. Krystal says that she wasn't sure if she wanted to teach, because she would "get too attached to the kids." She reports similar concerns with an exercise science job like gym teacher. She questions whether she wants to teach chapter, we explore these implications, along with strategies for addressing them. One of the challenges we face in this work, which frames this discussion, is balancing between alpha and beta errors (bias, prejudice) in approaching diversity.

Alpha prejudice (Hare-Mustin, 1987) and bias (Hare-Mustin & Marecek, 1988) exaggerates differences while beta prejudice (bias, errors) minimizes differences. Counselors committing alpha errors or bias assume that a client like Krystal's presenting concern *must* be related to her race, gender, sexual orientation, and/or religion, because difference is so significant and features prominently in counseling issues. Alternatively, a counselor committing a beta error is likely to assume that because we're all just people, Krystal's struggles could not be directly related to race, gender, sexual orientation, and/or religion. After all, they might reason, we are all the same under the skin.

As you read this, you may be saying to yourself that you would never do either of these things, but please note that these are extreme views used to highlight ends of a continuum. In day-to-day practice in CFC, these errors occur in much subtler and, therefore, insidious ways. Novice counselors—those with limited practice or reflective experience—may think concretely about these extremes and struggle to maintain balance. In practice with a client like Krystal, for example, they may struggle to know how to determine the role that her "categories of difference" play in her career-related concerns. They may initially vacillate between the two errors, first thinking that Krystal's sexual orientation must, for example, be key to her struggles and that it must be explored early as to its relation to selecting a career. The counselor may also swing to the opposite extreme by acting as if Krystal's sexual orientation plays no role in her career-related issue and, therefore, intentionally not ask about possible connections. This struggle is a natural part of the counselor development process and serves as a guide to help frame the discussion that follows in this chapter.

As you will see, I advocate for erring on the side of talking with the client about their categories of difference. For an example, a counselor might say, "Krystal, I can see that this career issue is important you, and it occurs in the context of your total lived experience. How do you see these career issues in relation to the other facets of your life that you have shared

at all. Wiping away tears, Krystal discloses that she feels like she has been "trying to fill some kind of hole inside me" by finding a meaningful job in which she can help people, but to a greater extent that her restaurant server job.

Alpha Bias: exaggerates differences

Beta Bias: minimizes differences

with me, like being a Black, Lesbian woman with conservative religious beliefs?" It is important to allow clients the freedom and room to determine the potential affect these characteristics have on their career-related concerns for themselves, rather than to impose the counselor's beliefs about their relevance on the client. So, multiculturally competent, CFC moves beyond recognizing generalized information about different cultural groups and toward a deep and abiding appreciation for and exploration of the client's lived experience. Fortunately, counselors have well-established guidelines for framing their thinking about what this means and how it looks in practice.

In 2009, the National Career Development Association (NCDA) approved the *Minimum Competencies for Multicultural Career Counseling and Development* statement, as it replaced the previous document, *1997 Career Counseling Competencies*. This highlights the organization's recognition of and appreciation for the role differences play across the career development range. The statement draws from the ACA Code of Ethics, the NCDA Code of Ethics and Multicultural counseling competencies. One way to ensure that CFC moves in lockstep with multicultural counseling standards is to explore and explicate each facet of the code. This supports counselors and counselors-in-training in understanding both their behavior and the rationale for those behaviors. Table 8.1 provides the introduction to the code, while the rest of the code is broken down and discussed below.

From the competencies statement above it is important to highlight the following passage:

> ... practice in ways that promote the career development and functioning of individuals of all backgrounds. ***Promotion and advocacy of career development for individuals is ensured regardless of age, culture, mental/physical ability, ethnicity, race, nationality, religion/spirituality, gender, gender identity, sexual orientation, marital/partnership status, military or civilian status, language preference, socioeconomic status, any other characteristics not specifically relevant to job performance, in accordance with NCDA and ACA policy*** (emphasis added).

NCDA has been intentional in its broad inclusivity, which is important today as diversity as a concept has expanded to include individual differences. In order to clarify an understanding of each dimension, the following section elaborates on these, including implications for each.

**Age**—Chronological age of the person receiving services, recognizing that each age, or age range, represents a distinct stage of psychosocial development (Erikson, 1968), which has clear implications for career development (Super, Savickas, & Super, 1996).

**Culture**—Draguns (2016) draws upon Herskovits' 1948 anthropological definition of culture: "the distinctive, human-made part of the environment that encompasses both the artifacts created by the human species and the mental products that have accrued over many millennia" (p. 34). It is the shared characteristics, both historical and contemporary, that includes beliefs, traditions, and practices. In CFC, it may important to distinguish between big "C" culture, as just described, and small "c" culture of the unique individual sitting before us. As we proceed through the remaining categories and descriptors, keep in mind the interplay of these small "c" characteristics and the big "C" ones.

**Mental/physical ability**—Fabian and Pebdani (2013) offer insight into the challenges of defining and describing what have typically been identified as disabilities and how they relate to career work. They begin by noting that the concept of disability is a social construction, often construed in pejorative ways but that researchers have begun to challenge these conceptions (see Davis, 2010). Further complicating the picture of disability are the different definitions used by different governmental agencies where support and resources are involved (e.g., 2010 U.S. Census; Americans With Disabilities Act; Workforce Investment Act of 1998; Social Security Administration; see Fabian & Pebdani, 2013, for extended discussion of these discrepant views). Brammer (2012) highlights a critical component of disability by grouping this topic with what he calls the culture of appearance, describing the change in language from "disabled" to "differently abled" to "person with a disability." Disabilities encompass physical, mental, developmental, and medical issues. As such, one all-encompassing definition of disability remains elusive and justifiably so.

**Ethnicity**—McAliffe and associates (2008) define ethnicity as, "the recognition of common social ties among people due to shared geographic origins, memories of an historical past, cultural heritage, religious affiliation, language and dialect forms, and/or tribal affiliation" (pp. 13; 85). They assert that ethnicity is a silent presence in the room and must, therefore, be explored with clients early on. Ethnicity is distinguished from race as being cultured-based, whereas race is a phenotype that is socially constructed (McAuliffe et al., 2008).

**Race**—Drawing from the literature on the race, Brammer (2012) describes race as, "an anthropological concept used to classify people according to physical characteristics, such as skin and eye color, or the shape of certain body parts, such as head, eyes, ears, lips, or nose" (p. 18). It has been viewed as a way to justify oppression by groups in power and demean the race of perceived inferiors (Ponterotto, Casas, Suzuki, & Alexander, 1995).

**Nationality**—Often conflated with ethnicity, nationality is a person's state of citizenship (McAliffe & Associates, 2008).

**Religion/spirituality**—Two other terms that are often used interchangeably, religion refers to "the means and methods (e.g., rituals or prescribed behaviors) of the search [for the sacred] that receive validation and support from within an identifiable group of people" (Hill et al., 2000, p. 66, as cited in Pedersen et al., 2016). Spirituality, in contrast, is "seen as an innate need to connect to something larger, something that may be felt as divine, sacred, or out of the ordinary" (Pedersen et al., 2016, p. 479).

**Gender**—As the term is used in this context, gender refers to sex, or the biological state of sex, and, more specifically, reproductive organs associated with male reproductive biology and female reproductive biology.

**Gender identity**—As the term is used in this context, gender identity is actually gender as it is socially construed. Gender is the way in which an individual experiences their self in the world. Increasingly, gender is viewed as fluid or continuous, rather than dichotomous (Pedersen et al., 2016).

**Sexual orientation**—This term refers to "romantic, emotional, and/or erotic attractions to others that are expressed through behaviors, affectionate bonds, and romantic relationships"

(Pedersen et al., 2016, p. 276), whereas sexual identity denotes, "the way people understand themselves with regard to sexual orientation ... [and] can be fluid" (p. 276).

**Marital/partnership status**—Social exchange theory (Murstein, 1976), contends that "people's romantic choices, just like their market behavior, are motivated by a desire to maximize their earnings and minimize their losses" (Pines, 2005, p. 62). Pines continues, "The more rewards (such as love, support, or sex) that a relationship provides and the lower the cost (for example, doing what one does not want to do), the more satisfying the relationship is and the longer it will last" (p. 63). In contemporary times, couples increasingly appear to find partnerships that don't involve marriage to be more advantageous. This may be particularly true as attitudes toward gay marriage persist and limit access to this option.

**Military or civilian status**—In the United States, there are over 22 million veterans, not counting active service individuals (Killam, Degges-White, & Michel, 2016). Many of our nation's military personnel, active, reserves, and retired, face unique challenges. Over and above the regimented military culture, many service men and women have been displaced from their families and homes, often for extended periods of time, and a large portion of them have been exposed to trauma, either directly or vicariously. Furthermore, many military personnel are wounded or injured during their time in the service. Upon reentry into civilian life, their experience varied reactions from the community, from suspicion to fear. These individuals face compounding challenges in career development (Killam, et al.).

**Language preference**—An important consideration for building rapport with a client is identifying their preferred language, as opposed to assuming it based on demographics, accent, or other markers.

**Socioeconomic status**—Perhaps one of the most significant indicators of the cultural divide involves the financial and consequent social status and roles in the community. Finances and issues of financial mobility create "glass ceilings" and other invisible barriers (though they are very visible to those experiencing them!) that keep individuals locked into their "place" in society.

Any one of these areas by itself represents a potentially powerful influence over the counseling relationship. As any two or more are combined, the complexity increases exponentially, especially as those categories of individuality interact and intersect with those of the counselor. All this really means is that each client is unique, cannot be a spokesperson for any category of characteristic, and the individuality of the client is what is most relevant, requiring careful consideration of the person of the client, rather than the demographics. Now that this has been firmly established, we turn to the specific CFC competencies for diverse populations established by NCDA.

# NCDA Competencies

In an effort to move in sync with the multicultural career counseling competencies established by the NCDA, I have included the components in italics below, directly from the standards/competencies, followed by a brief discussion of each as to how they apply to CFC.

As discussed throughout this text, career counseling theory is one set of tools counselors can use. Another tool is the application of counseling theory to career-related client issues. The strength of career counseling theories is their specific application to career issues, but this can also be a limitation in that they may result in a myopic view of the client's concerns. For example, Krystal expresses her concern regarding selection of a career, yet her relationships and her own identity plays a part in her decision-making confusion. Because she has identified career as the presenting problem, that is where the CFC will begin, but it will also acknowledge that, in order to make appropriate progress, counseling may need to address these contextual issues as well. Another inherent limitation of career theory, like many theories is the target population, has been narrow and fairly homogeneous, missing the key roles that issues of oppression, marginalization, and prejudice play in navigating career issues (Fouad & Kantamneni, 2013; Melvin, Galles, & Lenz, 2012).

When it comes to counseling, counselors of all backgrounds and approaches are vulnerable to values imposition with clients. First and foremost, the power differential in the relationship means that counselors are in the role of authority, and therefore, in most cases, their opinions carry great weight in a session. Be aware that, in counseling, clients tend to answer almost any question a counselor asks, even if it's not a good question. Part of this is social convention—we feel pressure to answer when asked—but to a greater extent, clients feel a heightened sense of obligation to answer. This dynamic highlights the danger of counselors imposing their biases on clients, even unintentionally. Fortunately, the path forward is clear, if challenging: awareness. The vast majority of multicultural competency models begin with or at least include early on, awareness of one's biases (ACA, 2015,

https://www.counseling.org/docs/default-source/competencies/multicultural-and-social-justice-counseling-competencies.pdf?sfvrsn=20;

Pedersen et al., 2016). John Sommers-Flanagan describes counselor self-awareness as one of four critical questions counselors should ask themselves in working with clients: How are my biases or personal issues influencing my work? (2012,

*Career development theory: understands the strengths and limitations of career theory and utilizes theories that are appropriate for the population being served.*

*Individual and Group Counseling Skills: is aware of their own cultural beliefs and assumptions and incorporates that awareness into their decision-making about interactions with clients/students and other career professionals; continues to develop their individual and group counseling skills in order to enhance their ability to respond appropriately to individuals from diverse populations; is cognizant when working with groups of the group demographics and monitors these to ensure appropriate respect and confidentiality is maintained.*

*Individual/Group Assessment: understands the psychometric properties of the assessments they are using in order to effectively select and administer assessments and interpret and use results with the appropriate limitations and cautions.*

*Information, Resources, and Technology: regularly evaluates the information, resources, and use of technology to determine that these tools are sensitive to the needs of diverse populations amending and/or individualizing for each client as required; provides resources in multiple formats to ensure that clients/students are able to benefit from needed information; provides targeted and sensitive support for clients/students in using the information, resources, and technology.*

*Program Promotion, Management, and Implementation: incorporates appropriate guidelines, research, and experience in developing, implementing, and managing programs and services for diverse populations; utilizes the principles of program evaluation to design and obtain feedback from relevant stakeholders in the continuous improvement of programs and services, paying special attention to feedback regarding specific needs of the population being served; applies his/her knowledge of multicultural issues in dealing with other professionals and trainees to ensure the creation of a culturally-sensitive environment for all clients.*

*Coaching, Consultation, and Performance Improvement: engages in coaching, consultation, and performance improvement activities with appropriate training and incorporates knowledge*

cf. 19; 365). We as counselors cannot appreciate the effect of our worldview on our clients unless and until we know what that worldview is. As counselors, we are required to reflect on our own attitudes and beliefs (Multicultural and Social Justice Counseling Competencies, ACA, 2015).

Swanson and Fouad (2015) describe a 3-dimensional model (Fouad & Kantamneni, 2008) for understanding both the client's and the counselor's worldview. The first dimension includes characteristics specifically related to career: interests, needs, values, personality, abilities, self-efficacy, and aspirations, but of course, these also have broader application. For example, counselors with high professional aspirations may inadvertently view a client with lower aspirations as resistant, unmotivated, or even depressed, if the counselor views these client features through their own lens of normality. The second set of characteristics includes group-level differences, include gender, race/ethnicity, family/relationships, role models, social class, religion, and sexual orientation. The third dimension includes broader societal factors, like acculturation, cultural values, opportunity structure, discrimination, schooling, barriers, and labor market. All three dimensions interact to create innumerable permutations of individual experience.

Swanson and Fouad (2015) suggest using a genogram (family tree) that includes career- and education-related components to assist counselors and counselors-in-training to identify patterns of beliefs and attitudes, to identify origins of the same, and to clarify at the time what their current attitudes and beliefs are across all three dimensions, particularly as they apply to the world of work. In doing so, counselors can illuminate their thinking about career and how this thinking might affect their relationships and work with clients in CFC.

One of the first things counselors engaged in CFC recognize is that formal assessments represent one tool or way of obtaining information from clients. A concern is that, working a specialty area in counseling, we as counselors have become too reliant on quantitative career assessments. The Strong Interest Inventory is perhaps the most widely used career tool by counselors in general and career specialists in particular. Unfortunately, the saying that "when all you have is a hammer, everything looks like a nail" is apropos here: our field's ambivalence about addressing career-related issues plays out in the over-reliance on formal career assessments. This is a uniquely challenging issue for clients outside the normed group upon which these formal assessments were constructed. Hansen (2013) heralds the call for caution in using interest inventories specifically, but this can also be considered a broader admonition for counselors. In describing the challenges of inventories across gender, race, and ethnicity, she asserts that, "good counseling practice is essential" (p. 411). Swanson & Fouad (2015) reiterate that career instruments must be used and interpreted in light of the published norms, ensuring that counselors take into consideration any cultural conflicts in using them.

Information can be used to liberate or oppress. As mentioned earlier on in this text, one of the reasons counselors are reluctant to enter fully into the role of CFC is the errant assumptions about how informed they must be about career resources and the wider world of work. While it is true that counselors are expected to be informed about information, resources, and technology, having the most thorough, latest information is improbable. Rather than appearing to have all necessary information, career-focused counselors assist clients in exploring resources for themselves. They do assess and ensure that the client is conversant with technology before sending them off to do research (Sheperis et al., 2012).

One of the challenges most counselors face in working with groups of people and designing programs that serve a broad cross-section of individuals is making the materials appropriate for and applicable to all likely constituencies. In addition, counselors avail themselves of opportunities to learn from other professionals both about career-related issues, as well as diverse populations. Likewise, they share information with colleagues and other professionals regarding differences in populations served that increase social justice in CFC.

Counselors maintain a growth orientation with regard to their professional practice.

It may be no coincidence that just as the counseling fields have demonstrated ambivalence toward career counseling, research in the supervision of career counseling has also lagged. Luke & Redekop (2016) have discussed this phenomenon, the challenges facing counseling and counselor educators in this regard, and suggestions for remedying this.

One of the initial considerations of ethical practice in counseling is that counselors do not ignore or minimize—or as is

*of multicultural attitudes, beliefs, skills and values; seeks awareness and understanding about how to best match diverse clients/students with suitably culturally sensitive employers.*

*Supervision: gains knowledge of and engages in evidence-based supervision, pursues educational and training activities on a regular and ongoing basis inclusive of both counseling and supervision topics. Further, is aware of their limitations, cultural biases, and personal values and seeks professional consultative assistance as necessary; infuses multicultural/diversity contexts into their training and supervision practices, makes supervisees aware of the ethical standards and responsibilities of the profession, and trains supervisees to develop relevant multicultural knowledge and skills.*

*Ethical/Legal Issues: continuously updates their knowledge of multicultural and diversity issues and research and applies new knowledge as required; employs their knowledge and experience of multicultural ethical and legal issues within a professional framework to enhance the functioning of their organization and the image of the profession; uses supervision and professional consultations effectively when faced with an ethical or legal issue related to diversit, to ensure they provide high-quality services for every client/student.*

*Research/Evaluation: designs and implements culturally appropriate research studies with regards to research design, instrument selection, and other pertinent population-specific issues.*

currently a major topic in counseling, refer—based on our discomfort with or lack of knowledge in a particular domain of counseling.

It seems especially important in CFC that we, as counselors, make ourselves aware of the research approaches and processes used to gather pertinent information about the clients we serve. We have a keen responsibility to recognize the limitations of research in terms of its applicability and generalizability to our client populations.

# A Return to Social Justice in Counseling

Anderson, Peila-Shuster, & Aragon (2012) issue a call to return to career counseling's social justice roots. Citing Gysbers et al., (2003) they note five key issues in multicultural career counseling:

***Individualism***—It is not safe to assume that, when clients are making career-related decisions, those decisions reflect themselves and their needs only. In many cases, their choices may reflect the identity of their family, significant others, or broader culture.

***Autonomy***—Autonomy is a hallmark of ethically responsible CFC; over-focusing on individual autonomy can minimize the very real influence of systemic oppression.

***Affluence***—One of the important lessons I hope readers will take from this text is the privilege implicit to career exploration. As you go through your day and week, take a moment to look around at those working jobs that might be easily overlooked or taken for granted. Many people in our society simply need employment or income; reflecting on a career or vocation may simply be beyond their reach. Insisting that they aim for this may be a way of imposing our values on our clients. At the same time, we must not assume just by looking that we know what the career aspirations of our clients are, nor what they can achieve.

***Opportunity available to all*** is the view that hard work is all or most of what is needed in order to succeed. The implication is that those who have not succeeded have not worked hard enough. Society does not create a level playing field in which all have equal opportunity. This attitude can result in "blaming the victim" of oppression for not taking advantage of the opportunities that were never available.

***Linearity of the career-counseling process***—this tenet suggests that there are fixed rules for career development in which one applies Parson's model in a stepwise fashion, resulting in success: Learn about yourself, then learn about the world of work, and finally, put the two together, and create a vocational life worth living. Not only is this a reductive, naïve understanding of development in general, it also ignores that reality that many professionals actually back into their careers, rather that walking forward, intentionally, into success.

Anderson et al., (2012) provides a rubric for career-related bias in CFC. We all have biases and limited views, but without diligent self-reflection and supervision, we risk imposing these on our clients. Let's consider some ways this could happen with Krystal.

- What are some areas of privilege that you may have experienced in career development? What things *don't* you have to think about in addition to self-assessment?

- What do racial minorities have in common with people in lower socioeconomic status strata?
- What does career development look like for underrepresented racial and ethnic groups? How about for the *working poor*?
- How might you view the clients in the vignettes differently if, for example, Xavier was Mexican-American, or Alexa was an African American female living in poverty? How might it change from your initial considerations, if at all?

As we approach the topics of race, ethnicity, and poverty in CFC, there are several considerations to keep in mind as you read. The first is the need to recognize the fine line between cultural characteristics of racial group stereotypes. Clients are individuals first and must be treated as such, recognizing that there are cultural factors that influence perceptions of the world of work and their place in it, but as counselors, we don't know what those are until the client shares them with us. As a counselor and counselor educator, I cringe at the thought that someone reading this text or having taken a course in multicultural counseling would encounter a Black client, for example, and immediately think to themselves, "this guy is Black, therefore he has experienced ____, or needs ____ from me." This "Black guy" needs the same thing every client needs: empathy, genuineness, and acceptance. The second caveat is that differences within groups of people are often greater than those between groups. This means that a Black client, a Latina client, and a White client seeking career-related support will likely have more similarities to one another than to members of their own race who are not seeking career support. The question, then, as we proceed is "how can I use the information in this chapter to experience empathy, acceptance and genuineness with the client sitting across from me?"

One last caveat from McDonald and Hite (2016):

> While the nature of research often compels us to study diversity in discrete segments that propose to be singular in nature (e.g., gender, race, age), there are few singularities in reality. The concept of intersectionality reminds us that, as humans, we are mosaics of various types of identities (e.g., Black lesbian, deaf man over 50). Intersectionality also means that barriers that may exist as a result of one aspect of difference from the majority are potentially exacerbated when several variations are compounded (Schore et al., 2011). In any situation or for any individual, one aspect of identity may be more salient than the others or may prompt stronger reactions, but there is always the dynamic of a compounded effect. (p. 125)

## A Word about Race

In this section, we begin with the hard stuff. Racism, particularly from Whites toward Blacks, is so historically ingrained that it may have become part of our biology (Reynolds & Klik, 2016), in terms of White guilt and Black mistrust. One of the main reasons that African Americans are a unique population to work with in counseling in general, and CFC in particular, is that Whites once owned, sold, and abused Blacks. This will never *not* be a feature of the history of the United States. This historical reality exists in the context of, "it did not happen to you, so when are you going to let that slavery thing go?" The fact is, this may—should—never leave the collective unconscious of African Americans. To take it a step further, this oppression of an entire race has been so effective that Blacks now oppress Blacks, as inner cities become urban turf warzones. This has a profound effect on the vocational identity development of African Americans. Vocational identity development in the context of systemic oppression, affecting most facets of career development. In working with race in particular, it is important to consider the ways your biases may emerge through language, posture, and omissions.

## CFC Considerations

- Do not ignore the diversity markers of the individual sitting across from you.
  - Do ask the individual how they have experienced their diversity in the context of their career development.
  - Ex. "What role do you see your race playing in this process?"
- Do not assume that the diversity marker of the individual sitting across from you is the problem.
  - Do ask about the factors that have complicated, as well as clarified, their career development process.
  - Ex. Some persons of color describe challenges associated with their race in this process; others describe advantages to it. How do you see these things in your experience?
- Do not assume that you know the individual or that you can assume anything about their experience based on their category of diversity.
  - Do bracket any generalizations as just that, and clarify the individual's experience.
  - Ex. Some Black clients—would you prefer that I reference your race as "black" or "African American"?—describe a strong role that spirituality places in overcoming challenges. How important or relevant is this to you in our work?
- Do not assume that your intentions are perceived as pure if you are in the majority working with someone in the minority.
  - Do recognize and note that your privileged status (as the counselor, having a graduate degree, being of a majority or different race, and so on) may come into play during your work together.
  - Ex. I'll ask you to keep me in check as we work together. There may be times I offer feedback or suggestions that seem unrealistic to you based on your experience, and you may begin to think I cannot relate to you. Would you call me out on those things?

Table 8.1. Demographic Distribution of U.S. Population (U.S. Census Bureau, 2011)

| Group | Population |
|---|---|
| Women in the U.S. | 51% or approximately 153 million |
| People of Color | 36% or approximately 108 million |
| Lesbian, Gay, and Bisexual Individuals (18–45) | 2.6% or approximately 8.8 million |
| Individuals living in poverty | 16% or approximately 48 million |
| Foreign born individuals | 13% or approximately 40 million |

# A Word about Gender

Can you think of situations in which a group with superior numbers was defeated by a group of inferior numbers but with superior power? What does it mean to be a feminist career counselor in the modern age? How can CFC address the needs of the individual while also advocating for the population represented by the individual?

John and Rita Sommers-Flanagan open their chapter on Feminist Theory and Therapy (2012) by noting a trend in early psychiatric journals picturing females in before-and-after cleaning situations, promoting the virtues of antidepressant medications. The message is clear that for many years in mental health, women's role was to cook, clean, and rear children. As much as we, as a society, would like to distance ourselves from this past, the reality is that the glass ceiling and implicit expectations for 51% of the U.S. population are very much alive and well. For example, Flores and Bike (2014) summarize the issue citing multiple sources of information,

- Women earn less than men (U.S. Bureau of Labor Statistics, 2011). On average, women make 81% of the earnings of men.
- The glass ceiling continues for women in high-level executive positions. Specifically, women account for only 6% of corporate chief executive officers and other high-level roles (Matsa, 2011).
- Although more women are graduating from college than men (National Center for Education Statistics, 2012), women are underrepresented in science, technology, engineering, and math majors—academic disciplines that lead to highly lucrative professions (National Science Foundation, 2007).

This is the context in which females build a vocational identity and the market into which they strive for work and career success. CFC with women finds its starting point in feminist theory. Before we dive too deeply into this area, a caveat is in order. The term "feminism" evokes a variety of reactions from most people and, typically, a negative one. But feminism is not an implicitly pejorative term. In fact, it is a hopeful one inspired by a number of philosophical perspectives that promote social justice. Consider the face of feminism on display during the

March for Women. Women from all walks of life participated in a public outcry for equality and justice. The primitive notion that feminists are pitchfork-wielding women descended from Amazonian tribes seeking to prove their superiority of men is a fable promulgated by those fearing true equality. The reality is closer to it being an extension of the Civil Rights Movement in the United States that advocates for a level playing field for all individuals. So, as you read this chapter and see terms like feminism, try to resist the urge to frown and instead, reflect on the times you might have wished to begin a race at the starting point on the same starting line as others, rather than beginning a lap behind.

In a recent graduate counseling course, I asked the 16 students in attendance if they believed women were inferior to men. Only one student looked up at me as if I were crazy, indicated her strong belief they women are not inferior to men. The rest of the class made no visible response and certainly none spoke out. In fairness, my students have learned to treat my questions with a degree of skepticism, but the fact remains that only 1 in 16 challenged the question. In order for counselors to conduct effective CFC with females, they must acknowledge the context in which women seek to fulfill their purpose.

### Neuro-Informed, Multiculturally Competent, Career Focused Counseling

It is a fact of neurobiology that the human brain is wired to be biased. As shocking as this is to read (and write, for that matter) it remains that, as humans, we harbor prejudice against those who are different from us, and even those whom we presume are different from us. This is an evolutionary biological survival tactic. Elsewhere, I have summarized the literature on this phenomenon (Luke, Redekop, & Moralejo, under review), so I discuss its implications for career-focused counseling here. The human brain prefers homeostasis—a state of balance—so when someone who is "other" comes along (and this is experienced differently depending on the type and degree of difference), it upsets homeostasis. It forces the brain to assess for threat by comparing the stimulus (person that is different) to emotion-laden memory in the amygdala, determining whether the hypothalamus releases neurochemicals for fight, flight, or freezing. In CFC, clients representing categories of difference have often experienced being the other in regards to the world of work. Three features bear highlighting in the recognition that neuroscience research that leads us to conclude that we, as counselors, cannot feign the core conditions of empathy, genuineness, and positive regard:

## Summary

The history of career counseling is rooted in social justice. In CFC this takes place on two levels: individual and societal. Clients deserve to be treated with dignity and respect, and counseling provides a safe environment for them to explore possible selves. This is one reason I advocate for a professional ethic that invites career-related issues into the counseling session, regardless of presenting problem. CFC stands on the front lines of social justice by advocating for clients to self-advocate to take steps to become more of themselves. The second way counselors can advance social justice is at the community level. Every time a client challenges their worldview that accepts the status quo, humanity takes a step forward. This means that CFC challenges the social structures that view individuals as members of "that group" and limits the resources, access, or services based on group characteristics.

Counselors speak truth to power in their communities to promote the vocational identity and development of every member. We are at the vanguard of balancing alpha and beta errors among individual clients and social systems.

# References


Anderson, S. K., Peila-Shuster, J. J., & Aragon, A. (2012). Cross cultural career counseling: Ethical issues to consider. *Career Planning and Adult Development Journal*, *28*(1), 127.

Bandura, A. (1986). *Social foundations of thought and action: A social cognitive theory*. Englewood Cliffs, NJ: Prentice Hall.

Bandura, A. (1997). *Self-efficacy: The exercise of control*. New York, NY: Freeman.

Brammer, R. (2012). *Diversity in counseling (2nd Ed.)*. Belmont, CA: Cengage Learning.

Brosch, T., Bar-David, E., & Phelps, E. A. (2013). Implicit race bias decreases the similarity of neural representations of black and white faces. *Psychological science*, *24*(2), 160–166.

Chojnacki, J. T., & Gelberg, S. (1994). Toward a conceptualization of career counseling with gay/lesbian/bisexual persons. *Journal of Career Development*, 21, 3–10.

Cikara, M., Bruneau, E., Van Bavel, J. J., & Saxe, R. (2014). Their pain gives us pleasure: How intergroup dynamics shape empathic failures and counter-empathic responses. *Journal of experimental social psychology*, *55*, 110–125.

Davis, L. J. (2013). The end of identity politics: On disability as an unstable category. *The disability studies reader*, 263.

Draguns, J. G. (2015). Counseling encounters in multicultural counseling: An introduction. In P. B. Pedersen, W. J. Lonner, J. G. Draguns, J. E. Trimble, & M. R. Scharron-del Rio (Eds.). *Counseling across cultures* (7th ed.), pp. 31–50. Thousand Oaks, CA: Sage Publications.

Erikson, E. H. (1968). *Youth and crisis*. New York, NY: WW Norton & Company.

Fabian, E. S., & Pebdani, R. (2013). The Career Development of Youth and Young Adults with Disabilities. *Career Development and Counselling: Putting Theory and Research to Work, 2nd ed.*, (pp. 357–384). Hoboken, NJ: John Wiley & Sons.

Fassinger, R. (1996). Notes from the margins: Integrating lesbian experience into the vocational psychology of women. *Journal of Vocational Behavior*, 48, 160–175. doi:10.1006/jvbe.1996.0016

Flores, L. Y., & Bike, D. H. (2014). Multicultural career counseling. In F T. L. Leong, L. Comas-Díaz, G. C. Nagayama Hall, V. C. McLoyd, & J. E. Trimble (Eds). *APA handbook of multicultural psychology, Vol. 2: Applications and training*, (pp. 403–417). Washington, DC: American Psychological Association.


1. Implicit bias is a natural, brain-based state—Studies show that our brain responds in ways that are outside of consciousness (see Iacoboni, 2009, for review), and so, bias is not always accessible via introspection (Brosch, Bar-David, & Phelps, 2013). For example, a client characteristic may trigger a visceral reaction in the counselor, leading the counselor to shift into an advice-giving mode in career-focused counseling.
2. In group/outgroup perception—Individuals identify with groups, in part for self protection. Studies show that our brain registers reward when we observe a member of our "group" do well (Cikara, Van Bavel, & Saxe, 2014); it registers disgust when a member of the other "group" does well (Cikara & Van Bavel, 2014; see Bergh et al., 2016, for extended discussion of in and out/group biases).
3. Developmental racism—All models of racial identity development contain stages of acceptance, even of one's own race. Studies show that our brains are constantly scanning for threats in the environment, especially if we a) have been wronged in the past or 2) have an underdeveloped regulatory system (Kubota, Banaji, & Phelps, 2012).

While this may seem dire upon first glance, it actually means that those visceral responses with have to the "other" is brain-based, somewhat natural, and developmental. The path for career-focused counselors is to own these experiences instead of denying, hiding, or shaming one's self, and move toward active behaviors that support the "other."

http://dx.doi.org/10.1037/14187-023

Fouad, N. A., & Kantamneni, N. (2008). Contextual factors in vocational psychology: Intersections of individual, group, and societal dimensions. *Handbook of counseling psychology, 4,* 408–425.

Fouad, N. A., & Kantamneni, N. (2013). The role of race and ethnicity in career choice, development, and adjustment. *Career development and counseling: Putting theory and research to work,* 147–183.

Gysbers, N. C., Heppner, M. J., Johnston, J. A., & Neville, H. A. (2003). Empowering life choices: Career counseling in cultural contexts. *Career counseling: Process, issues and techniques*, 50–76.

Melvin, B., Galles, J. A., & Lenz, J. G. (2012). Assessing career readiness in culturally and ethnically diverse populations. *Career Planning & Adult Development Journal, 28*(1).

Hansen, J. C. (2013). Nature, importance, and assessment of interests. In S. D. Brown and R. W. Lent (Eds.) *Career development and counseling: Putting theory and research to work*, 387–413.

Hare-Mustin, R. T. (1987). The problem of gender in family therapy theory. *Family Process, 26*, 15–27.

Hare-Mustin, R. T., & Marecek, J. (1988). The meaning of difference: Gender theory, postmodernism, and psychology. *American psychologist*, *43*(6), 455.

Herskovits, M. J. (1948). *Man and his works: The science of cultural anthropology*. New York, NY: AA Knopf.

Hill, P. C., Pargament, K. I., Hood, R. W., McCullough, M. E., & Larson, D. B. (2000). Conceptualizing religion and spirituality: Points of commonality, points of departure. *Journal for the Theory of Social Behavior, 30*(1), 50–77.

Iacoboni, M. (2009). Imitation, empathy, and mirror neurons. *Annual review of psychology*, *60*, 653–670.

Killam, W. K., Degges-White, S., & Michel, R. E. (Eds.). (2016). *Career Counseling Interventions: Practice with Diverse Clients*. New York, NY: Springer Publishing Company.

Krieshok, T. S., & Black, M. D. (2009). Assessment and counseling competencies and responsibilities: A checklist for counselors. In E. Whitfield, R. W. Feller, & C. Wood (Eds.) *A counselor's guide to career assessment instruments* (5th ed.) (pp. 68). Broken Arrow, OK: National Career Development Association.

Kubota, J. T., Banaji, M. R., & Phelps, E. A. (2012). The neuroscience of race. *Nature neuroscience*, *15*(7), 940–948.

Lent, R. W., & Brown, S. D. (2013). Social cognitive model of career self-management: Toward a unifying view of adaptive career behavior across the life span. *Journal of Counseling Psychology*, 60, 557–568. doi:10.1037/a0033446

Lent, R. W., Brown, S. D., & Hackett, G. (2000). Contextual supports and barriers to career choice: A social cognitive analysis. *Journal of Counseling Psychology*, 47, 36–49. doi:10.1037/0022-0167.47.1.36

Liddle, B. J., Luzzo, D. A., Hauenstein, A. L., & Schuck, K. (2004). Construction and validation of the lesbian, gay, bisexual, and transgendered inventory. *Journal of Career Assessment*, 12, 33–50. doi:10.1177/1069072703257722

Luke, C., & Redekop, F. (2016). Supervision of co-occurring career and mental health concerns: Application of an integrated approach. *Career Planning and Adult Development Journal, 32*(1), 130.

McAuliffe, G. (2008). *Culturally alert counseling: A comprehensive introduction*. Thousand Oaks, CA: Sage.

Malakh-Pines, A. (2005). *Falling in love: Why we choose the lovers we choose*. New York, NY: Routledge.

Melvin, B., Galles, J. A., & Lenz, J. G. (2012). Assessing career readiness in culturally and ethnically diverse populations. *Career Planning & Adult Development Journal, 28*(1).

Murstein, B. I. (1976). *Who will marry whom?: Theory and research in marital choice*. New York, NY: Springer.

National Career Development Association. (2015). ***NCDA Code of ethics***. Broken Arrow, OK: Author. Retrieved from http://ncda.org/aws/NCDA/asset_manager/get_ le/3395.

Ponterotto, Casas, Suzuki, & Alexander (Eds.) (1995). *Handbook of multicultural counseling*. Thousand Oaks, CA: Sage.

Pedersen, P. B., Lonner, W. J., Draguns, J. G., Trimble, J. E., & Scharron-del Rio, M. R. (2015). *Counseling across cultures*. Thousand Oaks, CA: Sage Publications.

Ratts, M. J., Singh, A. A., Nassar-McMillan, S., Butler, S. K., McCullough, J. R., & Hipolito-Delgado, C. (2015). Multicultural and social justice counseling competencies. AMCD: Alexandria, VA.

https://www.counseling.org/docs/default-source/competencies/multicultural-and-social-justice-counseling-competencies.pdf?sfvrsn=20

Reynolds, K. J., & Klik, K. A. (2016). New developments in prejudice research: from its neural basis and impact on well-being to prejudice reduction. *Current Opinion in Psychology, 11*, 115–119.

Sangganjanavanich, V. F., & Headley, J. A. (2016). Career development of transgender college students pursuing gender transition. *Career Planning and Adult Development Journal, 32*(1), 161.

Sheperis, D. S., Perepiczka, M., & Limoges, C. (2012). Individual and group assessment and appraisal. In D. Capuzzi & M. D. Stauffer (Eds.) *Career Counseling: Foundations, Perspectives, and Applications*, 153–196.

Super, D. E., Savickas, M. L., & Super, C. M. (1996). The life-span, life-space approach to careers. In. Brown, D., Brooks, L. *Career choice and development*, 121–178.

Swanson, J. L., & Fouad, N. A. (2015). *Career theory and practice: Learning through case studies*. Thousand Oaks, CA: Sage publications.

Velez, B. L., & Moradi, B. (2012).Workplace support, discrimination, and person–organization fit: Tests of the theory of work adjustment with LGB individuals. *Journal of Counseling Psychology*, 59, 399–407. doi:10.1037/a0028326

https://www.census.gov/quickfacts/table/PST045215/00

http://www.census.gov/newsroom/facts-for-features/2016/cb16-ff01.html

## Figure/Table Credits

Tab. 8.1: U.S. Census Bureau / Public Domain.

CHAPTER NINE

# Groups at Risk: Aging, Veterans, Disability

### Chapter Goals

- Introduce risk factors for specific groups of clients in career-focused counseling (CFC)
- Identify the career-related needs specific to adults in transition
- Identify the career-related needs specific to veteran and enlisted clients
- Identify the career-related needs specific to clients with disabilities

## Introduction

Groups at risk represent a significant portion of clients that counselors engaged in CFC will encounter. They are more likely than others to face challenges related to career development. The phrase "groups at risk," as used herein, is not intended to be oppressive, patronizing, or otherwise condescending; it is intended to highlight the unique ways in which career-related concerns interact with certain other factors. Counselors are agents of social justice and advocacy, so recognizing risk factors for clients is an important part of their role in CFC. There are many risk factors to choose from, and there will be one or two that you may wish were contained in this chapter. The ones selected represent a large swath of the potential career clients with whom counselors will be expected to work effectively. The three of focus in this chapter are mid-career, older adult individuals experiencing some career transition; military veterans, including the growing number of combat veterans; and individuals with disabilities. All of these groups can and do contribute substantially to society, within and outside of the world of work. At the same time, the approaches to the complexities surrounding career development need appropriate nuance in CFC in order to honor the experiences of individuals from these groups and support their autonomy in this process. For this chapter, three separate vignettes are used to guide the discussion.

As you think through the ways you would interact with individuals from these groups, it may help to consider the following. Krumboltz and Chan (2005) prefer the term *transition counseling* to career counseling because of career counseling's (over)emphasis on making a decision. Instead, they advance five considerations for counselor training, and these considerations bear greatly on the populations discussed in this chapter:

1. Expand the goal. This means shifting from deciding to exploring what a satisfying life would look like.
2. Include all aspects of life. This means eschewing a myopic view of work in favor of exploring personal and family issues related to work and the life one wants to live.
3. Make training more comprehensive. While applied to counselors, this consideration is really the heart of CFC: addressing the individual while they consider the role work will play in the life they desire to create.
4. Deal with all transitions. Career or work may be the focus at a given time in counseling, but transitions occur in ways that create a broader context in which career transition takes place. Counselors can and must address these as well.
5. Build a long-term relationship. Making a career decision must not be the conclusion to counseling, nor should failure to make a decision represent a failed counseling experience.

These reminders help counselors keep in mind that risks are often temporal states rather than character traits. We begin with a vignette about an adult in transition.

## Opening Vignette

Walt is a 50-something-year-old male who is seeking counseling related to career dissatisfaction. He has become increasingly frustrated with the path he has been on for the past 25 years in the sales and marketing field. He initially entered the work world assuming he would be with the same company for his whole career, working his way up the corporate sales ladder. Over time, however, Walt felt he was passed over for promotions by other sales associates. In response, he has made several employment changes within the same industry. He has made a somewhat satisfactory income due to his willingness to work hard and learn new tricks of the trade. For the last few years he has felt increasingly restless in his work and feels disillusioned by the world of work. He wants to make a change, but has a variety of concerns. Finances are top of the list, as he has two high school–aged children who will be heading to college in the next couple of years, and he also worries about retirement accounts for he and his wife. Walt also confides that he worries that he is getting too old to be viable in the job market, that sales is a "young person's game." Yet, he is miserable in his current situation, and his wife is concerned about him.

# CFC with Adults in Transition

## Overview

There are three primary groups of adults seeking employment: adults reentering the workforce, which includes homemakers and veterans; welfare to work adults; and adults experiencing job loss (Bobek et al., 2013). This last category is the one wherein Walt finds himself. Bobek, Hanson, and Robbins (2013) summarize the issues facing adults looking to change careers: "organizational downsizing, rightsizing, outsourcing, fluctuating markets, advances in technology, changes in opportunity structures, and increased job skill demands" (p. 655). They also note that across demographic characteristics of adults in transition, three common traits are shared among these groups. They include, a) "conducting a realistic self-appraisal of existing skills, (b) recognizing the need for career adaptability, and (c) dealing with the psychological effects related to financial difficulties and job uncertainty" (p. 661). These challenges can result in physical and psychological stress and distress, making it all the more important that counselors view CFC from a holistic perspective.

## Challenges to and Opportunities for Career Development

In working with a client such as Walt, there are several considerations to highlight as we begin to address his concerns. First and foremost, career transitions offer opportunities for re-evaluating one's life. While a counselor would be ill-advised to celebrate this with a client like Walt prior to empathizing with him and hearing him out, this is important to keep in mind. Many times, our clients find themselves thrust into situations that force change, change that they may never have initiated on their own. Yet, these times of transition can usher in reflection on one's path, along with the potential to redirect the course of life. In session with Walt, this delicate balance might be approached in the following way:

Co: Walt, thanks for coming in today. Perhaps you could tell me what's on your mind today?

Cl: I've just been feeling down a lot lately. My wife insisted that I come in to talk about it with someone.

Co: So, you have felt down, and your wife has "encouraged" you to attend counseling. You may be having mixed feelings about being here then.

Cl: Well, I guess it couldn't hurt, but I don't really see how this is supposed to help.

Co: Help with what exactly? Being down? Or is there more?

Cl: Oh, there's more! I've been struggling with my job. I mean, I do fine with the work, and we make a comfortable living ... (pauses).

Co: Go on, if you're comfortable.

Cl: This is just not what I thought work and life were supposed to be!

Co: (nods silently)

Cl: I work in sales, and the world of sales has really changed over the past few decades. I've switched companies a couple of times—not something I ever thought I'd do—and I just feel empty at work.

Co: If I'm understanding you correctly, you entered the field with certain expectations that have not been met.

Cl: (nods)

Co: And the pay-offs or rewards you thought would come with the work are less than you desired?

Cl: That's right. I've actually just been laid off from my

most recent position—I have not been able to bring myself to tell my wife, yet—and it has me questioning what the point of it all is.

Co: I'm so sorry to hear about your loss. That has to hit pretty hard!

<<remainder of session spent processing emotions associated with this bad news>>

... Continues next session ...

Co: Walt, I wanted to pick up a thread from our talk last time. You mentioned your disillusionment with the way your life, and work life specifically, was headed.

Cl: Yes.

Co: What would it be like if this was the nudge you needed to reevaluate some things in your life and to explore other options for yourself?

Cl: I don't know. What do you mean?

Co: Well, you've described your expectations for work, how they were not met, and how you have felt stuck for some time. Yet, you remained in that rut, if you will. Now your current circumstances have forced you to make some kind of change.

Cl: They certainly have!

Co: And while this is not what you would have chosen, I wonder if there is a way we could leverage this to create new opportunities along a different path—one of your own choosing, but building on the wisdom you've gained over the years in the world of work.

Cl: That sounds good, but I have a mortgage, a family, two kids getting ready for

As you read this, you may recall how it felt to be told you were too young or inexperienced to be considered for a job. This occurs quite often for high school students and young adults. Well, the inverse can be true for adult in transitions, except that, instead, they can be considered overqualified and/or too old. To be overqualified is to be perceived as expecting more compensation for the work than the position pays. It also means that job satisfaction will be low for an over-qualified individual, and they will be unlikely to remain in the position for long, or they will struggle to accept supervision from a younger, less-experienced supervisor. Adults in transition may also be perceived as less able to be flexible in the workplace and to keep up with current trends; instead, they may be viewed as "set in their ways." In the first instance, over-qualification may be a legitimate reason for not hiring an adult. However, the second instance is age discrimination and is legally protected. The Age Discrimination in Employment Act of 1967 (ADEA) offers legal protection for adults 40 years of age and older from discrimination on the basis of age. You may want to read more about this law at the following webpage:

The Age Discrimination in Employment Act of 1967 (ADEA)

It is vital, however, for counselors to be aware that just because a law exists, clients can still be victims of workplace discrimination—both real and perceived. Clients like Walt, who perceive that they have been passed over for promotions related to their age, need to understand their rights under the law. While CFC does not offer legal consultation, which would be outside our scope of practice, we can provide clients with resources as they explore options for self-advocacy. In addition, counselors assist clients in processing these negative experience as they look to rebuild a path to future success.

## CFC Interventions

Despite its ubiquity in modern society, job loss and its effects on individuals and their families are remarkably understudied (Thompson, Dahling, & Chin, & Melloy, 2016). When thinking of what clients like Walt need during these times, empathy is the logical first step. Walt has experience in identifying a career and exploring work, but is at a very different developmental stage than those starting out in a career. In addition, the trauma of job loss hits individuals in unique ways, yet the effects can have common characteristics. For example, Walt has had success in his career and while he has had to change companies to continue climbing the ladder, he has attained an enviable level. However, at this point in his transition, he is facing the bottom rung of the ladder again if he chooses a new direction; if he continues his current direction, he faces the same changes in a new context. He may face symptoms of anxiety, depression, continued low life satisfaction, and the like (Paul & Moser, 2009). Understanding the differences in the challenges Walt faces, contrasted with those of a new college graduate, will help support the relationship between Walt and the counselor.

Any intervention will need to take into account the complicating factors associated with job loss as described above. Walt needs more than just a job. He may need a new career, but he also needs the support of those around him. One way to accomplish this may include a number of family sessions in which the family attends counseling with Walt and learns from him. In addition, he can see how this loss and transition has affected his family. They may serve as mutual support for one another. A caveat to this involves any shame or self-doubt that accompany this loss; he may struggle initially to participate this way. Another way of offering both social support and career resources is Web resources like www.ilostmyjob.com. These types of sites offer empathic understanding and community support through information and resources targeted to the experience of adults in transition due to job loss. Exploring sites like these in session will empower Walt and his family to communicate about the collateral challenges associated with job transitions. It also reminds the counselor that the counselor is not responsible for getting Walt another job or convincing him to do anything.

college, and retirement to think of.

Co: You're right. You have a lot to consider. And, we know that you can pick back up on the rut-path at any time.

Cl: Yeah, but that's not the life I want!

Co: So you're weighing the risks and benefits of making a change or staying where you are. That sounds like a good starting place for our work together. What do you think?

Cl: I'd like to work that through.

## Opening Vignette

Damian is a 28-year-old military veteran who was honorably discharged from the United States Army 6 months ago. He served for 10 years, having enlisted during his senior year of high school. After several stateside posts at various bases around the country, Damian was deployed to Afghanistan for the last 3 years of his service. While he was never involved in any offensive maneuvers, he was a scout who regularly patrolled war-torn streets and neighborhoods, attempting to "keep the peace." He was never wounded in action but saw a number of fellow soldiers become wounded, and many of those became disabled as a result of their work there. As a private, first-class, the majority of his training was combat-related. He shares in session that he had hoped to received advanced training and education, but as he sits with you, frustrated about his state of unemployment, he adds that he feels ill-equipped to find and obtain gainful employment.

# CFC with Veterans

## Overview

Servicemen and women provide the nation with a sense of security and safety, peace in times of upheaval. Ironically, that service to the nation has costs for many enlisted personnel while directly serving, as well as after their service. The concerns facing veterans reentering the workforce include "culture shock, identifying transferable skills, lack of job preparation and job search skills, and financial concerns" (Bobek et al., 2013, p. 658; Simpson & Armstrong, 2009). There are myriad challenges to reintegration into civilian life, and career-related issues are just a component of that complex of tasks. At the same time, these veterans have a wealth of knowledge, skills, and experiences that can facilitate their successful transition. These transitions take place in a world where the battles are fought with different strategies, tactics, and even weapons, so even the most skilled can feel unprepared and overwhelmed. Like many veterans, Damian is experiencing a very common, and distressing, re-entry process. In this section, we look more closely at those challenges and identify strategies for supporting the work of career development with these keepers of the peace.

## Challenges to and Opportunities for Career Development

*Not understanding the world of work as it exists outside of military culture and structure.* Many of those enlisted personnel who find success or a home in the military are either drawn to or become acclimated to the military culture. This includes a clear chain of command, rigid rules and structure and often swift consequences for noncompliance. These individuals have become highly proficient in these environments, drawing satisfaction from attention to detail. During the transition back to civilian life, many veterans find the world of work to be the opposite: ambiguous rules and leadership, unclear expectations, and capricious maintenance of standards (Killam, Weber, Michael, & Luke, 2016). This represents hardships that most civilians will never confront (though it is very true that these work environments cause others stress, as well).

*Not feeling understood by the civilian population, as well as being viewed with mixed emotions by the populace.* It is an unfortunate reality that stereotypes of military veterans pervade society's collective unconscious. Popular press and media present many veterans as unstable, raging killers, most of whom have post-traumatic stress disorder (PTSD). This is unfortunate for many reasons, not the least of which is that this inaccurate portrayal leads civilians to view veterans with an unhealthy level of skepticism. The majority of veterans transition back to civilian life and are productive members of society. Adding to the complicated picture of veterans is the pop psychology notion of PTSD. It is important for counselors to know and actively inform others that PTSD is not something you pick up from military service. It is a complex diagnosis and one not lightly assigned. For example, the lifetime prevalence of PTSD in the general population is between 6.8–7.8 percent. In one study of Gulf War Veterans, the prevalence of PTSD was estimated to be 10.1%, while the prevalence of those serving in Operation Enduring Freedom and Operation Iraqi Freedom was 13.8%. Granted, these are high rates—almost double the general population—but not a rate that represents a specific threat to others. In fact, a common feature of PTSD is depression and anxiety, yet the popular narrative is of the angry combat veteran looking to pick fights with co-workers. Now imagine that you are the veteran in the room, coping with all the transitions in your life, while trying not to read into the looks from others who wonder if you are a Rambo waiting to explode. Luke and Michael (2016) identify myths about veterans that counselors need to attend to in their work with this population:

- All military personnel are angry and aggressive—they have to be—and therefore so are veterans.
- All veterans have PTSD and are therefore likely to 'go off' at work.
- All veterans have trouble reintegrating back into civilian life and therefore back into the workplace.
- The skills needed to be successful in the military are vastly different than the skills needed to succeed as a civilian employee.
- All veterans are 'high maintenance' in that they have a lot of physical and mental health issues to contend with.
- You can be successful without good people skills.
- There is a perfect job waiting out there for you.
- Working hard and keeping your nose clean will guarantee success. (p. 228)

*Finding a sense of identity—individual and vocational—outside of the military.* Many enlisted personnel entered the military right after high school and, therefore, had limited opportunities to continue their education (Killam, Weber, Michael, & Luke, 2016). The period of emerging adulthood (18–29 years of age) is a critical time for identity and career development. Consistent with the developmental upheaval of this time period, veterans between the ages of 18–24 have the highest rates of unemployment (Boutin, 2011), in some cases approaching triple the national average (Robertson & Brott, 2013). The military and, at times, unemployment becomes the context in which these developmental tasks are approached.

*Degree of concomitant stress and distress that accompany both transition from military to civilian life and the impact of their experiences in the military.* While it is imprudent to stereotype veterans and their experiences, it is prudent to assess for complicating factors when engaged in CFC. Veterans do struggle with transition to civilian life, and this can result in stress, depression, anxiety, financial problems, homelessness, and disability—visible or invisible. Two additional complicating factors include combat veterans and veterans with disabilities (Clemens & Milsom, 2008).

# CFC Interventions

Keim and Day (2016) describe an intervention designed to help veterans address issues of transferring military skill development to the civilian world of work:

**Activity Directions**

1 Ask the clients to briefly list the types of training, leadership experiences, and skills they developed while in the military on a piece of paper.

2 Explain that you are going to do an activity together to help them better understand how employers understand these skills and what terms they use for the same experiences.

3 State for the client: *If you think of developing your career like building a house, you already have a strong foundation of training that prepared you for your military occupation. The framework of that house was built with skills and experiences that are particular to military service, and therefore you use military terms to describe what you did. Let's use these sticks to represent the frame of the house—its walls, supports, and roof. Label each of the main skills that you demonstrated in your military position on one side of each stick.*

4 When this part of the activity is completed, assist the client to identify similar terms used in the civilian world to describe the experience or skill set described on each of the sticks.

5 The client would then label the stick on the opposite side with the civilian term. Putting these together by taping them to a piece of paper in the shape of a house, the client can then see how he or she has "reframed" the career house that the client has already made on his or her own life. The client can then see it literally from the employer's perspective as well.

6 These new terms for military skills and experiences can be used to assist the client to develop a resume that fits a civilian job expectations and descriptions. (p. 235, italics in original)

# CFC with Clients with Disabilities

## Overview

A concept introduced in an earlier chapter is a concept I have used in other writings (see Luke, Redekop, & Moralejo, in press): projective sympathy. It is the orientation of this chapter that the layers of oppression and marginalization that differently abled individuals face begin with projective sympathy. Consider the following application of this phenomenon to the case of Alexa. Alexa has cerebral palsy (CP), a congenital or acquired neuro-muscular disorder that results in difficulties related to movement and coordination affecting gross and fine motor movements (www.cerebralpalsy.org). For Alexa, this means that, while she is ambulatory, her gait is askew; she has a visible limp, and she walks quite slowly. When she sits down, her leg muscles spasm, causing some visible muscle tremors. She is in almost constant pain, resulting in the need for her to shift sitting positions often. One factor that often goes unnoticed is her ability to function at quite a high level given her pain and speed. For her, success is defined a little differently than for those who do not have CP, in terms of pain management, ambulation, and so forth. Yet, Alexa has fairly clear career goals—she wants to be social worker.

As you read this description you may have an initial experience that is common for counselors and people in general: You may wonder what Alexa's subjective experience of having CP is, but then you may wonder what it would be like for you in her situation. You imagine how you would feel in her situation; this is sympathy. As you, consciously in some cases, unconsciously in others, reflect on what this experience might be like for you, the tendency of many is to then transfer the feelings back onto Alexa (projection) as if this is how Alexa feels. You then begin to respond, or not, to her as if her experience of CP is what yours would be if you were her (projective sympathy). Whether or not you agree that this is something you would fall prey to (despite the growing body of neuroscientific research demonstrating its almost

### Opening Vignette: Alexa, 21, with a disability

*Returning to an earlier case, Alexa, imagine that she informs you that she has cerebral palsy. Consider how this would (or would not) alter your recommendations as you read the introductory material to this section and reflect on the vignette.*

Alexa is a 21-year-old college student working in a local restaurant who comes to you for career counseling. She tells you that she switched from a major in special education to one in exercise science. After some inquiry, you learn that she initially chose special education, because a family member did that, and she then chose exercise science, because she ran cross-country all 4 years of high school. When asked what she wants to deal with in counseling, Alexa says, "Stress. Thinking about getting a job after graduation has been making me worry." She goes on to tell you that she switched out of special education after her first semester taking upper-division classes in her major. Alexa says that she wasn't sure if she wanted to teach, because she would "get too attached to the kids." She reports similar concerns with an exercise science job like gym teacher. She questions whether she wants to teach at all. Wiping away tears, Alexa discloses that she feels like she has been "trying to fill some kind of void inside" by finding a meaningful job in which she can help people but to a greater extent that her restaurant server job.

universality), imagine how this could complicate the working relationship—in counseling, as well as in the workplace.

Now imagine that I am the counselor working with Alexa, and I have unwittingly engaged in projective sympathy. Pause and consider why this could severely limit the working relationship, first, in terms of why projective sympathy is inappropriate and, then, in terms of the behaviors evoked in me from this process.

*Reasons this is ineffective.* The first reason that projective sympathy is an ineffective strategy for understanding Alexa is, most readily apparent, I am not her. Alexa's experiences are her own, and pain in particular, is incredibly subjective. Another reason is that, not having lived with a condition like CP for an extended period of time, I have not had the opportunity to acclimate to the pain and physical realities of it. This means that I do not have the experience of dealing with the things that Alexa has, wherein she has built in competence and awareness of the boundaries of her competence in various daily domains. Thirdly, this lack of experience with CP also means that I have not had to live with the "looks" from others, in addition to behavioral, social, emotional, and other responses from others: looks of pity, comments belying assumed incompetence, attributions of courage for living this way, limited (or pity-based) social invitations due to the discomfort of others, and on and on. These reasons, along with many others (as I do not have CP) have shaped Alexa's view of herself and her way of being in the world. Her individual identity and vocational identity are intricately interwoven.

*Behaviors.* Now, consider how I might treat Alexa in the presence of projective sympathy. I might begin by going out of my way to accommodate her in the office, signaling my belief about her capabilities. This type of statement must be balanced with the requirement to be sensitive to individuals—all individuals—so it is equally unwise to act as if there is nothing different. (This is, perhaps, the disability equivalent of "colorblindness" with White perspectives of African Americans.) Alexa does have CP, and this does affect her movement and sitting position, so acting as if it is not part of her experience is equally limiting in effective CFC. In addition, I might begin to circumscribe (Gottfredson, 1981; 2005) career options on Alexa's behalf, rather than listening for her own perspectives. Here again, I may react by overcompensating, acting as if there are no limits. I might also overcompensate for her perception of limits by becoming her cheerleader.

As severe as the above discussion may seem, disability evokes powerful reactions from people, including counselors. Even the term *disability* if rife with cultural baggage. It is unfortunate that, in all of career services, we advocate for clients putting their best foot forward, but for some among us, that "foot" is a *dis*, typically without the individuals consent, depending upon whether the disability is hidden or visible (we take up this discussion further below).

# Challenges to and Opportunities for Career Development

1 Federal policy regarding disability benefits and access to health insurance

Persons with disabilities often find themselves in a double-bind, wherein their status as disabled, and the benefits to which they are entitled, are placed in jeopardy when they attempt to work. Working part-time and the income it generates, for example, may disqualify an individual from receiving aid in the form of health insurance. In these cases, working and the subsequent loss of benefits, becomes a disincentive. Part-time employment rarely comes with benefits. Even full-time employment for many either does not include health insurance or is so cost prohibitive that "living on disability" becomes the only viable option for many. The resulting ambivalence toward employment, along with the loss of satisfaction that accompanies gainful employment, increase the complexity of CFC.

2 Employer attitudes and discrimination

Laws do not change attitudes, and attitudes lead to behaviors (Ajzen & Fishbein, 1977). In addition, not all disability is perceived the same way. Some are more stigmatized than others (Fabian & Pedani, 2013). There are differences in perceptions and reactions—covert and explicit—to disabilities that are congenital and those that are acquired, those perceived as communicable or contagious, and those seen as "legitimate" and those that are not. Discrimination based on disability, much like sexual harassment, perhaps, can be subjective and result in recrimination as a result of self-advocacy. Discrimination is wrong—illegal—but present, and even the possibility that it could happen can cast a pall over an individual's experience of the world of work. It is a form of privilege for those of us without a protected disability that our competence as a prospective employee will not be questioned as a result of the way we walk into the office (from a disability) or other condition that exists independent of my skills.

3 Lack of adequate preparation for the workplace

Depending upon the salience of a disability in a person's lived experience, preparation for the world of work may have been placed on low priority. Fabian and Pebdani (2013) identify from the literature the likely impact: "(a) limitations in early career exploratory experiences, (b) limited opportunities to develop decision-making abilities, and (c) poorer vocational well-being (Loprest & Maag, 2007; Moore, Konrad, Yang, & Ng, Doherty, 2011)" (p. 363).

4 Professional attitudes toward employment

Systemic oppression continues to challenge access to training and career options for individuals with disabilities. For many employers employing individuals needing extensive workplace accommodations (circumscribed in the ADA, 1990), these can be disincentives to employing certain candidates. Often, too, the question for these candidates moves from "what do you want to do?" to "what *can* you do?," a questions these individuals may have regularly asked themselves. Career-focused counselors encounter clients under these conditions, wherein employment issues may be less about any challenge their disability creates in performing the work, and more about navigating institutional attitudes and behaviors toward their disability (Fabian & Pebdani, 2013).

**Table 9.1. Summary of Legislation and Resources Related to Persons with Disability**

| Name | Description |
|---|---|
| **Sections 501 and 505 of the Rehabilitation Act of 1973** | "This law makes it illegal to discriminate against a qualified person with a disability in the federal government. The law also makes it illegal to retaliate against a person because the person complained about discrimination, filed a charge of discrimination, or participated in an employment discrimination investigation or lawsuit. The law also requires that employers reasonably accommodate the known physical or mental limitations of an otherwise qualified individual with a disability who is an applicant or employee, unless doing so would impose an undue hardship on the operation of the employer's business" (US EEOC; https://www.eeoc.gov/laws/statutes/) |
| **Title I, American with Disabilities Act (ADA) of 1990** | "This law makes it illegal to discriminate against a qualified person with a disability in the private sector and in state and local governments. The law also makes it illegal to retaliate against a person because the person complained about discrimination, filed a charge of discrimination, or participated in an employment discrimination investigation or lawsuit. The law also requires that employers reasonably accommodate the known physical or mental limitations of an otherwise qualified individual with a disability who is an applicant or employee, unless doing so would impose an undue hardship on the operation of the employer's business." https://www.eeoc.gov/laws/statutes/index.cfm) |
| **The Genetic Information Nondiscrimination Act of 2008 (GINA)** | "This law makes it illegal to discriminate against employees or applicants because of genetic information. Genetic information includes information about an individual's genetic tests and the genetic tests of an individual's family members, as well as information about any disease, disorder or condition of an individual's family members (i.e. an individual's family medical history). The law also makes it illegal to retaliate against a person because the person complained about discrimination, filed a charge of discrimination, or participated in an employment discrimination investigation or lawsuit" (US EEOC; https://www.eeoc.gov/laws/types/genetic.cfm) |

# CFC Interventions

There are several considerations for counselors engaged in CFC with Alexa. As you review them, reflect on which one represents the greatest challenge for you in thinking about clients with disabilities.

1. Alexa's career development issues are just like everyone else's in terms of stages of development; they just present in the context of CP. Her dreams and goals are somehow reduced; there is no intrinsic dream-mitigation system that helps her aim lower "because of her condition." She is just as susceptible to dysfunctional career thoughts as anyone else. She does not has special compensatory powers that, though she struggles to walk, she does not have heightened senses.
2. She may or may not have career goals beyond "helping people like me."
3. She desires to be human first.
4. She appreciates recognition through modification in the workplace that sitting still in an office chair at a desk for 8–10 hours a day will not work as well for her as it might for others.
5. She does not want your pity; nor does she want your congratulations for accomplishing basic tasks (e.g., "you did great sitting in that meeting").

Keep in mind the importance of using Person-First Language—use language of individuals, not a characteristic that limits their essential being. In other words, "View disability as a characteristic, not an essential personal attribute, that might need to be considered in understanding career issues and designing interventions" (Fabian & Pebdani, 2013, p. 377). As with all individuals, it is imperative that the counselor seek a greater understanding of the client's experience of the world.

## Neuro-Informed CFC

Trauma is an area of counseling with which most counselors will work, whether clients explicitly describe a traumatic event or not. The client risk factors described in this chapter represent a continuum of trauma, from everyday microaggressions toward individuals with disabilities to combat-related trauma, with job transitions falling somewhere between the two. Neuro-informed counseling speaks clearly to trauma in the brain and its relevance to CFC. It should first be noted that the experience of trauma is both individual in nature, but it also has universal attributes. It is individual in that trauma is often based on perception. For example, while 25% of combat veterans will develop PTSD (compared with rates in the general), 75% will not. While the numbers are staggering and represent a crisis in the U.S., a large number of individuals who are present for an event will not experience it in ways that result in trauma. One neural mechanism of trauma is the almost indelible neural-based impression it makes. Bessel van der Kolk, a leading researcher in the neuroscience of trauma, explains it this way:

> Immediately after a traumatic event, almost all people suffer from intrusive thoughts about what has happened ... These intrusions help them either to learn from the experience and plan for restorative actions (accommodation), or to gradually accept what has happened and readjust their expectations (assimilation) ... One way or another, the passage of time modifies the ways in which the brain processes the trauma-related information. Either it is integrated in memory and stored as an unfortunate event belonging to the past, or the sensations and emotions belonging to the event start leading a life of their own, When a person develops PTSD, the replaying of the trauma leads to sensitization; with every replay of the traumatic event, which started out as a social and interpersonal process, comes to have secondary biological consequences that are hard to reverse once they become entrenched. (2012, p. 8)

This is the point at which neuroscience collides with CFC. Clients who may appear resistant or reluctant to move forward in career-related behaviors, may actually be paralyzed by trauma. It is as if the brain has figuratively limited motor movement to protect the individual from inadvertently walking off the cliff of trauma again. Unless and until the brain's protective mechanisms have been unlocked, the individual may remain intractable.

# Summary

There is an ever-present danger in identifying any specific group to use as an example of increased risk in society, be they adults in transition, veterans, or persons with disabilities. Individuals vary in their social and vocational needs, so counselors must seek to be sensitive to these variations from person to person. For example, one client in CFC may seek to feel understood regarding their struggle as a person with a disability or as a veteran. At the same time, the very next client may desire to be viewed as absent these particular characteristics. The challenge for counselors is not to apply one lens to all clients. It is to learn to individualize their approach to their clients as they seek to learn about the needs of the client in front of them.

# References

Ajzen, I., & Fishbein, M. (1977). Attitude-behavior relations: A theoretical analysis and review of empirical research. *Psychological bulletin*, *84*(5), 888.

Anderson, M., Goodman, J., & Schlossberg, N. K. (2011). *Counseling adults in transition: Linking Schlossberg's theory with practice in a diverse world*. New York, NY: Springer Publishing Company.

Bobek, B. L., Hanson, M. A., & Robbins, S. B. (2013). Counseling adults for career transitions. In S. D. Brown and R. W. Lent (Eds.) *Career development and counseling: Putting theory and research to work* (2nd ed.) (pp. 653–682). Hoboken, NJ: Wiley.

Boutin, D. L. (2011). Effective vocational rehabilitation services for military veterans. *Journal of Applied Rehabilitation Counseling, 42*(2), 24.

Bullock, E. E., Braud, J., Andrews, L., & Phillips, J. (2009). career concerns of unemployed us war veterans: suggestions from a cognitive information processing approach. *Journal of Employment Counseling, 46*(4), 171–181.

Clemens, E. V., & Milsom, A. S. (2008). Enlisted service members' transition into the civilian world of work: A cognitive information processing approach. *The Career Development Quarterly, 56*(3), 246–256.

Cornish, M. A., Thys, A., Vogel, D. L., & Wade, N. G. (2014). Post-deployment difficulties and help seeking barriers among military veterans: Insights and intervention strategies. *Professional Psychology: Research and Practice, 45*(6), 405.

Fabian, E. S., & Pebdani, R. (2013). The career development of youth and young adults with disabilities. In S. D. Brown and R. W. Lent (Eds.) *Career development and counseling: Putting theory and research to work* (2nd ed.) (pp. 357–384). Hoboken, NJ: Wiley.

Gottfredson, L. S. (1981). Circumscription and compromise: A developmental theory of occupational aspirations. *Journal of Counseling psychology, 28*(6), 545.

Gottfredson, L. S. (2005). Using Gottfredson's theory of circumscription and compromise in career guidance and counseling. *Career development and counseling: Putting theory and research to work,* 71–100.

Krumboltz, J. D., & Chan, A. (2005). Professional issues in vocational psychology. *Handbook of vocational psychology, 3,* 347–370.

Killam, Weber, Michael, & Luke (2016). Veterans. In W. K Killam, S. Degges-White, & R. E. Michel, (Eds.), *Career counseling interventions: Practice with diverse clients* (pp. 73–77). New York, NY: Springer Publishing Company.

Loprest, P., & Maag, E. (2007). The relationship between early disability onset and education and employment. *Journal of Vocational Rehabilitation, 26*(1), 49–62.

Luke and Michael (2016). Interventions for veterans. In W. K Killam, S. Degges-White, & R. E. Michel, (Eds.), *Career counseling interventions: Practice with diverse clients* (pp. 225–239). New York, NY: Springer Publishing Company.

Moore, M. E., Konrad, A. M., Yang, Y., Ng, E. S., & Doherty, A. J. (2011). The vocational well-being of workers with childhood onset of disability: Life satisfaction and perceived workplace discrimination. *Journal of Vocational Behavior, 79*(3), 681–698.

McAllister, C. P., Mackey, J. D., Hackney, K. J., & Perrewé, P. L. (2015). From combat to khakis: An exploratory examination of job stress with veterans. *Military Psychology, 27*(2), 93–107.

Paul, K. I., & Moser, K. (2009). Unemployment impairs mental health. *Journal of Vocational Behavior, 74,* 264–282. doi:10.1016/j.jvb.2009.01.001

Robertson, H. C., & Brott, P. E. (2013). Male veterans' perceptions of midlife career transition and life satisfaction: A study of military men transitioning to the teaching profession. *Adultspan Journal, 12*(2), 66–79.

Robertson, H. C. (2013). Income and support during transition from a military to civilian career. *Journal of Employment Counseling, 50*(1), 26–33.

Simpson, A., & Armstrong, S. (2009). From the military to the civilian work force: Addressing veteran career development concerns. *Career Planning & Adult Development Journal, 25*(1).

Tanielian, T. & Jaycox, L. (Eds.). (2008). *Invisible Wounds of War: Psychological and Cognitive Injuries, Their Consequences, and Services to Assist Recovery.* Santa Monica, CA: RAND Corporation. Retrieved from http://www.ptsd.va.gov/professional/PTSD-overview/epidemiological-facts-ptsd.asp

Thompson, M. N., Dahling, J. J., Chin, M. Y., & Melloy, R. C. (2017). Integrating job loss, unemployment, and reemployment with Social Cognitive Career Theory. *Journal of Career Assessment, 25*(1), 40–57.

Van der Kolk, B. A., & McFarlane, A. C. (Eds.). (2007). *Traumatic stress: The effects of overwhelming experience on mind, body, and society*. New York, NY: Guilford Press.

Yamamoto, S. H., & Alverson, C. Y. (2016). Individuals With Disabilities in Self-Employment Through Vocational Rehabilitation Predictors of Successful Case Closure From 2008 to 2012. *Journal of Career Assessment*, 25(3), pp. 450–466.

# CHAPTER TEN

# Career and Mental Health Disorders

**Chapter Goals**

- To identify the intersections of career issues and mental health
- To explore four primary categories of mental health issues likely to emerge in career-focused counseling (CFC)
- To appreciate the reciprocal impact of career and mental health
- To apply a developmental, wellness-based philosophy to career and mental health

## Introduction

This text is primarily about CFC, so it may initially seem a bit odd to find a whole chapter about mental health. The simplest reason for this is that mental health issues pervade many cultures, and their combined impact exacts a heavy toll in the domain of work, both in terms of work hours lost, under- and unemployment, and medical bills. Besides the intuitive validity of this notion, there is growing empirical support for this, as well (Heppner, O'Brien, Hinkelman, & Flores, 1996; Pace & Quinn, 2000; Robitschek & DeBell, 2002). In addition, career-related issues can take their toll on the mental health of employees and job seekers (Anderson & Niles, 1995; Swanson, 2002). Therefore, this chapter drills down into this relationship by exploring four main diagnostic categories of mental health: anxiety, depression, stress and trauma, and addiction.

**Reintegrating Career and Mental Health.** Statistically speaking, counselors, whether in the community or schools, have a high likelihood of encountering clients and students who have directly or indirectly experienced anxiety, depression, trauma and stress-related, and substance use disorders, according to the Diagnostic and Statistical Manual of Disorders (DSM-5; APA, 2013). To facilitate making connections between career and mental health issues, Table 10.1 includes a breakdown of the categories of mental health issues discussed in this chapter and their impact on career-related dynamics. This table is meant to be a guide only in thinking about the intersections of mental health on career; it is in no way a comprehensive description. It is also important to note that counselors, while aware of risk factors, also proactively explore protective factors that work can provide for mental health issues. Counselors are wise, however, not to jump straight to discussions of protective factors before making clients feel heard and understood.

**Table 10.1. Potential Impacts of Mental Health on Career-Related Domains**

| | Work Performance | Career Decision-Making | Job Satisfaction | Protective Factors |
|---|---|---|---|---|
| **Anxiety Related Disorders** | Hypervigilance leading to fatigue and irritability | Avoidance, leading to premature commitment or delayed choice | Anxiety diminishes satisfaction in numerous life domains; career is a prime example | Work provides a creative outlet to relieve stress, increase sense of purpose and meaning, focus attention, inoculate against external, personal stressors, provides opportunities for structure, productivity, short and long-term rewards |
| **Mood Related Disorders** | Decreased concentration, leading to limited attention to detail | Passivity, past orientation, impacting future planning | Depression limits perspective for deriving satisfaction from work | |
| **Stress and Trauma Related Disorders** | Reactivity and distractedness leading to mistakes, errors | Chronic and acute stress similarly impact critical thinking and problem solving capacities | As performance and engagement decrease, so does satisfaction | |
| **Addictions** | Besides on-site inebriation, lethargy, and paranoia, hang-overs and lateness | Long-term planning often gives way to short-term behaviors and making up for past behaviors | Work becomes a means to an end, and often as a last resort | |

In approaching the topic of career and mental health issues, students and new practitioners (seasoned ones, too!) often wrestle with which issue to address first, to address one and not the other, or to try to address both concurrently. Anderson and Niles offer guidance that will guide the discussion throughout this chapter,

> Although some career counseling theorists suggest that noncareer issues must be resolved before counseling for career decision making (e.g., Brown & Brooks, 1991),

> the findings of this study suggest that clients often choose to address both career and noncareer concerns throughout counseling. (1995, p. 244)

Anderson and Niles' study and quote highlight the reason for this book and this chapter, in particular: career *is* personal (Betz and Corning, 1993; Subich, 1993), and it is a component of mental health and school counseling. As you read this chapter, I invite you to reflect on Swanson's (2002) baseline assumptions as they provide a guiding compass in the (re)integration of career and mental health into *CFC*:

1 Clients who seek help for issues that are primarily career related are similar on a number of relevant dimensions (e.g., psychological distress) to clients who seek help for other issues.

2 Counseling sessions for clients who seek counseling for primarily career related issues also contain noncareer content, and counseling sessions for clients who seek counseling for noncareer issues also contain career content.

3 Counseling primarily focused on career issues is more effective if salient noncareer issues also are addressed. Similarly, counseling primarily focused on noncareer issues is more effective if salient contextual career issues also are addressed.

4 Counselor and client in-session behaviors are fundamentally similar regardless of whether clients seek help for primary career issues or for noncareer issues (or, more broadly, whether the content of counseling sessions is career or noncareer in nature).

5 The nature and course of therapeutic change is similar regardless of the client's presenting issues.

6 The process of supervision is similar regardless of whether the counselor is delivering counseling that is primarily career or noncareer in nature. (p. 818)

In January 2016, the Career Planning and Adult Development (CPAD) journal published a special issue on the relationship between career and mental health. This was done for a very practical reason: career and mental health issues, respectively, pervade one another. As you read this chapter and continue to reflect on your own career development, try to imagine a career-related issue that does intersect with mental health. As I write this, I expect there will be immediate exceptions that come to mind, so I will attempt to circumscribe the question in order to clarify: Counselors approach client issues from a wellness-based, developmental perspective as described in Chapter 1. In the current context, development involves an ongoing process of growth and change, which, in turn, involves identifying and overcoming natural (and unnatural) barriers and challenges. Counselors facilitate this process by working to unlock the inherent potential in individuals and guide them to resources to accommodate areas of weakness. Career development is simply another domain of development that counselors facilitate. Because of that, every career issue is a developmental issue, and every developmental issue is an opportunity to benefit from counseling. Keep this in mind as you ask yourself the opening questions again.

# Neuro-Informed CFC

The field of neuroscience has continued to increase in its influence on related fields—and counseling is no exception. Monthly, new articles on the integration and application of neuroscience to counseling appear. Currently, however, there is little effort directed at the role of the integration of neuroscience into counseling applied to CFC. While this presents a great opportunity to think and write and work in this area, it also means that there is little direct work to lean on. Instead, I offer extrapolations from existing work in related areas. In order to set the context for applying neuroscience integration to career-related issues, it is important to review the types of work that are ongoing.

In the first instance, Interpersonal Neurobiology (Siegel, 2006; Siegel, 2012) is a specific theoretical orientation and treatment modality based on the ways neurobiology inform our understanding of early relationships and their impact on later functioning (or dysfunction) (Luke & Michael, 2016). This theory offers great promise in applying neurobiological findings to the work counselors perform (e.g., Badenoch, 2008). Siegel offers three foundational principles for understanding interpersonal neurobiology:

> 1) A core aspect of the human mind is an embodied and relational process that regulates the flow of energy and information within the brain and between brains; 2) … the mind is a process that emerges from the distributed nervous system extending throughout the entire body, and also from the communication patterns that occur within relationships; 3) The structure and function of the developing brain are determined by how experiences, especially within interpersonal relationships, shape the genetically programmed maturation of the nervous system. (Siegel, 2012, p. 3)

A second, preeminent empirical approach is one articulated by Sarah Feldstein Ewing, called simply the translational approach to understanding the mechanisms of psychosocial interventions on mental health issues (Feldstein Ewing & Chung, 2013; Feldstein Ewing et al., 2011; Feldstein Ewing et al., 2013). Feldstein Ewing's work has focused on exploring and understanding the neurological mechanisms that underlie psychosocial interventions, specifically for addictions. In other words, the translational model seeks to explain what is happening in the brain when psychosocial interventions (like Motivational Interviewing) are implemented, and where these processes are taking place in the brain.

The two approaches described above represent, to a certain extent, two ends of the empirical integration continuum. Feldstein Ewing's work represents a highly empirical approach that moves closely with the laboratory data. Siegel's work, while immensely popular and practical in many ways, can be seen as moving closer to the philosophical, even while orienting itself toward the neuroscience of relationships. Somewhere in between these two bookends, is a middle approach, first articulated by Luke (2015); this perspective seek to bridge the above continuum by offering additional options for counselors without an extensive training in neuroscientist (Feldstein Ewing is indeed a neuroscientist; Siegel is a clinical psychiatrist and researcher).

The metaphoric-analogical approach (Luke & Michael, 2016) to neuroscience integration takes the information gleaned from the current understanding of the brain and central nervous system and offers numerous metaphors for human behavior. This approach is quite practical in that it offers clinicians another tool for communicating with clients about their presenting issue, without, perhaps paradoxically, adding unnecessary complexity. For example, humans see with their brains, not with their eyes (Luke, 2015). This is true in that the electrical stimuli received by the eye is essentially meaningless until those stimuli travel down the optic nerve and into the occipital lobe of the brain where it is processed. This is an incredibly complex process, the details of which are unnecessary for making the point with clients: what they see in others and in the world is a mere interpretation of how their brain is making meaning of those things. The visual system, therefore, becomes a metaphor for how we often misinterpret environmental cues.

This approach to integration also helps to explicate the neurological mechanisms of thoughts, feelings, behaviors, and relationships, which provides clients with an explanation of sorts regarding their experiences. This approach demystifies experience by offering a plausible explanation for previously inexplicable experiences. For example, for clients who struggle with behavior change, Hebb's rule (Hebb, 1949)—captured at least in part by the slogan, "neurons that fire together wire together"—contains an explanation for why change is so difficult. Over time and repeated behavior, stronger neurons strengthen weaker ones that fire synchronously, increasing the likelihood that the weaker impulse will be strengthened and fire again. This reduces the judgment and character focus of clients who have struggled to change. While it does not exculpate them from owning their behavior, it can ease the emotional burden of failed attempts to change. These approaches are naturally limited and incomplete, reflecting the state of the "art" of neuroscience integration into counseling. However, these models will guide the discussion of neuroscience integration as relevant to CFC.

**Appreciating Diversity—Levels of Differences.** CFC draws upon the expertise of the counseling field to approach clients and students as individuals ... and individuals in context. There are well-documented differences in mental health and career issues among large diversity groups, including groups differentiated by race, gender, and sexual orientation (MacDonald, 1997). Counseling cannot be fully effective when these issues are minimized or unattended to. At the same time, each individual's experience of these social markers impacts how and to what extent they will contribute to career and mental health issues. It is often the interaction of factors that create the largest effect on a client's functioning (Slattery & Park, 2012). We also know that within group differences often exceed between-group differences (Pedersen et al., 2015). Additionally, challenges of a particular sub-group are subsumed under a larger social or other factor, such as socioeconomic status (Sue & Sue, 2003). This is especially true in CFC where poverty—driven by un- and under-employment, as well as downward pressure exerted by socio-political systems—create incredible—often virtually insurmountable—barriers to physical, mental, and vocational health and wellness (McAuliffe et al., 2008). As you read about mental health issues in this chapter, please keep these considerations in mind.

## CAREER AND ANXIETY DISORDERS

Whether you plan to work in a school, college, community center, or other location and whether you call yourself a guidance counselor, a clinical mental health counselor, or a career consultant, you will encounter anxiety in the individuals you serve. One of the challenges in this work is discerning the extent to which the anxiety you see or perceive is the result of the career issue you are addressing or the genesis of it. Unfortunately, you cannot necessarily try both at the same time.

The metatheoretical model (Luke, 2015), offers another approach to thinking about clients' presenting problems by honoring numerous theoretical frames, while also recognizing the contributions of relational, transtheoretical, common factors-based models and the growing literature on the efficacy of the relationship in effective outcomes (Freud, 1910/1961; Rogers, 1959; Lambert & Barley, 2001; Prochaska & Norcross, 2014). For example, anxiety is an abstract concept that describes several categories of phenomena; the metatheoretical approach serves to make this more concrete in considering treatment approaches. Furthermore, the ***Neuro-Informed, CFC*** box below contributes additional concretization of anxiety.

In order to address these domains effectively and accurately, a neurological understanding of anxiety is vital. While discussed in further detail below, a brief overview will lay a strong foundation. Anxiety, neurologically, is the brain's way of preparing the body to deal with existential threats (death) (Ledoux, 2003). Regardless of the source or interpretation of the stimulus, once the stimulus is processed by the limbic system as a threat, the sympathetic nervous system takes over. Biologically and genetically, the person may be predisposed to what occurs neurologically: the excitation of the sympathetic nervous system that stimulates physiological arousal. In terms of experience, anxiety can produce and be produced by experiences that trigger neural and physiological arousal in response to a perceived threat. To begin, anxiety is most certainly an affective experience. It is often described as butterflies in the belly, nervousness, feeling unsettled, or some fear of impending doom. Cognitively, anxiety is a confused state of uncertainty, difficulty finding direction, and impaired judgment. Behaviorally—and this is key for effective treatment—anxiety is the set of fight/flight/freeze actions that the behaviorists have long described as experiential avoidance (Wolpe, 1973). Anxiety can also result from the environmental triggers that signal some threat. Relationally, anxiety can certainly result from interpersonal interactions that indicate rejection or otherwise conditional acceptance. Lastly, the socio-cultural milieu can barrage the individual with messages of perceived threats. All of these factors interact to create both the vulnerability and floridity of anxiety. Regardless of whether the anxiety is a cause of career-related distress or results in it, there are markers that can assist counselors in intervening. And, this is the crucial point: recognizing the presence and role of anxiety in the client is a key to effectively treating them. This is true whether the client is seeking assistance for career decision-making anxiety or generalized anxiety that results in difficulties on the job.

To summarize, anxiety is the brain and body's response to a perceived threat. These perceptions are informed through the other domains. Therefore, an individual might enter counseling with an anxiety-priming experience, environment, biology, thought process, relational patterns, or socio-cultural milieu. These lead to, arguably, the most visible outcome of anxiety: behavior. The fight, flight, or freeze response that clients display upon entering therapy is a continuation of pre-entry patterns of behaving. Most notably, when anxious, humans avoid whatever is related to the anxiety (Hayes, Pistorello, & Levin, 2012). This avoidance takes many forms but, again, is most obvious through the ways in which people fight, flee, or freeze up in the face of anxiety. Here's how this looks in CFC.

# Recognizing Anxiety in CFC: Community Counseling

Donna is a 22-year-old female and recent college graduate with a degree in sociology. She makes an initial appointment for counseling to discuss career options and job search strategies. She is currently employed 30-plus hours per week at the same restaurant she worked at throughout college as a server. As you begin discussing areas of occupational interest with her, she becomes tearful and begins describing a history of social anxiety. In college, she became increasingly withdrawn from social activities and isolated herself because of her anxiety. She describes her friends as really outgoing and, as a result, were pairing up with romantic partners and having less time for her. Due in part to her anxiety about social situations, she describes a very passive approach to meeting people and building relationships. She got to where she only attended classes, arriving right as they started and leaving immediately after they ended. She states that, at least while she was in school, she had to be around people, but now that only comes through her job. She describes her work as surprisingly productive, as she is able to give excellent customer service, but that the social interaction drains her; after her shifts, she retreats to her apartment instead of going out with coworkers. As she continues, it also becomes apparent that she has a poor self-concept (low self-esteem to some). Despite making solid grades throughout high school and college, having a close set of friends in both settings, and being considered a valued employee, she describes chronic self-doubt, with periods of acute doubt. This combination has prevented her from following through on career-related information she heard from advisers, career professionals visiting her classes, and from her family as well. In fact, in spite of other supportive characteristics of her family, her inability to find a "sociology job" has validated their rhetorical, skeptical question throughout, "What are you going to do with a degree in sociology?" Donna is feeling a tremendous amount of pressure to find a job—and preferably a satisfying one—but has a lot of self-doubt and is, therefore, skeptical of achieving success in this area. After hearing this information in the first session, you attempt to summarize her goals: "It sounds like you want to transition from your current 'college job' to a more major-related professional occupation, but your anxiety about social interaction and your self-doubt have you kind of paralyzed. Is that accurate?" In affirmation of the accuracy of your summary, Donna bursts into tears, mumbling about how this feels hopeless.

In reflecting on Donna's case, consider your response to the following: Is Donna's problem a career problem or a mental health problem? Where would you begin: the career/job search issue or the anxiety? What about self-esteem? Would your answer to the above question depend on the setting you're in? Would you explore career options and refer for "counseling?" When examining the timeline of Donna's issues, what can this tell you about the primary problem? Can Donna's social anxiety, self-esteem, and career development be addressed concurrently in counseling? What would it take for you to be/feel competent to attempt this with her? Where would you like to begin in working with Donna? What does she need right now?

**Case Conceptualization for Donna.** One of the primary ways of identifying anxiety issues involves framing the fight, fright, or freeze response. This mnemonic is easy enough to remember and say, but it can be more challenging when identifying it in the client sitting across from you in counseling. Recall that from a neurobiological perspective, anxiety is a response to some threat, real or perceived (see Box 4.1 below). Therefore, the range of behavioral responses will present in a variety of ways. All of these represent behavioral avoidance, regardless of whether the presenting problem is primarily career related or not. This is just one way to frame anxiety, and in terms of one category of anxiety disorder (space will not permit a thorough discussion of every disorder nor every permutation of anxiety symptomology).

**Fight.** When thinking about Generalized Anxiety Disorder (GAD) as an example, one of the criteria is irritability. Clients can appear ill at ease, almost combative when describing their experience of anxiety. The key in spotting anxiety that presents this way is recognizing the bias many hold that anxiety is weak, passive. It certainly can be and does involve those things, but it absolutely can present as anger and hostility, especially around the source of the anxiety.

**Flight.** Active avoidance characterizes the flight response. Clients can be evasive when discussing issues related to the anxiety source. They also distract themselves and the counselor by jumping topics, presenting the crisis of the day, or feigning a lack of understanding regarding direct feedback about anxiety from the counselor. These clients retreat from challenges that evoke anxiety. Even the language used in the DSM-5 to describe anxiety—restlessness, muscle tension—brings to mind a readiness to run in a prey species (even contrary to human nature as a predator).

**Freeze.** The essence of freezing is inaction. They "forget" their homework. They appear to stall out whenever contemplating a change in behavior. The GAD criteria includes difficulty concentrating or mind going blank and being easily fatigued—two examples of freezing.

Perhaps the first step in understanding Donna's situation and how to proceed is becoming aware that Donna's anxiety is not a sudden result of graduation from college. Graduation has become the catalyst or has exacerbated her underlying anxiety. In other words, the career situation in which she finds herself has raised her own awareness of an unresolved issue with anxiety. CFC starts with where the client is, in terms of the issue the client identifies; they also know that there is typically far more going on clinically than those presented in the initial disclosure. Donna needs a supportive relationship to enable her to be more forward in identifying and attaining her goals. Naturally, despite her job search orientation, her tearful presentation indicates that her emotion systems are overloaded, so she does not need facts related to effective job search strategies, at least not at this point. The counselor intervenes at the affective domain, because that is where her client is. Meeting Donna where she is emotionally is what permits the counselor to operate authentically while shifting the session toward other domains that will need attention in order for her to make satisfactory progress. For example, Donna's approach to relationships (avoidance), combined with the expectations she perceives from her parents (relationships and socio-cultural factors) combine to activate her fight/flight/freeze response, two of which she has already demonstrated in the first 10 minutes of the session: flight and freeze. Once relationally affirmed in the counseling context, the counselor will be able to address other components of treatment based on the counselor's orientation. One example is that a more cognitively oriented counselor may explore with Donna how her thought patterns regarding relationships and career are limiting her ability to take action. The point here is that counselors recognize the likely path that clients will need to take to realize their goals, but they don't accept the natural pressure to direct every step. The process of the relationship, combined with refined goals in collaboration with the client, will direct the steps. It is obvious to the counselor in the case, as it is to Donna, that at the end of the day, Donna will have to take some action (from this perspective, inaction is still related to action).

# Recognizing Anxiety in CFC: School Counseling

Claire is a 16-year junior in a suburban high school. While meeting with you, her school counselor, regarding her senior schedule, she expresses anxiety—almost panic—about what comes next for her. She "knows" she must go to college upon graduation but feels lost about the steps and ambivalent about the process. When pressed, she discloses that she has always had a sense of "free-floating" anxiety, that something is always about to go wrong. She worries about her parents' health, her siblings' well-being, and the perception others have of her (whether she's a good-enough person, or not). Each approach the school counselor attempts in refocusing Claire on decision-making and demystifying Claire's career myths is parried by her "what ifs." Rather than progressing in formulating her schedule, Claire is actually beginning to hyperventilate and increase her verbalizations that "this is never going to work out!" Here are some things to reflect on related to Claire's case: Claire is unable to complete her schedule, and while she's not having a full-blown panic attack, she is beginning to decompensate. What might you do next? Your other students are lining up for their scheduling session, so how might you intervene? While Claire's anxiety has a historical component to it, it the discussion of college and career that set her off. Is this a career issue or mental health issue? At your particular high school, there is really no time or mechanism built into your schedule for one-on-one personal counseling. What can you do for Claire in this moment, and what might you do next in order to support her? Once Claire regains her equilibrium but is still unsure of college/career related issues, how would you want to proceed: address the anxiety, push the schedule, or something else?

**Case Conceptualization for Claire.** Gati and colleagues (Gati et al., 2011) discuss research on the multi-faceted nature of career-related anxiety (Saka et al., 2008). It offers a unique perspective in a time where the term anxiety is used with great frequency. This multi-faceted perspective challenges the reductive nature with which anxiety can often be viewed. For example, "she's just anxious" or "don't be nervous about getting a job." Instead, it views anxiety with more of an approach to appreciation for the depths and complexities of this simple term.

In Saka and colleagues' model, anxiety about career is made up of four categories with several subcategories. Table 10.2 contains the highlights.

**Table 10.2. Summary of Dimensions of Career-Related Anxiety (adapted from Gati et al., 2011)**

| Cluster | Description | Subtypes |
|---|---|---|
| Cluster 1—Anxiety about the career process | Occurs just prior to beginning the process; perfectionism leading to anxiety | |
| Cluster 2—Anxiety about uncertainty of choosing | Contains 3 subtypes: | Uncertainty about the future |
| | | Anxiety about *being* undecided |
| | | Anxiety about low tolerance for ambiguity |
| Cluster 3—Anxiety about choosing | Contains 4 subtypes: | Perfectionism about choosing |
| | | Fear of losing other suitable options |
| | | Fear of choosing an unsuitable occupation |
| | | Anxiety about one's responsibility for the choice |
| Cluster 4—Anxiety about the outcome | Individual has alternatives but unable to actualize for fear of failure or not fulfilling expectations | |

The point for a school counselor engaged in CFC with Claire is to avoid reducing her anxiety down to something common or to assume that the counselor knows the cluster and/or subtype related to her anxiety. Anxiety, regardless of the cluster, often presents as avoidance (Wolpe, 1973). This avoidance is not character-based, but reinforcement-based. Counselors who miss this critical part may attribute incomplete counseling homework, passivity, and the like as resistance, laziness, or lack of investment. Instead, these behaviors can often be signs of anxiety, to which the student has become accustomed to dealing with through avoidance.

## Neuro-Perspectives on Anxiety and Career

Perception of Threat: from a brain perspective, perception is reality, in that all brain function is an interpretation of sensory stimuli and is based in experience. Once signals leave the sensory receptors, there is no longer any chance for objectivity in the sense that these impulses are framed by experience. For example, visual stimulus, seeing a frown on someone's face, contains the objective data of the physics involved in a face forming a frown, but after that, the meaning ascribed to that frown is totally subjective. "Are they frowning at me?," "Is it my fault?," "Is it my concern," etc. The anxiety response is governed by several key brain structures.

**Limbic System versus Cerebral Cortex**—The limbic system is the mid-brain, survival set of structures designed to protect the person from the threats described above. In contrast,

the cerebral cortex, and more specifically, the prefrontal cortex, processes high reorder information and deals with abstract reasoning and problem solving.
**Amygdala**—Almond shaped pair of structures that govern emotional responses and the emotional components of memory. This means that incoming stimuli are routed through the amygdala where they are compared with historical data on threats for a resemblance. Matches elicit a threat response signal. Non-matches equal non-threats and are routed along to the hippocampus for further memory-based functions.
**Hippocampus**—Acts as the executive control center for all memory, not as once assumed, for storage, but for coordinating storage in various parts of the brain and, later, retrieval.

# Summary

As we have just seen, anxiety comes in many forms, can be the result of career-related issues or the cause, and shows itself in CFC often via avoidance behaviors. Sensitive counselors attend to these dynamics and facilitate their client's navigation of the anxiety regardless of the specific ways it relates to their particular career issue. The key is that, regardless of the order of approach, anxiety in CFC cannot be ignored or swept aside; it must be dealt with in order for the client to achieve success in their career-related endeavors.

## Career and Depressive Disorders

Depression is first and foremost a clinical construct, not a real *entity*. Depression is a set of criteria that, when combined, result in a socially constructed phenomenon called depression (or any of depression's associated disorders). This is a vitally important distinction, because clinicians and especially clients give significant amounts of weight to this term and the role it plays in one's life. This is not to minimize the brutal impact of depression in the lives of individuals and their families, in addition to the economic impact in terms of treatment costs, lost wages, and decreased work productivity, to name a few. On the contrary, the gravitas associated with depression, both real and perceived, can make it difficult to treat. In CFC, this can also be problematic: for the client presenting with a dual "diagnosis" of depression and a career issues, is it better to promote treatment of the depression first, and then address the career-related issue, or vice versa? In the first instance, depression treatment can take months, if not years, depending on a variety of factors, including prevalence, pervasiveness, support systems, and so forth. What happens to the career issue in the meantime? In the second instance, addressing the career issue becomes quickly problematic due to the symptomatology of depression, particularly the cognitive and behavioral components (e.g., concentration, fatigue—physical and mental, inhibition and withdrawal, etc.). Waiting to treat depression may inadvertently stifle the CFC efforts. In Table 10.3, I have outlined parallels between depression and career-related issues in order to provide clarity in approaching this dilemma, at least from one perspective.

Table 10.3. Parallels in Depression and Career (Adapted from DSM-5)

| Depression Criteria/ Symptoms | Implications for Career | Protective Factor |
|---|---|---|
| Depressed mood (i.e., sadness or hopelessness) | Affective: Decreased motivation in goal orientation; limited follow through on exploration | Strength- and interest-based assessments can illuminate possibilities leading to hope |
| Decreased interest in what once was pleasurable | Cognitive: Interest; affect: pleasure—limited reward for pursuing and attaining goals (feeds back into motivation); fixation on outcomes rather than on process | Bring back to process, not outcome-only pursuits, allows focus on the here-and-now experience of joy-evoking activities without the pressure of a "result" |
| Appetite and weight—loss or gain (i.e., an indicator of poor self-care motivation) | Difficult to perceive career-related tasks when mindful eating is not a priority | Short-term purpose (e.g., informational interviewing, shadowing, visiting local career office) can trigger self-care (at least in the short-term) |
| Too sad to sleep; too sad to wake | Increased difficulty focusing on career related tasks when unrested; not waking to completed career-related tasks | Paradoxical intervention of forced waking to develop list of interests, abilities, skills, etc., can result in sleep (or helpful lists) |
| Slow-moving or restlessness | Behavioral: either creating such a level of distraction from task or inaction toward task | Career development activities encourage focus and mindfulness |
| Feelings physically drained or exhausted | Basic life tasks take enormous work, so career-related tasks are pushed out of awareness | Small steps in career planning can lead to big results |
| Low self-worth, guilt that does not fit their circumstances | Self-defeating thinking and feelings inhibit the belief that any of this (career-related behaviors) matter | CFC encourages meaning making, not meaning finding: it must be created, not discovered |
| Trouble concentrating or making decisions | Cognitive: When the career-related task involves decision making | Small, specific, concrete, short-term tasks in career development |
| Thoughts of death, thoughts of killing oneself, attempts on one's life | In Durkheim's scheme, suicide is the permanent exit from a social system | Career engagement, while not a "cure" for suicide, invites participation in the social system in tangible ways. |

Abbreviations: CFC = career-focused counseling.

Adapted from *Diagnostic and Statistical Manual for Mental Disorders, Fifth Edition*, pp. 160–161.

In Table 10.3 we see the complexity of depression as a construct, but also how any one of the criteria can significantly limit or even derail CFC. The counselor is left to decide where and how to begin. However, career-related topics can also serve as protective factors. For example, in the last criterion for depression, suicidal ideation, clients are looking for help, a way out. In Durkheim's scheme (1897/1951), suicide is a way to exit the social setting or social role. Carefully conducted, CFC can offer an alternate exit, one that allows an individual to exit a role, and re-enter with a new role. (No one is claiming that CFC is the most effective approach to treatment of depression or suicidality). When conducted in a supportive, accepting environment, clients with co-occurring issues, such as depression and career concerns, may experience the hope that comes with concrete plans for tangible goals. Recovering from depression can feel so abstract and incorporeal; whereas writing a resume, researching an employer, taking a career assessment, etc., can feel quite tangible, especially when those activities are harnessed to challenge any one or combination of depressive symptoms. And herein is the value of challenging the dominant model of depression as a construct: taken together, depression is overwhelming—almost by definition. When taken one symptom at a time, career-focused counselors have opportunities to move back and forth between presenting issues in order to balance strengths and needs.

# Recognizing Depression in CFC: Community Counseling

John is a 50-year-old man who presents for counseling, because he feels depressed. He attends counseling at the urging of his wife, because as she puts it, "he has no drive." The areas he once found joy in no longer hold any appeal for him. John was a plant manager in a regional factory leading a team of 25 tradespeople for the past 15 years. He enjoyed time off with his family, hobbyist-level woodworking, and gardening. In the last year, according to his wife (John is a little recalcitrant about being in "therapy"), his hobbies have fallen by the wayside, and his work quality and satisfaction have decreased. He sleeps or watches television in the evenings and on weekends, and struggles to wake up on time for work. He acknowledges that he feels "down" most of the time, but attributes this to aging and working hard. However, he also reports that the quality of his work has slipped, with his supervisees expressing concern about his availability to them on the floor of the plant. John's supervisor has insisted that John take corrective action, which includes counseling, but it was his wife's insistence that led to him following through (not even the threat of job loss or demotion motivated John to seek help). When asked about his goals for counseling, John states that he would not mind feeling better, but that he does not see that as likely. In reflecting on John's case, is John's situation a mental health or career problem? Should counseling begin with his work or his depression? If you said depression to the above question, where should you begin? Which symptom of John's depression is most salient to him? To his wife? His employer? How might John's job play in to his worldview?

**Case Conceptualization for John.** Case conceptualization involves exploring the client's view of the presenting problem against the backdrop of a biopsychosocial assessment. In the case of John, I intentionally use the term recalcitrant regarding John's motivation for counseling, because this is not a characteristic of John in general. John's apathy toward work and home life is not a condition of his character; rather it is a state of his depression. In working with John, we must begin at the beginning: ***what outcome is John looking for?*** John may or may not have lost his drive to perform at a higher level at his job. However, this is not consistent with his work performance history. This could mean one of at least two possibilities: Either John has lost interest in and satisfaction with his work, and persevering in it is having negative effects in other facets of his life, or John may, for myriad reasons, be experiencing a depressive episode that is impacting all areas of his life.

CFC assumes that the depression and the career issues are most likely related, at least at some level (Walker & Peterson, 2012). Working with John might entail crafting a timeline of his mood, work, and hobbies, attempting to identify when these shifts in his mood, behavior, and motivation shifted. When did John's malaise first become noticeable? In proceeding with John's treatment, it is important to identify other times in his life where he has experienced depression symptoms and the precipitating factors. Returning then to the first and pivotal question, the starting point for CFC with John is what he sees as the problem and what he wants to get from counseling.

## Recognizing Depression in CFC: School Counseling

Sydney is a tearful 13-year-old African American female in the eighth grade. She comes to your office following a career fair to discuss her feelings of sadness, irritability, and guilt and the sense that she is not and never will be good enough. She states that it has been this way for her since beginning middle school, but this year, it has gotten worse for her. Her family does not have the resources to send her to a counselor in the community, nor do they think counseling is the right way to go. They are concerned that the counselor will impose his own "White, middle-class values" onto her. Sydney has nowhere else to turn and wants to find a way through this fog she's in and has been in for the past two and a half years. She is not suicidal and denies self-harm, but she is clearly in pain. The fair triggered her feelings of hopelessness and helplessness regarding the future and her place in it. She reports being unable to concentrate on finding a career when school, friends, and family require so much energy from her, just to keep up. What if you are a White counselor working with Sydney. Knowing how her parents feel about this, what do you do? Sydney's tearful episode appears to have been triggered by the career fair; does this make it a career or mental health counseling issue? Do you believe Sydney's depression will subside if you can assist her in finding a career path? Will it remain if you can't? How might you use what you have learned so far about CFC in helping Sydney with her depression?

**Case Conceptualization for Sydney.** It is important to recognize the difference in races between the counselor and Sydney, as well as at least one explicit attitude about racial differences expressed by Sydney's father. This is important, in that racial attitudes are rarely this explicit, so the counselor is able to identify one racially charged area of counseling from the outset. However, as described earlier in this chapter, the sociocultural domain exerts influence, but primarily as it exists with the other domains. For example, Sydney's relationships with her family, friends, and school leaders also play a role in shaping her attitudes. Furthermore, it would not be accurate to assume, when working with Sydney, that her father's perspective (environment domain) represents a more universal "Black distrust of White." While this could be true and has empirical and anecdotal support (Helms, 1990, for example), the counselor needs to begin with Sydney as an individual in context.

In Sydney's current situation, she in an emotional crisis—apparently a non-life-threatening one—but a crisis nonetheless. This crisis appears to be based on her identity development issues that have been fomenting for a couple of years. This is not the time to try to help her make a decision; it is time to listen and reflect. Career-related issues often trigger emotional responses or exacerbate underlying mental health issues (see Multon et al., 2001, for discussion of psychological distress and career). It will be important, through this reflective, supportive process, to develop a greater understanding of how Sydney's goals connect the family values and goals, on one hand, with the "White middle-class values" she's getting at school. Her transition to middle school also seems to be a precipitating factor for her—also a time when increased emphasis is placed on charting a career course. Assuming that this is "just" teen depression, emotional reactivity, or vocational immaturity, while tempting, are not useful assumptions at this point (Rottinghaus, Jenkins, & Jantzer, 2009).

### Neuro-Perspectives on Depression and Career

In a previous work, I posed the question, "where is depression in the brain" (Luke, 2015)? Simply asking a question such as this can prod counselors' thinking in terms of treating specific criteria. For example, while it has come under increased scrutiny, the serotonin hypothesis offers a compelling look at the question of where depression is in the brain. For example, if we reframe the question to, "where are the criteria for depression in the brain?" This expands our thinking, because cognitive criteria (e.g., concentration, decision-making) are governed by different brain regions (orbitoprefrontal—cortex; pfc) from the affective criteria (e.g., mood, pleasure, guilt), which are governed more by the limbic system (e.g., amygdala, hypothalamic-pituitary-adrenal axis (HPA axis)). The behavioral symptoms (e.g., psychomotor agitation/retardation) are managed more by motivation circuits and the motor cortex). Basic life functions (e.g., sleep, hunger, metabolism) are controlled by yet a different set of structures (thalamus, hypothalamus).

# Summary

Depression is not one thing; it is a collection of neurological phenomena that exhibit their impact in behavior, cognition, and emotion and influence, among other things, career-related factors by extension. In order to be effective in CFC, it is important in clients who display symptoms of depression to provide a differential diagnosis. Career-related issues that are free-standing require a different approach than career-related issues that have their origin in depression or other mood disorders. Likewise, depressive-like symptoms can begin to abate when rooted in career-related issues.

## Career and Stress- And Trauma-Related Disorders

The first thing you will note in reading this section is that stress and trauma are listed together, which is a totally artificial conflation of these two clinical conditions. While stress can feel traumatic, and trauma is stressful, they often exist on separate ends of the continuum, if they share a continuum at all. So, why does the DSM-5 group them into the same section? Part of the reason is that, far from being polar opposites, as comes to mind with concepts such as continuum, it is more accurate to think of them as two sides of the same coin. Nowhere is this seen more clearly than from a neurological perspective, as we will see in the discussion below. In addition, stress can be acute or chronic; likewise, trauma can be acute, chronic, or both. Stress and trauma both change the functioning of the brain (Joels & Baram, 2009) and, with that, make concentration, problem-solving, goal-setting, and the like—all career-related tools and tasks—extremely difficult.

Coursol and colleagues explored the relationships between expectations for career counseling and career maturity among survivors of trauma and individuals who did not report experiencing trauma (Coursol, Lewis, & Garrity, 2001). In their study, trauma is described in terms of Shengold's (1989) description of soul murder, in which trauma can be massive trauma or deprivation of nurturance. In either case, the individual is developmentally arrested (Coursol, 2001) in terms of the individual's soul, psychological structure, and functioning (p. 134). Massive trauma, as that referenced in the DSM-5 for post-traumatic stress disorder (PTSD; American Psychological Association, 2013), involves exposure to actual or threatened death, serious injury, or sexual violence in a variety of ways. Shengold (1989) defines deprivation by juxtaposing it with child abuse, "Child abuse means that the child has felt too much to bear; child deprivation means that the child has been exposed to too little to meet his or her needs" (p. 1). Coursol and colleagues looked at massive trauma, finding that these survivors expected their counselors to be less empathic and understanding, which reflects DSM-5 criteria, as well.

Strauser and colleagues extended this work by examining trauma and career development among college students (Strauser, Lustig, Cogdal, & Uruk, 2006). In their study, career development included: 1) work personality, meaning behaviors that meet the interpersonal demands of the job: 2) vocational identity, or awareness of career interests, skills, abilities, and so forth: 3) career decision-making, in which an individual makes a good decision in terms of living out one's vocational identity; and: 4) job-seeking, or the ability to find the occupation or position that is the culmination of the first three tasks. They found that trauma did indeed negatively impact participants' ability to navigate the first three career tasks. They noted that trauma and dysfunctional career thoughts exhibit a strong positive correlation: more trauma often means more dysfunctional career thoughts.

Stress can exert an insidious impact on career development in that stressors can take many forms. In addition, stress is such a ubiquitous concept in popular culture that its effects can be minimized or overlooked (Bullock-Yowell, Peterson, Reardon, Leierer, & Reed, 2011). There is little doubt for anyone who has experienced career-related issues—searching, displacement, dissatisfaction, etc.—that they can be very stressful. Managing this stress is a key to successfully navigating these career-related issues. Likewise, stress in other domains of one's life can create difficulties both on the job and in career-related tasks (Bullock-Yowell et al., 2011; Multon et al., 2001; Spokane & Fretz, 1993). CFC assists clients in untangling the often cyclical nature of stress and its effects, which almost invariably create additional stress, and so on.

# Recognizing Stress/Trauma in Career—Focused Counseling: Community

Theresa is a 30-something single mother of two elementary-school-aged sons, Thomas, age 7 and Terrence, age 10. Theresa works 8:00 a.m. to 5:00 p.m. Monday through Friday as a receptionist/administrative assistant at a local pest-control company. She makes 12 dollars per hour, has health insurance (a rarity in this work), and receives basic child support from the boys' father, from whom she has been separated for 4 years. The boys see their father every other weekend. Theresa has sought counseling, because despite being able to tread water financially for the past few years, she is eager to return to community college to advance her education and employment prospects. She reports living constantly on the edge of the poverty line and often considers seeking public assistance to ease the burden, but also feels conflicted about "living off the government" when they are able to mostly "get by." She is further conflicted by the recent note from the elementary school that her eldest, Terrence, is thought to have a reading disability. And just last year, in the fourth grade, Terrence received three days in-school suspension for "shoving" another boy during lunch. Theresa states that she would like to focus on her own vocational development, because she thinks being able to afford an apartment in a "nicer area" may help her sons socially and behaviorally and would put them in a "school district with higher ratings." She asks you whether it is appropriate for her to pursue her career goals, vague as they currently are, when doing so would pull her from home more than she already is, possibly making things worse for her sons in the short term. As you think about your work with a client like Theresa, consider the following:

Theresa does not meet the criteria for a mental health disorder, but she definitely has psychosocial stressors impinging on her career decision-making. Is this a career or mental health issue? What do you make of Theresa's question to you as the counselor? What should your response be? What part(s) of Theresa's story "triggers" a reaction from you? How might you need to manage your own emotions and biases before responding to her request for help? How would you conceptualize Theresa's problem: psychosocial stressors impacting career-related issues or career-related issues limiting her options and, therefore, creating stressors? Does it matter? How so?

**Case Conceptualization for Theresa.** The third reflection question from the set above holds a key to the next steps in working with Theresa. She believes that her two options are in conflict, which is creating stress for her, and she desperately wants someone in authority to tell her the "right" thing to do. From a CFC perspective, there is no most right way, in any absolute sense; there is only the next step. It is analogous to the way humans walk: one step left of center followed by one step right of center, effectively countering the "error' in each previous step. Theresa wants the correct step, and depending on the counselor's own status and experience with career decision-making and tolerance for ambiguity, this could be a problematic question. There is virtually no way a counselor can know a client's situation so well that they could advise them on the right step to take; there is only taking action and making the necessary corrections. This is a foundational ethical principle for counselors.

One thing that cannot be ignored in Theresa's case, regardless of the direction of the problem—stress-based or career-based—is that, as of 4 years ago, Theresa's life situation shifted radically. Prior to her separation, her job, income and role in the family worked; it made sense to her and for her. But suddenly this arrangement, her job, and her role have changed. It would be reasonable to assume that there is value in exploring with her the potential impact this change in life role has had on her.

## Recognizing Stress/Trauma in CFC: School

Terrence is a 10-year-old male, referred to your office following a verbal altercation with another boy in his class that was then directed at the intervening teacher. We were introduced to him briefly in the case of Theresa, his mother, above. Terrence was involved in an altercation at the school in the year prior, so the administration is concerned about escalation. As you talk with Terrence, it becomes apparent that he is experiencing some stressors at home, and those may be impacting his behavior at school. As your meeting proceeds, the conversation turns to Terrence's parents and their occupations. He states that his mother does "something for the bug company" but that she does not like it and that "the pay sucks." When you inquire about his father's work, he pauses, breaks eye contact, and then remarks, "he hustles." Based on his body language, you know to proceed cautiously without appearing to pry—this is clearly personal, private information. "He makes money any way he can; and he's great at it. He can make more in one night than mom can make in two weeks at her crappy job." When you ask how he sees that difference, he tells you that his dad has to do something to be able to provide child support. When you ask Terrence about how he views work and what he wants to do when he grows up, his looks tells you that dad's way is the way for him as well. As you reflect on your meeting with Terrence, is it appropriate to incorporate CFC into your sessions? Why or why not? Has Terrence experienced trauma or stress, in terms of the descriptions in this chapter? How so? What can you, as the school counselor with your limited time to work with Terrence, do to help him with his worldview—a view that is very real to him and ever-present? How might you integrate behavior modification (curtailing the confrontational language and behavior) with CFC?

**Case Conceptualization for Terrence.** In considering Terrence's case, it's important to recognize that Terrence and his brother both experienced the same life event that their mother did when their father left the home. Suddenly, a family that was intact and financially balanced (for the most part) have become fractured and financially unstable. His mother, who was available to and for him in her previous role is much less available and at a time in which he is struggling to make sense of his identity. This perspective acknowledges Terrence as a victim of divorce but does not excuse any of his subsequent acting out behaviors in school. In contrast, it highlights the socio-cultural, experiential, environmental, and relational factors that are swirling around him as he acts on his thoughts and feelings—increasingly to negative effect.

This case intentionally eschews explicit physical or sexual forms of trauma, in order to highlight the subtler, often insidious, forms of relational and environmental trauma and trauma-related stress that affect students in K–12 settings. School counselors must maintain an appreciation for these dynamics as they seek to work with the career assumptions of students in Terrence's circumstances. Terrence's ideas about the world of work and his role in it are forming quickly: he sees his mother struggling to support them, working many hours at a low-status job, while his father presumably makes significantly more money at a higher-status (in certain circles) "job." The counselor must begin by empathizing with Terrence's perspective on the way the world works. The temptation here is to "set him straight" about respect for authority and honest work, yet we already have sufficient information about Terrence and his circumstances to know this will only reinforce his views. Instead, the counselor can empathically explore the threats to Terrence's sense of self that he is clearly experiencing and gently guide him through an inoculation approach to threat perception.

## Neuro-Perspectives on Stress/Trauma and Career

Stress is the brain's way of communicating to the body's support systems that a threat has been detected that requires specific action. The catalyst for this cascade of responses involves cortisol, the so-called stress hormone. Cortisol is the chemical current that carries response messages through the HPA axis. This system prepares the body to respond to threats. It performs this function very effectively ... in the short term. Over longer periods of time (prolonged stress states), Cortisol begins to exerts deleterious effects on the central nervous system. It degrades short-term memory, impairs concentration, disrupts digestion, and increases blood pressure (Garrett, 2015). It's important to note that all of these negative effects are highly facilitative in the short-term, when responding to environmental threats. However, when the system is "on" for extended periods, the consequences can become the focus of clinical attention. It is of critical importance that counselors recognize that this system activates whether the threat is real or perceived, because neurologically speaking, there is no difference. Consider the implications of prolonged stress, and its effects on the brain and central nervous system, on career-related tasks!

# Summary

During times of stress, clients are not in their right minds; to be more precise, they are not in their *prefrontal cortex* minds. Instead, they are in reactivity mode: we see this in Theresa trying to pry an answer from her counselor to the false dichotomy she has set up with her situation. The same is true for Terrence: he is reacting to environmental stimuli as existential threats and is acting on his protective instincts. Neither of these individuals is prepared to make reason-informed career decisions, and yet both of them are doing just that. They are forming polarizing views: "care for self" versus "care for family," "make legitimate money and be broke" versus "hustle and be successful." Regardless of the sequence of the stress/trauma response, counseling must focus on taking these clients out of their midbrain reactions and back to their prefrontal regions in order to make more effective decisions based on reasonable conclusions.

## Career and Addictions

Career-focused counselors face unique challenges when engaging in CFC with those struggling with addiction (Comerford, 1999; Henkel, 2011; Wood & Cato, 2012). There is a dearth of professional literature on how counselors can begin to address the complexities of these issues when intertwined. For this section, it is important perhaps to begin with an overview of addiction, both in terms of the DSM-5 diagnostic criteria as well as its clinical presentation. First and foremost, addiction is a behavior or set of behaviors. Also, this chapter addresses use disorders, rather than intoxication and withdrawal. In addition, the focus is on substance addiction, as opposed to process addictions, e.g., pathological gambling, pornography, Internet, etc., in part due to space limitations, but also because, from a neurological perspective, substance and process addictions are virtually indistinguishable (Fetting, 2011). Regardless of its precursors—and there are many—addiction is addiction because of the behavioral expression.

**Table 10.4. DSM-5 Criteria by Eight-Factor Metamodel**

| | | |
|---|---|---|
| 1. | *Uses more or for longer that intended* | *Behavioral* |
| 2. | *Wants to quit and tries to unsuccessfully* | *Cognitive/Emotion* |
| 3. | *Spends a lot of time and energy pursuing, using, recovering* | *Behavior* |
| 4. | *Wants to use very badly* | *Emotion* |
| 5. | *Fails to meet expectations in major areas of life, like work, family, socially* | *Sociocultural/ Relational* |
| 6. | *Keeps using even after negative consequences* | *Sociocultural/ Relational* |
| 7. | *Ignores major life roles and expectations* | *Sociocultural/ Relational* |
| 8. | *Uses when dangerous or precarious to use* | *Environment/ Bio-Physical* |
| 9. | *Ignores consequences of use and persists in using* | *Cognitive/ Bio-Physical* |
| 10.a. | *Has to use more to continuing getting "high"* | *Bio-physical/Cognitive/ Emotional* |

| | | |
|---|---|---|
| *10.b.* | *Ceases getting as "high" as before on same amount* | *Bio-physical/Experience* |
| *11.a.* | *Withdrawal symptoms* | *Bio-physical/ Cognitive/ Emotional* |
| *11.b.* | *Uses to cope with withdrawal* | *Bio-physical/Behavior* |

Adapted from DSM-5, pp. 490–491.

It takes only a cursory look at the diagnostic criteria for a "use" disorder to see the connections between addiction and career issues. By definition, in fact, addiction negatively impacts work-related activities (see criteria 5 and 7), not to mention the indirect impact of other criteria (3, 4, and 9). Likewise, career issues that are left unaddressed or unresolved lead to negatively coping behaviors, including alcohol/substance use (Henkel, 2011).

# Recognizing Addiction in CFC: Community

Eddie is a 27-year old male, finishing up an Associate's degree in computer science. He has only 13 credit hours to go to complete his degree but is struggling to finish. Eddie has been referred for counseling from his county's drug court for a driving under the influence citation (DUI) he received three months prior. Despite his referral, Eddie maintains that he does not have an alcohol problem (be blew a 1.4 on a breathalyzer when he was pulled over). He states that his goal is to figure out his career prospects, as he is not enjoying his program. He initially pursued an Associate of Applied Science (AAS) in computer science, because he wanted to develop video games. Recently, it was brought to his attention that his program actually trains students to work with computer hardware, not software, as Eddie wished. Furthermore, he also learned that an AAS degree would not transfer to a 4-year college like an Associate of Science would have. When asked about his academic advising experience at the community college that would have presumably covered these important issues, Eddie remarks, "I told them not to schedule me for Monday mornings, because I party pretty hard on the weekends." As a mental health counselor in the community, what is your responsibility to your client, in terms of his view of the presenting problem? The client? The referral source? What do you see is the relationship, if any, between Eddie's career decision-making process and his alcohol use? Does CFC in Eddie's case require that he "get sober" first? Assume that you feel strongly that you need to address Eddie's alcohol use, how might you use his version of the presenting problem—major and career—to also address his alcohol use?

**Case Conceptualization for Eddie.** Eddie is court-ordered for treatment; therefore, he is accountable in some way to the court for attending and completing counseling with you. At the same time, he does not see himself as having a substance use problem and is reluctant to discuss this with you. In this case, it is important to recognize that it is Eddie who is responsible to the court, not necessarily the counselor. However, he must demonstrate some progress (or at least participation in) drug-related treatment; the counselor documents this. A counselor would not be able to ethically document drug treatment if they only provided treatment for a career-related issue, for example. Unless when the client is in the precontemplation stage of change (Prochaska & Norcross, 2014), he will only demonstrate resistance to these interventions (Miller & Rollnick, 2013), so CFC may be the treatment of choice. After all, the client has acknowledged that career issues are most salient for him.

In working with Eddie, it becomes clear that he chose to attend community college somewhat arbitrarily and certainly chose his major without a lot of research. This has led to limited investment in the career planning process and the situation in which he now finds himself: halfway through a program that he neither desires nor is very successful in, without being able to transfer the majority of those courses to a four-year program. Based on the biopsychosocial assessment, the counselor may be able to determine that this is more the rule for Eddie than the exception. He acknowledges a pattern of taking passive approaches to developing the life he wants to live. This creates tension with the parts of him that want more out of life. It becomes clear to the counselor (and over time, it will to Eddie as well) that substance use is simply another method of passively engaging his life. Will this insight be enough to initiate lasting change for Eddie? Probably not, but it may move him toward contemplation, and even preparation, as he increases his awareness (Prochaska & Norcross, 2014) of the relationship between his avoidance behaviors and substance use.

## Recognizing Addiction in CFC: School

Angelica is a 15-year-old Hispanic American student in the 9th grade. You meet her during an advising class period in which you are teaching about the college application process and how it impacts course selection for sophomore year. You notice that Angelica struggles to attend to the class presentation, makes little eye contact, and seems generally disengaged. You approach her just before she darts out into the hallway. When you ask her about her behavior, she remarks, "I don't need to know this s**t; I'm not going to college!" As she says this, you notice a faint smell of marijuana, and notice some redness in her eyes. When you point this out, she gets very defensive and runs off down the hall. Recognizing the implications of being intoxicated at school, as well as the impact it will have on your ability to work with her, you consult with a colleague. You learn that Angelica is a first-generation American citizen whose parents only speak Spanish and work in service industries. Angelica would be the first in her family to attend college. You also learn that Angelica has struggled since coming to the high school with fitting in, and there's concern about her social group. Assuming you could get her into your office for a meeting, where would you want to begin with Angelica? Also, assume that as it turns out, Angelica was not "high" at school, but does have a history of marijuana use. Which would you address (first): drug use or her disposition toward college? Is Angelica's issue a marijuana use problem or a career development problem? How would you conceptualize separating the two? There are limited resources in the community for referrals, so you must address this issue with Angelica. What approach might have the greatest likelihood of connecting to her?

**Case Conceptualization for Angelica.** One place to begin exploring with Angelica is how being successful in high school and, subsequently, college affect her *familismo*—the concept of interpersonal connectedness of each individual with parents and extended family members in Latino and Hispanic culture. It may be that Angelica is experiencing intrapersonal tension about being successful in ways that are different from her parents and, therefore, is somehow showing disrespect to them. Of course, multicultural competencies in counseling call for caution in assuming that a client's presenting problem is primarily due to one's race, ethnicity, or national origin, while balancing it with the recognition that race always exerts some influence, whether overt or covert.

In working to engage Angelica, it is, again, important to ascertain what it is that she wants. Because she is initially, at best a reluctant client, what can the two of you agree on as to her goals (besides her goal to not talk with you about this)? She does seem to want a strong connection with her family, but the counselor may also find that she also wants a strong connection (success) in the broader "American" culture. This, it can be agreed upon, is a source of tension for her, and reconciling this conflict may be a reasonable goal. High school success and college represent movement away from her family. While marijuana use is not commensurate with her Hispanic heritage, aligning herself with peers who use and struggle in their career-related goals both directly and indirectly aid her avoidance of the core conflict: low achievement reduces the conflict. CFC embraces the discrepancy, in the tradition of Motivational Interviewing, and works through the relationship with Angelica to reconcile these two (apparently) discrepant parts of herself.

## Neuro-Perspectives on Addiction and Career

The neurological foundations of addiction have much to offer in the way of CFC with both Eddie and Angelica, in terms of the brain-based mechanisms related to addiction. In comprehending the brain-based features of addiction and its implications for CFC, Feldstein, Ewing, and Cheung (2013) say it best regarding the top-down/bottom-up processing pathways:

> The conceptual reviews converge in referencing two overarching processing pathways that are relevant to addictive behavior: "top-down" and "bottom-up" processing. Top-down processing refers to the role of cognitive control circuitry (which may involve, for example: orbitofrontal cortex, dorsolateral prefrontal cortex, and anterior cingulate cortex) in modulating the processing of sensory information (e.g., craving and response to reward). Bottom-up processing refers to the primacy of sensory information processing and salience of drug cues (circuitry relevant to the incentive salience system may involve, for example: the insula, ventral tegmental area, putamen, and caudate) relative to modulation of sensory processing by cognitive control systems. The interplay of top-down and bottom-up processes dynamically influences the onset, maintenance, and effective treatment of addictive behaviors. Ideas proposed in the conceptual reviews with regard to how specific interventions impact top-down and bottom-up processes may be controversial, but aim to provide heuristic frameworks to guide testing of novel concepts regarding brain-based psychotherapy mechanisms of change. (p. 330)

# Summary

Substance use contaminates even the clearest presenting problems and goals. Counselors must assess for the presence and impact of substances, both as a result and a cause of the presenting problem. Just as career and mental health exert reciprocal impacts on one another, so too do substance use disorders have mutual cause and effect relationships with career and mental health (Magura, Staines, Blankertz, & Madison, 2004).

# Conclusion

In the cases reviewed above, which factors become most salient? Hopefully, you noted that the most salient, relevant factor is the therapeutic relationship. After that, the point of entry depends upon the client's goals (which are also evoked in the context of the therapeutic relationship) and then by the counselor's theoretical orientation. As we have seen throughout this chapter, the lines dividing career and mental health issues, if there are any, are thin. Counseling often moves between the two.

# References

Anderson, W. P., J., & Niles, S. G. (1995). Career and personal concerns expressed by career counseling clients. *The Career Development Quarterly, 43*(3), 240–245. Retrieved from

http://search.proquest.com/docview/219436952?accountid=28833

Anderson Jr, W. P., & Niles, S. G. (2000). Important events in career counseling: Client and counselor descriptions. *The career development quarterly, 48*(3), 251.

Badenoch, B. (2008). *Being a brain-wise therapist: A practical guide to interpersonal neurobiology.* New York, NY: Norton.

Betz, N. E., & Corning, A. F. (1993). The inseparability of "career" and "personal" counseling. *The Career Development Quarterly, 42*(2), 137–142.

Blustein, D. L. (2001). The Interface of Work and Relationships Critical Knowledge for 21st Century Psychology. *The Counseling Psychologist, 29*(2), 179–192.

Braunstein-Bercovitz, H. (2014). Self-criticism, anxious attachment, and avoidant attachment as predictors of career decision making. *Journal of Career Assessment, 22*(1), 176–187.

Bronfenbrenner, U. (1977). Toward an experimental ecology of human development. *American psychologist, 32*(7), 513.

Bronfenbrenner, U., & Morris, P. A. (2006). The bioecological model of human development. *Handbook of child psychology.*

Bullock-Yowell, E., Peterson, G. W., Reardon, R. C., Leierer, S. J., & Reed, C. A. (2011). Relationships among career and life stress, negative career thoughts, and career decision state: A cognitive information processing perspective. *The Career Development Quarterly, 59*(4), 302–314.

Comerford, A. W. (1999). Work dysfunction and addiction: Common roots. *Journal of Substance Abuse Treatment, 16*(3), 247–253.

Coursol, D. H., Lewis, J., & Garrity, L. (2001). Career development of trauma survivors: Expectations about counseling and career maturity. *Journal of Employment Counseling*, *38*(3), 134.

American Psychiatric Association. (2013). *Diagnostic and statistical manual of mental disorders*. Arlington, VA: American Psychiatric Publishing.

Dipeolu, A., Hargrave, S., & Storlie, C. A. (2015). Enhancing ADHD and LD Diagnostic Accuracy Using Career Instruments. *Journal of Career Development*, *42*(1), 19–32.

Durkheim, E. (1951). *Suicide: A study in sociology* (JA Spaulding & G. Simpson, trans.). Glencoe, IL: Free Press.(Original work published 1897).

Feldstein Ewing, S. W., & Chung, T. (2013). Neuroimaging mechanisms of change in psychotherapy for addictive behaviors: emerging translational approaches that bridge biology and behavior. *Psychology of Addictive Behaviors*, *27*(2), 329.

Feldstein Ewing SW, Filbey FM, Hendershot CS, McEachern AD, Hutchison KE. (2013). Proposed model of the neurobiological mechanisms underlying psychosocial alcohol interventions: the example of motivational interviewing. *Journal of Studies on Alcohol and Drugs*, *72*(6):903–916. [PubMed: 22051204]

Feldstein Ewing, S. W., McEachern, A. D., Yezhuvath, U., Bryan, A. D., Hutchison, Feldstein Ewing, S. W., McEachern, A. D., Yezhuvath, U., Bryan, A. D., Hutchison, K. E., & Filbey, F. M. (2013). Integrating brain and behavior: Evaluating adolescents' response to a cannabis intervention. *Psychology of addictive behaviors*, *27*(2), 510.

Fenichel, O. (1996). *The psychoanalytic theory of neurosis (2nd ed.)*. New York, NY: Routledge. (Originally published 1946)

Fetting, M. (2011). *Perspectives on Addiction: An Integrative Treatment Model with Clinical Case Studies*. Thousand Oaks, CA: Sage.

Freud, S. (1961). *Five lectures on psycho-analysis*. (J. Stachey, Ed. & Trans.) New York, NY: Norton. (Original work published 1909–1910).

Gati, I., Gadassi, R., Saka, N., Hadadi, Y., Ansenberg, N., Friedmann, R., & Asulin-Peretz, L. (2011). Emotional and personality-related aspects of career decision-making difficulties: Facets of career indecisiveness. *Journal of Career Assessment*, *19*(1), 3–20.

Gelso, C. J., Prince, J., Cornfeld, J. L., Payne, A. B., Royalty, G., & Wiley, M. O. L. (1985). Quality of counselors' intake evaluations for clients with problems that are primarily vocational versus personal. *Journal of Counseling Psychology*, *32*(3), 339.

Hayes, S. C., Pistorello, J., & Levin, M. E. (2012). Acceptance and commitment therapy as a unified model of behavior change. *The Counseling Psychologist*, *40*(7), 976–1002.

Hebb, D.O. (1949). *The Organization of Behavior*. New York, NY: Wiley & Sons.

Helms, J. E. (1990). *Black and White racial identity: Theory, research, and practice*. New York, NY: Greenwood Press.

Henkel, D. (2011). Unemployment and substance use: a review of the literature (1990–2010). *Current drug abuse reviews*, *4*(1), 4–27.

Heppner, M. J., O'Brien, K. M., Hinkelman, J. M., & Flores, L. Y. (1996). Training Counseling Psychologists in Career Development Are We Our Own Worst Enemies? *The Counseling Psychologist*, *24*(1), 105–125.

Heppner, M. J., & Heppner, P. P. (2003). Identifying process variables in career counseling: A research agenda. *Journal of Vocational Behavior*, *62*(3), 429–452.

Joëls, M., & Baram, T. Z. (2009). The neuro-symphony of stress. *Nature Reviews Neuroscience*, *10*(6), 459–466.

Ladany, N. & O'Shaughnessy, T. (2015). Training and supervision in career counseling. In: Paul J. Hartung, Mark L. Savickas, & W. Bruce Walsh, (Editors-in-Chief) (pp. 375–387). *APA handbook of career intervention*. Washington, DC: American Psychological Association.

Lambert, M. J., & Barley, D. E. (2001). Research summary on the therapeutic relationship and psychotherapy outcome. *Psychotherapy: Theory, Research, Practice, Training*, *38*(4), 357.

Lara, T. M., Kline, W. B., & Paulson, D. (2011). Attitudes regarding career counseling: Perceptions and experiences of counselors-in-training. *The Career Development Quarterly, 59*(5), 428–440.

LeDoux, J. E. (2003). *Synaptic self: How our brains become who we are.* New York, NY: Penguin.

Luke, C. (2015). *Neuroscience for counselors and therapists: Integrating the sciences of brain and mind.* Thousand Oaks, CA: Sage.

Luke, C., Redekop, F., & Burgin, C. (2015). Psychological factors in community college student retention. *Community College Journal of Research and Practice, 39*(3), 222–234.

Luke, C., & Redekop, F. (2016). Supervision of co-occurring career and mental health concerns. *Career Planning and Adult Development Journal, 32*(1), 130–140.

MacDonald, G. (1997). Issues in multi-cultural counseling supervision. In: *Caring in an age of technology.* Proceedings of the international conference on counseling in the 21st century (6th, Beijing, China, May 29–30, 1997).

Magee, I. M., & Whiston, S. C. (2010). Casting no shadow: Assessing vocational overshadowing. *Journal of Career Assessment, 18*(3), 239–249.

Magura, S., Staines, G. L., Blankertz, L., & Madison, E. M. (2004). The effectiveness of vocational services for substance users in treatment. *Substance Use & Misuse, 39*(13–14), 2165–2213.

McAuliffe, G. (2008). *Culturally alert counseling: A comprehensive introduction* (Vol. 2). Thousand Oaks, CA: Sage.

Michael, T., & Luke, C. (2016). Utilizing a metaphoric approach to teach the neuroscience of play therapy: A pilot study. *International Journal of Play Therapy, 25*(1), 45.

Miller, W. R., & Rollnick, S. (2013). *Motivational interviewing: Helping people change.* New York, NY: Guilford Press.

Multon, K. D., Heppner, M. J., Gysbers, N. C., Zook, C., & Ellis-Kalton, C. A. (2001). Client psychological distress: An important factor in career counseling. *The career development quarterly, 49*(4), 324–335.

Pace, D., & Quinn, L. (2000). Empirical support of the overlap between career and mental health counseling of university students. *Journal of College Student Psychotherapy, 14*(3), 4–50.

Pedersen, P. B., Lonner, W. J., Draguns, J. G., Trimble, J. E., & Scharron-del Rio, M. R. (2015). *Counseling across cultures.* Thousand Oaks, CA: Sage.

Prieto, L. R., & Betsworth, D. G. (1999). Supervision of career counseling: Current knowledge and new directions. *The Clinical Supervisor, 18*, 173–189.

Prochaska & Norcross (2014). *Systems of Psychotherapy: A Transtheoretical Analysis* (8th ed.). Belmont, CA: Cengage.

Reiss, S., Levitan, G. W., & Szyszko, J. (1982). Emotional disturbance and mental retardation: diagnostic overshadowing. *American journal of mental deficiency.* 86(6), 567–574.

Robitschek, C., & DeBell, C. (2002). The reintegration of vocational psychology and counseling psychology Training issues for a paradigm shift. *The Counseling Psychologist, 30*(6), 801–814.

Rogers, D. R., & Whiston, S. C. (2014). Qualitative analysis of clinical notes do counselors ignore work and academic concerns? *Journal of Career Assessment, 22*(2), 207–220.

Rogers, C. R. (1959). A theory of therapy, personality, and interpersonal relationships, as developed from a client-centered framework. In S. Koch (Ed.), *Psychology: A study of a science. Vol. 3: Formulations of the person and the social context* (pp. 184–256). New York, NY: McGraw-Hill.

Rottinghaus, P. J., Jenkins, N., & Jantzer, A. M. (2009). Relation of depression and affectivity to career decision status and self-efficacy in college students. *Journal of Career Assessment, 17*(3), 271–285.

Saka, N., Gati, I., & Kelly, K. R. (2008). Emotional and personality-related aspects of career-decision-making difficulties. *Journal of Career Assessment, 16*(4), 403–424. doi: 10.1177/1069072708318900.

Shengold, L. (1989). *Soul murder: The effects of childhood abuse and deprivation.* New Haven CT: Yale University Press.

Siegel, D. J. (2006). An interpersonal neurobiology approach to psychotherapy. *Psychiatric Annals, 36*(4), 248.

Siegel, D. J. (2012). *The developing mind: How relationships and the brain interact to shape who we are.* (2nd Ed.). New York, NY: Guilford Press.

Slattery, Jeanne M & Park, Crystal L (2011). *Empathic counseling : meaning, context, ethics, and skill.* Belmont, CA: Brooks/Cole.

Spengler, P. M., Blustein, D. L., & Strohmer, D. C. (1990). Diagnostic and treatment overshadowing of vocational problems by personal problems. *Journal of Counseling Psychology, 37*(4), 372.

Spengler, P. M. (2000). Does vocational overshadowing even exist? A test of the robustness of the vocational overshadowing bias. *Journal of counseling psychology, 47*(3), 342.

Subich, L. M. (1993). How personal is career counseling? *The Career Development Quarterly, 42*(2), 129–131.

Strauser, D. R., & O'Sullivan, D. (2008). The role of developmental work personality in the employment of individuals with psychiatric disabilities. *Work (Reading, Mass.), 32*(2), 171–177.

Sue, D. W., & Sue, D. (2003). Counseling the Culturally Diverse (5th ed.). New York, NY: John Wiley & Sons.

Swanson, J. L. (2002). Understanding the Complexity of Clients' Lives Infusing a Truly Integrative Career-Personal Perspective into Graduate Training. *The Counseling Psychologist, 30*(6), 815–832.

Uthayakumar, R., Schimmack, U., Hartung, P. J., & Rogers, J. R. (2010). Career decidedness as a predictor of subjective well-being. *Journal of Vocational Behavior, 77*(2), 196–204.

Walker III, J. V., & Peterson, G. W. (2012). Career thoughts, indecision, and depression: Implications for mental health assessment in career counseling. *Journal of Career Assessment, 20*(4), 497-506.

Whiston, S. C., & Oliver, L. W. (2005). Career counseling process and outcome. In W. B. Walsh and M. L. Savickas, *Handbook of vocational psychology: Theory, research, and practice* (3rd ed.), 155–194.

Wolpe, J. (1973). *The practice of behavior therapy.* New York, NY: Pergamon Press, Inc.

## Figure/Table Credits

Tab. 10.2: Gati et al., "Summary of Dimensions of Career-Related Anxiety," Adapted by Chad Luke.
Tab. 10.3: American Psychiatric Association, "Parallels in Depression and Career (DSM-5)," Adapted by Chad Luke.
Tab. 10.4: American Psychiatric Association, "DSM-5 Criteria by 8-Factor Metamodel," Adapted by Chad Luke.

# SECTION THREE

# CAREER-FOCUSED COUNSELING IN EDUCATIONAL SETTINGS

## Opening Vignette

The role of a school counselor in career development is dynamic, though it can feel one-dimensional at times. School counselors spend great amounts of time building schedules and coordinating collge fairs. Because of this, it is understandable when we do not attend to the underlying career development needs of students. As we return to the case of Xavier and his now-familiar situation, try to imagine how he might appear in the context of a bustling high school campus. Think about how you might recognize his struggles while also considering the ways you can be strategic in addressing the needs of students like him. Here is a reminder of his case:

Xavier is a popular 17-year-old high school senior. He was referred to you for mood concerns, as he hasn't been paying attention in his classes. In an attempt to build rapport with Xavier, you ask him what he likes to do after school, to which he curtly replies, "I mind my own business and do my school work." When you ask if he has an afterschool job, he shifts in his chair and tells you that his grandparents won't let him get one, so he "can focus on schoolwork." Xavier goes on to disclose that he makes straight As in his largely Advanced Placement coursework. He says that his grandparents, whom he lives with, had to give up their educations at early ages in order to provide for their families. While he says he understands his grandparents' concerns, Xavier says he feels stressed

CHAPTER ELEVEN

# Career-Focused Counseling in K–12 Settings

### Chapter Goals

- Examine the developmental dynamics across the ages and stages of this population
- Describe how children process career-related information and the ways this informs career-focused counseling (CFC) with children
- Describe and discuss implementation strategies of the myriad Web-based tools for school-based, CFC

## Introduction

CFC in kindergarten through 12th grade (K–12) has a feel that is different than community-based CFC. The counseling skills and theories are the same, but the timing and tasks vary. In this chapter, we will consider an alternative approach to cultivating the *how* of CFC with children. Counselors are already equipped by this point in the text to begin applying career counseling theory in practice. Rather than starting from scratch, because we are discussing a new population, this chapter explores how fundamental career theories and principles may look with K–12 students. For this reason, this chapter begins with an overview of some of the resources available for school counselors.

# Guiding Resources for School Counselors

One advantage of working as a school counselor in a K–12 setting is that career development is built into the job description. Along with the expectation of addressing career-related issues in these environments, is that the concomitant resources will be available to ensure that this mission of school counselors is met. In this chapter, we begin by reviewing a few prominent resources that guide professional school counselor practice as it relates to CFC. Afterward, we examine how these resources might be extended to address additional developmental issues regarding K–12 vocational identity development. First, we begin with the American School Counselor Association's (ASCA's) National Model. The ASCA is a branch of the American Counseling Association and you may find additional information about this association, which is core to professional school counselor's identity, here:

https://www.schoolcounselor.org/school-counselors-members/about-asca-(1)

The executive summary for the ASCA National Model may be found by following this Web link:

https://www.schoolcounselor.org/asca/media/asca/ASCA%20National%20Model%20Templates/ANMExecSumm.pdf2

Sections of the document have been included in this chapter in order to direct our attention to key facets of the model. For example, what follows is ASCA's vision, mission, goals, and objectives statements that school counselors use as a guide for their identity and work. Two additional documents and their associated links follow the ASCA Model summary for reference.

about paying for college, as his grandparents struggle to survive off of social security and their relatively meager retirement funds. You ask Xavier what he wants to study at university, and he tells you he's too stressed about finances to think about that. He says, "I need to be able to pay for college before I decide what to study."

**Table 11.1. ASCA Vision, Mission, and Goals**

**ASCA's Vision**

The American School Counselor Association (ASCA) is the foundation that expands the image and influence of school counselors through advocacy, leadership, collaboration and systemic change. ASCA empowers school counselors with the knowledge, skills, linkages and resources to promote student success in the school, the home, the community and the world.

**ASCA's Mission**

The mission of ASCA is to represent school counselors and to promote professionalism and ethical practices.

**ASCA's Goals and Objectives**

- Professional development opportunities in areas of critical need are made available to all school counselors.
- Timely, relevant information exists to enhance school counselors' level of skill and professionalism.
- Legislative policy exists that supports school counselors and child advocacy.
- ASCA initiates and supports relevant research and evaluation in school counseling.
- Professional and ethical standards articulate the code of conduct and professional behavior for school counselors.
- Strategic partnerships with stakeholders exist to benefit school counselors and their students.
- Leaders at local, state and national levels champion and lead change initiatives.
- ASCA maintains an organizational structure and administrative functions that facilitate the accomplishment of the goals and objectives.

## ASCA Mindsets and Behaviors Document:

https://www.schoolcounselor.org/asca/media/asca/home/MindsetsBehaviors.pdf

## NCDA Career Development Policy Statement:

http://www.ncda.org/aws/NCDA/pt/sp/guidelines

These three resources are vital for 1) the cultivation of a professional identity of a school counselor, 2) development of ethical and efficacious practice in career development in the role of a school counselor, and 3) effective practice for any counselor addressing career-related issues with children and adolescents. A close examination of the literature on the career development of pre- and elementary school children reveals that we as a profession and as a society struggle to articulate how this could and should look in practice. The National Career Development Association (NCDA; 2005) has placed a stake in the ground to say that the two areas of emphasis in children's career development is, first and foremost, that children have their first experiences with work information through their parents and families. The second area is that it is vital at early ages to debunk gender stereotypes in the world of work for children. These are outstanding observations and calls to action, but they are limited to describing the "what" of career development in children.

At this early stage of this chapter, it is important to note that, while its title describes pre-K–12th grade children, it is not intended to imply that the developmental dynamics are the same on the youngest end of this range (age 4) as those on the oldest end (about 18). Therefore, this chapter looks across the developmental range to explore the stages, tasks, attitudes and experiences necessary for effective CFC in schools with these groups. As we examine in detail *how* to assist the career development of children, there are several considerations to keep in mind. The first is that not all development is created equally. As we saw in an earlier chapter, the world of an individual is made up of the confluence of numerous factors, so the child in front of you in this moment may vary widely from the child in the next moment. Second, there are vast overlapping bodies of empirical literature that describe the *what* of child development: cognitive, social, emotional, psychosocial, and so on. This chapter will not summarize them all. Not only would that likely be overwhelming to readers, but also, and perhaps more importantly, *how* can get lost in the shuffle. We will, however, reference these literatures as we go through. Lastly, this chapter assumes that children are little humans. This means that they have personality, identity, needs, desires, and so forth, just like every other human on the planet. Therefore, accessing career-related material and promoting development is a very human process. At the same time, as developmentalists asserted around the time of the industrial revolution in America, children are not miniature adults, and because of this, their personality, identity, needs, desires, and so forth must be approached differentially. We turn to this last point next.

As noted above, CFC as a field and society have struggled to make the transition from the *what* of career development to the *how* of career development with children. The field of play therapy has greatly informed our understanding of child development, language, and communication. As Magnusson and Starr (2000) assert, play is the work of children. Taking this a step further, play is the language of children (Landreth, 2012). Children, and younger children in particular, do not have the lived experience nor the linguistic ability to express

Child: Daddy, where is mommy going?

Dad: Mommy is going to work, honey.

Child: What is work?

Dad: It is a place that mommy does her job.

Child: Why does she have to go?

Dad: Mommy makes money from going to work.

Child: I have money in my piggy bank. I can give it to her so that she can stay home.

Dad: That's sweet, but it takes a lot more money than that.

Child: How much?

Dad: A lot.

Child: Then why don't you go to work?

Dad: Daddy stays home for work.

Child: Do you get money?

Dad: No, I get different things from staying home and taking care of the house.

Child: Mommy does that too. Why does she still have to go to work?

Dad: That's just how we've set up our family.

Child: Can I watch cartoons?

career-related interests or to respond to language-based career interventions. Consider the following conversation:

Children think about work in radically different ways than adults do, and this is vital to be aware of as we consider approaches to laying the foundation for career development with children. When children play, they are both working and communicating. The challenge for parents, guardians, teachers, and school counselors is that we want to either a) guide the play toward career-related themes or b) interpret the play in adult terms. In so doing, we miss valuable opportunities to connect to the child and let them develop fully through their play. Play is rarely quantifiable in that its end product is often only apparent to the child. In fact, it is the *process* of play that is so formative, not any particular result.

Linda Gottfredson (1981; 2005) has contributed a lot to our understanding of children's career development. One of her four stages of development involve children's orientation to size and power. This stage encompasses ages 3 to 5. It describes how children see the world compared with how adults see it. Try standing on your knees and moving throughout your house. Note the things you can now reach, along with those you can't. Take note of how the world looks from this vantage point. Stand next to an adult who is also standing; how do they appear? Gottfredson asserts that this is the experience of children as they move throughout their world: huge people with huge objects, and their task is to make their way through these grown-up environments using creative problem solving. Their thought process is intuitive, as opposed to being concrete (1981). This means they feel their way through problems. It further means that offering them worksheets or other concrete cognitive interventions may represent a misapprehension of their view of the world, which includes cognitive and social orientations. This is just one example of the call for differential approaches to fostering career development in children and represents but one of the many stages of development that occurs across the pre-K–12 experience. Now imagine this small, young child receiving career-related information from this huge adult, who uses language that is difficult to decipher. In the same way, it seems that adults often struggle to recall what these early experiences of life were like and impose adult logic on child thought processes. Elsewhere, I have referred to this as projective sympathy (Luke, Redekop, & Moralejo, in submission), wherein the parent takes how they think they would feel as a child and projects those feelings and thoughts onto the child. It seems to be a way of trying to parent ourselves into a more successful future.

In the following sections, we examine the highlights of career theory to elementary school students, middle school students, and high school students. We begin with an overview of the career development standards from the ASCA national model, summarized in Table 11.2.

Table 11.2. The ASCA Mindsets & Behaviors for Student Success: K-12 College- and Career-Readiness Standards for Every Student

*Each of the following standards can be applied to the academic, career and social/emotional domains.*

**Category 1: Mindset Standards**

**School counselors encourage the following mindsets for all students.**

**M 1.** Belief in development of whole self, including a healthy balance of mental, social/emotional and physical well-being

**M 2.** Self-confidence in ability to succeed

**M 3.** Sense of belonging in the school environment

**M 4.** Understanding that postsecondary education and life-long learning are necessary for long-term career success

**M 5.** Belief in using abilities to their fullest to achieve high-quality results and outcomes

**M 6.** Positive attitude toward work and learning

**Category 2: Behavior Standards**

**Students will demonstrate the following standards through classroom lessons, activities and/or individual/small-group counseling.**

| Learning Strategies | Self-Management Skills | Social Skills |
|---|---|---|
| B-LS 1. Demonstrate critical-thinking skills to make informed decisions | B-SMS 1. Demonstrate ability to assume responsibility | B-SS 1. Use effective oral and written communication skills and listening skills |
| B-LS 2. Demonstrate creativity | B-SMS 2. Demonstrate self-discipline and self-control | B-SS 2. Create positive and supportive relationships with other students |
| B-LS 3. Use time-management, organizational and study skills | B-SMS 3. Demonstrate ability to work independently | B-SS 3. Create relationships with adults that support success |
| B-LS 4. Apply self-motivation and self-direction to learning | B-SMS 4. Demonstrate ability to delay immediate gratification for long-term rewards | B-SS 4. Demonstrate empathy |
| B-LS 5. Apply media and technology skills | B-SMS 5. Demonstrate perseverance to achieve long- and short-term goals | B-SS 5. Demonstrate ethical decision-making and social responsibility |
| B-LS 6. Set high standards of quality | B-SMS 6. Demonstrate ability to overcome barriers to learning | B-SS 6. Use effective collaboration and cooperation skills |
| B-LS 7. Identify long- and short-term academic, career and social/emotional goals | B-SMS 7. Demonstrate effective coping skills when faced with a problem | B-SS 7. Use leadership and teamwork skills to work effectively in diverse teams |

*(continued)*

Table 11.2. (*continued*)

| Learning Strategies | Self-Management Skills | Social Skills |
|---|---|---|
| B-LS 8. Actively engage in challenging coursework | B-SMS 8. Demonstrate the ability to balance school, home and community activities | B-SS 8. Demonstrate advocacy skills and ability to assert self, when necessary |
| B-LS 9. Gather evidence and consider multiple perspectives to make informed decisions | B-SMS 9. Demonstrate personal safety skills | B-SS 9. Demonstrate social maturity and behaviors appropriate to the situation and environment |
| B-LS 10. Participate in enrichment and extracurricular activities | B-SMS 10. Demonstrate ability to manage transitions and ability to adapt to changing situations and responsibilities | |

https://www.schoolcounselor.org/asca/media/asca/home/MindsetsBehaviors.pdf

# Theory and Practice Considerations in Pre-K–12th Grade

**Trait and Factor Theory.** In Chapter 2 we discussed the various general applications of trait and factor theory to CFC. Here, we look more closely at how these approaches can inform CFC with elementary school students, children ages 3 to 8 or 9. For the sake of brevity, consider Parsons' (1909) formula, if you will, for career development:

***Self knowledge + occupational knowledge + true reasoning = career choice***

What does self knowledge look like across this age range, and how can we access it in elementary school children? The temptation may be to give them a modified interests inventory or to try and read career themes from observing their play. The challenge is that, in terms of child development, these interests are unstable, meaning that they vary based on context, emotion, and social influence. Further, they are often pre-verbal in nature. This means that asking children to put their "self" into words is neurobiologically impossible, depending upon the age of the child (Schore, 2012; Siegel, 2015). The ability to transform self-referential thoughts and feelings, while present, are primitive. This means that counselors need alternative ways to access this information and to expose children to options for self construal. Self knowledge at these stages of early childhood development occur in the context of relationships: parents/guardians, peers, and teachers/role models.

Because of the developmental dynamics of the identification-differentiation continuum, children are in a consistent state of social comparison, of me/not-me self-dialogue. Behaviors of important others in their environment shape this internal dialogue, and can support or limit self-concept and, by extension, self knowledge. For example, statements from parents like "you're just like your father" can impact the self-concept of children, especially depending on the tone and context in which it is said. In contrast, statements like "you are really your own person" can support the child's move toward individuation and differentiation.

Another point here is that vocational identity is the projection of self in the world of work (Super, 1990; Savickas, 2005), and the self does not fully develop until late emerging adulthood (Newmann & Newmann, 2015), self knowledge must focus on exploration and fantasy and directed away from concrete foreclosure. In other words, career development at these stages involve supporting the basic building blocks of becoming a fully functional human in society. It is also why gender-role job stereotyping is so important to watch for. Children are vulnerable to dichotomous thinking when it comes to work, as they infer from their environment what dad's job means for males. If dad works on cars, then that's the kind of work dads do, and since daddy is male, then males work on cars. Occupational knowledge at this point must be limited, as children have limited exposure to the myriad jobs available. In addition, their awareness of jobs and the vague concept of work is developmentally superficial, wherein they focus on the external, often stereotypic characteristics. Even in working with college students in career development, students often express a desire to work in a field they learn about from watching television, with no concrete conceptualization of the work involved nor the path to get there.

True reasoning is where the work of school counselors can make the most impact in developing successful future member of society who contribute through work. True reasoning at these stages involve developmentally appropriate problem solving and conflict resolution. Again, children learn this through play—play that is both individual and group. Games promote cooperation, communication, solution-seeking, and self-regulation skills that are vital both for school and future career success but also the development of the foundation of true reasoning. School counselors and community counselors working with children can each foster career development through processes that harness children's biologically pre-wired inclination to learn. Some may call this indirect career development, but for those in the population who have been to school or held a job, the skills and characteristics described above are very direct in their application indeed.

**Developmental Theory**. The most common application of CFC to elementary school–aged children is via developmental career theory (Zunker, 2016). This has intuitive appeal in that children progress through more developmental stages in a briefer period of time than adults, so these stages are often easier to track. Several tenets of developmental career theory can be gleaned from the literature in order for school counselors, in particular, to work most effectively with elementary school students.

*Development occurs in stages, but these stages are fluid.* School counselors can challenge the boundaries of stage-based development by offering information and skills training at the upward bound of a given stage. For example, they might offer a variety of age-based games that include games for the next age group, in order to provide students with opportunities to continue their challenge-by-choice behaviors.

*Stage progression occurs via the completion of specific and broad tasks.* School counselors can assess task completion in the context of play, noting stage-based task approach/avoidance as indicators of development. For example, playing games in small groups using story cubes can illuminate children's self-referential themes (as play is a projection of oneself onto characters and roles).

*Children are historical, context-dependent individuals (like everyone else), so their approaches to tasks at various stages emerge from their history of relationships and other experiences*. School counselors can use this information to help children turn around and shape their home environment and relationships. For example, children can ask questions of caregivers about attitudes and behaviors related to work but in language that children can understand. Effective school counselors recognize that a) children's home environments are the most influential for early career development, b) the primary access of influence school counselors have on the home is through their students, and c) they can support children's career development in the home through the student without putting the child in inappropriate positions.

**Social and Cognitive Theory**. One of the major contributions to the fields of psychology and education comes in the form of Bandura's (1977; 1997) work on self-efficacy. As discussed in an earlier chapter, self-efficacy is the belief in one's ability to accomplish a task. Self-efficacy is a valuable component of children's development in that is plays an important role in the effort one invests in a task and the duration of that effort. Self-efficacy is strengthened through four processes: personal mastery, vicarious reinforcement, verbal persuasion, and physiological arousal. In career development among elementary school children, these paths to self-efficacy might look like the following. Please keep in mind that career development at these ages and stages involve capacity-building in that many of the daily living skills in childhood lay the foundation for later stages of career development.

Personal mastery, as an example of the application of social cognitive career theory (SCCT) to elementary school students, essentially claims that success begets success: once an individual experiences success at a given task, they are more likely to believe that it will again be possible for them. This extends to foundational tasks for career development. For example, children can begin building a record of success in play, if you will. As they grow in their ability to create, design, and implement an image of their play goals, they can also increase their self-efficacy. School counselors work with children and can seize upon opportunities to inspire parents to identify these mastery experiences. The caveat is to praise the effort, problem solving, frustration tolerance, and perseverance that occur in play, as opposed to praising outcomes exclusively. Career-focused counselors understand and are keenly aware that clients may encounter setbacks and "no's" in their own career development and must, therefore, have the personal resilience skills that self-efficacy brings.

**Postmodern and Emergent Theory**. Postmodern approaches to career development involve both creativity and creation, regardless of whether it is Savickas's (2005) Career Construction Theory or Krumboltz's Happenstance Learning Theory (2009). Few among the groups described throughout this book are as creative as pre- and elementary school children.

They are unfettered by the rules of logic in their creative play (work). That is one reason some of us, as counselors, tend to cringe when we hear adults make comments like "that's not realistic" in response to children's fantasy play. The purpose of this creative exploration is to test reality and push the bounds of what is possible. By the time we are adults, the boundaries of what is possible are often firmly fixed. Mitchell, Levin, and Krumboltz (1999) enumerated curiosity among five key skills or characteristics to foster in clients to prepare them for serendipity, or Planned Happenstance, as he once called his theory (1999). If play is the work of children, then curiosity is the tool they use for their work. Children's play—their creative work—can be seen as a form of self-scaffolding, in which they push their own skills and understanding of the world, its rules and its limits.

This corresponds to Savickas's (2005) description of self and identity. According to Savickas, self is constructed through language—the words one uses to describe oneself. However, for children, language is a less-than-accurate way to construe self, due in part to brain development and also to the limited experience and repository of words available. This brings us back to the concept of play as the language of children—the self is both developed and communicated through child's play. Identity, then, as being the self in context, is the child's sense of self at play with adults, peers, and toys. The context Savickas describes extends beyond the social role as it would with adults, to the "social" contexts in which a child plays. The point here is that the career development for elementary school children may need to emphasize less language-based learning about career and more access to play that allows them to explore, fantasize, and create.

Young children in particular are highly dependent upon their environments and relationships for their development. Their early interactions with adults and careers can leave lasting impressions about how they must comport themselves as they think about work. Most of this development is unconscious, pre-verbal in nature, and therefore, requires attunement from caregivers, school counselors in this case, to decipher these emergent, but nascent, attitudes. School counselors are in strategic positions to influence the career development of children and pre-adolescents in elementary school, especially when they recognize the indicators of identity and vocational development. It is vital to take action in their development as young humans with similar and distinct characteristics of older children and adults.

# Theory and Practice Considerations in Middle School

This chapter provides an opportunity to conceptualize CFC with children and adolescents from multiple perspectives. For example, rather than revisiting the conceptual scheme from the previous section with elementary school aged children to early adolescents, we turn to examine Super's (1990) core considerations. Super (1990) and, later, Schultheiss (2005) provide useful conceptual schemes for targeting career-related interventions for middle-schoolers. "Nevertheless, the consensus from more recent research appears to be that interest patterns are rather variable from childhood to adolescence and gain relative stability in early adulthood" (Betsworth & Fouad, 1997; Hansen, 1984), supporting Fagin's (1953) assertion that "interest patterns are probably neither well differentiated nor very stable before age 15" (p. 172) (Hartung, Porfeli, & Vondracek, 2005, p. 405). Hartung et al., also assert that the literature on career development in childhood really picks up in middle school. In fact, it is 7th grade (around age 11-13) that children really begin to work outside their home and family for pay (as many as 75%) (Hartung et al., 2005). Therefore, along with the developmental changes that occur during the transition to middle school, work-related behaviors also change, adding to the complications—and opportunities—associated with supporting career development among pre- and early teenagers.

Super (1990) identified tasks related to this period of development: curiosity, exploration, information, key figures, interests, locus of control, time perspective, self-concept, and intentional (having a plan). These characteristics alone are sufficient for school-based counselors in shaping the career development of middle school students. Rather than provide prescriptive direction for creating individual, group, and classroom lessons plans, herein is a discussion of descriptive features of his and subsequent work (see Schultheiss, 2004; 2008). Naturally, school counselors are trained in the basics of lesson planning, classroom guidance, and organization and the administration of school counseling programs; these provide the foundations upon which CFC in middle and high school settings take place. For example, curiosity is a skill or characteristic emphasized by both Gottfredson (2005) to avoid premature circumscription and Mitchell, Levin, and Krumboltz (1999; Krumboltz, 2009) to allow the natural imagination of this age group to form the impetus for exploration. Exploration about one's self and the work world can address one's curiosity and lead directly to information-seeking. One excellent source of career-related information is key figures, those influential, inspirational, and grounded leaders in a youth's life that can assist them in both gathering accurate information, and determining how to use this information. This can help refine their interests, both personal and professional. Locus of control, a construct first articulated by Rotter (1966), is an estimate of one's ability to influence their environment. In other words, succeses are the outcomes of one's behaviors, the result of luck, an accident, powerful others, or on the other hand, hard work and self-determination. This belief about whether effort matters or not figures in the time orientation, wherein these students begin to see beyond the past and present and begin preparation for a future that is the product of their action. This purpose and preparation shapes their self-perception or self-concept and aids in aiming their efforts through being planful.

Middle school CFC takes the form of relationship-based reflection on activities that implicitly and explicitly connect to identity and vocational development. Drawing out these experiences and interests, patterns, and processes enables middle school students to learn to attend to their environment in meaningful ways. Therefore, upon entering high school, they are more practiced at self-reflection and environmental introspection, wherein they can begin to understand their role in the world and its relation to work.

# Theory and Practice Considerations

# in High School

In this section, we move toward middle and later adolescence in school settings for career development. As you read, please keep one primary thought in mind—one realization above all others—that regardless of how many inventories, activities, interviews, and so forth an adolescent may engage in as they prepare for graduation, very little in their life to this point can compare with the perceived enormity of choosing a career. Up to this point, they may have felt supported by teachers, counselors, parents or guardians, and friends, but there is something uniquely isolating about choosing a career. Part of this comes from the things we tell ourselves about such decisions. See if any of these self-statements resonate with you as you look back on your high school and college years. Some are explicit, others are implicit.

- I must make the right decision!
- This decision is permanent.
- The rest of my life is at stake.
- If I mess this up, it will be awful!
- There is no way I can make a decision this big!
- I don't know where to begin!
- I don't need a plan.
- This will sort itself out by graduation.
- I'm not planning to graduate high school or go to college, so this is a waste of time.

When working with these youth, it is vital that the counselor recognize the perceived weight of the process and, ultimately, the decision. The ability to self-regulate and tolerate ambiguity in the face of the set of steps is paramount in working with adolescents. It is important, as we address the following components of career development, as outlined in the ASCA model, that we assist students in sorting fact from fiction and identify barriers in their thinking to effective learning and planning. Adolescents, while they have typically developed more complexity in their cognitive processes, continue to struggle with thinking that any planning means all planning leading to a certain conclusion. One strength of school counselors is their foundation of counseling skills and methods from which they can draw on vast resources to help students, rather than throwing information at them to see what sticks. In CFC in high school settings, information is not the same as knowledge. Information is the raw material of knowledge, making it a necessary but insufficient condition for success. This first standard is skills-based and emphasizes the development of an orientation toward information-seeking with students, and is presented in Table 11.3.

**Table 11.3. ASCA Standard A**

| |
|---|
| *Standard A: Students will acquire the skills to investigate the world of work in relation to knowledge of self and to make informed career decisions.* |
| *C: A1 Develop career awareness* |
| *C: A1.3. Develop an awareness of personal abilities, skills, interests and motivations* |
| *C: A2 Develop employment readiness* |
| 1.C: B1 Acquire career information |
| 2.C: B2 Identify career goals |
| C: C1 Acquire knowledge to achieve career goals |
| C: C2 Apply skills to achieve career goals |

These steps coincide with Porfeli and Lee's (2012) three stages of adolescent career development: career exploration, career commitment, and career reconsideration. These stages bear discussion, since, despite their being reiterations of previous conceptualizations, they provide a succinct outline for understanding career development in middle and, in particular, high school.

In career exploration, identity exploration is inextricably interwoven, so interventions and experiences that affect one will likely—necessarily—affect the other. This means that the majority of a high school student's daily experiences in and out of school have bearing on their identity, and by extension, their career or vocational identity. Therefore, it is less an issue of creating experiences or utilizing disembodied career assessments and more about the process of drawing out the elements of identity as displayed in their day-to-day, moment-to-moment experiences. Once these are evoked and elucidated, they can be connected to career channels—channels providing a conduit between the self and the self at work.

Two types of exploration in children and adolescents: in-breadth, in which they explore multiple careers to discern interest, and in-depth, where they encounter a career that seems interesting, and they investigate it further (Porfeli & Lee, 2012). These in-depth and in-breath explorations become more self evident in light of the discussion of self in everyday experiences above.

Career commitment is the next step and involves thoughts, behaviors, and connection. "Commitment to a career is demonstrated in the decisions (that is, thoughts), choices (that is, behaviors), and vocational identities (that is, a personal connection to one's decisions and choices) that children establish" (Porfeli & Lee, 2012, p. 14). While decidedness in career development is generally associated with positive outcomes, it is not profitable for an adolescent to foreclose on the decision-making process just to have the decision made (Porfeli & Lee, 2012). The three components of career commitment speak to this dilemma: a student in high school must experience alignment in their thinking about the career decision-making process, leading to effective efforts toward making that choice and ensuring that it aligns with some version of their sense of self.

Career reconsideration is an important stage and one in which high school counselors and adolescent counselors in general play a critical role. Development is not static, at least not when on a healthful trajectory. Therefore, the individual can and should expect to grow and change. This means that well-thought-out decisions from middle school or earlier on in high school may not continue to be a good fit. It means that unless previous decisions and choices are revisited with an open mind, the implementation of a job choice may match a previous version of the individual rather than the current one. In addition, this offers an excellent opportunity to normalize the change process, recognizing that few choices are or need be permanent so as to inoculate the student/adolescent from angst associated with possible, often likely, changes upon arriving in college.

Here are these stages as they might present in working with Xavier. At the end of the transcript excerpt, you will find three key Web-based resources for use in these stages.

## Career Exploration

CO: Xavier, you've shared with me some of your current frustrations, and I can tell they have been getting you down. I wonder if we could change gears for a moment and talk a little about things that cause you less frustration.
CL: Like what?
CO: What things happen in your regular life that give you positive emotions?
CL: Like at school?
CO: At school, home, work, or wherever.
CL: It's hard to say. I don't think about that stuff much.
CO: That's probably a pretty good reason to think about it together, then?
CL: Sure. I really like history, though my classes are a little dull.
CO: What draws you to history?
CL: I really like reading about warfare—the circumstances leading up to wars and the ways armies maneuvered to gain position and advantage.
CO: Oh, those are interesting!
CL: I also like reading and learning about the stories of the civilian leaders and how they rose to power and how their actions affected the populace.
CO: Wow, you really do enjoy history!
CL: Yeah, but there's no jobs for a history buff.
CO: Well, hold on, we're not planning a career yet. I'm just learning about what you enjoy. Your face changes when you talk about your history-related interests.
CL: It is definitely a different feeling than frustration, unless I think about getting a job or majoring in college. Everyone says I should do what I love, but I can't see this as being more than a hobby.
CO: I can see this is weighing on you, so let's look a little closer. First of all, it could be that history remains in the hobbies domain. And that's great, because many people *work* a job and *live* at home, while others live through their career. What do you think the interests related to history say about you as a person?

CL: I've kind of only thought about how I can't pick a major or career. I think I really like the strategy component in warfare, and I like seeing how people problem-solved their life situations.
CO: It sounds like intentional, planful movements, along with the plight of humans overcoming obstacles?
CL: That's exactly right.
CO: So, then how might those interests show themselves in the ways in which you approach your daily life?
CL: Oh, I see! I'm pretty strategic in how I approach school, work, and money. One of the ways I am able to make such good grades, even when I'm feeling frustrated, is that I plan and strategize—I can be very efficient in my studies.
CO: And when you encounter a challenge like college major or career ...
CL: I can't seem to map out a strategy or direction.
CO: No wonder you're so frustrated—your main skills are being threatened in this task.
CL: Yeah, I'm used to being able to solve problems on my own.
CO: That makes me wonder if you've come across a historical precedent for the situation in which you now find yourself.
CL: How do you mean?
CO: Well, imagine a leader from a period you've studied with interest, either a warrior or political leader who found themselves up against new obstacles that did not have a clear path forward.
CL: There are tons of instances of leaders in this type of position.
CO: Any lessons you could learn?
CL: I get it. [discusses a couple of leaders with whom he identifies]
CO: I'm glad to hear you make these connections. When exploring careers, we are really exploring ourselves and making hypotheses about who we are in the work world. So, as we discuss major and career possibilities, it is really taking what you know about yourself and looking for ways to use their characteristics in work. Instead of "history jobs," let's discuss the jobs that relate to the characteristics someone interested in history might bring.
CL: I've never tried anything like that before!

## Career Commitment

CO: Xavier, you have had a couple of weeks to explore career domains on your own. I wonder how that was for you.
CL: I'm still not feeling totally confident but I have quite a few choices now.
CO: Really? What's that like for you?

CL: It is very different than before. I have looked for job areas using the resources you provided, paying special attention to work that involves strategic planning, human advocacy, and of course, reading and analytic skills.
CO: Wow, that *is* different than before! What have you found?
CL: Of course, there are the usual suspects: high school teacher, librarian, museum staff, archivist, etc. But then, I found a lot of jobs that require this kind of thinking, like FBI agent and law enforcement in general, law, business, management, and sales, in addition to health and human services.
CO: Now you have a bunch of potential options! We call this in-breadth exploration, in that you have identified quite a number of options. It seems you have experienced a lot of success with this.
CL: Yeah, it feels really good to feel like I have options. I still don't know what my major should be, and that's a little stressful, but I feel more confident in my ability to select something meaningful.
CO: That is great to hear. There are several things we can do to take the next steps. For example, here are additional resources that can help you identify specific job titles, college majors that align with those jobs, and more information on how to choose.
CL: Okay. It is still a lot to take in, but now I have a strategy!
CO: Good. Once you've spent some time exploring and taking some notes, perhaps you could bring what you find to our next session?

One Day, One Job website:

http://www.onedayonejob.com/about/

California Career Zone:

https://www.cacareerzone.org

Bureau of Labor and Statistics—K-12:

http://www.bls.gov/k12/

# Neuro-Informed CFC in Schools

Career and vocational development in K–12 settings is about exploration, as opposed to the information aggregation models often proffered. Children with secure attachment are free to explore, and through this exploration, they discover their own truths about the self in relation to the environment. This can lead to carving a place in the world to fit this sense of self.

Neurobiologically, these secure attachments are pre-requisites for whole-brain development (Schore, 2005) and brain-to-brain connection (Siegel, 2015). Consider Schore's words on the topic:

> Although the role of early expressed genetic factors is an essential focus of current study, it has become clear that genes do not specify behavior absolutely; prenatal and postnatal environmental factors play critical roles in these developmental origins. The social environment, particularly the one created together by the mother and infant, directly affects gene-environment interactions and, thereby, has long-enduring effects ... studies in neuroscience indicate that development represents an experiential shaping of genetic potential and that early experiences with the social environment are critical to the maturation of brain tissue. Thus, nature's potential can be realized only as it is facilitated by nurture. (2005, pp. 204–205)

Children's brains are at their most vulnerable throughout their school years, during which they experience periods of peak development. During these times, they need to be able to lean on those trusted others who can offer a regulated experience that mitigates their own developmental challenges. What this means in practice with CFC in schools is that, often, career development takes on the form of a sustaining relationship through which the child draws on the strength of the adult with whom they feel connected as they experience disequilibrium. Through these regulating relationships, their own brains become more regulated (Siegel, 2015), allowing for continued exploration and identity consolidation.

# Summary

If career development is truly a lifelong process that starts in childhood, the fields of career counseling and vocational psychology have come up short in terms of research on the early end of the spectrum of development (Howard & Walsh, 2011; Schultheiss, 2008). The literature that does exist highlights how childhood and adolescent career development requires all hands on deck: parents, teachers, and guidance counselors. Counselors really must enlist the help and support of parents and guardians in this process (Bryant et al., 2006; Cinamon & Dan, 2010). The challenges of career development and decision making among children and adolescents are particularly daunting as they represent unique, high-stakes decision making. These children and adolescents need wraparound support to navigate the process successfully without foreclosing prematurely on the process (Porfeli & Lee, 2012).

# References

American Counseling Association. (2014). ACA Code of Ethics. Alexandria, VA: Author.

ASCA National Model (n. d.). Alexandria, VA: American School Counselor Association.

Bandura, A. (1977). Self-efficacy: Toward a unifying theory of behavioral change. *Psychological Review, 84*, 191–215.

Bandura, A. (1997). *Self-efficacy: The exercise of control*. New York, NY: Freeman.

Betsworth, D. G., & Fouad, N. A. (1997). Vocational interests: A look at the past 70 years and a glance at the future. *Career Development Quarterly, 46*, 23–47.

Bryant, B. K., Zvonkovic, A. M., & Reynolds, P. (2006). Parenting in relation to child and adolescent vocational development. *Journal of Vocational Behavior, 69*(1), 149–175.

Cinamon, R. G., & Dan, O. (2010). Parental attitudes toward preschoolers' career education: A mixed-method study. *Journal of Career Development, 37*(2), 519–540.

Hansen, J. C. (1984). The measurement of vocational interests: Issues and future directions. In S. D. Brown & R. W. Lent (Eds.), *Handbook of counseling psychology* (1st ed., pp. 99–136). New York, NY: Wiley.

Hartung, P. J., Porfeli, E. J., & Vondracek, F. W. (2005). Child vocational development: A review and reconsideration. *Journal of vocational behavior, 66*(3), 385–419.

NCDA Career Development Policy Statement (n. d.). Broken Arrow, OK: National Career Development Association.

Fagin, B. (1953). Guiding the vocational interests of the child. *Education, 74*, 171–179.

Gottfredson, L. S. (1981). Circumscription and compromise: A developmental theory of occupational aspirations. *Journal of Counseling Psychology, 28*, 545–579.

Gottfredson, L. S. (2005). Using Gottfredson's theory of circumscription and compromise in career guidance and counseling. *Career development and counseling: Putting theory and research to work*, 71–100.

Howard, K. A., & Walsh, M. E. (2011). Children's conceptions of career choice and attainment: Model development. *Journal of Career Development, 38*(3), 256–271.

Krumboltz, J. D. (2009). The happenstance learning theory. *Journal of Career Assessment, 17*(2), 135–154.

Landreth, G. L. (2012). *Play therapy: The art of the relationship*. New York, NY: Routledge.

Luke, Redekop, Moralejo (in submission). From microaggressions to neural-aggressions: A neuro-informed counseling perspective. *Journal of Multicultural Counseling and Development*.

Magnuson, C. S., & Starr, M. F. (2000). How early is too early to begin life career planning? The importance of the elementary school years. *Journal of Career Development, 27*(2), 89–101.

Mitchell, K. E., Levin, S., & Krumboltz, J. D. (1999). Planned happenstance: Constructing unexpected career opportunities. *Journal of counseling & Development, 77*(2), 115–124.

Newman, B. M., & Newman, P. R. (2054). *Development through life: A psychosocial approach*. Stamford, CT: Cengage Learning.

Parsons, F. (1909). *Choosing a vocation*. Boston, MA: Houghton Mifflin.

Porfeli, E. J., & Lee, B. (2012). Career development during childhood and adolescence. *New directions for youth development, 2012*(134), 11–22.

Rotter, J. B. (1966). Generalized expectancies for internal versus external control of reinforcement. *Psychological monographs: General and applied, 80*(1), 1.

Savickas, M. L. (2005). The theory and practice of career construction. *Career development and counseling: Putting theory and research to work, 1*, 42–70.

Schore, A. N. (2012). *The Science of the Art of Psychotherapy*. New York, NY: WW Norton & Company.

Schultheiss, D. E. P., Palma, T. V., & Manzi, A. J. (2005). Career development in middle childhood: A qualitative inquiry. *The Career Development Quarterly*, *53*(3), 246–262.

Schultheiss, D. E. P. (2008). Current status and future agenda for the theory, research, and practice of childhood career development. *The Career Development Quarterly*, *57*(1), 7–24.

Siegel, D. J. (2015). *The developing mind: How relationships and the brain interact to shape who we are.* New York, NY: Guilford Publications.

Super, D. E. (1990). A life-span, life-space approach to career development. In D. Brown & L. Brooks, *Career choice and development: Applying contemporary theories to practice*, (2nd ed.), (pp. 197–261). San Francisco, CA: Jossey-Bass.

Wood, C., & Kaszubowski, Y. (2008). The career development needs of rural elementary school students. *The Elementary School Journal*, *108*(5), 431–444.

Zunker, V. (2016). *Career counseling: A holistic approach* (9th ed.). Boston, MA: Cengage.

# CHAPTER TWELVE

# Career-Focused Counseling in College and Emerging Adulthood

### Chapter Goals

- Identify the developmental needs of college students as they provide the context in which career-focused counseling (CFC) takes place.
- Discuss strategies for intervening in developmentally appropriate ways with college students and other emerging adults.
- Contrast earlier models of positivist career counseling with current CFC.

## Introduction

This chapter approaches CFC in the context of college in a little different way than might be expected. It continues using the lens of human development, a wellness orientation, prevention and early intervention, and client autonomy as foundational. But this chapter uses developmental theory that extends Erikson's work on psychosocial development that readers may not be familiar with unless they have taken a course in college student development. Throughout this chapter, CFC is viewed through the theory of Chickering and Reisser's (1993) model of development that they pioneered in their book *Education and Identity*. The theory frames the discussion of the challenges college students face in navigating college and how these challenges interact with major and career decision making. The model is not one of career development, per se, but it includes and elucidates the process of making these challenging decisions.

### Opening Vignette

Alexa is a 21-year-old college student working at a local restaurant who comes to you for career counseling. She tells you that she switched from a major in special education to one in exercise science. After some inquiry, you learn that she initially chose special education, because a family member did that, and she then chose exercise science, because she ran cross-country all 4 years of high school. When asked what she wants to deal with in counseling, Alexa says, "Stress. Thinking about getting a job after graduation has been making me worry." She goes on to tell you that she switched out of special education after her first semester taking upper-division classes in her major. Alexa says that she wasn't sure if she wanted to teach, because she would "get too attached to the kids." She reports similar concerns with an exercise science job like gym teacher. She questions whether she wants to teach at all. Wiping away tears, Alexa discloses that she feels like she has been "trying to fill some kind of void inside" by finding a meaningful job in which she can help people, but to a greater extent that her restaurant server job.

As you read this chapter, reflect on the developmental tasks that accompany this stage of development. Are there tasks that seem to need to be completed prior to addressing career issues? Are that tasks that seem to be more likely to be completed after addressing career issues?

# College Student Development Theory

Chickering and Reisser (1993) developed and extended Chickering's (1969) model of student development to assist college staff and faculty in better assisting individuals during this tumultuous time. Their work has generated considerable research in the field and has attained a status in the college student development literature akin to that which Erikson's psychosocial model has in developmental psychology. The basic premise of the theory is that college takes place during a key transition period in the life of an adolescent—though the label for this stage of development continues to be debated, I use later adolescence, emerging adulthood, and early pre-adulthood somewhat interchangeably. This stage has its own clear set of tasks, or vectors, in Chickering's approach, the navigation of which established the identity of the individual as they progress through college and launch into life beyond college. These vectors, of which there are seven, include the following: Developing Competence, Managing Emotions, Moving through Autonomy toward Interdependence, Developing Mature Relationships, Establishing Identity, Developing Purpose, and Developing Integrity. Table 12.1 contains a summary and overview of these vectors for reference. While these vectors appear to progress in a stepwise fashion, Chickering was adamant that they are not linear, are recursive, and can occur in any order. The value of this model for CFC rests in the reality that career development does not occur in a vacuum and is rarely, if ever, a standalone issue for emerging adults.

**Table 12.1. Seven Vectors for Student Development**

| | |
|---|---|
| Developing Competence | Includes competence in the following domains:<br>• Intellectual—using one's mind to master content and "building a repertoire of skills to comprehend, analyze, and synthesize" leading to "developing new frames of reference" (1993, p. 45)<br>• Physical—revolves around competence and self-discipline, related to the arts and athletics<br>• Interpersonal—includes the basics of "listening, cooperating, and communicating effectively" but also to "tune in to another person and respond appropriately" (p. 46). |
| Managing Emotions | • Describes the power of negative emotions to "derail" one's learning process and requires allowing negative emotions to flow such that the individual can "release irritations," "deal with fears," and "heal emotional wounds"<br>• Also challenges helpers to bring into awareness and then harness the power of positive emotions, which include "rapture, relief, sympathy, yearning, worship, wonder and awe" (p. 47) |
| Moving through Autonomy toward Interdependence | • Balances need for both dependence and independence in making choices and decisions in life<br>• "It [emotional independence] culminates in diminishing need for such supports and willingness to risk loss of friends or status in order to pursue strong interests or stand on convictions" |

| | |
|---|---|
| Developing Mature Relationships | • "Involves (1) tolerance and appreciation of differences (2) capacity for intimacy ... more in-depth sharing and less clinging" (p. 48) |
| Establishing Identity | • "Development of identity is the process of discovering with what kinds of experience, at what levels of intensity and frequency, we resonate in satisfying, in safe, or in self-destructive fashion" (p. 49)<br>• Involves seven components:<br>1 Comfort with body and appearance<br>2 Comfort with gender and sexual orientation<br>3 Sense of self in a social, historical, and cultural context<br>4 Clarification of self-concept through role and life-style<br>5 Sense of self in response to feedback from valued others<br>6 Self-acceptance and self-esteem<br>7 Personal stability and integration (p. 49) |
| Developing Purpose | • "Entails an increasing ability to be intentional, to assess interests and options, to clarify goals, to make plans, and to persist despite obstacles ... It also involves a growing ability to unify one's many different goals within the scope of a larger, more meaningful purpose, and to exercise intentionality on a daily basis" (p. 50) |
| Developing Integrity | • "Involves three sequential but overlapping stages:<br>1 humanizing values<br>2 personalizing values<br>3 developing congruence" (p. 50) |

Even a cursory look at the table highlights the complexity and volume of tasks required during the college years. There is one point to highlight above the others at this point: given the context of stages and tasks during emerging adulthood, it is terribly reductive to view career development as *merely* career decision-making, as if it exists apart from all the other domains of development vying for attention during this time. CFC with college students is necessarily holistic counseling, virtually impossible to divorce from the other components of the emerging self. Additionally, every individual a counselor encounters is unique, in that their process along these developmental dimensions will be widely variable. There is no room for cookie cutter approaches or interventions here! Chickering and Reisser's 1993 revision of Chickering's 1969 model highlights this well. Of note is the revision of the model based on the different developmental trajectories between men and women. This was the result of revisions to Kohlberg's (1981) theory of moral development by Carol Gilligan (1982; 1993).

# Developing Purpose

Developing purpose is Chickering's sixth vector, and while the theory claims to be more of a spiral, rather than linear, there is a sense in the literature that purpose and vocational identity develops after individual identity (Hammond, Michael, & Luke, 2017). This creates challenges for counselors in college settings addressing career-related concerns. However, this is a theoretical proposition; in practice, it may make more sense to facilitate development across vectors simultaneously. Therefore, this section concerns the developing purpose vectors, while also discussing its relation to the other vectors relevant for effective CFC. Developing purpose emerges from the process of exploring and, to an extent, answering identity questions (e.g., Who am I?) and prepares the way for the next questions: "Where am I going? What are my goals and ideals? What kind of life do I want to lead as I complete my college experience?" (Chickering & Reisser, 1993, p. 209).

The first step in addressing these questions with college student clients is to address the proverbial *elephant in the room*. The elephant, in this instance, is magical thinking that simply attending college culminates in answers to these questions and, along with the diploma, comes a career path. This is logical when we consider the vestiges of adolescent egocentrism (Elkind, 1967), such as "I'm special," no one can possibly understand *my* struggle," and "Consequences happen to *other* people; not me." The result is often passivity and ignoring opportunities to grow through engagement of the process using the resources available to them. Others recognize the need but feel completely overwhelmed by the prospect of taking action to create a future they cannot yet imagine. At the risk of losing the reader by mixing elephant metaphors, the age-old riddle of "how do you eat an elephant" rings true here: one bite at a time. It has also been said that actors work tirelessly for decades to become an "overnight success." Students must be supported in taking one step (bite) at a time, but they must take that step. One of the reasons they might not is related to change.

As alluded to in another chapter, change takes readiness (Miller & Rollnick, 2012; Prochaksa & Norcross, 2013). Imagine that many college students do not view career decision-making or career development as a problem to be solved. Or that it is a problem but not up to them to resolve. How might that student respond to offers of help and opportunities for skill development? To answer this, consider the last time you were offered help to address a problem you did not think you had or that you did not think was your responsibility to change. What was your reaction? I once worked at a college wherein every entering student was required to take the Strong Interest Inventory and Myers'-Briggs Type Inventory and to meet with a career counselor to discuss their results. Arguably, this is an incredible opportunity for these students to engage right away in a self-exploration process that can help clarify career direction. However, about 25% of students either did not take the inventories, did not show up to their meeting, or needed constant prompting to make it. Another 25% or so followed through but in a clearly perfunctory way. What made these students so reluctant to avail themselves of this opportunity? Some, as expected, felt they already had the answers to these questions, because their major was set and was clearly related to their future career plans: "I'm pre-med and I want to be a pediatric specialist." But for a large number of students, it is more likely that they were not ready to engage, as seen through comments like, "Why do we have to think about this stuff now?," "I just got here!," or "It will all work out." In these many instances, CFC must take a new tack.

Prochaska and Norcross (2013) suggest that individuals whware in precontemplation (no problem) and contemplation (problem, but not my responsibility) respond best to insight-oriented, experiential interventions to move them toward readiness. Miller and Rollnick (2013) go so far as to say that if, when working with a client, the counselor encounters resistance, it is the fault of the counselor for using interventions that do not match the stage of readiness the client is in. this is fascinating to contemplate as researchers and practitioners continue to scratch their collective heads over the vast under-utilization of career services and other resources available on college campuses. On the contrary, the last semester of college tends to bring a surge of students to career services offices in an attempt to accomplish in that visit what would have best been initiated and implemented over the previous 4 to 6 years. This is where CFC is not just the name of another book but is a paradigm shift. As counselors, we should be among the most effective at tapping into the intrinsic motivation of the individual.

This presents an interesting corollary between counselors and clients: counselors must be intentional about helping college students become intentional about their career—and life—development. Chickering and Reisser (1993) offer a succinct description of this: "To be intentional is to be skilled in consciously choosing priorities, in aligning action with purpose, in motivating oneself consistently towards goals, and in persevering despite barriers or setbacks" (p. 212). In translating this to practice, career-focused counselors work to draw out the client's internal sense of motivation, which leads more successfully to consistent, purposeful behavior. Several developmental considerations are relevant to moving counselors toward this end.

First of all, as noted previously, later-stage adolescents need effective help-seeking skills, yet also have the tendency to not seek help. Bridges (2014) notes:

> Although many students struggle with career-related issues in college, comparatively few engage the career services offered by their academic institutions for help with their difficulties. In addition, there is little research on the factors influencing students' decisions to engage in counseling for career-related issues, making it difficult to develop programs to enhance the students' use of career counseling services. (Ludwikowski, Vogel, & Armstrong, 2009, p. 408)

This is tied to adolescent egocentrism. Part of the process of individuation is the belief that they can do it on their own or that seeking help conveys weakness. Ironically, asking for help in college is both a belief and a skill tied to student success. College self-efficacy is the belief that a student can successfully complete tasks related to college. The College Self Efficacy Inventory (CSEI) is a measure of this construct and explores self-efficacy in four domains: course, roommate, and social (Solberg & O'Brien, 1993). Social self-efficacy in this context includes the ability to talk with professors and, ostensibly, to ask for help (Gore, Leuwerke, & Turley, 2005). Belief in ability often precedes action (Bandura, 1997), but it also precedes intention, which precedes behavior (Fishbein & Ajzen, 1975; Ajzen & Fishbein, 1980). The implications for CFC with college students is that building capacity for belief in one's ability (self-efficacy) in the domain of speaking with campus leaders (i. e., professors) may remove one barrier to help-seeking and increase the likelihood that help will be sought. In fact, self-efficacy related to college tasks has been found to be connected to others factors associated with student success (Luke, Redekop, & Burgin, 2014; Luke, Diambra, & Gibbons, 2014; Luke & Diambra, 2017, in press).

Another reason for the lack of help-seeking is the perception of weakness, as noted above. Anecdotally, as a former career center director, we experimented with the language students used to describe their career decision-making status. One group, when asked what their major was, labeled themselves as undecided, and their body language validated how such students perceived themselves and may be perceived by others, as reported by Ludwikowski, Vogel, and Armstrong (2009), as "indecisive, unmotivated, less intelligent, and unsuccessful" (p. 409). With the other group, we replaced "undecided" with "still deciding," and the results were striking. Students' body language changed—they opened their posture, stood taller, and made better eye contact—when they stated they were still deciding. In terms of identity and self-efficacy, the reasons have intuitive appeal. Students shifted their self-concept from what they cannot or have not done (i.e., "Un") to something more intentional (i.e., "still ... ") which implies direction and openness. Language has been a part of counseling interventions for decades and can be seen in Adlerian, Narrative, Solution-Focused, Cognitive-Behavioral, and many other approaches. Reminding clients that they can alter their perception of reality by adjusting their language is just another of the myriad ways CFC helps to prepare clients for change.

Duffy and Sedlacek (2010) reference Super (1990) and may connect to Chickering's developing purpose vector. Research on career calling, beyond its implicit religious associations, may highlight the value in searching for a sense of purpose within a college major and career direction. Rather than finding a calling and using it in work, it may be that selecting work and finding or creating the meaning within that work may be most expeditious in effective career decision-making among college students. Duffy and Sedlacek (2010) found that 40% of the students in a public, nonreligious university in their study felt strongly that they had a calling. They add the vital caveat that, for students who feel a sense of career calling or those seeking one, counselors explore what the individual students means by calling and how their goals for implementing this calling correspond (or not) with other career-related values, interests, skills, and personality. This is important, because Chickering and Reisser assert that having a sense of purpose is actually more motivating than just establishing goals.

Second, despite the apparent ubiquity of career information, college students continue to struggle in navigating it. Domene et al. (2015) offer an insight into online information overload for those students who are not secure in their career identity but who are seeking career-related information. Ironically, the volume of information decreases the effectiveness of the information-seeking process, as well as self-efficacy. This is unfortunate, because in an age of limited resources paired with virtually unlimited technology, career service resources are often outsourced to Web-based information, because it is so cost-effective, despite the fact that individual career counseling is most effective (Vertberger and Gati, 2015). In order to inoculate college students from information overload and saturation, career-focused counselors can assist students in increasing subjective well-being (Hartung & Taber, 2008) (i.e., contentment) and tolerance for ambiguity and uncertainty (Domene et al., 2015). These features of effective information management harken back to Mitchell, Levin, and Krumbotz's (1999) five characteristics of planned happenstance: curiosity, persistence, flexibility, optimism, and risk-taking. This approach offers a useful counterbalance to the intentionality described above. Students may be tempted to used intentionality as a way to hold themselves solely responsible for outcomes when it comes to managing information. In fact, the opposite is true in that planned happenstance theory emphasizes intentionality but toward preparation for desirable career options that one has no control in generating. To that end, Mitchell et al. (1999) offer the following Foundational Axiom considerations for career counselors:

> Anxiety about planning the future is normal and can be overcome; Plotting a career path is a life-long learning process that requires you to make innumerable decisions in response to unexpected events; Our [counselors] goal is to facilitate that learning process by discussing how your [client's] curiosity is excited, how you can take advantage of unplanned events, and how you can create future beneficial unplanned events. (p. 121)

**Table 12.2. Treatment Steps in Planned Happenstance**

| |
|---|
| Step 1: Normalize planned happenstance in the client's history. |
| 1 How have unplanned events influenced your career? |
| 2 How did you enable each event to influence you? |
| 3 How do you feel about unplanned events in your future? |
| Step 2: Assist clients to transform curiosity into opportunities for learning and exploration |
| 1 How is your curiosity excited? |
| 2 How have chance events contributed to your curiosity? |
| 3 How have you acted to heighten your curiosity? |
| 4 How could you explore the career implications of your curiosity? |
| Step 3: Teach clients to produce desirable chance events |
| 1 Tell me a chance event you wish would happen to you? |
| 2 How can you act now to increase the likelihood of that desirable event? |
| 3 How would your life change if you acted? |
| 4 How would your life change if you did nothing? |
| Step 4: Teach clients to overcome blocks to action. |
| 1 How have you been blocked from doing what you want to do? |
| 2 How could you find out how permanent that block is? |
| 3 How have other people overcome blocks like that? |
| 4 How would you begin overcoming that block? (Mitchell, Levin, & Krumboltz, 1999, pp. 121–122) |

Few approaches are as developmentally oriented, concrete, hopeful, and reality based as the foundations and steps just described. College students can benefit from being reminded that while the future is uncertain—for everyone—we can all takes steps to prepare for the unknown. What follows is an example of an exercise to demonstrate this dynamic, as illustrated in the case of Alexa. For this transcript excerpt, I turn back the clock to her first year in college, and initiate the intervention. Then, I return to the present in order to see how the intervention works during senior year. The intervention was alluded to briefly in Chapter 6 and has also been applied to career counseling with veterans (Luke & Michael, 2016). The activity is as follows:

Today Resume/Ideal Resume: Write your resume as if you are actually searching for a career-related position. Employers are seeking versatile, flexible, and talented people in and out of the specific profession who demonstrate leadership, civic or community involvement, and dedication. Show this in the most succinct and professional manner on your resume. Note your reactions to the content of your resume in relation to a position career future. (Often, these reactions are a little negative as students beginning college feel self-conscious about not having a lot (or any) relevant work experience). But part of this exercise is to assist you in not apologizing for your youth and lack of work and lived experience!

Next, write your "ideal" resume. This is an edited version of your current resume but written from the perspective of your last semester in college. In the next 4 to 6 years, what do you want your resume to have on it as it relates to a potential career future? What will you have accomplished that may be desirable to a prospective employer? Consider items such as the following:

- Practicum, internship, or cooperative
- Student organization membership
- Leadership positions on campus or in the community
- Part-time employment
- High grade-point average
- Volunteerism
- Double major
- Foreign language
- Study abroad

This list goes on and on. The point is to identify what you want to have on your resume by graduation and then chart a course, working backward, that increases the likelihood of those things coming to fruition.

### In Session with Alexa

CO: Alexa, I know that there are a lot of new things to experience as you begin this college phase of your life. We have already talked a little about how lost you feel in selecting a career path and the pressure you feel from your family—it is a lot of responsibility for a young adult.

CL: Yeah, I don't feel like an adult; I feel like a kid—even the students in my classes refer to us all as "kids."

CO: Well, there is not a lot of difference between childhood-type experiences in high school and college, in that it is really just the summer months that separate the two. It can be difficult to make the transitions involved. I would like to discuss with you the results of the activity you attempted, as I think it may inform a component of the transition. Would that be okay?

CL: Yes, definitely. It was not at all what I expected. I had to do a resume in high school, but we just downloaded a template and threw stuff onto it. I don't think it did much good.

CO: But this was somehow different for you?

CL: Yes. I used the Web resource you gave me and actually put some thought in it. Most of all, I found the ideal resume super helpful! It helped me to see that I won't always be inexperienced, but also that, if I want that future, I need to take some action now.

CO: Okay, so the future is not going to magically come

## Emerging Adulthood

Arnett (2000) has described the conceptual developmental stage of emerging adulthood. Emerging adulthood include the age range of 18 to 29 (though it is conceived of and communicated variably, at times from 18 to 24, the broadest range is used here). The tasks of emerging adults are situated between the completion of the high school years, where life was fairly clearly circumscribed for adolescents, and early adulthood, wherein liberty, personal responsibility for every facet of life, and entry into mature relationships and work predominate. In the center is a period of transition, and for many, that means college. Konstam et al. (2105) discuss the career issues and employment issues facing unemployed emerging adults. These individuals are characterized by feeling in-between, career instability, unemployment, and underemployment. They note that, according to the Bureau of Labor and Statistics (BLS; May 2013) that unemployment rates among emerging adults (18–24) was 11%, nearly double that of any other group. Even accounting for college enrollment effects on employment, this is a problematic trend. These lead to mental health issues and have almost inevitable negative effects on the identity development that is crucial to this stage. Vertberger and Gati (2015) used a powerful measure of addressing career decision making, the Career Decision-Making Profile (CDMP) that measures young adults' decision-making styles across 12 dichotomous dimensions:

**Table 12.3. Career Decision-Making Profile Dimensions and Polarities**

| Dimension | Polarity |
|---|---|
| Information processing | analytic vs. holistic |
| Information gathering | comprehensive vs. minimal |
| Locus of control | internal vs. external |
| Effort invested in the process | much vs. little |
| Procrastination | high vs. low |
| Speed of making the final decision | fast vs. slow |
| Consulting with others | frequent vs. rare |
| Dependence on others | high vs. low |
| Desire to please others | high vs. low |
| Aspiration for an ideal occupation | high vs. low |
| Willingness to compromise | high vs. low |
| Using intuition | high vs. low |

Results allow counselors to target assistance in more intentional ways. The value in these dimensions (and this instrument) is to identify the things holding back adolescents and emerging adults from seeking help. As you can see in Table 12.3, there are multiple factors that can lead to discouragement in help-seeking, many of which are attitudes or dispositions that must be addressed even in order to get these individuals into counselors' sphere of influence.

together, but it can come together.

CL: Yes.

CO: Did anything else stand out to you as you completed the exercise?

CL: Well, I realized a few things. When I thought about what I really want for myself 4 years from now, I noticed that they did not line up with my family's path.

CO: Oh, so you found some discrepancies?

CL: Yes

CO: What was that like?

CL: Believe it or not, it felt like a huge relief!

CO: Really? I believe you, but how so?

CL: Right now, I feel pressure to do what they do, probably because that is all I know. When I looked at the things I want on my resume, they seem to lead in a different direction, and that feels liberating.

CO: Oh. Great! Can you give me an example?

CL: I really want to study abroad—maybe France or Belgium—and that highlighted that I would like to learn French, which made me think of my major and what I like about French.

CO: And what did you learn?

CL: I think I feel a connection to the culture and the challenge of expanding my cultural horizons.

CO: How has this effected your view of your major and possible career futures?

CL: It seemed to open possibilities for a double major and new clubs to explore, and possibly a major in international business (mouth gapes opens in mock surprise).

CO: That does seem like a difference from exercise science.

CL: I know! But it makes sense to me. I even talked it over with my family, and they were actually supportive.

CO: You seem surprised.

CL: I was, but it turns out that they talked about their careers, because that's all they knew! They did not necessarily think I should be like them, but their careers were their only reference point. Crazy!

CO: But it makes sense.

CL: Yeah, I mean, I was putting all this pressure on myself to do something like them but that I did not really see myself doing. But I did not make the connection at the time.

CO: It sounds like you may have turned a corner!

# Crisis and Commitment in CFC

Erikson's psychosocial stage of development identifies ages 18 to 24 as later adolescence, or what has come to be known as the beginning of emerging adulthood (1968). The crisis at this stage is individual identity versus identity or role confusion. A crisis, "refers to the adolescent's period of engagement in choosing among meaningful alternatives" (Marcia, 1966, p. 551); whereas "commitment refers to the degree of personal investment the individual exhibits" (p. 551). James Marcia developed one of the most oft-cited theories of identity development (1964; 1966; 1993).

The theory is derived from Erikson's (1968) psychosocial stage of adolescent development. These four stages are Identity Achievement, Foreclosure, Moratorium, and Diffusion. An achieved identity is the result of a developmental crisis, wherein the individual has engaged the process of exploration and decision making; in addition, they have made a commitment to the decision through personal investment. A foreclosed identity is one in which there is a commitment without a crisis. The individual has personally invested in an identity without having explored and made autonomous decisions. Identity moratorium represents a crisis without a commitment, meaning the individual has actively explored, but may feel paralyzed, about committing to a particular path. Lastly, when individuals have neither experienced a crisis nor committed themselves to a path, they are said to be in identity diffusion or, in Erikson's term, role confusion. These individuals represent the lowest level of development, as the lack of exploration and engagement lead to role conflicts that are irreconcilable. Table 12.5 summarizes the stage rubric, an extension of Marcia's stages in Table 12.4.

**Table 12.4. Marcia's Stages of Identity Development**

| | | Crisis | |
|---|---|---|---|
| | | yes | no |
| Commitment | yes | Identity Achievement | Identity Foreclosure |
| | no | Identity Moratorium | Identity Diffusion |

In the context of the stage of identity development, a crisis in the career domain indicates engagement in the process choosing a career path. The commitment component involves a level of personal investment in the career path. Interestingly, in his conceptualization study, Marcia used an occupational prompt as part of the project.

> Examples of typical answers for the four statuses were: "How willing do you think you'd be to give up going into if something better came along?" and "A sample question in the occupational area was":
>
> > [Identity achievement] Well, I might, but I doubt it. I can't see what "something better" would be for me.
> > [Moratorium] I guess if I knew for sure I could answer that better. It would have to be something in the general area—something related.
> > [Foreclosure] Not very willing. It's what I've always wanted to do. The folks are happy with it and so am I.
> > [Identity diffusion] Oh sure. If something better came along, I'd change just like that. (Marcia, 1966, p. 553).

Table 12.5. Marcia's Stages in CFC

| Marcia's Stage | Brief Description | CFC Implications |
|---|---|---|
| Identity Achievement | Crisis and commitment: leads to integrated sense of self and purpose | Satisfaction with career path as it emerges from thoughtful exploration and reflection, along with a personal investment in the process. |
| Identity Foreclosure | Commitment without a crisis: leads to a sense of self not derived internally from exploration and engagement | Career path selection may represent parental influence or pressure, or it may be intolerance for the anxiety and ambiguity of not having a decision made. |
| Identity Moratorium | Crisis with no commitment: leads to role uncertainty as open-ended exploration fails to crystalize in whole self | Career path selection is postponed as long as possible, often the result of fear of making the wrong choice. There is a lot of academic major changes, at times to the extent that students are forced to graduate due to high amount of credit hours. |
| Identity Diffusion | No crisis or commitment: leads to difficulty even pursuing college but if they do, may appear to the "party animal" on campus | May present as ambivalent about anything related to personal development in terms of major, career, or other facets of growth in college. |

Abbreviations: CFC = career-focused counseling.

The challenge in CFC with college-aged students is to balance the goal (pressure) of making a decision with the need to delay decision making until it is right for the individual. It is easy for clients and counselors to fall off either end of these extremes. One value of college is that, whether students like it or not, it invokes a crisis. The question then becomes whether a commitment will follow, leading either to achievement or moratorium. Students in College for whom the experience does not represent a crisis—how does this happen—and what do we do with them?

Chickering and Reisser Stages add to the complexity of vocational identity development (developing purpose) at by enumerating the myriad tasks that accompany vocational identity and career decision making. Evans, Forney, Guido, Patton, and Renn (2010) offer a contemporary description of Chickering and Reisser's seven vectors of college student development. These include Institutional Objectives, Institutional Size, Student-Faculty Relationships, Curriculum, Teaching, Friendships and Student Communities, and Student Development Programs and Services. The implications of these factors mean that any one or combination may serve as both risk and protective factors for students in CFC.

Lastly, Chickering and Reisser issue three admonitions for working with college student populations. The first is the necessity of Integration of Work and Learning. This means that counselors and institutions work to assist students in connecting their academic work to their career development. Studies of college student success have validated this admonition. Luke, Redekop, and Burgin (2014) demonstrated that, among a sample of 1,200 community college students, those students who were better able to draw connections between their academic work and their work plans were more likely to remain in college. They also demonstrated greater career decision self-efficacy. Secondly, Recognition and Respect for Individual Differences emphasizes the need to view student issues as individual, though they exist in layers of context. This seems particularly relevant as an admonition, as the emphasis on generational dynamics and characteristics has become more popular (e.g., Millennials, Gen-X). The members of the groups should be viewed as individuals, in addition to the broader categories of differences, like race, gender, and socioeconomic background. Third, Acknowledgment of the Cyclical Nature of Learning and Development reminds counselors that students who may not have successfully navigated a particular task are still capable of returning to that stage and experience growth. Likewise, students who had been successful may also experience developmental regression as those who encounter multiple transitions or other stressors.

# Career and Neuro

Luke and Field (2017, in press) discuss the integration of career and neuroscience in terms of the neural correlates of identity in the brain and, by extension, vocational identity in the brain. For example, Freton, Lemogne, Bergouignan, Delaveau, Lehéricy, & Fossati (2014) describe brain structures and regions related to oneself or identity. Several structures are relevant to the current discussion. First, the precuneus is associated with autobiographical memory but has a unique feature to it. It allows the recall of self-referential memories from either the first-person or third-person perspective. What this means is that the individual recalling memories of self can observe these as their own (first-person) or as those of someone else (third-person). This has implications for the role of individual identity and vocational identity development. As Freton et al. note, third-person recall of positive past events have been implicated in depression (see Lemogne et al., 2006). Imagine if, in CFC, a client views their accomplishments as if watching a movie of someone else (third-person), how this might affect their ability to draw on these experiences as resources going forward. While there is not yet a way to non-invasively change the role of the precuneus in these individuals, an understanding of this self-referential phenomenon may help clients understand their view of their experiences.

In working with a client like Alexa, we might begin by inviting her to describe in visually-oriented language, how she views her early experiences as they relate to herself. We might then offer the briefest of descriptions of autobiographical memory and the role of the precuneus in first- and third-person memory retrieval and experiences. We can then hypothesize with her that one way that self-defeating thoughts limit the vocational identity development and forward-looking perspectives of individuals is by immersing oneself in the first-person perspective of negative experiences while also viewing positive experiences from the third-person perspective.

# Summary

The college-going years and the period of emerging adulthood, in general, include uncertainty in consolidating identity and directing this identity toward the world of work. For many, economic downturns provide a socially acceptable justification to extend this period of lower vocational commitment. Counselors can support the work of vocational-identity development by normalizing the angst associated with transitions of this sort. It is of practical assistance for counselors to understand developmental trajectories related to the brain, considering the amount of neural restructuring that is occurring.

# References

Ajzen, I. & Fishbein, M. (1980). *Understanding attitudes and predicting social behavior*. Englewood Cliffs, NJ: Prentice-Hall.

Arnett, J. J. (2000). Emerging adulthood: A theory of development from the late teens through the twenties. *American psychologist*, *55*(5), 469.

Bandura, A. (1997). *Self-efficacy: The exercise of control*. New York, NY: W. H. Freeman & Co.

Chickering, A. W. (1969). *Education and identity*. San Francisco, CA: Jossey-Bass.

Chickering, A. W., & Reisser, L. (1993). *Education and Identity*. San Francisco, CA: Jossey-Bass.

Domene, J. F., Landine, J. & Stewart, J. (2015). Emerging adults career transition. In P. J. Hartung, M. L. Savickas & W. B. Walsh (Eds.), *APA handbook of career interventions, Vol. 2: Applications*. Washington, DC: American Psychological Association.

Duffy, R. D., & Sedlacek, W. E. (2010). The salience of a career calling among college students: Exploring group differences and links to religiousness, life meaning, and life satisfaction. *The Career Development Quarterly*, *59*(1), 27–41.

Elkind, (1967). Egocentrism in adolescence. *Child Development*. *38*(4), 1025–1034.

Patton, L. D., Renn, K. A., Guido, F. M., Quaye, S. J., & Forney, D. S. (2016). *Student development in college: Theory, research, and practice*. Hoboken, NJ: John Wiley & Sons.

Evans, N. J., Forney, D. S., Guido, F. M., Patton, L. D., & Renn, K. A. (2010). *Student development in college: Research, theory, and practice*. San Francisco, CA: Jossey-Bass.

Fishbein, M., & Ajzen, I. (1975). *Belief, attitude, intention and behavior*. Reading, MA: Addison-Wesley.

Lemogne, C., Piolino, P., Friszer S., Claret, A., Girault, N., Jouvent, R., ... Fossati, P. (2006). Episodic autobiographical memory in depression: specificity, autonoetic consciousness, and self perspective. *Conscious Cognition 15*, 258–268

Gilligan, C. (1982). *In a different voice.* Cambridge, MA: Harvard University Press.

Gore, P. A., Jr., Leuwerke, W. C., & Turley, S. E. (2005). A psychometric study of the college self-efficacy inventory. *Journal of College Student retention, 7* (3–4), 227–244.

Greenleaf, Arie Todd. Human agency, hardiness, and proactive personality: Potential resources for emerging adults in the college-to- career transition." PhD (Doctor of Philosophy) thesis, University of Iowa, 2011. http://ir.uiowa.edu/etd/3310.

Hammond, M. S., Michael, T., & Luke, C. (2017). Validating a measure of stages of change in career development. *International Journal for Educational and Vocational Guidance, 17*(1), 39-59.

Kohlberg, L. (1981). The philosophy of moral development moral stages and the idea of justice. San Francisco: Harper and Row.

Konstam, V., Tomek, S., Celen-Demirtas, S., & Sweeney, K. (2015). Volunteering and Reemployment Status in Unemployed Emerging Adults: A Time-worthy Investment? *Journal of Career Assessment, 23*(1), 152–165.

Lane, J. A. (2015). Counseling emerging adults in transition: Practical applications of attachment and social support research. *The Professional Counselor (5)*1, 30–42.

Lehmann, I. S., & Konstam, V. (2011). Growing up perfect: Perfectionism, problematic internet use, and career indecision in emerging adults. *Journal of Counseling and Development: JCD, 89*(2), 155–162. Retrieved from http://search.proquest.com.ezproxy.tntech.edu/docview/858390679?accountid=28833

Ludwikowski, W., Vogel, D., & Armstrong, P. I. (2009). Attitudes toward career counseling: The role of public and self-stigma. *Journal of Counseling Psychology, 56*(3), 408.

Luke, C., Redekop, F., & Burgin, C. (2015). Psychological factors in community college student retention. *Community College Journal of Research and Practice, 39*(3), 222–234.

Luke, C., Diambra, J., & Gibbons, M. (2014). An exploration of complimentary factors in career and student development in the liberal arts. *College Student Journal, 48*(2), 209–220.

Luke, C., & Diambra, J. F. (2017). Identity integration via career development issues: Counseling college sophomores from moros to sophos. *Education, 138*(1), 363–370.

Marcia, J. E. (1966). Development and validation of ego—identity status. *Journal of Personality and Social Psychology, 3*(5), 551-558.

Marcia, J. E. (1993). The status of the statuses: Research review. In *Ego identity* (pp. 2241). New York, NY: Springer New York.

Miller, W. R., & Rollnick, S. (2013). *Motivational interviewing: Helping people change* (3rd ed.). New York, NY: Guilford Press.

Prochaska, J., & Norcross, J. (2013). *Systems of psychotherapy: A transtheoretical analysis* (8th ed.). Stamford, CT: Cengage.

Vertsberger, D., & Gati, I. (2015). The effectiveness of sources of support in career decision-making: A two-year follow-up. *Journal of Vocational Behavior, 89*, 151–161.

## Figure/Table Credits

Tab. 12.2: Kathleen E. Mitchell, S. Al Levin, and John D. Krumboltz, "Treatment Steps in Planned Happenstance," Journal of Counseling and Development, vol. 77, no. 2. Copyright © 1999 by American Counseling Association.
Tab. 12.3: Vertberger and Gati, "Career Decision-Making Profile Dimensions and Polarities," Adapted by Chad Luke.
Tab. 12.4: J. E. Marcia, "Marcia's Stages of Identity Development," Adapted by Chad Luke.
Tab. 12.5: J. E. Marcia, "Marcia's Stages in CFC," Adapted by Chad Luke.

CHAPTER THIRTEEN

# Applying Career-Focused Counseling to Counseling Students

### Chapter Goals

- To combine theory, ethics, diversity, and special considerations into a coherent whole that counselors-in-training can readily apply
- Use the process just described to support the career development of counselors-in-training by applying these principles to the reader
- Use the process described above to use effectively in career-focused counseling (CFC)

## Introduction

One of the major challenges in writing a career text (and reading one, for that matter) is in taking all of the information presented and combining it into a meaningful whole that can be used effectively with a client. In this concluding chapter, the intent is to wrap up the broad material presented in this text such that you feel increased confidence and competence to practice ethical, effective, CFC. To that end, this chapter provides a guide to your own career development as the reader. Once you are able to apply this material to yourself, you will be able to access greater depths of empathy for clients, leading to a reasonable, rationale process for moving them through career-related challenges (Busacca & Wester, 2006). Several models are available for this purpose, so this chapter draws on the best of them. The following categories of concrete resources are not intended to substitute for the counseling process but, instead, are there to support the calming work of counselors who are sitting with emotionally activated individuals. They should not

### Opening Vignette

Sydney is a 23-year-old graduate student in a clinical mental health counseling program. She is making satisfactory progress in her program and is enjoying her courses related to basic skills and human understanding. However, she has begun to question her choice in career paths as she learns more about the day-to-day work counselors perform. Sydney entered the counseling program right after graduating with a degree in psychology—a degree that she also enjoyed but struggled to identify desirable career paths for. As an undergraduate, she had often heard the quip that you can do anything and nothing with a psychology degree. But, like many undergraduates, she figured it would sort itself out by graduation. Upon graduation, she realized that the work she thought about doing required a master's degree, so she returned to school. Now, sitting in second semester classes, she has begun to wonder if this was the right decision for her. She hears the stories from the interns in the program and wonders if she has what it takes to do the work. To complicate matters, she is equally uncertain what she would do if she were to quit the program or change majors. Adding to the issue, Sydney is currently taking a course in career counseling, so she is experiencing internal conflict as she reads and reflects on the ways in which she is supposed to assist future clients in navigating the exact thing she is going through. She feels like a fraud, a hypocrite, and wants to just get out of the class and the program.

Adviser: Sydney, you have said that you know you want to help others, but you are feeling a little uncertain in the program.

Sydney: Yes. I want to help, but I also feel like I may have rushed into the graduate program. I'm not sure that this is the way I'm meant to help.

Adviser: In my role as adviser, I'm not going to treat you as my client (both smile). However, I have a few questions for you that come to mind, the answers to which may feel a bit like therapy. Are you okay with me asking them?

Sydney: Yes, of course. I'm stuck.

Adviser: Okay, well, first of all, what information do you feel is missing, either about yourself or the field, that might help you to better evaluate your decision?

Sydney: That's just it. I don't feel like I know enough to know what I'm missing or what I don't know.

Adviser: That makes a lot of sense to me. Try these: What would you like to know that would help you make a career decision or feel better about a decision that has been made? In other words, how has limited knowledge limited your ability to move forward? What kind(s) of knowledge would it take for you to be successful?

Sydney: Well, I'd like to know that I'm making the right decision, that I'm in the right program at the right time.

be the first thing that counselors run to, but they should be part of the counselor's knowledge/resource set.

# Applying Busacca's Taxonomy to Yourself

In the following sections, we look at how Busacca's (2002) model of career issues plays out for Sydney, the counseling student in the vignette. Note the ways in which you may (or may not) identify with her areas of struggle. You may recall that Busacca's taxonomy addresses three types each of inter-personal and intra-personal issues. We address the problem areas one at a time, viewing them first from the interpersonal perspective and then from the intrapersonal perspective.

***Interpersonal Problem Area 1: Lack of information.*** The interpersonal dimension of the *Lack of Information* involves identifying credible sources of information that can be used to fill in gaps in your career information. However, there are many times when you might have all the information needed to take the next step, but you do not know how to take that step. When this happens, additional information is not only *not* helpful, it can be counterproductive in that it is overwhelming. This creates its own problems. Two kinds of information are relevant to the discussion of your career development: information about yourself as a person, and information about the world of work.

## Sydney in Her Own CFC

Sydney is in a similar situation that many graduate students find themselves in. She knows she wants to help others, so as an undergraduate, she chose psychology. As she neared graduation, it became increasingly apparent to her that she would need additional training to help others in the way she envisioned. Attending graduate school moved from being one of several options, to one of necessity. Therefore, she applied to a number of graduate programs, received a few offers, and ultimately selected the one that was closest to her home. Now in her second semester, her head is spinning somewhat as she realizes her decisions have been a bit reactionary rather than proactive. She continues to desire a role in helping others, but lacks the self-knowledge and the knowledge about the ways she might help others that would help her feel more settled. In consultation with Sydney, the dialogue with her graduate adviser might appear as follows:

As this transcript excerpt highlights, not all information is created equally. Counseling students are just as vulnerable to unchallenged assumptions about whom they must be and what the field is like as any client. Assumptions and unchecked information is incredibly powerful in the lives of individuals, and one of the functions of CFC is to question sources and interpretations of this information.

***Intrapersonal Problem Area 1: Self-actualization.*** Sometimes the information you have about yourself is sufficient in quantity but not in quality. In order to match the information about oneself and the world of work, information about self-concept must be clear, which is often lacking. By the time you are reading this, and perhaps even because you are reading this, you may have a list of characteristics about yourself but are uncertain how those pieces fit together. It is at this point that the *self* continues to feel abstract and diffuse, leading to uncertainty about which pieces of information about oneself are relevant to career decision making. This process of self-actualization—the crystalized self—often benefits from the support of a trained process expert, like a counselor. A counselor is trained to listen to the components of self that you may not even be able to express verbally. They offer judgment-free feedback on the information you share through reflection, clarification, paraphrasing, and so forth that help you hear your own thoughts from another person. At this point, survey assessments may be inadequate, as many individuals have these pieces. Making sense of them is the role a counselor plays.

Adviser: Okay, so you would like some guarantees (both smile and nod). I don't have any of those to offer, but it helps to know that you are in need of some reassurance. Let's talk for a little bit about how you came to the helping professions. What is it about helping that attracted you to the counseling profession?

Sydney: (goes on to describe personal and professional experiences that have led her to this place.)

Adviser: That's a great description. Now, what do you think it takes to be successful as a professional helper? Counseling is just one example.

Sydney: I assume I need to have my life figured out before I can help others, and that just is not going to happen!

Adviser: So you have some unchallenged assumptions about what it means to be a counselor. It sounds like you may benefit from finding additional, credible sources of information about becoming a counselor. We can talk through some of these, but I wonder who you may know or get to know in the community who could help with your assumptions? Perhaps after you've spoken with them, we could meet again to take another look at the information you've obtained.

## Sydney in Her Own CFC

Sydney knows she wants to pursue a career in a helping role. She is convinced that the role of counselor fits best with her sense of self and her worldview. However, as she moves through her counseling courses, she finds herself feeling less confident about her plans compared with her classmates. She has interviewed a couple of counselors in the community and spoken with her adviser. While in the career counseling course,

CO: What brings you in today, Sydney?

Sydney: I'm a graduate counseling student. I am enjoying the program, but it is bringing up some things for me that I'm uncomfortable with, and I'm not sure what to do with it.

CO: Okay, so your program may be pushing some personal buttons for you as it prepares you professionally. Is that right?

Sydney: It is definitely pushing me.

CO: As a result of our work together, what you like to see happen? What will be different about how you think, feel, or act?

Sydney: I think I would be able to feel confident that counseling is the right path for me as an individual. I'm afraid that I won't be able to handle the stress or be able to help people the right way. I mean, am I supposed to be help people in less stressful ways?

CO: You have placed a lot of pressure on yourself to get this right. That's a lot of weight to carry.

Sydney: Well, I've seen my friends make career choices that weren't what they wanted, and while my parents just sort of fell into their jobs, they want me to be very intentional. They worry that counseling will be too stressful and pay too little and that I will have wasted a lot of time, money, and energy.

CO: So there's pressure coming from other sources as well. You want to make the right decision, help people, and feel confident that you are moving in the best direction for you. I have a question: regardless of

she has taken several career assessments. At this point, she has a lot on information about herself but is struggling with how these pieces of data come together to form her identity. After some time struggling with herself and the counseling role she wants to pursue as an extension of herself, Sydney seeks consultation with a counselor in the community.

***Interpersonal Problem Area 2: Lack of skill.*** This step is often framed in terms of position procurement but relates to the skills associated with putting into practice all the information described above. In other words, it may be that you really want to work in a career helping others, but without a complete understanding of how to skillfully implement the information you have about self and the world of work, you may default into something less than a good fit for you. It involves switching your mindset from thinking like a job- or career-seeker and thinking like an employer. For example, who is hiring helpers? It may be that helpers work as teachers, counselors, and ministers, but what other characteristics, skills, abilities, etc., might you possess that would fit with other forms of helping, like medicine, law, and physical therapy or other forms of helping, like through art, science, business, and leadership? The skill referred to here is putting yourself in the shoes of a hiring manager as you compile a summary of the skills, education, and other characteristics that you bring to bear on the position. The next skill is identifying the individuals and organizations that are doing the work you want to do. How did they get there, and what tips would they have for you? Ask them!

## Sydney in Her Own CFC

Through her consultations with her adviser and her counselor, Sydney has increased certainty about her path, at least for the immediate future. Imagine now that she is in her last semester of her master's program and is beginning to explore possible positions. There are two key documents in this process that can assist Sydney in taking the next steps toward employment: the cover letter and resume. Cover letters are letters of introduction. They represent a narrative description of the job-seeker's fit for a given position. They are invitations to the employer to read further—the resume—to learn more specifics about the prospective employee. The website https://www.livecareer.com/cover-letter-tips includes tips, samples, and templates for cover letters. While it is not recommended that someone like Sydney purchase a template, because she is new to this type of professional communication, seeing examples can be very helpful. Table 13.1 contains a cover letter that a graduating student like Sydney might use.

**Table 13.1. Sydney's Cover Letter Sample**

Dear (Hiring Manager),

I was very pleased to see your position of residential therapist on the website www.indeed.com. As an upcoming graduate with a master's degree in mental health counseling, I believe myself to be a good fit for the position described. My attached resume provides specifics on my experience, but I would like to take just a moment of your time to describe how I see this as a mutually beneficial opportunity.

First of all, I meet the educational requirements listed in the posting, but that is just the beginning. I am currently completing a 600-hour internship at a residential treatment facility, much like yours. During my time at the facility, I have led group therapy, carried a small caseload of clients for which I managed cases and led treatment. Through this extended internship, I have been able to demonstrate my growing clinical and relational skills. In addition, I have received increasing positive feedback regarding my clinical documentation, from intake to discharge.

As I researched your organization through your website, I was drawn to your mission statement and emphasis on wellness. During my undergraduate education, I was a part-time yoga instructor and feel strongly that a holistic approach to mental health is essential. I also noted that many in your leadership have clinical license credentials, indicating to me their history as clinicians. Through my leadership and involvement in the national honors society for counseling (CSI), I have gained an appreciation for managers with clinical experience.

In summary, I perceive that my skills and training, along with my unique approach to holistic helping, may make me a valuable member of your team. I would appreciate the opportunity to speak with you further about the position and how I might assist in advancing the mission of ACME Mental Health Organization.

Please feel free to contact me via email at Sydney.counselorwannabe@email.com or via phone at 555-555-1212.

Sincerely,

Sydney Rodrigues

whether counseling is the right path for you—and you might not know that for sure beforehand—what kind of person would you like to emerge from the program as?

Sydney: So you don't think counseling is right for me?

CO: Oh, is that what you heard me say? That explains the look of horror on your face (both smile, breaking the tension). I'm saying that since you cannot see the future, you may be trying to know something with a level of certainty that only accompanies hindsight. Regardless, you can move through this process in a way that honors yourself. What would that look like?

Sydney: Okay, I think I understand now, though I'll admit I'm a little disappointed that you didn't just say, 'don't worry, Sydney; I can tell you are going to make a great counselor—you're on the right path.'

CO: (smiles and nods) That would be something of a relief—if only that were the truth and my role. Thank you for your candor!

Sydney: I want to be the person who makes the best decisions with the information she has, knowing that there is the potential to make mistakes and to even have regrets.

CO: Sounds like the kind of counselor a client would benefit from working with. Let's take a closer look at some of those characteristics.

As you can see from Sydney's letter, the intent is to make a connection with the reader by describing characteristics that meet and exceed the requirements of the position. Further, Sydney is able to describe more of the qualities she has brought to the tasks of the work, further setting herself apart. You may also be thinking that Sydney has good leadership and volunteer experience, and you would be correct. It is important, as you read this, to consider the ways you can distinguish yourself in the program—and this at a time when you are already stretched thin. This can be challenging, but it is also very doable, if you are intentional. Much like the process described in Happenstance Learning Theory, looking for opportunities and preparing yourself to meet them will almost certainly help you see previously hidden ones. In moving toward that goal, we now explore the role of the resume in addressing the *intra* dimension of problem area two.

***Intrapersonal Problem Area 2: Lack of self-understanding and awareness.*** The list of accomplishments and skills listed on your resume is not the same thing as self-understanding and awareness. In many ways, this is what comes through in your cover letter, though resumes and cover letters are often discussed in the same context. The cover letter is a narrative view of who you are and what you can do for an organization. This goes beyond the resume lists and reasons you want the job and to the heart of why *you* are right for *this* job. This is a challenge for many and is the reason that hiring managers spend so little time on any resume or cover letter: they may have a stack of hundreds to peruse for a single position, and this is why self-understanding, in writing, is vital. Who are you, and how does this translate to what the organization has communicated through the position description? You may have wonderful experience, education, and/or skills, but if you cannot articulate the connection to what the employer's needs, your chances of getting an interview are reduced. Speaking of interviews ... the purpose of the resume and cover letter is to get you an interview, not the job. The interview determines whether you get you the job or not. The interview is the time to string together thoughts about yourself *in vivo*, and it is why it is imperative to practice these in a variety of circumstances. Not only does it smooth out the wrinkles in your presentation of self; it also helps you refine your understanding of yourself and clarifies the position you may want. Now that you have a clearer concept of the cover letter, let's look a little closer at Sydney's resume and how it sharpens her self-understanding and prepares her for an interview.

# Sydney in Her Own CFC

## Sydney's Resume

Sydney Rodrigues
12345 Uncertain Way
College Town, US

Work Experience
McDonalds during high school
- Took orders
- Completed orders
- Helped customers

Bath and Body Works during college
- Sold lotion
- Ran cash register

Academics
Bachelor's Degree in Psychology, 3.3 GPA
Master's Degree in Counseling, almost finished

Internship, Community Mental Health Center
- Completed intake paperwork
- Ran psychoeducation groups

Activities
Playing the flute
Pets

It may be obvious that this resume sample is an extreme example, but it is actually a fairly common one. The first thing to notice is the energy of the resume, almost like it was written with her eyes closed. This type of resume demonstrates a low self-awareness and limited self-valuing. As discussed in an earlier chapter, the resume can be used with clients to assist in developing a greater self-understanding as well as increasing their self-valuing perspective. For example, the

CO: Sydney, before we wrap up our session, I wonder if I could ask you to complete a task before our next session?

Sydney: Sure, depending on what it is (smiles coyly).

CO: I'd like to ask you to create a resume and bring it with you to our next session.

Sydney: I guess I can, as long as your expectations are low.

CO: Fair enough!

counselor may proceed in the following way with Sydney, combining both resume writing tips with self-concept work.

***Resumes in CFC.*** Use the most meaningful language to describe your experience. Rather than listing responsibilities in a generic way, use power verbs to communicate the unique qualities you bring to a position. Sydney has fallen prey to a common fallacy among job seekers: minimizing the value of their experience. In the example of working for McDonalds during high school, two considerations become apparent. The first is managing employment while a student. This can communicate motivation, time management, and reliability. Second, the way Sydney approached the position may be more important than her specific tasks. For example, she may have been recognized for being a team player, being extra responsive to customers, a quick learner, motivated to learn and grow, etc. Not only are these things valuable traits to employers, but they are demonstrable on a resume (never list characteristics you cannot provide evidence for).

Place the most relevant sections at the top of the resume. In Sydney's case, most employers seeking to hire an individual with a specific degree will want to check that off their list first. That means that Sydney would benefit from listing her educational experience first. However, because many applicants will also meet the educational requirements, she could also include educational information, accolades and relevant educational experience here. She does not need to include her GPA if it does not assist her in presenting the picture she wants to show. Sydney worked her way through undergraduate and graduate school, so her GPA suffered somewhat. However, instead of feeling self-conscious about this, she can describe it. In her revised resume that follows, you will find an example of how to present this. Next, Sydney will list her work experience. Since she has a variety of work experiences, some of which relate directly to the position for which she is applying and others that apply indirectly, she has options. The best option may be to divide her work experience into two sub-sections: "relevant experience" and "related or additional experience." This allows her to highlight her internship first, under relevant experience, and also describe other work experience that have shaped her and make her a unique applicant. Let's look at a revised resume for Sydney.

***Interpersonal Problem Area 3: Lack of experience***. It has been said that experience is something you get right *after* you need it, and this is very true for career development. There will be many times when the solution to a dilemma in your life makes perfect sense when viewed through the rearview mirror. And, it will always be this way. The trick, if you will, is to extract the meaning from past lessons and apply them to future decisions, even when they differ substantively. For many reading this book and on the journey to become a professional counselor, school counselor, or other human services professional, you may feel you have little experience to draw from. After all, this is likely your first time in a counseling-related master's degree program and seeking your first job in a new career path. In these situations, it may matter more that you can gain access to others with relevant experience in this area to combine with your experience of yourself in other domains of life. For example, you may never have interviewed for an internship in school counseling, but others have. In addition, you likely have experience pursuing something that you want and finding ways to do it intentionally. This, combined with strategic interactions with those who have gone before you in this area, can make for meaningful experience. You

## Sydney's Revised Resume

**Sydney Rodrigues**
**12345 Uncertain Way**
**College Town, US**

EDUCATION

Master's Degree in Counseling, May 2018
University Name and Location
3.4 GPA; worked 30 hours/week
Active Member of Chi Sigma Iota Honor Society

Bachelor's Degree in Psychology,
University Name and Location
3.3 GPA; worked full-time

RELEVANT EXPERIENCE

Counseling Intern, ACME Community Counseling Center, Location, Dates

- Increased efficiency and accuracy in completing clinical documentation, including biopsychosocial assessments, progress notes, and discharge summaries
- Facilitated process-based psychoeducational treatment groups
- Recognized for consistent professional behaviors and skilled interactions with clients and staff

ADDITIONAL EXPERIENCE

Sales Associate, Bath and Body Works, Location, Dates

- Provided excellent customer service
- Developed helping orientation by attending to staff and customer needs
- Increased multitasking, efficiency, and management skills through running cash register, inventory control, and schedule creation

ACTIVITIES AND SKILLS

- Playing the flute—6 years
- Pet-lover—interested in animal-assisted therapy

CO: Sydney, you've described times of enjoyment and satisfaction with your counseling program, as well as times, like now, in which you are experiencing self-doubt.

Sydney: Yeah, I mean, I felt really good at first, but I wonder how I can know that I'll be good at this and if I will enjoy it.

CO: First of all, as a counselor in training, you recognize that it is perfectly okay for you to have your feelings, thoughts, and experiences regarding your life.

Sydney: (sighs) I may have forgotten that this applies to me as well (smiles).

CO: We often do. Your current experiences can alert you to be reflective and to increase your self-awareness, but they may or may not be a call to change. However, they may be a call to some action.

Sydney: What do you mean?

CO: Well, this is your first graduate program and your first major career choice, right?

Sydney: I'll say! I feel lost!

CO: And that "lostness" is the call to act. I can sit here and tell you all day that what you are experiencing is normal, but you may not be inclined to believe me, in part, because so much seems to be at stake. However, you have two tools at your disposal that can support your own acceptance of this. The first is your past experience and the second is the experience of others.

Sydney: Well, that's part of the problem. I don't have any experience in the field,

do not have to operate in a bubble, on an island, or under any other metaphor that implies you have to do this all alone! Here is one example of how this type of conversation might go with Sydney in her own CFC.

## Sydney in Her Own CFC

Sydney is in a situation wherein she has committed to a master's program in counseling but wonders if she has the skills, experience, and characteristics needed to be happy and effective in the field. The first thing to note is that these experiences among students and novice counselors has been predicted in the counselor development literature. For example, Stoltenberg, McNeill, and Delworth (1998) described oscillation of trainee motivation, autonomy, and self- and other-awareness. Later, Stoltenberg and McNeill (2010) expanded on this idea, noting that novice counselors should except to question both their ability and desire to continue in this work. In other words, the types of experiences predicted by Stoltenberg and colleagues, and described by Sydney, is just information. It does not indicate fit or not; rather, it is a call to self-reflection and increased self-awareness. Let's look at how a counselor might use this with Sydney.

As you can see in the transcript excerpt, Sydney is experiencing a fairly common phenomenon among clients in CFC: minimizing or devaluing one's lived experienwce. Many times, therefore, the work of the counselor is to draw out client resources. They have lived with themselves all their lives, so the skills, qualities, and abilities become hidden from their view. In our role as counselors, we provide a type of mirror to reflect back what is there but has been neglected.

***Intrapersonal Problem Area 3: External and internal conflict.*** All five problem areas described thus far are developmental in nature; they are fairly common and require time, effort, and lived experience to navigate. Other challenges are more like barriers that vary from person to person. The locus of these barriers can be internal or external. About the time you begin practicum or internship, you may begin to ask what you have gotten yourself into. The answer is that you've walked into the next step in your career development. Your desire to help has run headlong into those who need help and the systems in place to facilitate this help. While being a little shell-shocked initially is very normal, these encounters also assist us in clarifying what it is we want to do in the world and where we want to do it. The sense that one wants or needs to help can come into conflict with the chosen mode of helping. It does not mean that you should not be a counselor, school counselor, human services professional, etc., but it does mean that you need a way to explore these conflicts and find a path that makes sense for you. Sydney has been working through her internal conflict, which is developmentally appropriate. She now begins to address an external conflict that has created anxiety for her and clouded her judgment.

One of the valuable contributions of CFC is what we just saw in the transcript excerpt: sitting with people in their struggles, while they experience trust and courage to go further with what may be the underlying barriers to living their lives successfully. This is a type of social justice, preventative counseling. For example, Sydney sought counseling for career confusion, and for many clients, information is the underlying need. For many others, however, the presenting problem may be a symptom of ineffective living strategies. CFC makes room for the client to explore these depths, if they desire.

# Putting It All Together ... for You

A litmus test for your ability to work with clients in addressing career-related issues is whether or not you can apply your approach to yourself. Many of you reading this text will be in a master's-level counseling program, and it makes me wonder: Where are you now? How did you get here? What were the influences that led you to graduate school? How about undergraduate? What led to your choice of major? Before college, how did you make decisions about yourself and your future in high school? What feelings emerge as you reflect on these questions? Where do you experience them in your body?

and it makes me wonder if I can get a job. Plus, I don't really know any counselors, besides you.

CO: Okay, this is a good start. The first thing I notice is that you immediately dismiss your life experience as irrelevant or not applicable to your current situation. Is that fair to say?

Sydney: Yeah, well, I have not worked anywhere but in fast food and retail.

CO: I wonder then, if you could describe a time at one of those jobs when you had to solve a problem in which you had limited resources.

Sydney: Oh, that. There are a lot of those, because at both jobs we were always understaffed. There was this one time at the retail store that my manager had left for a meeting. We had no key holder and a customer was there demanding a refund.

CO: Wow. What did you do?

Sydney: Well, the first thing was to move them away from the cash register and from other customers. I asked a co-worker to track down the manager, while I talked with the customer. She was so mad.

CO: I can tell from the look on your face as you recall this.

Sydney: It was tough. But, as I talked with her and started listing options, she started to calm down. I think she was not expecting a young sales person to be kind but firm. By the time the manager returned, the customer had settled down and even complimented me to my manager.

CO: That is a great story!

Sydney: That kind of stuff seemed to happen a lot to me.

CO: Now you're getting it!

Sydney: Getting what?

CO: How valid your experience is, both in informing your decision about this work and how you can apply these experiences for a job interview in the counseling field.

Sydney: I honestly never thought about it that way.

CO: Well let's keep up the momentum, then. Let's take a moment to identify professionals in the community who are doing the kind of work you may be interested in and reach out to them.

Sydney: You can do that?

CO: Yes, and so can you (smiles). And when you talk with them, be sure to ask them if they ever had doubts about their chosen path.

Sydney: I definitely will!

CO: Hi Sydney, I thought we might check in to see how things are going for you.

Sydney: Things are okay, but I did have a conversation with my family this past weekend that shook me up about my career.

CO: I'm listening.

Sydney: Well, you may recall that I came into undergrad as a business major. My parents run the family business, and they assumed that I would take my place with them after my bachelor's degree. Needless to say, they were not very happy when I switched to psychology. They thought I could still go into the business, but then I told them in my senior year that I wanted to get a counseling degree.

CO: How has that been?

# Guiding Reflections

Every person who picks up this or any career-related text brings along with him/her a slew of knowledge, based on personal experience, as well as the "knowledge" shared with them by others. This knowledge and experience shapes how you will encounter the words in this text. As you reflect on Sydney's story and apply the principles to your own career development, use the following to begin translating to your work with your clients:

1. Choose your own explanation.
   a. What theory best explains the answers to the questions above?
   b. How would you describe your path to the place you are now?
   c. What issues may need to be addressed as you move forward, and what theory best addresses these for you?
2. Choose your own application.
   a. What strategies or techniques have worked for you in the past?
   b. Do you find that you are more cognitively, affectively, behaviorally, or socially oriented? Which one works best for you? Which one(s) do you avoid most in order to not have to deal with them?
   c. Who in your life knows what works for you even when you can't or won't see it? Ask them.
3. Choose the results and work backward
   a. What is the result you want 5 to 10 years down the road?
   b. What steps, in reverse chronological order, need to be taken in order to get there?
   c. What can you do in the next 30, 60, or 90 days to bring this to fruition?
4. Choose your allies.
   a. As in 2.c., who in your life knows you well and will tell you the truth?

b. Who in the community is doing the work that you might want to do? How can you gain access to them?
c. What are the groups or agencies already in place that can assist you in your path?

5. Choose your strengths and weaknesses
    a. What do you already have going for you that you?
    b. How might you leverage your responses from 5.a. in order to move forward?
    c. As with the flagging the minefield techniques, what are the ways you are most likely to trip yourself up?
    d. What are the areas you've struggled to grow through?

The five steps above, along with the associated reflection questions can inform your future by honoring your past and present. In addition, they provide a guide of sorts in thinking with clients about who they are. In the next—and final—section, these five steps are expanded into a type of CFC taxonomy or rubric to guide you as you engage with clients.

# Putting It All Together ... for Clients

The structure of any counseling session is important both to counselors and clients. It can assist newer counselors in directing the session toward effective outcomes with clients. It also can provide a framework that substitutes for confidence in those early counseling sessions. The steps are drawn from counseling literature and clinical experience. You may decide in time to modify them to fit your style. Following the list is Table 13.3 that provides the steps, questions to the counselor, questions to the client, and broader considerations for CFC.

But first, the steps also serve to assist in dealing with a very challenging issue in CFC: "can you help me get a job?"

Many, if not most, counselors experience the angst associated with a client transferring responsibility for their problems

Sydney: Very tense. We actually try not to talk about anything related to school or my career. However, lately, they have been making more comments about what will happen if they want to retire. They also talk about wishing they had help in the business—help that they can trust, like me.

CO: How is that affecting you?

Sydney: I'm torn. I feel guilty that I'm not helping and that they feel let down. But I also don't want to do that job! I would be bored and depressed if that was my future.

CO: So you're feeling caught between your family's desires and expectations for you and your own values.

Sydney: Yeah. More than that, I don't know what I would say to a client who came to me about something similar.

CO: That is a terrific insight! Though it may also be a miserable feeling!

Sydney: It definitely feels more miserable than it does insightful.

CO: How does your family respond when you tell them about the pressure you're feeling from them?

Sydney: Oh, they don't know. I can't talk with them about this!

CO: Got it. You've been keeping your feelings to yourself. No wonder you feel overwhelmed!

Sydney: What do you mean? I do, but ...

CO: Well, you have all this relational-emotional energy where they are concerned, but you have not been about to advocate for yourself with them.

Sydney: You don't know my family.

CO: Okay. If I knew them, I might better understand why you don't talk with them.

Sydney: Yeah! I guess you could stand up to them, but I can't.

CO: What is it you see in me that is not in you? It seems like you've taken some kind of stand by going to grad school for counseling.

Sydney: Yeah, but actually talking about this stuff with them is scary. You seem like you'd be calm and counselor-y and have the right words.

CO: Maybe, but they are not my family. What would it look like for you to be calm, counselor-y, and to have the right words with them?

Sydney: First of all, I would not get flustered when they give me the look of disappointment or use the condescending tone. Those things set me off every time!

CO: Set you off?

Sydney: It shuts me down, and I just stop talking.

CO: Okay. So being more counselor-y might mean not shutting down and staying engaged, even though it's uncomfortable?

Sydney: Yes. I want to not feel guilty for making my own decisions about my life.

CO: There it is!

Sydney: There *what* is?

CO: The calm, counselor-y "right words." You just said what you need! Let's look at the ways you might communicate this. But first, I have to thank you for exploring the deeper levels of career confusion that you've been experiencing. That takes a lot of courage, and I respect that.

to the counselor. Perhaps nowhere is this more pronounced than when a client pops the question: "How am I going to get a job? Can you help me?" Counselors not well-trained in CFC may, understandably, respond with a knee-jerk reaction like referring the client, giving them a career assessment, of clarifying the scope of their practice (e.g., "I don't do career counseling" or "I can help you explore some options, but I can't help you get a job"). First thing's first. It is not the counselor's job to get a client a job. It is the client's responsibility. While we would never express this to a client in this direct a fashion, it is important for the counselor to internalize this truth. It will assist in responding reflexively instead of reacting with defensiveness. Secondly, the job loss/job search process is anxiety-provoking for almost everyone and tends to trigger those around the individual (e.g., "I'm glad that's not me," "I guess I should help, but how?," and "This makes me feel guilty that I have a job, and now, they don't"). Counselors are process experts—individuals trained to help facilitate the process of individual growth. As such, we focus on processes, like strengths, movement, challenges, relationships, and resources. At the same time, it is typically not enough to describe to a fellow human in pain a process without offering something more concrete from which they can act.

1. Relationship-building
2. Quiet yourself and ready yourself to meet the client where they are (Sommers-Flanagan & Sommers-Flanagan, 2012).
3. Hear the client's concerns
4. Conduct a positive assets search
5. Identify the client's goals
6. Identify barriers to achieving the client's goals
7. Identify confounding factors
8. Select a theory appropriate to the client
9. Apply career-related interventions
10. Evaluation: What is the client's here-and-now response? (Sommers-Flanagan & Sommers-Flanagan, 2012)

Table 13.2. CFC Taxonomy (Rubric)

| | Questions to the Counselor | Questions to the Client | Considerations |
|---|---|---|---|
| Relationship Building | • What does this client need in this moment to feel safe, trust? | No questions! Exude warmth and welcome | Note that clients with career-related issues often feel like failures for asking for help in this area |
| Quiet yourself and ready yourself to meet the client where they are | At each stage of CFC, ask yourself:<br>• What am I doing?<br>• Why am I doing it?<br>• How are my biases coming into play?<br>• What is client's here-and-now response? | • Do you have any concerns *before* we get started? | Clear from your mind questions like "How are you?" because clients will tell you, whether you are ready to begin or not. Try substituting "It is nice to see you," "Thanks for coming," or "I hope you are well" |
| Hear Client Concerns | • Is there anything left over from the previous session that needs to be addressed?<br>• What does the client think is the problem? | • What brings you in today?<br>• What's on your mind?<br>• How might I help? | Yours and the client's perceptions of the problem may be very different—this is not the place to point out discrepancies. Hear them! |
| Positive Asset Search | • Do you believe the client is capable of success?<br>• How has the current concern overshadowed their capabilities and self-efficacy? | • You have some heavy things on your mind. But you also have some things going for you. Tell me about them?<br>• What about you has kept the situation from getting worse? | Counselors view clients developmentally, meaning that in spite of the "problem" they bring to counseling, they also bring numerous strengths—it's up to the counselor to remind the client of these without minimizing their concerns. |
| Client Goals | • What is the nature of the goals the client articulates? | • If our time together is successful, what will be different? What will you be doing differently? | • What do you do when the client doesn't know? |
| Barriers to Success or Flagging the Minefield | • What patterns have you noted in the client's behaviors that indicate self-sabotage? | • What has prevented you from using your strengths in this area?<br>• After our session, what is most likely to derail you from moving toward your goals? | Believing that clients are capable is balanced by the fact that they may not have been using these capabilities. |

(*continued*)

Table 13.2. (***continued***)

| | Questions to the Counselor | Questions to the Client | Considerations |
|---|---|---|---|
| Identify the career-related issue | • What is the career component embedded in the client's concerns? | • What would you like to address in counseling that specifically relates to work? | It is useful not to assume that the problem the client "leads" with is the concern they want to address. It may or may not actually pertain to career and work (e.g., money, family, meaning, security, etc.). |
| Identify confounding variables and complications | • What does the client's body language tell you about the effects of the career issue? | • What other things have been going on prior to the work situation?<br>• How has the work situation affected other areas of your life? | Career issues and mental health issues are often intertwined: one can cause or exacerbate the other. Given the amount of time clients often wait to seek help, assume there may be related issues with which to contend. |
| Select a theory appropriate to the client | • What theory best addresses the clinical picture you've gleaned from your relationship with the client?<br>• Have you worked with the client to select a theory, and thereby bolstered client autonomy? | • How would you explain how you got here? And where would you like to go next?<br>• Here are a few explanations that might fit; I wonder if we could explore them together? | Please note that, in selecting a theory, you may decide to use *any* counseling theory that serves the client—career specific, or not. |
| Apply career-related interventions | • What needs to be addressed first in working with this client: career or something else? | • I wonder if you'd be willing to try something? | Assessments tend to be the go-to intervention, but use them judiciously, as a precise approach, not a blunt instrument that you apply to every client with career-related concerns. |
| Evaluation | • How does the client's response to the intervention inform you of its efficacy beyond client report? | • Rather than asking if it worked (yes or no question), try something like, "what did you like/dislike about the activity/intervention/homework? | Not all interventions will work for all clients, even those with similar career-related issues. If the client does not connect with an intervention, process, step back, and re-evaluate. |

Abbreviations: CFC = career-focused counseling.

# Summary

As we come to the end of this chapter and the end of this book, I would like to leave you with some thoughts. First, CFC is both personal counseling and personal. Second, CFC is often an entrée into other, even more personal issues with clients (Luke & Redekop, 2016). Career-related issues can be a way that clients "test" the counseling relationship for safety before going into underlying issues. Third, as we saw with Sydney, career issues can both create additional client concerns and can be a symptom of additional client concerns.

Finally, CFC is and should be a social justice act, wherein the counselor explores ways the client can be more fully human in the world. The result of this is more satisfying work that contributes to the client's sense of self and to society's forward movement.

# References


Busacca, L. A. (2002). Career problem assessment: A conceptual schema for counselor training. *Journal of Career Development, 29*(2), 129–146.

Busacca, L. A., & Wester, K. L. (2006). Career Concerns of Master's-Level Community and School Counselor Trainees. *The Career Development Quarterly, 55*(2), 179–190.

Luke, C., & Redekop, F. (2016). Supervision of co-occurring career and mental health concerns: Application of an integrated approach. *Career Planning & Adult Development Journal, 32*(1).

Sommers-Flanagan, J., & Sommers-Flanagan, R. (2012). *Clinical Interviewing: 2012–2013 Update.* Hoboken, NJ: John Wiley & Sons.

Stoltenberg, C. D., McNeill, B., & Delworth, U. (1998). *IDM supervision.* San Francisco, CA: Jossey-Bass.

Stoltenberg, C. D., & McNeill, B. W. (2010). *IDM supervision: An integrative developmental model for supervising counselors and therapists.* New York, NY: Routledge.

# Index

## D

## W



## Z

Lightning Source UK Ltd.
Milton Keynes UK
UKHW030623190122
397355UK00006B/138

9 781516 513291